Love and Conflict in Medieval Drama

The Plays and their Legacy

LYNETTE R. MUIR

CAMBRIDGE
UNIVERSITY PRESS

CAMBRIDGE UNIVERSITY PRESS
Cambridge, New York, Melbourne, Madrid, Cape Town, Singapore, São Paulo

Cambridge University Press
The Edinburgh Building, Cambridge CB2 8RU, UK

Published in the United States of America by Cambridge University Press, New York

www.cambridge.org
Information on this title: www.cambridge.org/9780521827560

© Lynette R. Muir 2007

First published 2007

Printed in the United Kingdom at the University Press, Cambridge

A catalogue record for this publication is available from the British Library

ISBN 978-0-521-82756-0 hardback

Contents

Illustrations

Acknowledgements

This study of non-biblical, serious plays from the tenth to the sixteenth centuries, and their legacy to the Renaissance drama, has only been made possible by the assistance of many friends and colleagues from all round the world.

Individual contributions are acknowledged in the relevant endnotes but I also owe a huge debt to those who have helped find and organise the source material and the lay-out of the different sections. Thanks are especially due to Elizabeth Williams who has provided me with much information on the development of the romance and the difference between a theme and a motif in folklore and fairy tale. Peter Meredith, John Tailby and Penny Robinson have read and corrected various sections and Alan Hindley has been of great assistance in identifying the morality plays that are based on relevant stories. Alan Knight has provided copies of unpublished plays from Lille and Nerida Newbiggin has made available much Italian material (courtesy of e-mail) including unpublished plays. Elsa Strietman has furnished (and translated where necessary) much of the Dutch material.

Photographs from the History Roll MS have been provided by the Brotherton Library, whose staff have been consistently helpful in finding and obtaining books for me. The illustration of a performance of the Dutch play of Esmoreit was kindly provided by Meg Twycross, and this and other photographs have been prepared for publication by Gavin Fairpo who has also kept my computer going. Diana Wyatt has undertaken the preparation of the bibliography. The editors for the Cambridge University Press, especially Victoria Cooper and Rebecca Jones, have been endlessly patient and helpful.

The important role played by French drama in the evolution of the European theatre in the period between 1450 and 1550 is emphasised by the sheer volume of material composed and performed. Many of the texts used here have been made available by one scholar and I want to acknowledge our debt to him by dedicating this book to my good friend and colleague, Chevalier des Arts et Sciences, Graham Runnalls.

Abbreviations and short titles used in
the text and notes

AASS: *Acta sanctorum*: Collegit Joannes Bollandus *et al.* 61 vols. Brussels, 1965–70.

Abruzzese: V. De Bartholomaeis. *Il teatro abruzzese del medio evo.* Bologna, 1924.

Best, *Bidermann*: Thomas W. Best. *Jacob Bidermann.* New York, 1975.

Black: Nancy B. Black. *Medieval narratives of accused queens.* Gainesville, Fla., 2003.

Boysse: E. Boysse. *Le théâtre des Jésuites.* Slatkine repr. Geneva, 1970.

BSS: *The book of saints. A dictionary of servants of God canonised by the Catholic Church.* Compiled by the Benedictine monks of St Augustine's Abbey Ramsgate. Sixth edition, London, 1989.

Bullough: Geoffrey, Bullough. *Narrative and dramatic sources of Shakespeare.* 8 vols. London, 1957–75.

Cangé: (Cangé MS) *Miracles de Notre Dame par personnages.* Ed. G. Paris and U. Robert. SATF. 8 vols. Paris, 1876–93.

CFMA: Classiques Français du Moyen Age.

Cohen, *Mons*: Gustave Cohen. *Le livre de conduite du régisseur . . . pour le mystère de la passion à Mons en 1501.* Paris, 1925.

Creizenach: W. Creizenach. *Geschichte des neueren Dramas.* 3 vols. Halle, 1911–23.

D'Ancona: A. D'Ancona. *Sacre rappresentazioni dei secoli XIV, XV, XVI.* 3 vols. Florence, 1872.

De Bartholomaeis: V. De Bartholomaeis. *Laude drammatche e rapprezentazioni sacre.* 3 vols. Florence, 1943.

De Bruyn: Lucy. De Bruyn. *Woman and the Devil in sixteenth-century literature.* Tisbury, 1979.

EDAM: Early Drama, Art and Music.

Edelman: Nathan. Edelman. *Attitudes of seventeenth-century France towards the Middle Ages.* New York, 1936.

EMD: *European Medieval Drama.*

Florentine drama: *Florentine drama for convent and festival*. Ed. and trans. J. W. and B. C. Cook. Chicago, 1996.

Harbage: Alfred Harbage. *Annals of English drama, 975–1700*. London, 1964.

Henrard: Nadine Henrard. *Le théâtre religieux médiéval en langue d'oc.* Geneva, 1998.

HLF: *Histoire littéraire de la France.*

Hüsken, *Everaert*: W. M. N. Hüsken. *De spelen van Cornelis Everaert*. 2 vols. Hilversum, 2005.

IMR: International Medieval Research.

Lancashire: Ian Lancashire. *Dramatic texts and records of Britain: a chronological topography to 1558*. Cambridge, 1984.

Lancaster: H. Carrington Lancaster. *Théâtre francais du 17e siècle*. Part I, 1610–35, 2 vols. Part II, 1635–42. 2.vols. Baltimore, 1992.

Lanson: G. Lanson. Etudes sur les origines de la tragédie classique en France. *Revue d'histoire littéraire de la France*, 10 (1903).

Lebègue: G. Lebègue. *Etudes sur le théâtre français*. Paris, 1977.

Legenda: *The Golden Legend of Jacobus de Voragine*. Trans. Granger Ryan and Helmut Ripperger. New York, 1969.

Lille: *Les mystères de la procession de Lille*. Ed. Alan Knight. 5 vols. (I–III pub.). Geneva, 2001– (in progress).

Loukovitch: K. Loukovitch. *L'évolution de la tragédie religieuse classique en France*. Paris, 1933.

Mainte belle œuvre faite: *Mainte belle œuvre faite*. Etudes offertes à Graham Runnalls. Orleans, 2005.

McCabe: W. H. McCabe, SJ. *An introduction to the Jesuit theater*. The Institute of Jesuit Sources, Missouri, 1983.

McKendrick: Melveena McKendrick. *Theatre in Spain, 1490–1700*. Cambridge 1989.

Meredith and Tailby: P. Meredith and J. Tailby, eds. *The staging of religious drama in Europe*. EDAM. Kalamazoo, 1983.

Metz, *Sources*: G. H. Metz. *Sources of four plays ascribed to Shakespeare*. Columbia, 1989.

Mystères: L. Petit de Julleville. *Les mystères*. 2 vols. Repr., Geneva, 1969.

Newbigin: N. Newbigin. *Feste d'Oltrarno. Plays in churches in fifteenth-century Florence*. 2 vols. Florence, 1996.

PMLA: *Publications of the Modern Language Association.*

Repertorium: M. M. Hummelen. *Repertorium van het Rederijkersdrama, 1500– c. 1620*. Assen, 1968.

Répertoire: L. Petit de Julleville. *Répertoire du théâtre comique en France au moyen âge*. Repr., Geneva, 1967.

Rouanet: L. Rouanet. *Autos, Farsas y Coloquios del siglo XVI*. 4 vols. Barcelona and Madrid, 1901.

Sachs: Hans Sachs. *Werken*. Ed. A. V. Keller and E. Goetzer. Bibliothek des literarischen Vereins, Stuttgart, CIV–CXXIV. Stuttgart, 1866–92.

SATF: Société des Anciens Textes Français.

Spel en Spektakel: *Spel en Spektakel: middleeuws toneel in de Lage Landen*, ed. H. van Dijk and Bart Ramakers. Amsterdam, 2001.

Stegmann: A. Stegmann. *L'héroisme Cornélien*, II: *L'Europe intellectuel et le théâtre, 1580–1650*. Paris, 1968.

Szarota: E. M. Szarota. *Das Jesuitendrama im deutschen Sprachgebiet*. 3 vols. (in two parts each). Munich, 1979–83.

TIE: Theatre in Europe. A Documentary History.

TIE *Medieval*: *The medieval European stage, 500–1550*. Ed. W. Tydeman. Cambridge, 2001.

TIE *German*: *The German and Dutch theatre, 1600–1848*. Ed. G. Brandt. Cambridge, 1993.

TLF: Textes Littéraires Français

Ukena: E. Ukena. *Die deutschen Mirakelspiele des Spätmittelalters. Studien und Texte*. 2 vols. Bern, 1975.

Valentin: Jean-Marie Valentin. *Le théâtre des Jésuites dans les pays de langue allemande (1554–1680)*. 3 vols. Bern, 1978.

Viel Testament: *Le mystère du Viel Testament*. Ed. J. de Rothschild. 6 vols. SATF. Paris, 1878.

V & A: Victoria and Albert Museum.

Weaver: E. B. Weaver. *Convent theatre in early modern Italy. Spiritual fun and learning for women*. Cambridge, 2001.

Worp: J. A. Worp. *Geschiedenis van het Drama en van het Toneel in Nederland*. 2 vols. Rotterdam, 1903.

Wright: Stephen Wright. *The Vengeance of Our Lord. Medieval dramatizations of the Destruction of Jerusalem*. Pontifical Institute of Medieval Studies, Toronto, 1949.

Introduction: staging the stories

The plays discussed in this companion volume to *The biblical drama of medieval Europe* are based on many kinds of serious stories from medieval sources: saints' lives and miracles, romances, epics and historical events from the siege of Troy to the Hundred Years War. The only biblical plays included are a few from Lille on the victories of Joshua, not previously available.[1] Polemical and morality plays are limited to examples relevant to the stories being discussed, and I have excluded (with a few exceptions) plays of situation rather than story, especially farces and Shrovetide plays.

What then is left after these omissions? The answer is a very substantial body of serious medieval plays on love and war, especially in French and Italian, with smaller but still significant collections in Spanish, German, English and Dutch. The varying amounts of medieval drama surviving from different countries has been vividly described by Peter Meredith: 'Where French language drama has hundreds of thousands of lines of texts (much still unedited) . . . England has a handful, an armful, perhaps a scaffold load.'[2] An imbalance in the number of references to the different language groups when discussing the stories is therefore inevitable but no attempt has been made to measure the relative quality of the plays – that is a task for the reader.

In a recently published article, Graham Runnalls, the acknowledged expert on medieval French play texts, has made it quite clear that to suggest that French medieval drama stops around 1500 is 'frankly absurd'.[3] Runnalls is referring here not only to religious drama, both biblical and hagiographic, but to the whole range of plays from miracles to farces. I have therefore taken the year 1550 as the end of half a millennium of medieval plays, and the beginning of the first century or so of retellings of these stories on both amateur and professional stages, which I have called the 'legacy'.[4]

In *Aspects of genre*, a study of the characteristics of late medieval French drama, Alan Knight distinguished between the serious plays which were historical and therefore based on true stories, and the comedies and farces which were fiction.[5] Among the serious group he lists the Bible, saints' lives and profane history such as the fall of Troy. Plays are also based on the narrative epics and romances. The plays discussed in this volume cover a wide range of subjects and forms but all belong to this 'serious' drama. They also include a genre principally found in earlier centuries: the miracle play, whose stories must also by definition be history, though as will appear they do not necessarily fit into any of Knight's categories. In contrast to the biblical drama whose source is indisputable, these plays have a variety of backgrounds, both religious and secular, but they have one thing in common: they are never original, which helps to account for the large number of plays on the same or similar subjects.[6] It is the minor variations in these stories over the centuries that reflect the changes in the theatrical world of different parts of Europe at the end of the Middle Ages and the beginning of the early modern period.

For convenience, the plays have been divided into four groups, according to subject matter. The divisions are based on the important collection of forty miracle plays found in the fourteenth-century Cangé MS, composed for performance at the annual meeting and dinner of a Parisian confraternity dedicated to the Virgin Mary, one each year from 1349 to 1382 (excluding 1354 and 1358–60 – years when Paris was under siege).[7] In an article for the *Histoire littéraire de la France* (XXXIX), the eminent French scholar, Alfred Jeanroy, pointed out that although all the plays are introduced as a 'miracle de Notre Dame' and contain an obligatory scene in which the Virgin Mary is honoured by the heavenly host singing specially composed *rondeaux*, more than half the plays are based on stories that have no connection with the Virgin. Jeanroy therefore divided the plays into four divisions: 'Légendes mariales' (seventeen plays); 'Légendes de saints' (eight plays); 'Légendes romanesques et héroiques' (eleven plays) and 'Légendes historiques romancées' (four plays).

The first group are straightforward dramatisations of well-known Marian miracles.[8] But the Virgin Mary has no real connection with the saints' lives in group two, or with most of the historical events in group four, while many of the plays in group three are based on well-known stories from romances, such as the falsely accused queen, which were told and retold all over Europe in both religious and secular forms.[9] These Cangé groups do not, of course, include all the subjects treated in the book, many of which were added in the fifteenth and early sixteenth centuries, including the theatre of cruelty inspired by the classical plays of Seneca but also reflecting the violence of the Passion and martyrdom scenes in the medieval plays.

WHO STAGED THE MEDIEVAL STORIES?

Saints' plays, like biblical subjects, were usually staged by religious communities or civic groups, but were rare in the celebrations of Corpus Christi, except as part of a procession.[10] There were a few examples of more personal arrangements. For example, in Metz in 1468, a play of the newly canonised St Catherine of Siena was commissioned by one Catherine de Baudoiche. The role of the saint was taken with great success by a girl of eighteen.[11] Stories on secular subjects, or presented in the form of miracle plays, might also be organised by trade guilds or religious confraternities, literary guilds or *Puys* (the title probably developed from the fact that the earliest such group was founded at Notre Dame du Puy in Valenciennes (Hainault). These *Puys* were most frequently found in the thirteenth and fourteenth centuries in northern France and the Low Countries. There was also a *Puy de London* modelled on the continental ones.[12]

Some of them were dedicated to poetry and music rather than drama, but others continued staging plays through to the sixteenth century. A morality, 'De la dame à l'Agneau et de la dame à l'Aspic' was presented as part of the ceremony at the meeting of the *Puy de la conception de la vierge* (also called the *Puy de palinods*) in Rouen in 1520. The play has an interesting double form: the conflict between the *Dame à l'agneau* (lamb) and the *Dame à l'aspic* (serpent) is not merely a struggle between the Virgin Mary and the Devil, it is also a clash between Rouen, whose crest was a Lady with a Lamb, and the Viper, the crest of Milan against whom Francis I had just declared war. I am grateful to Alan Hindley for finding me a copy of this interesting play. Further details of the *Puys* and an interesting account of the confraternity of the 'guilde des Archers' of Antwerp in 1493 is provided by Nigel Wilkins in an article based on a picture of the *Schuttersfeest* or 'fête de la guilde des archers du maître de Francfort (1493) et la musique des confréries'.[13]

Early drama in the Low Countries was also staged in both Dutch and French by many different street or neighbourhood groups. Nothing is known of the staging of the famous Dutch romances the *Abele spelen* (skilful plays) composed in the late fourteenth century. From about 1430 onwards, however, drama was mainly in the hands of the Chambers of Rhetoric, groups of fifteen to twenty men of all degrees from carpenters, to build and decorate the waggon stages, to the literate members, including clergy and doctors, who composed and directed the plays. Frequent contests were organised between the different Chambers of Rhetoric, on given subjects with valuable prizes.[14]

Some of the Italian plays are based on the lives of local saints such as St Guglielma, and were part of the very popular convent drama.[15] They also provided material for court entertainment in many Italian cities. In the sixteenth and early seventeenth centuries, many German analogues of the French and Italian plays were created by the prolific cobbler and Mastersinger, Hans Sachs, and his fellow Nuremburger, Jacob Ayrer. Sachs not only composed more than 4,000 *Meisterlieder* to the strictly observed rules for both poetry and music, but plays of all kinds, including fifty-eight tragedies and seventy comedies, many based on stories by Boccaccio.[16] In other parts of Europe, similar stories were dramatised for the newly developing public theatres by professional authors such as Shakespeare, Lope de Vega, Hardy and Rotrou.[17]

By the fifteenth century an important contribution to the drama was also made by the Latin plays performed in schools and colleges. The desire to teach the boys to speak Latin fluently, and debate and discuss before an audience, encouraged this practice. In the sixteenth century, with the founding of the Society of Jesus in 1555, this academic drama spread all over Europe, with every one of the more than 500 Jesuit colleges staging at least two plays a year. Only a small proportion of the Jesuit drama was printed and a few other plays survive in the original manuscripts; but it has been calculated that even over only one century (and the Jesuits were active from 1550 to 1773) if all the plays had survived: 'yet an elementary mathematical operation – allowing for repetitions of some plays – sets the sum total of plays, conservatively, at nearly one hundred thousand'.[18] Details of the many plays performed in the German colleges can be found in the *perioche* or summaries prepared for the parents and other members of the audience who had no Latin.[19] The late development of public theatre in Germany, partly as a consequence of the Thirty Years War, meant that Jesuit drama had a much wider and more general audience in Germany than in France or Italy.[20]

In contrast, the audience for the plays performed at the Paris Jesuit Collège de Clermont was distinguished by its social status and included ladies although they knew no Latin. The *entractes* were occupied by ballets on a related subject or scenes in French. Elegant refreshments were also served and the audience and performances were commented on by the social newspapers of the period. The college was renamed Collège Louis-le-Grand in 1683 by Louis XIV, who had attended plays there for many years (accompanied in 1651 by Charles II of England and the duke of Gloucester). Other French colleges adhered more closely to the Jesuit principles of no women in the audience and exclusive use of Latin.[21]

Saints' plays continued in school and college drama and, put on by travelling players, in the provinces but in the seventeenth century the public theatres of Europe became increasingly addicted to national, historical and classical subjects for the tragedies, and the eighteenth century added the bourgeois drama with its stories of love and conflict.[22] Subsequent developments of medieval traditions will be considered in the Conclusion.

PART ONE

War in Heaven: saints and sinners

Saint: A dead sinner revised and edited.

(Ambrose Bierce)

The majority of the texts in the first two chapters are described as saints' plays or miracles, the former mostly dealing with martyrdoms and conversions to Christianity, from the early church to the Reformation, and the latter with the sins and repentance of individual Christians.[1] The focus is usually on a single character whose soul is the object of a tug-of-war between the forces of Heaven, often led by the Virgin Mary, and those of Hell.

Saints' plays may be divided into three main groups: martyrdom plays, plays about hermits and the work of Confessors and founders of religious orders.[2] Extant saints' plays from the tenth to the end of the fifteenth century are numerous in French, Italian and Spanish, rare in German and English and unknown in Dutch. A unique play on a Celtic saint is the Cornish play of St Meriasek (*Beunans Meriasek*). The only surviving text is early sixteenth century but the saint, who probably dates from the seventh century, is depicted as a contemporary of Constantine.[3] The sixteenth-century school drama included a very large number of Latin saints' plays from all parts of Catholic Europe.

CHAPTER I

The noble army of martyrs

There are too many martyrdom plays to consider them all in detail, so only a selection of the most popular or interesting ones can be mentioned here.

THE VIRGIN IN THE BROTHEL AND OTHER FEMALE SAINTS

The earliest surviving saints' plays are the six Latin ones composed by the German nun, Hrotsvitha of Gandersheim, Saxony, in the tenth century.[1] She specifically claims Terence for her model and their importance and originality deserve separate treatment.[2] Three of her plays are based on the legends of martyrs: *Callimachus* is an original story based on a brief reference to a miracle of John the Apostle (*Legenda* 27 December); the other two are hermit plays. Only the first four will be discussed here.[3]

One feature that is striking in Hrotsvitha's martyrdom plays is the use of humour. In *Dulcitius*, a young man who believes he is embracing three Christian virgins, servants of St Anastasia and imprisoned in his kitchen, is in fact embracing dirty pots and pans, the maidens are untouched (St Anastasia, *Legenda* 25 December). He emerges so blackened no one recognises him.[4] After vain attempts by soldiers to strip the girls naked they are finally executed.

Failure to accept offers of marriage by men of rank is nearly always the start of the troubles for these young Christian women. In addition to Dulcitius, Hrotsvitha uses the theme in *Gallicanus* which is the story more usually named after SS. John and Paul (*Legenda* 26 June) and dramatised by Lorenzo de Medici for the boys of a school in Florence: *SS. Giovanni e Paulo* (D'Ancona, II).[5] In *Sapientia* on the other hand,[6] the emperor is threatening a mother and her children, Faith, Hope and Charity, with martyrdom if they do not recant, and he asks her how old the girls are. She asks the children:

'Shall I puzzle his dull brain with some problems in arithmetic?'

FAITH: 'Do mother, it will give us joy to hear you.'

SAPIENTIA: 'O emperor, Charity has lived a diminished evenly even number
      of years; Hope a number also diminished, but evenly uneven; and Faith an
      augmented number, unevenly even.'   (trans. p. 137)

The emperor (not surprisingly) is bewildered and asks for explanations.
Sapientia obliges with a rather patronising lesson in mathematics.[7] The
English translator is somewhat critical of this scene and the continued
impertinence of the daughters during their martyrdom, and claims that
only Dulcitius 'was obviously designed to provoke laughter' – a modern
audience would disagree I think.

The story of *Callimachus* is not humorous nor a martyr play, but is based
on the motif of desire. Callimachus is overwhelmed by his passion for
Drusiana, a Christian woman in a celibate marriage, and attempts to
become her lover. When she refuses, he threatens to trap her somehow.
She prays to Christ that she may be able to keep her vow of chastity and
immediately collapses and dies. Her distraught husband, Andronicus,
has her buried and sends a messenger to St John the Evangelist. Meanwhile Callimachus, tempted and helped by a servant, Fortunatus, goes to
the tomb, desperate to touch her body. When they open her sarcophagus
he tries to kiss the corpse but a great serpent appears and kills both men.
When St John and Andronicus arrive, they find the tomb open and the
two dead men lying there. St John revives Callimachus who tells of a
vision of an angel; he confesses his sin and is filled with remorse. John
then revives Drusiana and is persuaded by Drusiana and her delighted
husband to revive Fortunatus also, but when the latter learns that Drusiana is alive and Callimachus has become a Christian, he rejects life: 'I
would rather not exist than see them swelling with grace and virtue.' St
John compares him to the tree which only bore bad fruit and was cut
down. Fortunatus' wounds reopen and start bleeding and he dies again
and is damned. John comments: 'nothing is more terrible than envy,
nothing more evil than pride'. They prepare to celebrate the conversion
of Callimachus.

Other heroines who suffer because they will not marry include St
Dorothy (*Legenda* 6 February; cult suppressed in 1969). Cioni lists eleven
editions of the play of *Santa Dorotea vergine e martyre* and she is the subject
of a rare English saints' play, Massinger's *The Virgin Martyr* (1620). The
Dorotheaspiel fragment (ed. Ukena) is one of the few extant saints' plays
in German. For some virgin martyrs the brothel is not just a threat.[8]
In the thirteenth-century Provençal play of *St Agnes* (*Legenda* 21 January),

when she refuses her suitor and declares her intention of being a celibate Christian, she is placed, naked, in a brothel and immediately grows a complete covering of long hair.[9]

In Troterel's *St Agnes* (1615) the brothel miracles are not shown on stage (Lancaster, I, i, p. 104). A similar fate (without the miracle of the hair) befalls *S. Teodora* (*Legenda* 11 September; D'Ancona, II).[10] In the story of *Grisante y Daria* (D'Ancona, II), Daria is sent into a brothel but a lion 'escaped from the amphitheatre and stood guard at the door of the house of sin' (*Legenda* 25 October). When a man approaches the brothel the lion seizes him and Daria preaches Christianity and converts him. Finally the prefect orders Daria and the lion to be burnt. Daria allows the terrified lion to go where he likes provided he will harm no one. Grisante and Daria are finally executed.

One of the most popular female saints in Europe, St Barbara, was dramatised many times, including two very substantial versions in French.[11] In contrast to the virgins already mentioned, her father incarcerates her in a tower to prevent her making an unsuitable marriage. This is probably a variation on the classical story of Danae, though in this case it is a priest who manages to make his way into her dwelling and convert her to Christianity so that she insists on having three windows in the tower to represent the Trinity. When she finally refuses to marry the man of her father's choice and declares her Christianity, her father has her head cut off and he himself is immediately struck down by a thunderbolt, making St Barbara, among her many other responsibilities, the patron saint of artillerymen.[12]

Other popular female martyrs include Catherine of Alexandria, Apollonia and Cecilia. All had plays in Italian and some in French or Spanish also. St Catherine is the only female saint to feature regularly in Jesuit drama.[13]

THE CHURCH TRIUMPHANT: ST STEPHEN AND HIS SUCCESSORS

Among the well-known male saints to be martyred on stage are St Laurence on his gridiron, Crispin and Crispianus, the shoemakers from Sens, who are unhurt when put into boiling oil,[14] and St Christopher.[15] Some of the multi-day French martyrdom plays are extremely elaborate with special effects, machinery and false bodies.[16] Animals are also a popular adjunct to the scene. In the fifteenth-century Provençal play of St Pons (Henrard, p. 294) the martyr has to face giant bears and several plays

show the saint faced by lions.[17] In *St Ignace* (Cangé, XXXIV), the executioners bring on the lions coupled together as if they were hounds, then
sick them on to Ignace: 'hu! hu! sur lui! sur lui!'. Although they knock
him down and kill him, they will not eat him despite the encouragement
of the emperor. A similar scene occurs in the *Rappresentazione di S. Ignazio*
(D'Ancona, I) but in Castellano Castellani's *S. Venanzio*, the lions bow
down and worship the saint and all the onlookers are converted.[18] The
terminal execution usually takes place off stage.

Three martyrs' lives show interesting variety and detail in their stories
(some of which are now generally accepted as fiction) and were also
staged over a long period of time. St George, St Eustace and St Genesius
will be studied individually, from the medieval plays through to the mid-
seventeenth century.

THE THREE FACES OF ST GEORGE

St George is unique among saints for having not merely two roles, as martyr and miracle worker, but a third, for in the sixteenth century the Byzantine warrior and dragon slayer moved on from being merely the patron
saint of England and acquired English nationality, with English parents
and a birth place and burial place in Warwickshire.[19] This makeover will
be considered in Part Three with the other popular heroes.

Little is genuinely known about the early life of George, neither his
place of origin nor his date of birth. As Dom Leclercq puts it: 'Né à? En?
Mort à? en?'[20] The executioners struggle to finish off this exceptionally
tough martyr (the *megalomartyros* of the Eastern Church) for seven years
before killing him by the only known successful method of dispatching a
saint: they cut off his head.[21]

In his detailed study of this most important member of the *état-mayor* or
top section of the warrior saints of the Byzantine church, Walter points
out that the early accounts of his life and martyrdom are totally spurious.
Although frequently presented in icons or other Byzantine art forms,
often on a horse, the killing of the dragon was not linked to him before
the eleventh century and George did not move into the Roman Western
Church until the early crusades. In the later Middle Ages he became
one of the busiest saints in Europe, patron of, among other regions,
Portugal, Germany, Aragon (for a time he ousted Santiago), Genoa and
Venice, protector of Ferrara and one of the Fourteen Holy Helpers. He
was known in England from Saxon times but became England's patron
when Richard I put his crusading army under the protection of St George.

Edward III founded his Order of the Garter under George's patronage in 1348.[22]

Not surprisingly, therefore, plays of St George are extant or mentioned in many languages either as martyr or dragon slayer.[23] The former include a Catalan *Passio de Sant Jordi*, and an Italian *S. Giorgio martyre e cavaliere di Cristo* – Cioni lists twelve editions from 1495 to 1608.[24] Several French performances are recorded from about 1420 but no texts have survived and it is not certain whether they were martyr or dragon-slayer plays.[25] The latter role is treated in a late fifteenth-century German *Hübsch spiel von St Jörgen und des künigs von Libiba tochter*; a Dutch *Spel van St Jooris*; a Catalan *Consueta de Sant Jordi* and a Spanish *Auto de Sant Jorge quando mato la serpiente*.[26] There is also a school play from Cologne of *Georgio dracontomachia* by Moller in 1598 and a Jesuit dragon-slaying play from Gratz in 1630.[27]

St George also appeared in many processions in Spain, Germany and England, sometimes together with that other dragon conqueror, St Margaret. In Valencia in 1407 and 1408 they have a dragon each (see Meredith and Tailby, pp. 121–2), but sometimes they share one, as in the 1533 procession in Bergen op Zoom, where St Margaret and her lamb are followed by a fire-breathing dragon, which is followed by St George on horseback.[28] In London in 1521 he actually frees St Margaret from the dragon by choking it (Lancashire, 969:12).[29]

THE NEW JOB, OR THE SUFFERINGS OF ST EUSTACE

Eustace, like St George, was a Byzantine warrior whose story was translated into Latin in the tenth century and retold in *The Gesta Romanorum* (CX) and many vernacular versions.[30] He was a very popular figure in the Middle Ages and plays of his adventures are recorded in several languages though few are extant.[31] Cioni lists ten editions, variously entitled a 'rappresentazione' or a 'festa di Santo Eustachio', between 1495 and 1606. A stage direction ends the 1495 edition: 'Sono messi nel toro & una nughola viene da cielo; e l'anime loro enporte cantando'.[32] A performance of a 'devotione de Sancto Eustachio primo chiamato Placito, romana' on 25 June 1503 on the piazza di Santo Francesca in Orvieto. is recorded in the diary of Tommaso di Silvestro.[33]

The Provencal *Moralitas sancti Heustachi* survives in a manuscript of 1504 and is linked also with a performance of a *mystère* of St Eustache in Avignon in 1453.[34] The texts mostly follow the story from the *Legenda* (20 September) which gives an abridged version of the Latin *Vita*, but

the *Moralitas* has interesting additions based on the *Vita*, some of which
are included – in italic – in the following outline, based on the analysis
by Chocheyras.[35]

Placidus, a Roman soldier in the army of Trajan was a heathen but
given to works of mercy (on the way to venerate an idol he gives alms
twice to the poor) and therefore 'merited to be lighted unto the way of
truth' (*Legenda*). His wife is also a good woman and he has two fine sons.
One day he is out hunting and follows a great stag to the depth of the
forest where it turns at bay and he sees a vision of a crucifix between
the horns from which Jesus speaks to him and converts him.[36] Placidus
is told to go to the bishop of Rome to be baptised and take his wife and
sons with him, then return the following day. When he tells his wife she
reveals she too has had visions. At their baptism they all change their
names and Placidus becomes Eustace, his wife Theospis and his sons
Agapitus and Theospitus.[37]

When Eustace returns to the forest the following day Jesus tells him
he will have to imitate Job. He is warned that his baptism will have
much angered the Devil who will pursue him with many woes but if
he perseveres he will finally win glory. Then Eustace is asked to choose
between immediate suffering now or later in his life. He chooses the
former but asks he may be given the virtue of Patience.[38] In a scene
in Hell the devils decide to avenge themselves by inciting Trajan to
persecute the Christians and making Eustace into another Job. Eustace's
troubles soon begin. The servants are struck down by plague and their
house and lands are sacked by robbers.[39] Ashamed of their condition,
Eustace and his wife and family flee the Roman court and board a
ship.[40] The captain demands payment for their trip – Eustace has no
money so the captain says Theospis must remain as a surety and when
Eustace refuses, threatens to have him thrown overboard. For the sake
of the children Eustace leaves the ship, but while they are crossing a
torrent, one of the children is carried off by a wolf and the other by
a lion. Eustace is kept from suicide by God's providence. One of the
children is saved by ploughmen and the other by shepherds from the
same village, who chase away the wolf and the lion and take the child
into their homes. The wolf and the lion go to hell and explain their
lack of success on the fact the children are baptised.[41] Bereft of wife and
children, Eustace settles in a nearby village where he works for fifteen
years, not knowing his sons are growing up in the village nearby. God
also protects Theospis – the captain is struck dead before he can harm
her.

Meanwhile the Roman army is suffering from the loss of its best commander and the emperor sends out men everywhere to find Placidus. Two come to his village and he recognises them and lets himself hope that he might one day see his wife again though the children were eaten by wild beasts. A voice promises him he will soon be reunited with his whole family. He returns to court and the service of the emperor and seeing the army short of soldiers sends out recruiting officers to bring in likely young men, among whom, naturally, come his sons. On their way to Rome they stop at a poor inn kept by their mother and after much talking there is a grand recognition and reunion. The mother accompanies them back to court and all the family are reunited. The emperor Trajan dies and as he is not baptised he goes to Hell. The new emperor is his son Hadrian. Placidus wins a victory for Rome but on his return Hadrian wants Placidus and his family to sacrifice to the gods and he refuses. When the emperor finds him adamant he orders the whole family to be sent to the lions in the arena.

At this point in Desfontaines' play (Act V, scene 6), Hadrian, addressing Theopisto, one of Eustace's sons, comments ironically:

> O le noble trépas! O l'illustre tombeau
> que fournit un lyon et qu'appreste un bourreau!
>
> (O what a noble death, what illustrious tomb
> furnished by a lion and prepared by an executioner.)

The lion of course does not harm the saintly family, so Hadrian orders them to be put into a brazen bull heated red-hot. According to *Legenda*, when it is opened they are dead but their bodies and clothes are unharmed (this is surely an echo of the Three Holy Children and the burning fiery furnace). Christians bury them and build a church on the site. One of the Jesuit plays ends with their being received into Heaven by angels, but most play versions end with their being led away to a martyrdom, which is reported not shown.

MIME AND MARTYR: THE STORY OF ST GENESIUS

According to the *Passio S. Genesii*, he was an actor in the reign of Diocletian who was violently opposed to the Christians and willingly agreed when the emperor asked him to present a play mocking their beliefs and practices, in order to turn the general public against them. To prepare an effective play he questioned Christians about their faith and sacraments, especially baptism. In the middle of the first performance,

'Our Lord touched the heart of Genesius and illumined him with a ray of his light.'[42] As a result he now was eager to be baptised and when, in the play, they prepared a mock baptism scene, he publicly declared his conversion and desire for the real sacrament, describing how, at the moment when they were about to pour the water over him, he had had a vision of angels with a book listing all his ill deeds, who told him they could be expunged by repentance and baptism. As the water touched him he looked again and the book was blank. Diocletian was furious and had Genesius tortured to make him recant but in vain. Genesius wanted to be properly baptised before he died but this was refused him. He was consoled by a Heavenly assurance that he had been baptised in blood.[43]

The earliest of many plays on Genesius is the fifteenth-century French *Vie de St Genest* which follows the *Passio* fairly closely. The play opens with a long *diablerie* and, speaking through the *ydole* (presumably a statue of a Roman god), the devils encourage Genesius to urge the emperor (unnamed) to suppress this blasphemous cult. Interestingly, the play-within-a-play is omitted altogether. There is a brief scene with the other mimes, during which they only talk of music and musical instruments, then a stage direction: 'tunc statim ludant mimi et Genesius coram Imperatorem' (then immediately the mimes and Genesius play before the emperor (l. 830).[44] Afterwards, Genesius soliloquises on the strength of the faith of the martyred Christians and begins to wonder how they can be so sure of their belief. Eventually he goes to a priest who instructs him in the faith and, seeing he is converted, baptises him. Jealous courtiers denounce him to the emperor. Then follows a lengthy series of theological discussions between Genesius and Diocletian, including one on the nature of the Trinity, alternating with tortures on the stage. Genesius has a final vision of Christ, his soul is taken to Heaven and angels come and bury his body. The play ends with another *diablerie* as Satan and his followers console themselves for the loss of the soul of Genesius by seizing that of the emperor.[45]

The story became popular in the sixteenth and seventeenth centuries with both Jesuit and secular authors from Spain and France.[46] The only Italian play (Cioni has no reference to Genesius) is the *San Ginesio* written c. 1624, by Michaelangelo Buonarottti the Younger, nephew of the artist, for the convent of St Agata in Florence where his two nieces were nuns.[47]

In Lope's *Lo fingido verdadero* (The feigned truth) composed about 1608 and printed in 1621, the first act deals exclusively with the story of Diocletian's accession to the empire.[48] In Act II, Genesius and his fellow actors are introduced and there is stress on their relationships to one another. Genesius, who is much in love with Marcella who, however, prefers Octavius, emphasises the fact that he cannot enact an emotion he does not feel personally – an actor must be completely absorbed by his role – acting and life are inseparable. Diocletian having asked for a play, Genesius offers him a variety of subjects and finally it is agreed they will perform a play of love and jealousy during which Genesius, absorbed in his feelings for Marcella, constantly uses her real name rather than that of the character she is playing. At the end of the play they learn Marcella and Octavius have run away together and are married. Genesius is devastated.

In Act III, Diocletian asks Genesius to write and present a play about 'a baptised Christian, because I've heard it's one of your best roles'. Genesius debates how he should play the role: 'How shall I move, what kind of facial expression, what gestures shall I use to win their praise'? he becomes absorbed in the part and declaims: 'Holy martyrs pray to Christ . . . give me baptism, Lord.' At this moment music plays and doors open high up on the stage revealing a painting of Mary with God the Father holding Christ in his arms and surrounded by angels and martyrs. Genesius does not see it but continues his introspection and finally exclaims 'What a lot of nonsense I'm talking, and all because I want to give a convincing performance.' An off-stage voice tells him he will not play the role in vain, for he will be saved.

Genesius is now in a confused state and when the play begins he keeps improvising and changing the lines he had given to the actors, adding more and more references to the truth of his conversion to Christianity. A second time the Heaven opens and angels perform the rite of baptism. Genesius declares 'You play the mercy of Jesus and I will play the martyrdom of Genesius.' The Heaven is closed. Diocletian comments 'That scene was outstanding.' But the play soon becomes chaotic to Diocletian's displeasure and Genesius admits the fault is his. He denies the Roman gods and Diocletian sentences him to death and departs with his companions. As in the *Passio* the other actors are questioned by the captain but manage to convince him they are not Christians. Genesius is shown crossing the stage on his way to martyrdom as they prepare to leave Rome and Octavius speaks the tag: 'Here ends the play of the supreme actor.'

In contrast to Lope's emphasis on Genesius as an actor, Rotrou in *Le véritable St Genest* [49] lays all his emphasis on the conversion of Genesius which takes place during a command performance of the martyrdom of St Adrian to celebrate the betrothal of Diocletian's co-ruler Maximin (Act I).[50] It is not originally intended as a satire of the Christians but to show off Genesius' acting skills, praised by the bride-to-be Valerie: 'on vante surtout l'inimitable adresse / dont tu feins d'un chrétien le zèle et l'allégresse' (they praise, especially, the inimitable skill with which you feign the zeal and enthusiasm of a Christian).

Act II shows the actors preparing the theatre and revising their lines, and it is during this run-through that Genesius, feeling himself become Adrian, also begins to believe as Adrian did: 'Christ me propose une gloire éternelle, contre qui ma défense est vaine et criminelle.' He then begins to hesitate but the Heaven opens with a blaze of fire and a voice is heard encouraging him to continue in his conversion.[51] The play then begins and the spectators are enthralled by what they see, as Genesius gives a superb performance as Adrian. For the next three acts, the play-within-a-play continues with Genesius altering the words and causing great difficulties for the other actors as he gradually changes from an actor to a convinced Christian. He finally puts off the role of Adrian and declares his own conversion and beliefs. Diocletian who has become angry at the chaos on the stage orders him to be arrested and the other actors interrogated. They each declare what roles they play and insist they do not share Genesius' sudden change of heart. Marcelle who had played Adrian's wife, Natalie, in the play, visits him in prison and tries to persuade him to give up his beliefs for the sake of all the actors but he is immovable. Diocletian declares his anger at the way the Christians continue to rebel against the gods despite all the punishments he has meted out. He gives orders for the painful execution of Genesius as the others exit weeping.[52]

The exact date of Desfontaines' play, *L'illustre comédien*, is not known but it was approximately contemporary with that of Rotrou. It differs from all the other plays in that Desfontaines was himself an actor as well as an author[53] and the text is full of superb speeches for both the Christians and the emperor. The action all takes place in Diocletian's Palace and opens with Diocletian lamenting the dangers to the empire of the presence of this sect of Christians which undermine his whole authority: 'C'est paroistre Empereur, et souffrir en esclave.' His councillor, Rutile, urges him to use 'raison' not torments when dealing with the Christians: 'Let reason and example be used instead / turn the scaffolds into splendid stages / and show them by mockery / the falsity and deception of their religion.'

This suggestion leads to a paean of praise for the great actor, Genesius. Diocletian agrees and asks for such a play to be prepared. Genesius is delighted because he himself had been driven from his home by his father's conversion to Christianity. It is decided to base the play on this theme and Genesius comments on the absurdity of their 'mystère nouveau qu'ils appellent Baptème'.[54] The roles are distributed among the members of the troop and the play opens with a long love scene between Genesius and his beloved Pamphilia, then, after a brief interval where Diocletian praises the performance, Genesius is converted on stage but no one else sees the angel and the bright light. A lengthy sequence follows as he tries vainly to convert the other actors, but only Pamphilia is converted. The tortures are off-stage but Pamphilia's death speech is reported by a messenger. Then follows a monologue of despair by Diocletian as he is surrounded by ghosts and wailing; the sky is like fire and the earth covered in blood. He has a vision of Heaven where the martyrs appear crowned and carrying palms. He asks their pardon and begs them to ease his agonies – he will build them magnificent mausoleums and add them to the number of his gods to show later centuries their innocence and his contrition.

El mejor representante San Ginés, written before 1655, by three *Ingenios* (authors) was printed in 1668. It follows the general lines of Lope's play with some additional characters and details and is certainly one of the sources of a later Genesius play, recorded from Madrid. In 1741, in celebration of the birthday of the emperor, the 'compañia de Joseph Patra' staged Urueña's *Ingenio y representante S. Ginés y S. Claudio*, a magnificent spectacle which lasted three days.[55] Urueña's play was published under the title *Ingenio y representante S. Ginés y S. Claudio* in 1771.

On the first day, Genesius and his company present before the emperor Diocletian a play on the story of Aeneas and Turnus from *Aeneid* Book x. The action includes the battle between Aeneas and Turnus, watched by Lavinia. On the second day, back-stage scenes introduce the complicated love-interest of Genesius and Pauline, loosely based on Lope's play and including also some elements from the *Passio* and the *mistere*. Genesius is learning his lines for the performance of the play on Christian baptism and falls asleep. The Heaven opens and St Michael appears with a company of angels. He urges Genesius to reject the old gods whom Michael has chained and accept the true God. Genesius, moved, asks to behold God but learns he must first be baptised. He is sent to Claudio (a priest of Mars, newly converted and now secretly a Christian priest) who will teach Genesius what he must know. The Heaven closes and Genesius awakes.

The court enter and take their places and the play of the baptism begins. Claudio dressed as a priest, Pauline as *Glaube* (belief) and other actors as sacristans with the necessary 'apparat' and Genesius in a white tunic accompanied by Guilt (*Schuld*) come on stage. Helped by Claudio and *Glaube*, Genesius makes a full declaration of faith. Michael appears again, accompanied by angels and a dove which breathes a cloud of 'gassa' on Genesius' head. Genesius is then baptised by Claudio while the other actors wonder what has happened as they keep changing the text (as in Lope). Claudio and Genesius then declare their Christianity and demand martyrdom. Diocletian has the whole group arrested and swears to avenge the gods.

On the third day the Devil tries to tempt the imprisoned actors to recant but fails. Diocletian tries both threats and promises of rich rewards but in vain. A final tableau shows Genesius on a cross with a lance through his breast and the beheaded Claudio at his feet. Above is St Michael with the souls of the martyrs, and angels bearing crowns and palms. The Devil falls into the underworld while the heavenly quire greets the martyrs.

There is no Genesius play in Dutch, perhaps because in the Protestant countries there was opposition to non-biblical religious drama, but an interesting defence of the subject was made by the Catholic Dutch author Vondel in the preface to his play *Lucifer* (1564). 'Vondel reminded his readers that even plays which appeared to abuse Christianity could be morally useful.[56] As the legend of St Genesius attested . . . a man's mockery of Christ may well result in his conversion.'

Though there is no play in German, the story of Genesius maintained its popularity with the Jesuits in Germany throughout the seventeenth century and even later. Balde, a noted Jesuit poet, composed in 1629 for the college at Innsbruck (where he had just been appointed professor of rhetoric) a play on the themes of Play and Reality which includes an episode of Genesius (*Jocus serius theatralis*, in *Euphorion*, 66 (1972), pp. 412–36). *The Felix catastrophae Genesii* was performed in Munich in 1680. It follows the *Passio* fairly closely, including the mock illness and appeal for help from the gods and, when they fail, from Christ. In contrast to *St Genis*, this mock baptism proves a real one and Genesius suffers martyrdom as a truly baptised Christian.[57] An interesting Spanish play of the mid-seventeenth century, by Alejandro Arboreda, which treats of the Spanish conversion of the Incas of Peru exists in two versions: *El mas divino remedio y Aurora de san Ginés*.[58]

No discussion of the Genesius material would be complete without a consideration of Massinger's *The Roman actor*, written shortly after the publication of Lope's *Fingido verdadero*. Villerejo (p. 339) claims that Massinger is strongly influenced by Lope's play but Edwards and Gibson, editors of the collected *Plays and poems* of Philip Massinger feel that 'a stronger case has been made by Dr Betha Hensman that the inset play was constructed from three of Seneca the Elder's Controversiae'.[59] It is certain that the story of emperor Domitian and his love for Domitia whom he forcibly (but not unwillingly on her part) takes from her husband whom he subsequently has executed; and the love that Domitia develops for the popular actor, Paris, are from Latin sources. Nor can it be overlooked that the two plays take place in the reigns of different emperors. On the other hand both plays are based on the relationship between a Roman emperor and his favourite actor and include one or more inset plays as a result of which the actor offends the emperor and is eventually put to death by him.

The major difference between Lope and Massinger is that the latter is not writing a religious play but a historical one, but there are certain episodes that suggest Massinger was familiar with the story of Genesius, and most probably through Lope's play. It is interesting, for example, that he should introduce in Act III:2 the episode of the senators who are tortured on stage because they have dared to criticise Caesar for putting to death the philosopher Thrasea – a true incident but which took place in the reign of Nero not of Domitian. The dialogue in the torture scene echoes many a martyr play. Caesar warns them of the power of the emperor to send their souls "'groaning to the stygian lake, / prepared for such to howl in, that blaspheme / the power of princes that are gods on earth". The prisoners reply with the standard martyr claim that there is no fear of death for those "that know / What 'tis to die, well taught by his example / For whom we suffer."' Even the torture instruments specified by Domitian, 'the hangman's hooks', are mentioned in the *Passio S. Genesii*: 'They placed him upon the rack, rending his flanks with claws of iron.'[60] Domitian, whose hangmen 'torment them still smiling' becomes increasingly angry at the impassivity of his victims: 'I am tortured in their want of feeling torments.' This whole scene has no place in the action of the play and serves only to characterise Domitian and prepare for the final scene of the play-within-a-play, where Domitian, finally convinced of Domitia's love for Paris but unable to bring himself to kill the woman he still loves, undertakes a role in the action of the play in order to avenge himself by killing his favourite actor.

CHAPTER 2

White martyrdom – the hermits

In the period leading up to Constantine's declaration of Christianity as the legal religion of the Roman empire, a group of ascetics lived lives of great hardship in the deserts of the Near East especially in Egypt. The sufferings of these Desert Fathers are sometimes referred to as the White Martyrdom, as by extremes of asceticism they repelled attacks both physical and mental by the hosts of Hell.

THE DESERT FATHERS

Two plays in this group are by Hrotsvitha.[1] The first play, *St Paphnutius*, is a faithful dramatisation of the story of St Thais the courtesan (*Legenda* 8 October). *Abraham* is a variation on the same story and loosely based on the legend of St Mary of Egypt (*Legenda* 2 April). It begins with the hermit, Abraham, bringing up as an ascetic his orphan niece, Mary. When she is eighteen, a false monk seduces her. She deeply repents the loss of her virginity but then falls into the sin of despair and goes back to the world.[2] Determined to save her, Abraham plans to dress as a worldling and go in search of her even if it means he must eat meat and drink wine – both of them anathema to the ascetic hermit. From then on the play closely follows the story of Thais. Abraham learns from a friend who has been searching for her that she is now a prostitute in a brothel. He borrows soldier's clothes and a horse from the friend, together with a hat to cover his tonsure: a typical Hrotsvitha touch of humour! He takes his solitary gold piece and goes to the brothel and buys Mary's company for the night. When they are alone he reveals himself to her and finally overcomes her shame and despair and persuades her to undergo the penance which will save her. They return to the desert and after many years of deep repentance and harsh penance she dies in the odour of sanctity.

In contrast to these stories of the hermit acting in the world, there are also plays of the lives of the hermits themselves. The most important of them and the founder of the movement, St Anthony the Great (*Legenda* 17 January; also known as St Anthony Abbot and St Anthony of Egypt), was the subject of many legends, including the story of his being tempted by the seven deadly sins but resisting them all, even when Gluttony seized the saint's favourite pig which the devils killed and cooked but failed to distract the saint from his prayers.[3] There is an Italian play on *Anthony Abato* by Antonia Pulci composed about 1490 and reprinted ten times by 1600.[4] It includes the story of how one day Antony saw a great lump of gold lying on the ground 'but he shunned it as if it were fire' (*Legenda* p. 100).[5] Antonia Pulci developed this reference into the story, famous as the basis of Chaucer's Pardoner's tale, of the three thieves who squabbled over a treasure and finally all killed each other.[6] In contrast to the fairly short and straightforward Italian play, is the large-scale Provençal *Mystère de Sant Anthoni de Viennes* from the Briançon region to which the relics of the saint had been brought in 1070 and where the order of Antonines was founded. Henrard[7] gives a detailed analysis of the play, which survives in a copy made in 1503 and edited by l'abbé Guillaume. It is nearly 7,000 lines long and the first half shows the young Anthony with his family, the sermon which led to his decision to become a monk and events in preparation for the change. Interspersed are elaborate scenes in Hell and in Heaven. The second part of the play follows closely the saint's life as told by St Jerome, with his reception into a monastic order followed by a long period as a solitary hermit where he undergoes the famous scene of the temptations. Then he is guided to leave the hermitage and travel around Egypt establishing many solitary hermits in different places – the first such organisation in the history of Christianity. When he is with St Paul, his greatest disciple, an episode is inserted in the text from the *Vita Pauli*, in which the two men share manna brought to them by a crow. In the *Mystère*, however, Gabriel is given the task and immediately responds: 'I will send it to him certainly by the dove.'[8] Shortly after, St Paul dies and two lions appear from the desert, dig a grave and bury him – a fairly common scene in hagiography.

The visit to St Paul is also the subject of the *Auto della visitacion de Sant Antonio a Sant Pablo* (Rouanet, LXXVI). The opening scene tells how St Anthony, who believed he was the first hermit to live in the desert, learns that he had a predecessor, St Paul. He sets off to visit Paul and meets a centaur with whom he tries to converse by signs without success and a *Satiro* (satyr) with whom he converses about God. St Paul then enters and invites Anthony into his cell (*hermita*), and Anthony meets his disciples. St Paul is dying and three angels enter to take his soul. Two lions then appear and dig his grave with their paws. St Anthony and the disciple bury St Paul and sing a final psalm.

ST ONOFRIO AND OTHER HAIRY HERMITS

The Italian play of *St Onofrio* describes a monk who leaves his monastery to go into the desert and live a strict ascetic life. Sometime later, his former abbot, S Panuzio, also sets off for the desert. He eventually finds Onofrio but does not recognise him – he is covered in hair and blackened by the sun. Onofrio tells him of his life and the fact that he has been sixty years in the desert and will soon die. Panuzio prays with him and angels bring them bread and wine to make their communion. Onofrio dies and two lions appear, dig his grave and bury him. Panuzio prepares to take his place in the desert.[9]

There are also plays of a group of male hermits who sin and then perform great penance, living like beasts on all fours and covered only with hair. The oldest play on these 'hairy hermits' is the *Vie de Saint Jehan le Paulu* (Cangé, xxx).[10] The play opens with Jehan listening to a sermon on the Virgin Mary which moves him to become a hermit. While living in the forest, he accepts as servant one Huet, not knowing that he is a devil in disguise. One day the king's daughter who is out hunting gets separated from the huntsmen, loses her way and is benighted in the forest.[11] She comes to the hermitage for shelter and Huet, seeing an opportunity at last to cause Jehan to sin, suggests Jehan should offer her a share of his pallet, with the inevitable result. The next morning the delighted devil suggests the only way to avoid being punished by the king is to kill the princess and put her body in the well where no one will find it. Jehan agrees and when they have disposed of the body Huet rejoices: 'Now I have you in my toils, wicked murderer! I can go away happy!' Jehan comes to his senses and, horrified at what he has done, he prays to the Virgin for help and promises as penance to speak to no one, to go on all fours like an animal and to live like they do by eating grass.

The action then moves on to seven years later, to a house where the wife is in labour and gives birth to a son. Preparations are made for the christening. Back in the forest, Jehan is still maintaining his penance and God sends the Virgin Mary to comfort him and assure him of eventual pardon. The king decides to go hunting again and sets off for the forest with his huntsmen, who see Jehan and take him for a strange animal 'une beste la plus sauvage que sachiez'. While they surround and capture Jehan the king is moved to lament his long lost daughter. The king orders them not to hurt the beast but to bring it back to the palace alive. The hunting party and the christening party meet and the infant calls out to Jehan to stand up and come to the church and baptise him. The king realises they have caught not a beast but 'un saint homme penancier'. He tells Jehan to stand up as bidden by the child, and tell him the reason for his penance. Before he begins, Jehan begs mercy of the king who promises to grant it. Jehan then narrates the whole story (eighty lines). Then he sends the mother and child to the church and promises to follow them soon. He and the king visit the location where the princess was killed and invoke the help of the Virgin Mary. The courtiers all kneel near the well and pray. God and the Virgin both descend, accompanied by angels singing a rondeau, and Jehan begs them to restore the princess to life. God agrees and Jehan calls out to her and she answers. One of the courtiers offers to go down the well and with God's help he will bring up the princess. He does so and the princess explains that her soul was replaced in her body, and all the time she was in the well she was comforted by a beautiful lady – the Virgin herself. Rejoicing, the whole party set off for the church to christen the child and give thanks to God and the Virgin Mary. The king promises he will see Jehan is made a bishop.[12]

Another play on the subject is from the sixteenth century and is in Dutch.[13] Based on a *volksboek*, it attributes the story to the English St John of Beverley. The cast list is much smaller than the Cangé version: the princess (and all the court therefore) is replaced by Jan's sister whom he rapes when he is drunk and then murders. The Devil is included but, as is normal in the sixteenth century, the Virgin Mary does not feature in the play and her place is taken by *Stemme uuten Hemel* (voices from Heaven). The cast list also includes the *Bisshop van Cantelberghe* (Canterbury) and *Dat Kint* (the child). There is no known reason for this change of protagonist and the legend is quite unknown in England, but it was probably based on one of the German narrative versions of the story, described by Williams.

There is also a French play of St John Chrysostom (Cangé, VI) in which he is falsely accused of seducing the king's daughter (who, like Potiphar's wife, had in fact tried in vain to seduce him) and is banished to the desert where only a miracle saves him from the wild animals. His innocence is established but he is later again falsely accused of writing a letter against the king – actually the writer was the Devil. He is banished to a monastery and his hand is cut off but the Virgin Mary gives him a new one.[14] This story is actually a legend of St John Damascene and is dramatised in a

Jesuit play, based on the iconoclast controversy in which John supported
the use of ikons against the iconoclast emperor Leo Arminius: *S. Joannes
Damasceneus a B. V. Maria Restituta dextera Sanatus*, performed at Ingolstadt
in 1692 (Szarota, III, 2, p. 2119). The perioche for the play (III.1 pp. 643–8)
makes it clear the Virgin does not appear on stage.

BARLAAM AND JOSAPHAT

Linked with the lives of the Desert Fathers is the immensely popular
legend of SS. Barlaam and Josaphat (*Legenda* 27 November), based on a
story of the childhood of the Buddha which was christianised by St John
Damascene.[15]

Plays are extant in many languages including two French, *Barlaam et
Josaphat* (Cangé, XXI, and the three-day *Mystère du roi Advenir*), and two Italian, one, *Barlaam e Giosafatte* attributed to Bernardo Pulci (D'Ancona, II),
and another composed for the *Socci Perettano* in 1581.[16]

At the beginning of the Cangé play the queen has just died in childbirth
and her husband, the king of India, asks the astrologers about the future
of his infant son. One of them says that he will become a Christian –
a sect which the king hates. To avoid this, Avenir says he will be taken
to a 'manoir' where he will live secluded from the world with its poverty,
sickness and old age.[17] Then follows a long sermon which converts Barlaam (who, uniquely, is here a member of the royal household) and he
determines to become a Christian and go to the desert as a hermit. The
king sends for news of his son. The messenger finds him now a grown
man, closely resembling his father, and takes the good news back to the
king that he lives a happy life with much singing and dancing. The king
is also told of Barlaam's departure.[18] Furious, he sends one of his knights
to search the desert and bring Barlaam back with him to the court. The
king promises Barlaam he will not be harmed if he tells the reasons for his
departure and the hermit then preaches to the king at length, angering
him more and more, but the king keeps his word and allows Barlaam to
leave in safety.

The scene changes back to Josaphat who says he has lost all appetite
and love of life from being cooped up in isolation all the time. The king
says he may go out but his companions must keep him away from signs of
mortality or poverty. Inevitably he sees beggars, one a leper and one very
old, and learns of death. Alone he meditates on these tragedies and God
sends Gabriel to Barlaam with instructions he shall go to Josaphat and
convert him to Christianity. Barlaam disguises himself as a merchant and

gains access to the prince by claiming he has a jewel that can heal many ills. The scene of the conversion includes a lengthy speech by Barlaam on the dual nature of Christ as Man and God. The converted Josaphat wants to join Barlaam in the desert but is told this will cause persecution of Christians by the king and he must wait. Josaphat accepts this but when asked to sacrifice to the gods declares he is a Christian. The king is furious and one of his knights suggests they arrange a debate between Nachor, disguised as Barlaam, and the pagan doctors who will appear to convert Barlaam to their gods. Josaphat however recognises Nachor and when they are left alone together, he succeeds in converting Nachor to Christianity. The king's next ploy is to send a company of girls to be with Josaphat all the time.[19] Tempted by them, Josaphat invokes the Virgin Mary who comes to comfort and strengthen him. Eventually the king himself is converted and Josaphat takes his father and all the court to Barlaam to be baptised.

The three-day *Mystère du roi Advenir*[20] is fairly similar in the development of the story but the first day has much cruelty and killing of Christians; there are also later scenes of attacks on Christians and battles. After the failure of Nachor's debate the king gives up his efforts. He hands over half the kingdom to Josaphat but banishes him. Eventually all ends well and having completed his task of bringing Christianity to the whole land, Josaphat joins Barlaam in his hermitage till his death.

The Italian play of *Barlaam e Giosafat* (D'Ancona, II) is preceded by a lengthy essay on the Indian origin of the story and its development. The story line is similar to the Cangé text except that when the *donzella* comes to tempt Josaphat she first begs him to marry her which he refuses because vowed to celibacy; she then offers to convert to Christianity if he will spend one night with her. At this point he prays for help and an angel tells him he will overcome the temptations. The king gives half the empire to Josaphat to christianise and is himself eventually converted and baptised by Josaphat. Father and son both abdicate and go to the desert. Josaphat finds Barlaam in a cave (*spelunco*) and an angel announces his imminent death. Afterwards Josaphat buries him then returns to his cell.

Lope's *Barlan y Josafa* is traditional in the first two acts but has an original third act which influenced Calderon's *Vida es sueno*. In contrast to the *Roy Advenir* there is no violence on the stage and only references to the killing of Christians. While Josaphat is confined to the tower, the king sends music, dance and rich things to keep him contented. Barlaam is a hermit taken to India to help and convert the prince by an angel. Like

Habakkuk, he is lifted up by his hair (cf. Daniel 14). The scene of the debate with the false Barlaam is reminiscent of the plays of St Catherine of Alexandria. In Act II there is a major role for Leucipe, the woman who nearly seduces Josaphat but instead becomes a desert hermit herself. Act III takes place exclusively in the desert, with peasants and women trying to tempt the hermit, Josaphat. The play ends with Leucipe's death in a state of grace and bells ringing.

ST BERNARD OF MENTHON

Few plays exist of the development of the early religious orders pioneered by St Benedict of Monte Cassino, but there is an interesting two-day French play of the fifteenth century which tells of the foundation of the great monastery at the top of the alpine pass by which invaders from Hannibal to the Goths had crossed from Italy to France and vice versa. In the tenth century, both the great pass of Mont Joux called after a statue of Jupiter (*Jovis*) erected there by the Romans centuries before, together with a small hospice for travellers to rest at, as well as the smaller neighbouring pass, was infested by bands of *sarrasins* who attacked the pilgrims on their way to Rome.[21]

Bernard, the son of an aristocratic and wealthy family at Menthon, near Annecy, is a fine scholar and very devout. He wishes to enter religion but his father insists he marry the daughter of a neighbouring *seigneur*. Having invoked the aid of the Virgin Mary and St Nicholas, Bernard runs away the night before the ceremony.[22] With the continuing support of the Virgin, Bernard becomes first a canon and then archdeacon of the diocese of Aosta. In Day Two he travels widely in all parts of the mountainous area. The story is interspersed with scenes of the devils in the mountains working with and for an idol (the old Roman statue of Jupiter), and attacking all the pilgrims on their way across the Alps towards the tomb of St Peter in Rome. Eventually, Bernard arranges for the whole town to meet in prayer before going up to the pass to destroy the idol and the devils. Jupiter's idol is seized, bound and thrown into the abyss. Having cleared the pass of these evil forces Bernard sends for masons and carpenters to build a bigger and better hospice and eventually establishes a monastery on the site. Meanwhile he has purged the small pass which will also bear his name: le petit Saint-Bernard. His parents learn of the holy man called Bernard from Menthon, they are reunited with their lost son and make donations to the building funds. The *meneur de Jeu* then announces they will skip to the end of Bernard's life and stage his death and his miracles. The play concludes with an appeal to the audience to contribute to the upkeep of the hospice which serves so many travellers. It is probable therefore that the play was written for and performed at the Grand St Bernard monastery.

ST GUILLAUME DU DESERT AND GUILLAUME D'AQUITAINE

These plays are set in twelfth-century France but begin with a confusion between two characters of similar names. The village of St-Guillem-le-desert (not far from Montpellier) is the location of the hermitage in which, according to legend, Guillaume *al cort nez*, count of Aquitaine, one of Charlemagne's paladins and the central figure in the *chansons de geste* of the *Cycle de Guillaume d'Orange*, passed his last years.[23] William of Gellone was canonised in 1066 (AASS 28 May). The author of *St Guillem du desert* (Cangé, XI) actually tells the story of quite a different and later William of Aquitaine, a violent fighter, and a contemporary of St Bernard of Clairvaux with whom he quarrels because William supports Anacletus the anti-pope.[24] Bernard finally goes to see William and threatens him with a brandished crucifix to such effect that William falls in a swoon.[25] When he recovers, he confesses his sins and asks Bernard for penance.[26] He is sent from one hermit to another in search of absolution, one of them has a coat of mail riveted on to his body as a form of hair shirt to be worn night and day. He is then passed on to the pope, followed by the patriarch of Jerusalem who absolves him and tells him he is to remain for the rest of his life in penance in a hermit's cell.[27] Two scenes then follow which are loosely based on episodes from the *Moniage Guillaume* (which is part of the cycle of *Guillaume d'Orange*). Two of his former household come to beg Guillaume to return to the world and save his land from destruction. Guillaume refuses, but because he hesitates for one moment he is struck blind by God. After William has repented his sight is restored.[28] He then goes away to an even more remote place but there is attacked and badly beaten by Satan and Beelzebub and left unconscious. At this point the Virgin Mary makes her statutory appearance in the play. Attended by singing saints and angels she and God descend to earth. Mary heals William and promises him imminent death and salvation. Two unknown men, Albert and Regnault, come to the hermitage. They attend the dying William, then bury his body while his soul is carried up to Heaven by SS Agnes and Christine.

There is no other medieval play of William of Aquitaine but there is a two-day German play of the sixteenth century from Lucerne. The first day text survives and there is a detailed stage plan which clearly indicates that the character and events are the same as in the Cangé play.[29] The story was also very popular with the Jesuits in Germany. Szarota (III, 2, pp. 28–30) lists three plays on the theme, *Guillaume Loricatus* (*Le Cuirassé*, Bale 1691),[30] *G. Eremita* (Munich 1703) and *G. Poenitens* (Eichstatt 1706). William also featured in a debate-play on War and Peace in Feldkirch in 1675 (Eichstatt).

CHAPTER 3

Soldiers of Christ: the Church militant

There are a number of medieval plays, mainly from Italy, on saints of the twelfth and thirteenth centuries, especially Dominic, Francis and members of the religious orders who struggled to deal with the decay in European Christianity and the growth of heresies.

ST FRANCIS OF ASSISI

There are three Italian plays of the life of St Francis. One by Antonia Pulci[1] is a rapid survey (800 lines) of the main incidents in the saint's life including his parting with his father, visit to the pope and to the sultan, the giving of the stigmata and finally his death. According to Cioni, the other play, the *Rappresentazione di San Francesco come converti tre ladroni* (based on a story in *The little flowers of St Francis*, ch. xxvi) was printed a dozen times between 1490 and 1620. There is also an Italian play on Francis receiving the stigmata.[2] He speaks to the brothers of the glory of the angels who see God and refers to the *serafino ardente* (burning seraph). Christ appears to him 'In serafica forma . . . de la mie passion ti fo segnato' (in form of a seraph . . . I will mark you with the signs of my Passion).[3] Quotes interesting staging details for the receiving of the stigmata from a Catalan Corpus Christi *Consueta de Sant Francesc*. The play was performed on a two-level stage and Frances was on the upper level. A curtain was drawn across and when it reopened 'se mostrera Francese ab les nafres a les mans, peus y coste' (Frances appeared with the wounds in his hands, feet and side).

Italian Francis and his Friars Minor were important in the revival of Christianity by their personal example, Spanish Dominic's contribution was the founding of the Order of Preachers.[4]

ST DOMINIC AND THE ORDER OF PREACHERS

The French *Mistere de l'Institucion de l'Ordre des Freres Prescheurs*, printed in the early sixteenth century, is more of a *moralité* than a saints' play.

It opens with a scene of Heresy and the Devil seeking to lead each of the three estates, Eglise, Noblesse and Labour, away from the true faith and into heretical beliefs. While obstinacy covers the three estates in her great cloak, Dominic prays for the world and the sinners there, that they may repent. God appears holding three lances, Death, War and Famine, which he will loose on the sinful world. In a scene taken from the legend of St Dominic (*Legenda* 4 August), the Virgin Mary then enters and begs for mercy for the world. God reminds her of all he has done for Mankind even to submitting to death on the cross but all in vain, man is incurable. Finally the Virgin introduces her servant, Dominic, who will by his preaching succeed in breaking the stranglehold of Obstinacy over the estates. God accepts and promises not to use his lances. The rest of the play narrates incidents from the founding and development of the Order of Preachers, especially the story of St Regnault who is struck down by illness, but when Dominic prays for him the Virgin descends in traditional miracle style with her escort of angels and heals him. He becomes one of the leading preachers in the order and indeed dominates the rest of the play at the expense of Dominic.[5]

A play from Orvieto[6] based on the *Legenda* (4 August) describes how Dominic is sent to school in Palencia and when there is a famine in the area he sells his books and clothes to buy food for the poor. The other students follow his example. While in Rome he is visited by SS Peter and Paul and then by the Virgin who tells him to create an order under her patronage to preach the true faith. Many join him and put on the black and white Dominican habit. While preaching in the south of France he is challenged by a group of unbelievers *I Patarini* (a thirteenth-century synonym for Cathars) who ask him by what authority he claims his book (the Bible) contains the only true law? Dominic tells them to throw the Bibles into the fire but they are unharmed, and he explains that God is greater than the normal laws of the universe. Most of them swear not to reveal the miracle but one is converted and later tells the story. They are converted and abandon their heresy.

Bologna was one of the strongholds of the Dominicans during the schism of the fourteenth century and it is also the location of the tomb of the Founder, a magnificent structure in the church of St Dominic. It is not surprising therefore that there should also be a play of St Dominic from Bologna, the *Turbamento di Jesu Christo*, an unpublished fifteenth-century play on the same subject as the scene in the French *Mistere* between God and the Virgin but introducing both Dominic and Francis. The risen and ascended Christ expresses his anger at the sins of the Church and his determination to put an end to the sinful world he had redeemed. He is described as having three lances in his hand and, in a scene reminiscent of the preliminaries to the Flood, declares his intention of sending destruction on the earth: 'and God seeing that the wickedness of men was great on the earth . . . repented him that he had made man' (Genesis 6:5–6; for 'made' read 'redeemed'). There is then a debate similar to the Trial in Heaven in which Justice encourages Christ's actions, but Mercy holds him back, literally, from hurling the lances. After much argument on Man's sinfulness, Mercy sends for the Virgin to come and plead for mankind. She agrees with her Son that the world is very sinful but explains that she has taken steps to remedy this. She opens her cloak and reveals SS Dominic and Francis who are to be the means of reforming the sinful world. Christ agrees that the preaching of these two and their followers will be effective and foretells the giving of the stigmata to St Francis. The play ends with Justice withdrawing her demands for Man's punishment.[7] The addition of St Francis in the play links up with the *Legenda* in which it is a Franciscan friar minor who relates to a group of Dominicans the story of the vision. It is also noteworthy that a statue of the saint from Assisi is included on St Dominic's tomb.

According to a tradition going back to the fifteenth century, the devotion of the Rosary was founded by St Dominic and features in two plays, one French and one Dutch. In *Le marchand préservé de mort* (Cangé, XI), an uncle sends his nephew off to Bruges to learn to be a merchant with the help of an experienced older man, Polet. The nephew tells Polet to go ahead and he will join him shortly. Then the nephew begins to recite his 'sautiers', a series of psalms in honour of the Virgin Mary which he had promised he would repeat every day. Mary sees that a thief and murderer is lying in wait for the young merchant and descends from heaven with her escort to protect the young man. After her departure, the thief tells the nephew he will kill him if he does not hand over the beautiful lady who had been with him. The bewildered nephew cannot undertstand what he is saying until the thief mentions the 'chapel' she had put on his head. He finds he has been crowned by a wreath of roses and realises it was the Virgin who had been there. Although desolate that he had not seen the Virgin he tries to convert the thief and persuades him to visit a hermit who will instruct him. The thief narrates to the hermit how he had seen the Virgin crown the youth with a chaplet of roses which she had gathered one by one from his mouth as he was reciting his prayers.[8] The nephew thanks the Virgin for her great kindness and for converting the thief but laments that he had not seen her as well. She descends again

with her escort of singing angels. The play ends with the hermit, the thief
and the nephew setting off together to visit the great shrine of the Virgin
at Rocamadour. Cornelis Everaaert's *Maria Houdeken* composed in 1509
is based on the same legend but all the cast are allegorical figures and
there is no appearance of the Virgin herself.[9]

A number of plays treat of other Dominican saints including St
Catherine of Sienna. The first recorded play on Catherine was performed in Metz in 1468 – only seven years after her canonisation in
1461 – and is noteworthy as the earliest known example of a woman (an
eighteen-year-old girl) taking the leading role in a public play.[10]

That preaching against heresy could be dangerous as well as difficult
is shown in an Italian play on the story of St Peter Martyr.[11] He was born
in Verona of Cathar parents and the play shows him being converted
by the schoolmaster. After much argument he leaves home and goes to
the Dominican priory where he is accepted as a friar. The rest of the
play consists of dialogues between various Dominicans and finally the
pope sends Peter to preach in Milan. The text ends here. Peter's many
miracles (listed in the *Legenda* 29 April)[12] are omitted as is his murder while
on a preaching tour against the Cathars in 1252. He was canonised the
following year.

St Thomas Aquinas (28 January), one of the great Doctors of the
Church, studied at the university of Paris and spent the rest of his life
teaching and writing his famous *Summa theologica*. The three-day *Legenna
di Sancto Tomascio*[13] is one of the most important of the texts from the
Abruzzi region collected and edited by de Bartholomaeis. It opens with
St Dominic imploring the Virgin to send him more fellow workers. She
foretells the birth of Thomas (c. 1225) son of the countess of Aquina
who will be *dottore serrano* (angelic doctor – the sobriquet of St Thomas).
The Virgin, with her customary escort of angels, is sent to the castle of
Aquina to bear witness to the future greatness of the child. It is decided
to send him to the Benedictines at Monte Cassino to be educated. He
delights everyone by his piety and scholarship. The first day ends with
his setting off for Naples to complete his education. Day two continues to
describe his growth and his determination, against the will of his parents,
to join the newly founded Order of Preachers (as the Virgin had foretold
in the play before his birth). He becomes a bone of contention between
the pope and the emperor but finally all is settled. The third act mostly
takes place in Paris where Thomas studies with Albertus Magnus, the
leading theologian of the time. The act includes a well-known story of St
Thomas being entertained to dinner by the king of France (St Louis). To

the horror of the other guests Thomas goes off into a trance considering how to defeat the Manichean heresy and finally declares 'contra maniceei me concluso éne' (that should settle the Manichees). When his attention is brought back to the present, he apologises profusely to the king who simply instructs one of his secretaries to go and write down St Thomas' train of thought before he forgets it.

When he has returned to Naples, Thomas is trying to understand the book of Isaiah and prays to God for help from SS. Peter and Paul. The two saints are sent to his aid. Other episodes include the pope's summons to him to compose the liturgy for the new Feast of Corpus Christi.[14] The play ends with his death in 1274 and some post-mortem miracles. He was canonised in 1323.

THE SOCIETY OF JESUS AND SAINTS OF THE COUNTER-REFORMATION

Although many early saints' lives continued to be dramatised through to the eighteenth century or even later, a new and important group of dramatists with additional subject matter emerged in the middle of the sixteenth century: the Order of Jesus, better known as the Jesuits. Reference has already been made to their plays on the earlier saints but they also contributed a substantial number of new ones, the earliest being Hermenegildus, the son of the visigothic king in Seville in the sixth century. He was brought up as an Arian but married an Austrian princess and became a Catholic. When he returned to Spain, his father, urged on by his second wife and her son, tried to force Hermenegildus to return to Arianism and when he refused he was executed in 586. A thousand years later in 1585 the Jesuits in Seville (where the college bore his name) succeeded in having him canonised.[15]

Hundreds of plays on the founder of the Jesuits, Ignatius of Loyola, were written and performed in the colleges in 1622, the year he was canonised. They also introduced a new group of martyrs, the Jesuits, who worked in the Far East. These plays were very popular with the teachers in the colleges because one of the order's principle aims was to prepare members for martyrdom.

Other schools also had regular theatre performances. In 1546 Ralph Radcliffe founded a school at Hitchin (just north of London) complete with a regular theatre 'in which his schoolboys gave annual performances of both Latin and English plays'.[16] Among the list of moral and bib- lical subjects including Judith and Job, Patient Griselda and Titus and

Gisippus, there appears the damnation of John Huss the Bohemian priest who became a Wycliffite and was burnt for heresy in 1415.

In a rare play on Protestant martyrs, the *Tragédie du sac de Cabrière* tells the true story of the massacre of the Vaudois in the town of Cabrière in southern Provence in 1540.[17] With the spread of the Reformation the leaders of the French protestants fled to Geneva to join the Calvinists and the last surviving community of this primitive sect was attacked by the local chief justice, the seigneur Oppède, a fanatical Catholic. They held out in their walled town against the attacking forces till Oppède persuaded them to surrender by guaranteeing their safety. When the gates were opened Oppède's forces surged into the town, hacking the men to pieces in the square and locking the women and children in the church to which they then set fire. The victims of Cabrière were listed in the Reform Church's *Histoire des martyrs* by Crespius.[18] (*Sac de Cabrière* Introduction, pp. 8–9).

Another victim of the quarrel of church and state is portrayed in the little known *Tragédie du Bon Kanut roy de Dannemarch*, which was composed in French in 1575 and survives in two manuscripts.[19] Canute the fourth, the nephew of the English king Canute, was a great supporter of Christianity in Denmark and in 1086 was killed in a church by a group of dissatisfied knights, led by his brother, who resented his policy on tithes. He was canonised in 1101.[20]

Among the plays on political martyrs of the Reform and Counter-Reform there are a number on Sir Thomas More including the English play by Munday and Chettle composed c. 1590.[21] The religious reasons for More's execution are not specified and the political clash between him and king Henry is discreetly treated. Several performances of Jesuit plays of *Thomas More* (*Thomas Morus*) in Luxembourg, France and Germany are recorded by Stegmann between 1620 and 1630. *Henricus Octavus* (1624) by Nicolaus Vernulaeus, head of the trilingual college in Louvain, treats Henry and his clash with More and others from a wider point of view: in Henry 'we are shown a magnanimous person whose gradual disintegration of character is set forth so convincingly that we never lose sympathy for his plight as a human being under the strain of decision'.[22] The subject was also popular on the public stage and in Paris, Pujet de la Serre's *Thomas Morus* was an enormous success. Richelieu saw it three times. It was published in 1642.[23]

Vernulaeus' plays also include *Thomas Cantuariensis* (1625), who, like More, was a martyr to conflict between church and state.[24] It is interesting but not surprising that no English play of the English martyr is

extant, though many references are recorded in the fourteenth and fifteenth centuries especially in East Anglia. In Canterbury there was a
'dramatization of Thomas Becket' annually in the first half of the sixteenth century with records of expenses for costumes and staging which
suggest a substantial play on the subject.[25]

Saints who were significant not so much in the spread of Christianity
as in the early history of Europe, such as St Sylvester who converted
Constantine and St Remi who converted Clovis, king of France, are
treated in Part Four.

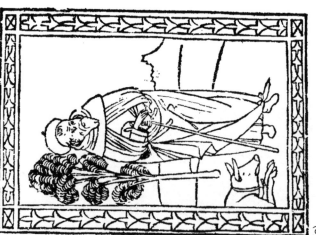

1 (a) St Anthony the Great with his pet pig. (b) St Eustace goes hunting.

2 (a) The 'hairy hermit' is captured by the huntsmen. (b) St Jan van Beverley seduces his sister, then kills and buries her.

(a)

(b)

3 (a) The Devil tries to kill Mariken before she can repent. (b) Her uncle's prayers save Mariken's life.

(a)

(b)

4 (a) Theophilus, the Devil and the Virgin Mary. (b) The Jew obtains a Host from the woman and then tortures it.

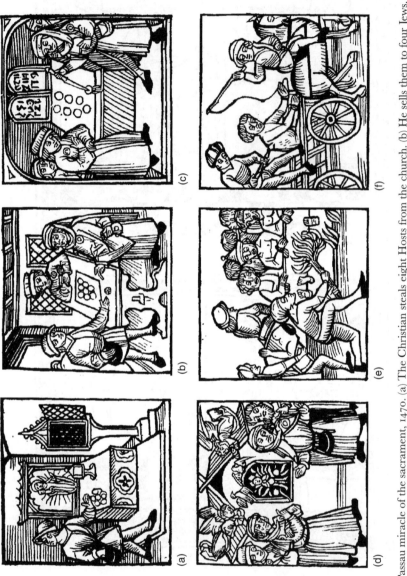

5 The Passau miracle of the sacrament, 1470. (a) The Christian steals eight Hosts from the church. (b) He sells them to four Jews. (c) The Jews stab the Host. (d) When the Host is put in an oven it becomes a child. Angels and doves fly out. (e) The Jews are burnt at the stake. (f) The Christian is tortured with heated iron hooks.

PART TWO

Miracles of salvation

Miracle plays may be divided into those included in a play of the saint's life, and the so-called post-mortem miracles, where the deceased saint reappears as a helper in need. Two saints' lives include miracles – St Meriasek and St Genevieve of Paris.[1] Post-mortem miracles by St James of Compostella and St Andrew were also dramatised.[2] The only saint to feature in both kinds of play is St Nicholas.[3]

By far the most important miracle worker in the drama, however, is the Virgin Mary, narrative versions of whose miracles are found in Latin from a very early date and in vernacular from the twelfth century, though the earliest extant play is late thirteenth century.[4] Miracles of Our Lady easily outstrip Nicholas in quantity (though not necessarily in quality) with more than fifty plays from France, and others from Italy and Spain. There is also the one interpolated in the Cornish play of St Meriasek, which tells how a woman stole the Christ Child from the Virgin's statue because the Virgin Mary had not helped her son who had been taken prisoner. An *auto del nino perdido* was performed in 1600 by the students of the *colegio trilingue* in Salamanca, but the author was criticised by the local Inquisition for employing improper language because he implied that the Virgin did not know that she was 'sinless' (*no tenia peccado*) because she said: '*Yo debo de ser culpada, o miserores / fueron merecedores de tal pena*' (I should be considered guilty, my misdeeds / merited such suffering).[5]

The power of the Virgin and her sometimes idiosyncratic justice is in marked contrast to St Nicholas' more orthodox methods. While the former is involved in rescuing penitent sinners who have been devoted to her,[6] Nicholas is primarily concerned with giving physical help to the poor and needy, and converting the Jew or the pagan.

CHAPTER 4

Miraculous conversions of Jews
(and a few pagans)

The Jew, presented as an extra-biblical character, makes his dramatic debut arguing with and being convinced by Isaiah, in the dialogue intercalated into the prophet sequence in the twelfth-century Anglo-Norman Adam play.[1] Jews subsequently feature in miracle and sacrament plays in Latin, English, French, German and Italian, sometimes as sober members of society fulfilling their traditional role of money-lenders, and potentially saved by conversion to Christianity, sometimes as the villains of the piece. In the following survey the miracles of St Nicholas and the Virgin Mary involving a Jew are grouped by themes in order of the play texts, not according to the date of the narrative sources.

ST NICHOLAS AND THE *ICONIA* PLAYS

The earliest play in which the *Iconia* (or statue of the saint) has an important role is found among the works of the wandering scholar, Hilarius, composed early in the twelfth century. The central character here is Barbarus, a pagan who has obtained possession of an image of St Nicholas, in whose 'magical' powers he has learned to trust.[2] Barbarus sets out on a journey, leaving the image as guard over the treasure in his house but robbers come and, finding the door open, steal all the goods. When Barbarus returns, he first laments the loss of the property, and then denounces and beats the image. St Nicholas, in his own person, visits the robbers, and, with threats of disclosing their crime, commands them to return the plunder which was under HIS protection. When the robbers have carried out this command, Barbarus joyfully and penitently gives thanks to the image. St Nicholas himself appears again and converts Barbarus.

This early account of the *Iconia* miracle stresses the conflict between pagans and Christians as the reason for the central character to have a devotion to St Nicholas, which makes the choice of Barbarus a logical one and also explains the extensive development of the crusading elements at the beginning of the next play. The *Jeu de St Nicholas*, c. 1200, by Jean Bodel of Arras was written for performance on the vigil of the feast. This, the earliest vernacular miracle play extant, also draws on the Latin source including the preliminary description of war between the Vandals and the Christians during which the pagan learns of the latter's veneration for the image of St Nicholas, and acquires it for himself. Bodel transfers the period to the crusades and introduces the character of the Christian owner of the image, who is captured by pagans. Their king, who already has an idol called Tervagant, is impressed by the prisoner's description of the powers of St Nicholas and determines to try them. When he discovers the thieves have stolen the treasure, the king threatens not the statue but its owner. He also attacks and beats his own statue – thus rearranging rather than omitting the incidents of the legend. However St Nicholas forces the thieves to return the treasure though neither here nor in any of the other versions of the *Iconia* are the thieves reformed or punished. At the end, Tervagant is destroyed and the pagan king and his followers are baptised – if not entirely converted.[3]

At this point in the evolution of the theme, a major change occurs, for in the next play, from the thirteenth-century MS of the Fleury play book (which includes four St Nicholas plays), the pagan and the crusades have disappeared for ever and are replaced by a Jew and when the story is recounted in the late thirteenth century (*Legenda* 6 December), the central character is Judeus not Barbarus. All the other plays of the *Iconia* miracle feature the Jew not the Barbarus.

This change perhaps echoes the passing of the crusading fervour of the *chansons de geste* and the beginning of the scenes of everyday life typical of much early drama. The opening rubric of the Fleury *Iconia* informs us that a certain Jew has been accustomed to venerate an image of St Nicholas hidden in his house, and that he has become rich. As the play opens the Jew is setting out upon a journey, leaving his possessions in an unlocked chest under the protection of the image. When he returns to find them gone he laments the loss of his riches, deplores his past confidence in St Nicholas and promises the image a beating – tomorrow, because he is too tired tonight. Meanwhile St Nicholas visits the robbers and threatens them with criminal punishment if they do not return the stolen goods to the owner that night. At the restoration of his possessions the Jew rejoices, and calls upon the bystanders to give praise to St Nicholas.

An Iconia of a different kind appears in one of a list from a Dutch rhetorician's group in the fifteenth century which includes *Item, het spel van den Smet van Cameroen*. In this story, attributed by Gautier de Coinci to St Jerome, a Jew visits the house of a Christian acquaintance and sees there a picture of the Virgin Mary which the Christian venerates. The Jew angrily rejects the idea of the great God being born of this *mariole* and throws the picture in the privy. At once his soul is carried off by devils – there is no conversion here! The picture is rescued unharmed by the Christian, and to his awe and delight oil begins to flow from it which serves to heal all illnesses. In another version of the story it is specified that the painting grows breasts from which the oil flows – a distinctly Salvador Dali picture!

MERCHANTS AND MONEY-LENDERS

Money plays a major role in other miracle plays which all lead, eventually, to the conversion of the Jews. In an Italian Marian miracle play, Agnolo's Christian wife prays to the Virgin Mary for the conversion of her husband, (alternately described as *Agnolo ebreo* or *Agnolo pagano*),[4] who is more concerned on how to invest forty 'dinari'. She urges him to give his money to the poor and God will return it a hundredfold.[5] Eventually he does so and the Virgin arranges for him to acquire a fish with a rich jewel inside. Agnolo is, naturally, delighted and converted. In Bidermann's play of *Jakob the usurer*, Jakob is a greedy and dishonest money-lender but devoted to the Virgin and says his Rosary regularly. When he dies the scales are heavily weighted against him till the Virgin Mary adds the rosary which makes his good deeds weigh most and he is saved (Best, *Bidermann*, p. 56). An amusing Protestant variant of this theme is the earliest of Sach's *Fastnachtspiele* loosely based on a Boccaccio story (Decameron I:6). A simple but rich man hears in church the reference to the hundredfold repayment and commiserates with the miserly monks who in the next life will be drowned in the hundredfold return they will receive for the three cauldrons of swill which they give the poor every week.[6]

   The sixteenth-century play of *St Nicholas et le juif* is based on a story commemorated in one of the twelfth-century windows of York Minster and included in the *Legenda*. It tells how a Christian borrowed some money from a Jew, giving him his oath on the altar of St Nicholas that he would repay it as soon as possible. As he was slow in paying, the Jew demanded his money; but the man declared that he had returned it. He was summoned before the judge, who ordered him to swear that he had repaid the money. In the meantime, the man had placed the money that he owed in a hollow staff, and before giving his oath, he asked the Jew to hold the staff for him.[7] Whereupon he swore that he had returned the money and more besides. Then he took back his staff, the Jew handing it over all unaware of the trick.[8]

On the way home the defrauder fell asleep on the roadside and was run over by a chariot, which also broke open the staff in which the gold was hidden.[9] Learning this, the Jew ran to the spot; but although the bystanders pressed him to take his money, he said that he would do so only if, by the merits of St Nicholas, the dead man was restored to life, adding that in this event he himself would receive baptism and be converted to the faith of Christ. Immediately the dead man came back to life, and the Jew was baptised.

There is a strong influence of farce in this dramatised version of the story. The Christian and his wife talk of behaving like Pathelin (who bought cloth and pretended to have been ill in bed all day when the seller came for his money) and, at the wife's suggestion, they borrow the money without any intention of giving it back. The legal set-up is also treated humorously, with the indignant Jew being told he will have to pay the costs of his suit to get his money back. Throughout the play, the Jew is seen as the goodie and the Christian and his Lady Macbeth of a wife, are the villains of the piece. Though the former, on being restored to life, confesses his sins and asks the Jew's forgiveness there is no indication of a similar act by the wife.

A very different story, though also involving a business deal between a Christian and a Jew, is found in the miracle of the *Marchand Chretien et le juif* (Cangé, XXXV) probably performed in 1377.[10] A rich bourgeois of Constantinople, named Audry, who has a great devotion to Our Lady has ruined himself by his extravagant hospitality and his many charities. Finally to help a friend marry off his daughter, he goes to a Jew named Mossé, to borrow money, and complains (like Timon of Athens before and after him) that none of his so-called friends or relatives will help him in his plight. Mossé agrees to lend him money to restore his fortunes if he has a guarantor. Audry names Jesus and his Mother. Mossé remarks that he cannot believe that the man who was crucified could be God but he is prepared to concede him the status of a prophet.[11] They go into a church and Audry swears before an image of the Virgin and Child that if he has not repaid the money by the date due he will become the Jew's slave for ever.[12]

Audry goes abroad and soon begins to make money and sends home well-laden ships. But it is only on the eve of the day he must repay the money that he remembers the bond and cursing himself for his stupidity he puts the money in a coffer addressed to the Jew, throws it into the sea and implores Jesus to make sure it arrives in time. The following day, Mossé's servant is walking by the sea and sees the coffer floating but cannot get hold of it. He tells his master who takes it without difficulty, finds it full of gold, takes the money and hides the coffer under his bed. The source makes it clear he knows it is from Audry, the play leaves the matter open.

When Mossé learns of Audry's return to Constantinople, he goes to claim his debt, or, since Audry has not paid, he says, to claim him as slave. Audry insists he has paid and takes Mossé to the statue whence a voice explains what has happened. Astonished and repentant, Mossé is converted, baptised and gives all his goods to the poor.

It is obvious that the *Merchant of Venice* and this rather different casket story have some elements in common.[13] In both plays the hero has borrowed money to help a friend or friend's daughter to get married; in both the hero makes a bond with a Jew. In Cangé, however, the Merchant is not bartering his life but his freedom, and it is Audry's own fault the money is not returned, not ill fortune as in the case of Antonio, and belated thought for his friend as in the case of Bassanio. In both texts the hero is rescued by a female intercessor, either the Virgin Mary or Portia: 'a Daniel come to judgement'![14] At the end of the *Merchant*, Shylock is forcibly converted; in the miracle play the Jew converts willingly.

In all these plays, the theme is riches and loss of riches, involving a falling out with God or his saint (no one ever blames the Virgin!) and a final conversion and reconciliation. They mostly include an image, with or without an altar, so that the theme of the *Iconia* protecting the owner's treasure underlies also the money-lender plays.

CHAPTER 5

Sacrament plays

Jews also appear but in a very different role in the sacrament plays. Although the emphasis on the Eucharist in the 1215 Lateran Council and the subsequent declaration of the Bull setting up the feast of Corpus Christi in 1264[1] was so important for the development of medieval drama, especially in England and Spain, plays which actually treat of the sacrament do not appear before the end of the fifteenth century.[2]

THE PARIS MIRACLE OF THE PROFANED HOST

According to tradition, in Paris in 1290, a Jew tried to 'kill' the Host he had obtained by blackmailing a Christian woman. She had pawned her skirt with him and could not afford to redeem it to wear to Mass on Easter day. He attacked the Host with knife, lance and hatchet before throwing it in a cauldron of boiling water from which rose up a crucifix. He was betrayed to the authorities by his own wife and son who were horrified and converted to Christianity. The Jew himself, unrepentant, was condemned and burned. The 'miracle' was commemorated in historical records and represented also in enamels and stained glass. A Mass was said in honour of the Host ever year on Low Sunday in the Chapelle des Miracles built over the site of the Jew's house (24 rue des Archives) which had been razed to the ground. As late as 1685 a plaque on the commemorative chapel read: 'Ci-dessous le juif fit bouillir la sainte hostie' (In this place the Jew boiled the sacred Host) and in 1328, Clemence of Hungary left £10 to the 'couvent ou Dieu fut bouilli' (the monastery where God was boiled).[3]

By the fifteenth century the miracle was the subject of an annual procession and tableau, as described in the *Journal d'un bourgeois de Parisi* in 1444:

Item, fut faite une des piteuses et la plus dévote procession que on eust oncques veue à Paris car l'évesque de Paris, celui de Beauvais et deux abbés portèrent le corps de Nostre Seigneur, de Saint-Jehan en Grève sur les espaules; et de là allèrent aux Billettes querre à grant révérence le quanivet de quoy le faux Juif avoit dépicqué la char de Nostre Seigneur, et de là furent portés avec la sainte croix et autres reliques sans nombre a Sainte-Catherine du Val des Escolliers; et y avoit devant plus de cinq cents torches allumées, et de peuple bien neuf ou dix mille personnes, sans ceux de l'église; et avoit après ces saintes reliques, tout le mistère du Juif, qui estoit en une charrette, lié, ou il avoit espines comme se on le menast ardoir; et après venoit la justice, sa femme et ses enfants. Et parmy les rues avoit deux eschaffaux de trés piteux mystères. Et furent les rues parées comme à la Saint-Sauveur.

(There was a procession in Paris, one of the most touching, the most devout, that there had ever been. The bishops of Paris and of Beauvais and two abbots bore on their shoulders the Body of Our Lord from St-Jean-en-Grève and went from there to *Les Billettes* to fetch, most reverently, the little knife with which the false Jew had cut up Our Lord's flesh. From there these were carried, together with the Holy Cross and countless other relics, to St-Catherine-du-Val-des-Ecoliers. In front went more than five hundred burning torches and at least nine or ten thousand people, not counting the clergy. After the holy relics came the whole Mystery of the Jew; he was shown bound in a cart with thorns in it as if he were on his way to be burned; next came the judge; then his wife and children. There were two platforms put up in the streets with very touching mysteries on them and the streets were decorated as they are at Corpus Christi.) (p. 330)[4]

The miracle was not dramatised in France until the early sixteenth century. Three printed editions survive of the *Mystère de la Sainte Hostie*, one from 1512–19(?); a second from c. 1531 and a third from 1547–66.[5] Runnalls suggests that the play was probably written for and performed (in Paris) by a Confraternity whose foundation is mentioned in the text of the earliest edition. It was performed in Metz in 1513, and the chronicler Philippe de Vigneulles describes the *secrets* and *feintes*, in great detail. For example, when the Jew stabbed the Host 'sortit grand abondance de sang . . . comme se ce fut ung enfant qui pissoit' (there came out a great quantity of blood . . . like a child pissing). Another performance, but with no details, is recorded from Laval on Corpus Christi and the day after it in 1533.[6] The second day may have included the episode in the play in which the woman who stole the Host flees to Senlis and lives there seven years working in a hostelry. She bears an illegitimate child which she kills and is finally brought to justice and burned. She dies repentant and absolved.

THE FLORENTINE SACRAMENT PLAY

The Italian sacrament play was composed in the late fifteenth century. The main lines of the story are similar to the French miracle but there are significant differences of detail. The woman in the Florentine play is a victim of her husband's gambling since in this play it is he who takes her skirt and pawns it to get money to pay his debts. Moreover, in this play the Jew is discovered not by his wife and family (who do not appear) but by the river of blood which runs out of his house. He is arrested and executed, impenitent, but the woman is saved by a personal intervention of St Thomas Aquinas who appears in a dream to the king and urges him to accept the woman's penitence and free her.[7]

THE CROXTON SACRAMENT PLAY

In the English Croxton sacrament play the miracle is described as taking place in the city of Eraclea in Aragon and being 'presented at Rome in the yere of our Lord, a thowsand fowr hundred sixty and one' (p. 59). A major difference with the earlier legend is that this miracle is seen as a 'playe of the conversion of Ser Jonathas the Jewe by Myracle of the Blyssed Sacrament'[8]. The thief in this play is a greedy merchant, Sir Aristorie, who makes a bargain to sell the Jew a Host for a hundred pounds. He gets the priest drunk, takes his key and goes to the church and steals the Host from the tabernacle. The Jews torment the Host in a series of incidents which follow the events of the crucifixion – beating, stabbing, nailing – and eventually put it in an oven (burial?) from which it bursts forth in the form of the crucified Christ (resurrection).[9] All the Jews are converted at these marvels. They confess their deed and after penance are baptised by the bishop. The priest and the merchant also do penance and the latter, who sees his sin as one of 'coveitise', is ordered to cease all buying and selling.

Throughout this sequence, there is none of the French violence and horror at the sin of the thief or the torturers. The tale is a moral and spiritual warning not a denunciation leading to death. As such it sounds most improbable for an event in the violently anti-Semitic Spain of the late fifteenth century. F. E. Barns in a Chicago dissertation of 1926 suggests that the change of location of the incident from Paris to Aragon 'was made in the text played in Rome before Leonore of Aragon in 1473, which the English writer may have seen or heard about'.[10] Since there is no city of Eraclea in Aragon, or reference to a miracle of the sacrament anywhere in the region, it seems more likely that the location had been confused with the distinguished spectator. The casual way in which the merchant steals the wafer, and is treated with incredible leniency at the end of the story, is hardly credible in the land of the Inquisition, but it is possible that the basis of the play is an event in Passau, Germany, in 1471. The story is portrayed in a detailed series of twelve pictures in a broadsheet, beginning with a picture of a merchant (called Christoff) taking eight wafers from the pyx on the altar while the adjacent tabernacle has its door wide open. He sells them to the Jews. The later scenes also fit the story well: there are four Jews involved, the wafer is stabbed and bleeds and when put in the oven and burned, two angels and two doves fly out. So far there are similarities but the end is quite different and much more credible in view of the extreme sanctity of the Host. The Jews are tortured and executed and Christoff is set on a waggon and torn with heated hooks.[11] An Italian play is listed by de Batines which seems to be on the same subject: *La rappresentazione di un miracolo del Corpo di Cristo*, he says, is quite a different play from the one about the women and her skirt and treats of 'un Cristiano che vende l'Osta consacrata ad un Giudeo' and the miracles that follow.[12]

THE BOLSENA MIRACLE

A play from Orvieto, based on the Bolsena miracle, tells how a German priest who has doubts of the Real Presence of Christ in the Eucharist is sent by his confessor on pilgrimage to Rome. On his way home he stops in the little town of Bolsena (near Orvieto) and goes to celebrate Mass in the church of St Christina. Two bystanders see him fall, rush forward and see the miracle: blood is dripping from the consecrated wafer on to the corporal. The pope is summoned, declares: 'We have here a great miracle of the "Corpo di Cristo"', and summons Thomas Aquinas to compose the Propers for a new feast.[13]

THE DUTCH SACRAMENT PLAY FROM NIEUWERVAART

The Dutch *Spel van der heiligen sacramente* from Nieuwervaart has some of the elements of the Bolsena miracle play mixed with scenes reminiscent of the Jews torturing the Host in the other plays. It tells the story of the miraculous discovery in 1300, in a ditch near the town of what appears to be a eucharistic wafer. Since there is no mud on it, the finders, a man who was digging in the ditch and two passing women, decide it must be a consecrated Host and kneel down and venerate it. They take it to the pastor and it is reverently placed in the church. The local bishop is informed. Meanwhile the devils, *Sondich Becoren* and *Belet van Dueghden* (Sinful Attraction and Prevention of Virtue), are desperate at the discovery, knowing Lucifer will be furious with them for allowing it to happen.

The bishop's envoy, a certain Macharius arrives in the town with instructions to test the wafer and decide if it is genuine. His first speech shows his doubts: he does not believe that it was found buried in mud because it still looks so fresh, though he also admits that God could have done this if he had wished. He rejects the devils' suggestions he should burn it or throw it in water since if it proves to be genuine, the whole world would know he had put it to that test and probably he would be burned himself (ll. 405–6). Interestingly, he does not explicitly, or even implicitly, say why he does not want to drown it or cut it into pieces (as suggested in l. 416) for it to reassemble if it is a genuine Host. Finally he decides to stab it five times (i.e. with the five wounds of Christ). If it does not bleed anywhere he will not take it to be the real sacrament (ll. 424–5). The testing takes place in the presence of the pastor and the three 'finders' and at the fifth stab blood flows. All are appalled at what Macharius has done and he runs away muttering that the bishop told him to test it. All the others kneel in veneration.

The story spreads around the province and many miracles are per-formed by the Host, from healing the sick to converting the heathen. The bishop admits his sin in not accepting the Host without proof and gives up his diocese. The local overlord, the count of Nassau, decides the Host should be taken to the city of Breda so many more people can see and venerate it. The play ends with rejoicing and honouring of the Host. A Brotherhood of the Sacred Host performed the play regularly – their coat of arms shows the Host's arrival in Breda in 1449.[14]

CHAPTER 6

Your adversary the Devil: the saved and the damned

In a number of medieval plays there are trial scenes of groups or individuals in which the argument is presented as a direct conflict between the powers of good usually, but not exclusively, represented by the Virgin Mary and the powers of darkness personified as one or more devils.[1] The oldest play is the fourteenth-century *Advocacie Nostre Dame*, a fragment (about 500 lines) based on a poem of the same name which has survived in several MSS.[2] The trial takes place after the Resurrection and the Harrowing of Hell. The devils, represented by Satan, claim their right to fallen mankind has been unjustly taken from them.[3] The introductory part of the poem explains that this trial shows that Our Lady is our best advocate and praises her powers. A day is set for the matter to be tried, with God the Son acting as judge and the Virgin Mary as advocate for mankind. The legal arguments are extensive and include Satan's valid claim that the Virgin Mary is not 'an acceptable advocate because (a) women are not allowed to plead in court and (b) she is the mother of the judge'.[4] The final judgement is that the Devil can have only those people who have not repented of their sins.

In a number of texts, including the play interpolated in the Dutch play of Mariken van Nieumeghen (see below), the Devil's representative is Mascaron or Mascheroen. He first appears in a Dutch poem by Jacob van Maerlant composed about 1261 and later features in a Catalan narrative trial of the fourteenth–fifteenth century possibly derived from a play. There is also a sixteenth-century Latin text – notable for extremely elaborate legal arguments – in which the Devil is called Ascaron.[5] An interesting feature of the Catalan text is the Virgin Mary's defence of her right to plead even though she is the mother of the judge because she is not an ordinary mother: 'although I am a mother I am not a mother like the others for I am a mother without corruption [i.e. immaculate] and I became pregnant without harm [i.e. without original sin] and I gave birth without pain'.[6]

CHILDREN OF THE DEVIL

The possibility of the Devil fathering a human child was widely believed in the Middle Ages, one of the most famous examples being the enchanter Merlin, whose mother 'having allowed the sun to go down on her wrath' failed to say her prayers at night and was therefore vulnerable to the sexual attack of a Devil. When she confessed what had happened to a priest, he gave her penance and absolution and warned her the child must be baptised as soon as it was born. Merlin was thus protected from the Devil though he retained supernatural powers.[7]

The best-known 'child of the Devil' is probably the eleventh-century Robert le Diable (also known as Robert of Normandy, and sometimes said to be the father of William the Conqueror).[8] The Cangé miracle (XXXIII), based on a slightly different version of the tale from the narrative *roman*, stages a vivid series of acts of violence by the young man: he sacks a nunnery, an abbey and a rich peasant's house and terrorises the countryside till his father banishes him. Finally Robert interrogates his mother who confesses that, desperate at having no child, she appealed to Hell for the child Heaven had not sent her.

Thereafter Robert is only concerned to expiate his crimes and save himself from damnation. The rest of the play shows his travels to Rome in search of pardon, his extensive penances and finally, in good romance form, how he lives as a fool[9] at court but incognito saves the city from a Saracen attack and finally cures the emperor's daughter of dumbness. A hermit comes to court, tells Robert he is pardoned and that he is to marry the princess and found a lineage 'qui réjouira le paradis'.[10]

A very different 'son of the Devil' is the central character of the earliest Latin humanist play, Alberto Mussato's *Tragedy of Ecerinis*[11] composed in 1314 to warn the Paduans of the dangers of the civil wars between Guelph and Ghibelline which raged in Italy. Ezzelino (Lat. Ecerinis, 1194–1259), the Ghibelline lord of Verona, was a real person to whom Mussato has given a diabolical background. The model for the form of the play with its messengers and chorus and limited number of actors in any one scene (never more than three) is of course the tragedies of Seneca which were to become so important an influence on the theatre of Europe two centuries later, but Mussato in his own time is unique.[12]

In the opening scene of the play, his mother describes vividly the moment of Ecerinis' conception making it clear that his father is the Devil:

A sulphurous mist invaded the atmosphere and formed a cloud.
Then a giant flash, like lightning, illuminated the house and thunder
followed . . . Then I am seized and violated.
O the shame! I suffer an unknown adulterer.   (p. 10)[13]

Then follows a description of a monster with horns and a mane of
thick bristles whose nostrils vomit flames, 'and a constant fire licked
his beard' (p. 12). Alberico, the younger son, is then told his birth was
equally monstrous. Ezzelino is delighted, and declares they are born of
the gods and their father is a greater god than Mars, the father of Romulus and Remus. Both brothers swear to live lives worthy of the Devil's
children. Having gone apart while the chorus speaks, Ezzelino 'summons his father, Lucifer' to come and possess him. He declares he has
always denied Christ and hated him and calls on the Furies to be his
companions and helpers and finally cries: 'Acknowledge me, Satan, and
test the temper of your son.' Here and throughout the play Christian
and classical deities are mixed – Ezzelino refers indifferently to his father
as Lucifer or Vulcan and in the second act, where the Chorus and the
Messenger describe the horrors of the war which Ezzelino is leading and
the plight of the inhabitants of Padua and Verona, they too follow this
mode, asking Christ whether he only finds joy in the delights of highest
Olympus and reminding him of the divine wrath that fell on Sodom and
Gomorrah.

In Act III, Ezzelino tells his brother of his plans and his determination
to advance and overrun the whole of Lombardy. 'The sins of nations
demand avenging hands' he declares, preparing to move on and on till
all Italy is under his yoke. Alberico responds with even greater claims;
he will go on to conquer all France and the Western land of the evening
sun. The brothers continue their violence and tyranny despite the effort
of Frate Luca to persuade Ezzelino to turn to mercy and goodness so
he may escape damnation. Ezzelino sees himself as the wrath of God
and recalls the plagues of Egypt, the conquests of Nebuchadnezzar and
the violence of 'the noble house of the Caesars whence Nero of happy
memory was born; [God] let it happen willingly' (p. 8).

In Acts IV and V the tide turns against Ezzelino as Padua rallies its
citizens: this is the example Mussato wanted to give his fellow countrymen. Having broken faith with his allies and alienated his followers Ezzelino sets out for Milan but the other cities unite against him
and attacked from both sides the 'wavering old tyrant' is taken prisoner.

'Resisting in vain. Someone struck him on the head, fracturing his skull.'
He is taken to prison, refuses food and medical care and dies unrepentant.
His body is buried in Soncino. In Act v the Messenger and the Chorus
describe the capture and death of Alberico with his wife and family, who
are thrown in the fire. The play ends with a chorus of thanksgiving: 'From
highest Olympus has come love which put an end to evils done; the cruel
tyrants rage has died and peace has been reborn' (p. 64). The Devil does
not appear to claim Ezzelino's soul though it obviously belongs to him
but the situation is quite different in the two other miracle plays on the
subject of the Devil's children.

The miracle of *L'enfant voué au diable* (Cangé, I. 1332) tells of a couple
who for devotion to the Virgin swear to live in chastity.[14] Tempted by the
Devil, the husband forces his wife who angrily swears that if she conceives
as a result she will give the child to the Devil. In due course she has a
son. When the Devil comes to claim him, she wins him seven years of
life (and then a further eight) by promising not to have him baptised.[15]
When the youth learns of his history he goes to the pope for help; he is
sent on to hermits and eventually to one Honoré.

The Virgin herself now intervenes. In the Cangé version she challenges
the Devil's claim to the boy in a trial before 'God' personified as Jesus. The
verdict is that as the mother did not have the father's agreement to the act
it is invalid and the boy is saved. In Gautier de Coinci's poem however,
the boy is snatched away from the hermit during Mass so that the hermit
upbraids God and the Virgin: 'Ha, wake up then, Mother of God, sweet
lady Mary you are sleeping too much.'[16] The Virgin responds so quickly
that when the hermit has finished his prayer he hears the boy say *Amen* –
he is back. In this version, the visit to Hell is described by the hermit
in advance – indicating what the Virgin can and will do: 'Hell would
not be so bold as to dare detain you (he tells the youth) for she is the
Lady of Heaven and Hell, there is no iron door, however strong, that she
could not quickly break it in bits. If she gets a bit angry she is so fierce
and vigorous that with a glance or a look she makes all Hell tremble.'
This echo of the *Advocacie* and the Harrowing of Hell would fit with a
description of a play on this subject in Metz in 1512, in which instead of
the trial scene, we are told that three devils come to claim the boy. God
gives the Virgin permission to go, accompanied by Gabriel, Michael and
Raphael, and bring him back from Hell (*Mystères*, II, p. 102).

One of the St Genevieve plays tells how a mother, having failed (from
laziness apparently) to have her child baptised, is distraught when he is
deliberately drowned in a well and then seized by the devil; she invokes

Genevieve's help.[17] In this play there is an actual tug of war between Gabriel and Satan for the soul (the customary mummet, no doubt). The Devil loses, despite pointing out that he has a just claim to it and appealing to God! Gabriel asks the Devil if a man condemned to death can be pardoned? 'Yes', says Satan. 'By whom?' 'His lord or king.' 'Exactly', says Gabriel, 'and the devils are only God's minions to carry out his sentence!'[18] With a touch of humour another devil points out that St Genevieve has the backing of the Virgin Mary and God dare not go against his mother or he would catch it properly!

THE DEVIL'S PARAMOURS

The idea of the Devil as the seducer of women is also reflected in three very different plays: Hildegard of Bingen's *Ordo Virtutum*, the German *Spiel von Frau Jutten* (better known as pope Joan) and the Dutch play of *Mariken van Nieumeghen*. Hildegard of Bingen's play was composed about 1151[19] and tells the story of salvation through the use of allegorical figures. The Virtues try to persuade Anima (the representative of Humanity) to accept the need for humility and chastity but Anima, tempted by the Devil, rejects the strict way of life they recommend: 'it is too grievous for me to fight against my body' (28). The Devil, (*shouting to Anima*) advises her to 'Look to the world: it will embrace you with great honour (48–9), and when the Virtues mourn for the loss of innocence he tells them that 'whoever wants to follow me and do my will, I'll give him everything' (60). This scene is obviously echoing the temptation and fall of Adam as well as the temptations of Christ. Anima succumbs to the Devil's wiles.

In scene 2 the Virtues describe their individual characteristics – Patience for example is the pillar that can never be made to yield, 'as my foundation is in God' (152–3). In the third scene Anima laments what she has done and appeals to the Virtues who beg her to come home but she feels unworthy: 'a burning sweetness swallowed me up in sins, so I did not dare come in (167–8). With the help of Humility the Virtues raise up the wounded and weak Anima and strengthen her so that when the Devil declares 'I shall fight you and bring you down (210–11), Anima declares she will fight him face to face. She is too strong for him, now, and the Virtues bind the Devil and Victory declares: 'the age-old snake is bound' (227). The play ends with a chorus of rejoicing by the Virtues and all the Souls.

This play, the earliest of what might be called moralities, is unique in many ways not least in making a female figure the subject, rather than the ubiquitous Mankind or Everyman, Humain Ligneage or Elkerlich, all of whom are presented as male.[20] These plays are too numerous to consider them all, so I shall just mention one unusual late one, the fifteenth-century French play of *Les enfants de Maintenant*, a unique version of the parable of the Prodigal Son.[21] Two brothers are sent by their parents to be educated by Discipline at the school of Instruction but they are led astray by the son of Malle Aventure and indulge in gambling and the pleasures of Luxure. One brother, Finet, sinks ever lower and finally ends on the gibbet of Perdition. The other, Malduict, repents his way of life, and turns to Discipline by whom he is punished then absolved. The closing short tableau shows Malduict, the shining-faced repentant sinner-cum-reformed scholar, receiving his parents' forgiveness.[22]

Ein schön spiel von Frau Jutten,[23] composed by Dietrich Schernberg in 1480 but only surviving in the revised edition printed in 1556 by Silesius, a Lutheran preacher, with the intention of showing up the weakness of the papacy, is based on the legend of 'pope Joan', the reality of whose existence is still the subject of debate.[24] According to the legend, Joan left England (or Germany – there are two accounts of her nationality) with her lover, to study in Athens, dressed as a man and calling herself Johannes.[25] Having become an established scholar she went on to Rome where her learning soon made her a respected figure, then a cardinal and, in due course, on the death of Leo IV in 855, she was made pope as John VIII. Her sex was discovered when she gave birth to a child in the middle of a procession. She was put to death and her name was removed from the list of popes but occasional references appear in chronicles and records over the centuries.

Schernberg rewrites the legend in many ways. The play begins with a lively scene in Hell where the devils, led by Lillis, the mother of Satan, determine to attack the Church through this English woman whose ambition and pride make her easy prey to a suggestion of diabolical help in achieving her ambitions. Joan makes a verbal (not written) pact with the devil *Unversun* and with her lover (called simply *Clericus* and thought by some to be a devil, see de Bruyn, p. 153) sets off for Paris where they meet a scholar who instructs them in the Trivium and then awards them scholars' gowns. They then go on to Rome, are favourably received by the cardinals and in due course made cardinals themselves. When the pope (referred to here as Basilius though the legend usually cites him as Leo)[26] dies, Johannes is unanimously elected pope by the cardinals and crowned with the triple tiara (l. 700). All these scenes are short and with only the barest semi-narrative stage directions, mostly connected with costume or properties, no mention is made anywhere of scenery or locations. Much of the dialogue is stilted and formal. Soon after Jutta's coronation, however, the play livens up again. A man brings his son to Jutta to be exorcised and she is terrified of the devil who, we are told, tells Joan she is pregnant, though it is not in the dialogue.[27] Unable to defeat the Devil, Joan begs the assembled cardinals to pray with her for the boy. *Unversun* tells her to stop chattering, but eventually leaves the boy and disappears. The scene moves to Heaven, where Christ complains about Joan to his mother, and insists it has gone on too long and Joan will die a painful death and be damned. After a plea by Mary he consents to a compromise – Gabriel is summoned and sent to Joan to tell her she will die and has the choice of earthly shame now or the pains of Hell hereafter. Joan, who is already penitent, chooses the earthly shame and prays to Christ and the Virgin Mary for pardon for all her sins. There follows a long dialogue between Joan and Death during which she prays to God for pardon, reminding him of the many sinners he has already forgiven including not merely Mary Magdalene and St Peter – both frequently invoked (see *Cenodoxus*, below) – but every one from Adam to the penitent thief, Theophilus, Longinus and St Paul. She gives birth on the stage while singing praise to the Virgin Mary. The crowd take up the child and *Unversun* comes to carry off her soul to Purgatory (p. 68). The cardinals decide to purify Rome by a procession with candles and banners.[28] In the *Fegefeuer* of Purgatory, Joan laments while the devils rejoice and torment her with burning drinks for about a hundred lines, and then the Virgin Mary and St Nicholas both intercede for her to Christ who sends Michael to rescue her and bring her safely to Heaven. The devils try to keep her but Michael sweeps them aside with his sword and the play ends with Joan in Heaven rejoicing and praising Christ, the Virgin Mary and St Nicholas.

Although the Lutheran editor tried to use the play as a mockery of the papacy, the text is against him: the brief dialogues mentioned give little scope for satire or even criticism, except for Jutta herself.[29]

Mariken van Nieumeghen whose earliest known text is dated 1515, is better known in England as Mary of Nemmegen, from the 1518 English narrative translation of the Dutch play. Both versions were printed in Antwerp.[30] The play, considered a masterpiece of medieval Dutch drama, takes the form of a Marian miracle play. Mariken is sent to market at Nieumeghen, by her uncle, a priest, who, knowing she will not be able to return safely that night, tells her to stay over with her aunt. Unfortunately for Mariken, her aunt is a witch and deliberately refuses to house her niece but sends her out in the dark where she meets and is seduced by a devil, called Moenen, who changes her name to Emmeken because her own is that of the Virgin. She becomes his mistress and helper for seven years. At the end of this time a miracle play, the Play of Masscheroen, is performed in the town, on a waggon in the midst of the square. To Moenen's disgust, Mariken insists on watching the play in which Masscheroen, Lucifer's advocate, appears in the court of Heaven to claim the souls of fallen mankind.[31] The Virgin pleads, eventually successfully, for a period of grace for them in which to amend. When Mariken shows signs of being moved by this,[32] Moenen tries to kill her before she can repent – he carries her high in the air and then drops her, but she is not killed as he had planned, thanks to the constant prayers of her uncle, who has been praying for her throughout the seven years. With her uncle she travels to Rome where the pope gives her a stiff penance to perform before she can be pardoned: she has three heavy iron rings fastened round her neck and her arms and is told when they melt and fall away it will be a sign her sins have been forgiven. She returns to Holland and enters a convent in Maastricht devoted to sinners like Mary Magdalene, where she remains many years, praying and weeping till one day an angel comes and removes the rings as a sign she is pardoned.

DOUBT AND DAMNATION

During the Council of Trent and the Counter-Reformation, the debate on grace and freewill was raging in Catholic Europe, especially between the two main religious orders, the Dominicans and the Jesuits, though both were united against the Protestant views of Luther and Calvin. This debate forms the main theme of a number of plays from different sources including a major Spanish play, *The doubter damned*, by Tirso de Molina and a rare Marian miracle play from Sweden.

The Swedish play 'Of a sinner who found mercy' (*De uno peccatore qui promeruit gratiam*) which dates from about 1492, is the oldest play extant in any Scandinavian language.[33] The pattern of the play is not unusual: a sinner called Vratislaus goes to Sir Procopius and confesses that he has sinned so grievously that he cannot be pardoned. Procopius agrees the sins are great and advises Vratislaus to seek the help of the Virgin Mary assuring him she will not refuse her help but in fact she literally turns her back on him. However, when he declares he will stab himself to death and thus condemn his soul to Hell, the Virgin Mary relents and turns the dagger aside with her hand. She then takes him to the throne of the Judge (*domare*) and implores her Son to forgive her penitent. At first

Christ refuses because of the gravity of his sins which included cursing by Christ's Wounds[34] and disregarding the agony on the cross. Mary admits the sins but begs for mercy and in traditional style 'pleads her breasts' where she nursed the infant Jesus. Christ relents and pardons Vratislaus and the Virgin Mary sends him off with a reminder to think of her whenever he is tempted.[35]

A very different treatment of salvation is found in the Florentine play of *Uno Monaco qui ando al servizio di Dio*.[36] The unique plot tells how a young man leaves home, against his parents' wishes, to serve a *santo padre* in the desert. He is not misled by the temptations of the Devil, but serves so faithfully that the old man begs God to assure him that the young *monaco* will go to Heaven. An angel comes to him to say that in fact the young man will be damned. Deeply distressed the *santo padre* tells the young man of this but he answers that if his damnation is the will of God, he accepts that as freely as all other acts of God. The angel returns and tells the *padre* that this total submission to the will of God has assured the young man's ultimate salvation.

The dangers of a lack of faith in God's goodness is illustrated in Tirso de Molina's *The doubter damned (El condenado por desconfiado)*[37] described by the editor/translator as 'perhaps the greatest theological drama in Spanish theatre, if not in world theatre' (58). Paulo, a holy hermit, lives in the wild with a companion, Pedrisco (the standard comic character, always grumbling but sure of God's goodness). Paulo tells Pedrisco he has had a fearful dream: he saw Death shoot his arrow in his heart and then his soul arrived at the gate of Heaven and saw the recording angel weigh his deeds and his sins far outweighed his ten years of pious living in the desert. Distraught, Paulo implores God to answer his prayer and tell him if this is a true version or a work of the Devil. Taking advantage of his lack of faith in God, the Devil appears to him in the guise of an angel and sends him to a nearby town where he will find a certain man called Enrico whom he must observe closely for 'the end that he shall have will be thine too' (221). Paulo is delighted and certain the man he sees will be a man of great goodness: 'some holy person he must surely be, / of that I have no doubt' (225–6).

Paulo and Pedrisco set off for the city where they discover, to Paulo's horror, that Enrico prides himself on being the most wicked man in the world: he steals, fights, kills and generally sins but has one redeeming feature which Paulo does not discover, his devotion to his old father, whom he has always cared for and from whom he has concealed the wickedness about which he usually boasts. Paulo decides that since Enrico is obviously damned, then he himself is also and therefore he has no reason to go on living his sober life.[38]

At the end of Act I, he tells Pedrisco they are going home and will become bandits. Paulo receives a further message, this time from a genuine messenger of God, a shepherd boy who assures him that God's 'love is such that if the sinner said: / 'O Lord I've sinned, I've sinned so many times.' / God would embrace him in his loving arms, / such is God's way. (1093–5). Paulo tries to believe that there might be mercy then for Enrico and, therefore, for himself, but he doubts and thereby condemns himself. Most of Act II is concerned with Enrico and building up the picture of his wickedness. Finally he is captured by Paulo and his bandits and the two confront each other. It now becomes clear that despite his sins, Enrico has not lost his faith in God's mercy and is sure he will be pardoned, but Paulo cannot believe this and the Act ends with a dialogue which sums up the difference between them:

> ENRICO: I may be bad but I have faith in God.
> PAULO: My sins are legion, and my faith is gone. / I can no longer trust.
> ENRICO: That want of trust / will lead you to your doom.   (1429–31)

In the short final act, as Paulo gradually sinks further into crime and sin, the shepherd reappears, and in a vision Paulo sees the soul of Enrico, who has been hanged for his crimes but died confessed and shriven, carried up to Heaven. Then Justice catches up with the hermit-become-bandit and Paulo is killed by some peasants. He appears to Pedrisco, enveloped in flames and declares he has no one but himself to blame: 'I lacked faith and doubted God's great love'(2019).[39] Like Don Giovanni centuries later, 'He sinks into the stage and flames rise through the hole.'[40]

CHAPTER 7

Who sups with the Devil: the rash bargain

In most of the plays so far considered the sinner is eventually saved and, having done penance, is assured of Heaven. A rather more varied fate befalls those who strike a rash bargain with the Devil.

THEOPHILUS AND OTHER MIRACLES OF THE VIRGIN

The best-known and most striking of all the stories of the triumph of the Virgin Mary over the Devil is surely that of Theophilus who sold his soul to the Devil in exchange for riches and status. The theme first appears in Greek and then is found in Latin from the ninth century.[1] The Latin account tells how in the year 537 there was in Sicily a man named Theophilus who was the bishop's *vicedominus* – a priest whose job was to look after the secular possessions of the diocese. When the bishop died the whole populace wanted Theophilus to succeed him, but he declined, feeling himself unworthy. Soon afterward, the new bishop dismissed Theophilus, who thereupon became so angry and concerned about his new poverty that he sought the assistance of a certain Jewish sorcerer. The Jew summoned the Devil, who appeared with all speed and, at his command, Theophilus renounced Christ and his mother, forswore the Christian faith and wrote down his abjuration in his own blood, sealing the paper with his ring, and giving it to the demon. Theophilus later bitterly regretted what he had done, and appealed to the Virgin who rebuked him sternly, commanded him to renounce the Devil and to profess Christ the Son of God and the whole Christian faith. When he woke from a swoon he found the paper he had given to the Devil placed upon his breast.

Compared to this fairly simple version, the twelfth-century French poem by Gautier de Coinci is more than 2,000 lines long, and enriched with both visual action and verbal imagery. The scenes with the Jew, especially, are much elaborated. He promises to take Théophile to see his 'lord and master' and leads him to a 'théâtre' outside the town where Théophile has a vision of fire and devils making a great noise and celebration. They are wearing black cloaks and carrying their lord in a procession. The reference to theatre and the scene described are reminiscent of the vision of Thurkill with its description of a Hell theatre where the devils hold 'theatrical sports'.[2] Théophile has an audience with the Devil, renounces God and his mother, and hands over his 'charter' sealed with his ring. He is restored to power and the Jew continues to visit and urge him on to further wickedness but as soon as Théophile repents, the Jew and the Devil disappear from the scene.

Rutebeuf's play, based on Gautier's poem,[3] is short, only 662 lines but there is a vivid picture of Théophile's anger and he threatens God himself: 'I can't get at God because he's out of everyone's reach. Oh! if anyone could grab him and give him a good beating, he would have done a great day's work.'[4] The scene of the charter is very short and the Jew is replaced simply by one 'Salatin qui parloit au diable quant il voloit.' In Théophile's presence, Salatin summons up the Devil with abracadabra nonsense words and it is clear that it is he, not the rather puny figure of the Devil, who is in charge. The name Salatin suggests that the intermediary here is a pagan rather than a Jew, but the polyglot invocation of the Devil includes some words in Hebrew. Similarly, when Théophile bids Salatin farewell, saying: 'may the God you believe in and adore defend you if you keep your word in this' he could be speaking to a Jew or a Saracen.[5] Théophile has to pay homage 'mains jointes' and become the Devil's 'hom'. He then hands over the letters he has written (without having been told to).

Then follow extended scenes of repentance. Théophile explicitly admits that he renounced God for 'un peu d'avoir' – and there is a long sequence of lamentations, and prayers to the Virgin. Having finally accepted Théophile's repentance, the Virgin promises him his charter back and we see her go to the Devil and demand it in round terms: Give it up or 'je te foulerai la pance!' (I shall trample on your belly!) (v. 585).

There are several Theophilus plays from the fifteenth century. The three German plays are all from north Germany and present an interesting variety of villains.[6] In text H, Theophilus speaks direct to Sathanas and has a long and friendly conversation with him; Theophilus asks the Devil for wealth and fine clothes, like a nobleman. He is ordered to renounce God and the Virgin Mary, refuses the latter but finally gets what he wants. Later he is converted by a sermon he hears and repents. He quotes as pardoned sinners, Mary Magdalene and St Peter.[7] After he has wept for three days the Virgin Mary goes to her child, Jesus and asks forgiveness for Theophilus. Then she goes to demand the letter from Satan. He claims it is lost but is forced to find and return it. When Theophilus wakes from sleep he finds the charter lying on his breast.[8]

In text S, nine canons discuss who should be the new bishop. Having been demoted, Theophilus meets a *magister yn nygromanticia* (master of magic) who knows all the 'black arts' (*swarte kunst*). Theophilus cries out and asks if there is a Devil who will appear openly to him and he offers to show him allegiance. Satanas appears and there is no further reference to the necromancer. Once again the repentance is linked to Mary Magdalene with mention of the seven devils whom Jesus cast out of her.[9] In another traditional motif, the Virgin Mary, when pleading with Jesus, bares her breasts which gave him suck (l. 887).[10] Again the Devil claims he has lost the letter but is forced to restore it.

Text T is different again. It begins with a musical invocation for silence for two voices. Then follows the opening discussion between named clergy all with different functions such as prebendary, cellarer and so on. This time, when he is angry at being demoted, Theophilus meets a pair of Jews, Isaac and Samuel, in a *bierkeller* (shades of Faust!) and with their help he summons up a Devil. The renunciation of God (he absolutely refuses to renounce the Virgin Mary) is done verbally, with Theophilus repeating each line after the Devil. He then prepares and hands over the charter. In a scene that anticipates the Faust plays, Theophilus receives money and rich clothes and declares he will now be a fine fellow (*fyn gesell*) and do whatever he likes. The MS is unfortunately incomplete and ends with a *silete* and song as they set off to overthrow the bishop who first rejected Theophilus.

The Italian *Teofilo* was first printed in the late fifteenth century with several more editions in the sixteenth.[11] It is long – 1,600 lines – and very detailed. Original touches include the Devil at the beginning tempting a priest to malign Theophilus to the bishop so that he deprives him of his office; urging Theophilus to anger and sending him to the Jewish enchanter, Manovello, who leads him to a cross roads, draws a circle round them and summons up Beelzebub. Devils carry in a chair and Beelzebub seats himself. After Theophilus has sworn allegiance, Beelzebub sends a Devil called Farfalletto to the bishop to tell him Theophilus was maligned and thus arranges his reinstatement. When the Jew and Theophilus meet and part they commend each other *a Dio!* After Theophilus' repentance, the Virgin sends an angel to demand the charter back.

The story of Theophilus was also a favourite with the Jesuits.[12] Seven performances of a Theophilus play are recorded between 1585 and 1601; only the text of 1596 by Matthaus Rader has survived.[13] Rader's play begins with Theophilus' rebellion against his loss of status and follows the medieval story closely.

In the *Theophilus* performed in Ingolstadt in 1621[14] and based on the account in Vincent of Beauvais' *Speculum historiale*, the action takes place during the reign of Justinian and is considerably enlarged to make a five-act play with numerous clergy, parasites and peasants, as well as devils, angels and virtues, so that Theophilus only makes his pact in Act IV. The intermediary between Theophilus and the Devil is a certain Chaldean magus or *zauberer*. Restored to power Theophilus attacks his enemies and avenges himself all round. In Act V his Conscience (a frequent character in Jesuit plays) becomes active again and eventually there is a struggle between the Devil Astaroth and Theophilus' guardian angel for the bond. Theophilus is urged to appeal to the Virgin Mary who appears in person and finally pardons Theophilus and gets back his bond.[15] This play is distinguished by the first appearance on the scene, both literally and figuratively, of that most famous maker of bad bargains: Faust. The Theophilus play ends with a scene of Faust and another celebrated damned character, Hieronymus Scotus, lamenting from Hell.[16]

Before looking at the Faust plays and their influence, there remain two pre-Faustian interesting and very different versions of the rash bargain to consider, one from France and one from Spain.

The miracle of the *Chevalier qui donna sa femme au diable* probably dates from the fourteenth century, the heyday of the Marian miracle plays in France, but has only survived in sixteenth-century printed editions.[17] A rich young knight is determined to lead a life of luxury and comfort and is particularly keen to be admired for his grandeur and generosity. Despite the pleas of his wife and with the help of two sycophants to whom he gives huge gifts of money he eventually finds himself destitute and abandoned by his so-called friends.[18] At this point the Devil decides to take a hand, convinced he can trap his victim despite his wife's faithful devotion to the Virgin Mary to whom she prays constantly for her husband to amend his way of life. The Devil offers the despairing knight all the money he can spend in exchange for a letter in which he swears to hand over his wife to the Devil. After very little hesitation the knight agrees, provided he does not have to hand her over for seven years.[19] He accepts the order to renounce the Trinity but absolutely refuses to renounce the Virgin Mary under any circumstances. The Devil accepts his refusal, the bargain is struck and the knight hands over his letter promising his wife to the Devil after seven years. Then, even richer than before, he resumes his luxury life style and even welcomes back the 'friends' who deserted him when he was poor. The day comes to fulfil his pact and the knight regrets bitterly what he has done but can see no way out of it as he must recover his letter. He orders his wife to accompany him and they set off. The wife is very uneasy and begs her husband to allow her to go into the chapel and pray to the Virgin. After some hesitation he agrees provided she does not linger too long. In the chapel, the wife urgently invokes the Virgin begging her protection for both herself and her husband. In Heaven the Virgin accepts her prayers and begs God's grace for her suppliant and the husband. God willingly agrees that the wife should be protected from the Devil but is unwilling to pardon the knight. Eventually the Virgin wins the day and herself descends to earth and, leaving the wife in a trance in the chapel, takes on her appearance and rejoins the knight. When they reach the Devil he is furious with the knight and blames him for bringing the Virgin Mary with him instead of his wife. Knowing he cannot now win the wife he still tries to hold on to the knight by his written pact but eventually, of course, Mary triumphs and the Devil declares 'tu ruines l'enfer!'. After a long scene of thanksgiving, the knight leaves Mary and goes to awaken his wife to whom he confesses the whole plot and wins her forgiveness.

THE DEVIL'S SLAVE

In great contrast to this fairly traditional Marian miracle play, the Spanish *El esclavo del demonio (The Devil's slave)* by Antonio Mira de Amescua, published in 1612 and probably first staged in Madrid c. 1608,[20] is a variant on the Theophilus–Faust theme written from a strictly Catholic viewpoint for the public stage and using all the special effects beloved of the Golden Age of Spanish drama. In a complex tragi-comedy with a plot of rape, love and misunderstanding, not one but two characters sell themselves to the Devil but ultimately repent and win pardon. The first to succumb to the idea is Don Gil, a holy man who, carried away by unexpected lust for the beautiful Lisarda, tricks her into believing he is the lover with whom she is preparing to elope and rapes her. He then comes to his senses, realises he is damned and decides he might as well continue a life of wickedness since 'I damned as I am have heard the voice of Hell itself and still have lost my faith.' Lisarda, who believes her lover has betrayed her, decides to accompany Don Gil on condition he

will help her avenge herself. It is significant that both blame themselves
for their fall: Don Gil for the sin of pride in believing he was good by
his own efforts and Lisarda because she was a disobedient daughter and
going to elope.[21] The two, disguised as highwaymen terrorise the local
countryside. Among those they rob are Lisarda's sister, Leonor. When
Don Gil sees her he is totally enamoured and declares 'I'll give my very
soul to possess you, Leonor.' At once the Devil appears in the guise of
a young man, called Angelio, and accepts the offer. Don Gil is at first
terrified of the Devil who points out that as he is predestined to go to
Heaven it does not matter what he does – this is clearly an attack on
the Calvinist doctrine on predestination – and offers him everything he
wants if he will become his slave. Don Gil decides he has already done
most of the things asked of him and agrees to sign a bond in his own blood
and become Angelio's slave in exchange for instruction in necromancy.
He is taken off stage by two other devils while Angelio tries to attack
Lisarda as well. Don Gil returns with an S branded on his cheek. The
devils assure Angelio he has signed the bond. Lisarda asks Don Gil why
he is branded and he tries to persuade her to join him in learning to do
evil, but warns her there are conditions.

The following dialogue is particularly interesting:

GIL: You'll have to renounce God.
LIZ: I'll do it twice if need be!
GIL: And the Mother of God as well.
LIZ: I cannot agree to that.
GIL: Isn't God greater than she?
LIZ: Of course He's greater. But if I now renounce both, who will intercede for
     me if I later repent?[22]

The complicated plot unwinds slowly in the next two acts. Lisarda has an
opportunity to revenge herself on her lover but her gun misfires. She takes
this as a sign from Heaven and gives up her vengeance and determines to
return to God if she can: 'I can be Mary Magdalene.'[23] To obtain money
for a poor woman, she has herself sold as a slave and reappears on stage
disguised and also branded, like Don Gil, but her brand says 'Slave of
God.' The woman sells her to Lisarda's own father. Meanwhile Don Gil,
still enslaved, reminds the Devil he promised him Leonor if he became
his slave. Angelio reassures him and Leonor enters. Don Gil carries her
off to his cave but reappears soon after with a figure wrapped in a shawl
declaring he must have light to see the woman he loves – he unwraps her
and 'the skeleton falls through a trap door in the stage'. Don Gil realises

the emptiness of what he wanted. At this first sign of grace a voice off stage calls to him: 'Man, Oh sinful man. Your life gives me pain. Change you life!'

When Don Gil accuses the Devil of giving him only an illusion the Devil responds with 'when have the joys of this life been otherwise?'. Angelio then disappears (by use of a turntable on stage) and is replaced by a fearful Devil, to an accompaniment of skyrockets and gunfire. Don Gil, finally recognising his folly and guilt, refuses to be overwhelmed by this and begs the help of his guardian angel. A battle is seen in the air between an angel and a Devil suspended above the stage on machines, then an angel enters and gives Don Gil back his contract. He addresses himself in words that interestingly show his pride is still in working order: 'Gil . . . if your sin was amazing, let your penance amaze even more.' The play ends with all the misunderstandings ironed out. Don Gil makes his final appearance in the black and white of the Dominicans. He announces Lisarda's death and promises 'As a monk in Spain's chief religious order, I'll show the world how I've changed.'[24] He exits and Lisarda is shown in a tableau as a corpse kneeling in the garden next to a crucifix and a skull.[25]

DR FAUSTUS

The historical personage behind all the various Faust legends seems to have been a German necromancer and conjuror Georg Faust (1480?–?1538) whose more mythological career was finally standardised by the appearance in 1587 of the *Historia von D. Johann Faustus, dem weit beschreyten Zauberer und schwarzkünstler*, compiled by Johann Spies. It was from an English translation, known as the English Faustbook that Marlowe obtained the basic material for his most famous and successful play, *The tragical history of Dr Faustus* (1588–93).[26]

Dr Faustus has a number of the characteristics of a medieval morality play, including the appearance of the Seven Deadly Sins, Lucifer and other devils. But in contrast to the Theophilus plays it is essentially a Protestant not a Catholic text. Indeed the scenes of Faust mocking the pope and other continental religious dignitaries were generally seen as an attack on the Catholic Church and many of the traditions associated with saints and the Mass.

In 'Marlowe's Doctor Faustus as an inverted Saint's life', Susan Snyder concludes that it is 'an anti-saint play' in which the traditional themes of conversion, good works and entry into Heaven are represented respectively by Faust's bargain with the Devil; his central conjuring tricks and other apparently pointless activities; and his final death and damnation.[27] If *Faustus* is an anti-saint play, the *Tempest* is in some ways an anti-Faust play complete with the bad spirit, Caliban and the good spirit, Ariel. When Prospero, brooding on the wrongs done him by Alonso and Sebastian, uses his studies of magic to prepare a bitter revenge on his brother and the other traitors, it is an unearthly spirit whose words are the turning point. Ariel suggests that if Prospero saw the villains' suffering 'your affections / would become tender,' adding: 'Mine would, sir, were I human' (V:1). Prospero responds immediately: 'And mine shall . . . The rarer action is in virtue than in vengeance' and immediately afterwards moves into his great speech in which he renounces not merely vengeance but his use of magic powers. When just after this, he is talking to Alonso about the supposed death of Ferdinand he tells the grieving king he has not 'sought her help of whose soft grace / for the like loss I have her sovereign aid'. To a medieval spectator this would surely have referred to the Virgin Mary – Prospero is talking of Patience.[28]

It is the final scenes of *Dr Faustus* which are the most interesting from the religious point of view: Faust tries to repent, realises his danger but is constantly pulled back from a real act of contrition by the Devil's threats of *physical* suffering: Faust's agonised cry 'I do repent and yet I do despair: Hell strives with grace for conquest in my breast' is met by a threat from Mephistopheles: 'Revolt or I'll in piece-meal tear thy flesh' (p. 41). Faust immediately surrenders to the threat – he is unable to face martyrdom. Despairing of grace, Faust is damned like the Judas of the passion plays, for both of them despair. The Reformation controversies between faith and works, grace and predestination are all bound up in this final struggle between Faust and the Devil but now there is no omnipotent Virgin Mary to sweep in with her attendant angels and trample on the Devil's belly.

Marlowe's play was very popular in seventeenth-century Germany to which it was taken by the English touring companies or 'comödianten' who provided most of the public theatre performances there during the troubled times leading up to the Thirty Years War. The earliest known performance, by a company led by Greene, was at Graz in 1608.[29]

The previous year had seen the publication in England of another story of a pact with the Devil, Barnaby Barnes, *The Devil's charter*, published in 1607: 'as it was plaide before the King's Maiestie upon Candlemasse night'. It is primarily a historical play about the Borgias but it opens with a splendid mimed scene of the Devil sending images of successful men to Roderigo Borgia. Finally 'after more thunder and fearful fire' a Devil appears dressed as pope 'in robes pontificall and with a triple crowne on his head'. He is followed by a notary carrying paper, pen and small knife (with which he slits Roderigo's sleeve and draws blood). In return for the papacy, which he wants above all for the benefit of his sons, Cesare and the duke of Candia, and his daughter, Lucretia, Roderigo signs the pact in blood for a period of eleven years and eight days after which he will die. The rest of the play, compèred so to speak by a Florentine commentator, tells of the violent acts and successful wars of Alexander VI and his family. Finally at a banquet the Devil exchanges the wine bottles, so that the poisoned ones, intended for the guests, are drunk by Roderigo and Cesare. The latter will recover but the Devil appears to the former and tells him his time is up – Roderigo claims he has eight years left but the Devil shows him that the eight refers only to days, of which this is the last. After a scene of fire and noise and devils triumphing, Alexander disappears to hell and the remaining cardinals arrange for his poison-swollen body to be displayed to the people of Rome as he receives his just deserts.[30]

Some sixty years later a German Faust play, very similar to Marlowe's version, but with a few interesting additions among the devils, was performed in Danzig and is described in a journal: 'First Pluto comes forth out of Hell and calls one devil after another: the Devil of Tobacco [is this the result of King James' famous attack on smoking?], the Devil, of Whoring, among others the Devil of cunning.' The usual story of the pact and the twenty-four years in which the Devil serves Faust, concludes with a spectacular Hell scene: 'Pluto arrives and sends his devils to fetch Dr Faust which indeed happens and they cast him into Hell and tear him to pieces. It is also shown how he is tortured in Hell being pulled up and down, and these words are seen in fireworks: *accusatus est, judicatus est, condemnatus est* (TIE *German*, Doc. 58, p. 73).[31]

These last words are particularly interesting because they feature in a Jesuit play, *Cenodoxus* by Jacob Bidermann, based on a legend connected with St Bruno, the founder of the Carthusian order, and one of several plays from different countries which, outside of the main Theophilus/Faust group describe events leading to the damnation of the principal character.[32] Where Faustus succumbs to lechery and wealth, *Cenodoxus* suffers from a more lethal and subtle sin: spiritual pride.

Bidermann's celebrated play, first performed in Augsburg in 1602 and later frequently acted at the Jesuit college in Munich, shows Cenodoxus as an apparently worthy and saintly man, given to prayer and alms-giving in public but mean and self-satisfied in private.³³ The play includes both angels and devils who constantly struggle for his soul, and the death of Cenodoxus is followed by series of scenes of the judgement, when even Cenodoxus' guardian angel has to admit he cannot defend him against the Devil's claims that a man so absorbed in his own self-glorification and spiritual pride belongs in Hell and not in Heaven. The judgement scenes are followed by a scene of the townsfolk carrying Cenodoxus' bier through the crowds which include St Bruno, one of the many people who believed in the integrity and righteousness of Cenodoxus. Suddenly the corpse speaks 'Ah! Ah!' All cry 'God save us what miracle is this?' Cenodoxus cries again and continues: 'before God's fearful judgement seat, I AM ACCUSED!'. The crowd, including Bruno, exclaim with wonder and horror. Bruno adds: 'how he rose up, His face all pale with death . . . And words wrenched out and forced from death-bound jaws!' They decide to postpone the funeral till the next day and the scene returns to the Heavenly judgement seat. There St Michael, St Peter and St Paul all refuse to defend him – he is unanimously condemned: 'Guilty is evil, godless Cenodoxus.' Next day, the funeral cortège reassembles in great distress wondering at the fate of the man they all admired. Cenodoxus' corpse lifts his head again and declares 'JUDGEMENT IS PASSED ON ME BY GOD'S JUST JUDGEMENT.' On Bruno's advice they again postpone the funeral; back in Heaven Christ passes judgement: 'Then undergo your proper punishment / To endure the flames prepared for the archfiend.' On earth the crowd collect round the corpse for the third time, preparing for the final rites. Once again Cenodoxus speaks, ordering them to abandon the funeral and the prayers. Cursing the mother who bore him, he declares 'BY GOD'S JUST JUDGEMENT I AM ETERNALLY DAMNED.' Bruno and his friends lament this fatal end and Bruno declares 'I leave this ominous corpse; and being unable to save another, seek my own salvation.' He and his companions decide to escape from the dangers of society, and live a life of mortification and prayer.³⁴

A Spanish play on the life of St Bruno (1032–1101), *El mayor desengaño* by Tirso de Molina was published in 1627. Act III, scene 6 includes the episode of the death of the man believed to be so holy, identified here as Raimundo Diocrès, a preacher and teacher in Paris where Bruno is living and himself also acquiring great fame as a preacher and teacher. The scene takes place on stage with the great crowd including the king and queen of France. As a result of this incident in 1084, Bruno leaves Paris to found a small and very strict community which grew into the

Carthusian order. The authenticity of the legend has been both attacked and defended by later writers; see the *Preambulo* to the play (ed. cit. II, pp. 1182–3).

Other Jesuit plays on those who die unconfessed, and therefore unpardoned, include two stories from Bede's *History of the English Church and people*, ch. 14: Ametanus and Humphredus have visions of their place in Hell after death but still die unabsolved.[35] In contrast there is a play by Georg Bernhardt of the well-known story of the Irish soldier, Tundal, whose vision of Hell leads him to repentance (Szarota, I, 2, p. 1816).[36]

Szarota points out the distinction between the Irish and the English in Jesuit drama: the former confess and are saved, the latter are damned. Is this the result of the Henrician declaration of independence, or merely the general Protestant attacks on the Society of Jesus?

PART THREE

Conflicting relationships: love, hate and marriage

In the preface to his *tragi-comédie*, *Clitandre* (1630), Pierre Corneille defends his introduction into the play of scenes which in classical tragedy were recounted by a messenger: 'Instead of the messengers they introduce to narrate the marvellous things which befall their characters I have put the events themselves on the stage . . . preferring to delight the eye rather than vex the ears.' This therefore explains my title, which is also based on a description in the Chester play of the apparently miraculous deeds of Antichrist: 'these are not miracles but marvellous plays'.[1]

CHAPTER 8

Happily ever after: friends and lovers

Many of the stories centre on the marriages or would-be marriages between persons of high rank in different European and Middle Eastern countries.[1] They can be divided into two main groups: those which end with the marriage of the lovers and those which treat of the problems of the already married, especially in stories of the falsely accused wife, or the woman scorned. Some of the themes were treated by many different dramatists and only a selection can be quoted. (Stories of rape and murder are considered as a separate group under the heading of the theatre of cruelty.)

THE HEROINE IN THE HAREM

This section treats of the numerous plays of lovers separated but eventually reunited, including many stories involving a scene with a Saracen or Turkish harem.[2] The best-known romance on this theme is probably that of *Floire et Blanchefleur*. A young pagan boy and a Christian girl are brought up as brother and sister, fall in love, are separated but finally reunited, marry and live happily ever after. Versions of the tale, which probably came from the East, are found in many languages[3] but the earliest surviving play on the theme is the Italian *Sta Rosana* found in two versions, one from Florence and one from the Abruzzi.[4]

Though the names have been altered, the Italian *Rosana* is a faithful two-day version of the romance.[5] The first day tells the story of the heroine's parents. The pagan king and queen of Rome, Austerus and Rosana, have no heir, which much troubles both them and their court who advise imploring the god Mars. The queen suggests, however, they invoke the Christian God and if their desire is granted, undertake to become Christian. The king agrees and the queen sends for a hermit who tells them God cannot be bribed but if they believe in Christ and accept baptism, God will surely hear them. After some debate and questioning they go to the temple where the hermit challenges the idol, Pantaleus, which admits to being a devil and then collapses. The king is converted and both are baptised.[6]

The hermit tells them that as penance for their past sins, they must make a pilgrimage to the Holy Sepulchre and they prepare to do so, leaving the seneschal in charge of Rome but taking an army as they have to cross Caesarea whose king is their defeated enemy. However, despite their precautions they are ambushed by the king of Caesarea and Austerus is killed. The pregnant queen is treated kindly and taken in to the king's own house; his queen promises she will be well cared for and sent home after the birth of her child. An angel tells Rosana she will have a fair and virtuous daughter who will suffer much but remain a chaste maiden. At the same moment as Rosana gives birth to a daughter, the queen of Caesarea has a son. Rosana commends her child to her maid to be baptised and brought up as a Christian. Then she dies. By order of the king of Caesarea the two children are sent to the same wet nurse to be cared for. A survivor of the battle sends word to Rome and orders all the armies to assemble to avenge this defeat. The angel sends the audience home till the next day.[7] There is none of this detail in Hans Sachs' play of *Florio und Bianceffora* (1551) which begins here and only mentions the early part of the story in the prologue. Sachs' version is distinguished by a complete absence of the Christian element. Divine assistance is provided by Venus though she does not appear on stage.[8]

Day two contains the story of the young couple called here Ulimentus and Rosana. After fifteen years the king sends for them and finds his son handsome and well grown – and deeply in love with Rosana and she with him. To break up this unfortunate relationship they plan to send Ulimentus to Paris to learn arms and dancing and tournaments. He is in despair at leaving Rosana but she persuades him to obey his parents. She baptises him, they plight their troth and he departs. The queen now shows herself the typical jealous mother. Fearing her son will pine away for love, she determines to have Rosana killed. [Sachs here introduces a scene in which the seneschal arranges for Bianceffora to appear guilty of attempted poisoning of the queen. On her way to execution, Floire appears, having been transported and given a sword by Venus.[9] He rescues Bianceffora then disappears again. She says her rescuer was godlike.] The king is reluctant to kill her [in Sachs, the queen dare not kill her because of a dream vision of Venus] and he suggests selling her to the sultan's merchants when they next come there. Rosana is carried off secretly from the palace garden.[10] After three days the merchants and Rosana arrive in Babylon and she is put under the care of the innkeeper and his wife. Then she is taken to the sultan and undergoes a chastity test based on the old tradition of the cup that only a virgin can drink from without spilling wine.[11] Rosana passes the test easily and is sent to the harem in the care of one Alisbech. An angel appears to her and assures her the Virgin will help her preserve her honour: the sultan is immediately struck down with a mysterious illness.[12]

Meanwhile Ulimentus has returned from Paris much angered. The king is deeply distressed but the queen tries to persuade him Rosana is dead. He rejects them both and the king, repenting of what he has done, gives Ulimentus all the money and soldiers he needs to go in search of Rosana. He sets off but leaves the army hidden and goes alone into Babylon where he meets the innkeeper who tells him where Rosana is to be found. The innkeeper's wife visits Rosana in the harem under pretext of selling a dress to the inmates. She tells Rosana that her 'brother' has come to rescue her. Ulimentus succeeds in bribing Alisbech with promises of much money and a chance to start a free life elsewhere. They set off together, pursued by the sultan's men. Ulimentus' soldiers meet them, however, and after a battle (off stage) the sultan's army is defeated. The party reach Rome and Ulimentus consents to pardon his mother if she becomes a Christian. All ends happily.

In Sachs' play, Florio learns that Bianceffora has been sold as one of the hundred maidens sent to the sultan as tribute. Florio manages to get into the tower in a basket of roses, but is caught and going to be killed; he asks that they may die in each other's arms. Florio reveals his identity and turns out to be the stadtholder's nephew. The couple are sent home to Spain where a general reconciliation takes place.

In two of the Dutch *abele spelen*, *Esmoreit*, and *Gloriant*, the religious roles are reversed and the eponymous Christian hero woos and wins a Saracen princess who converts to Christianity. Unlike the French and Italian plays, however, the Dutch plays use their source material very freely, and the plays cannot be considered as simple dramatisations of a romance source.[13]

Esmoreit opens with the birth of the hero to the king and queen of Sicily, which angers Robbrecht, the old king's nephew and previously his heir. Meanwhile, in Saracen Damascus, an astrologer, Platus, foretells that a child born in a far country will one day kill the king. To prevent this, Platus sets out to find the child and bring him to Damascus to be brought up in their faith. Meanwhile Robbrecht has stolen baby Esmoreit in order to kill him and – to ensure there is no future heir – arranges for the queen to

be condemned as having killed her child. She is imprisoned. Platus meets
Robbrecht with the child and purchases it from him. Esmoreit is taken
to Damascus and handed over to the king's daughter, Damiet, to bring
up. He grows up with and falls in love with the girl he believes to be his
sister (the age discrepancy is ignored). In an orchard, Esmoreit overhears
Damiet saying she loves him and that he is a foundling. Determined to
find out who he is, Esmoreit sets off, wearing on his head a cloth that
had been wrapped round him as a baby. He comes to Sicily and the
queen's prison. She identifies the cloth and her son. Meanwhile, Damiet
has set out with the soothsayer to try to find her lover and comes to Sicily,
disguised as a youth, in time to cause the downfall of Robbrecht and the
reinstatement of the queen. Esmoreit and Damiet will marry and govern
the two countries when she has converted to Christianity.

Gloriant is a very different tale though it includes many themes already
mentioned. Gloriant, duke of Brunswick (Bruuyswijc) is a very proud
man, who refuses to marry and give his dukedom an heir because he
considers no woman worthy of him. His courtiers warn him that Venus
will be revenged on him for his pride. Meanwhile in an Eastern country,
the beautiful Florentijn, daughter of the Red Lion of Abelant,[14] has
decided that the only man worthy of her love is the Christian hero,
Gloriant, of whose pride and valour she has heard. She sends him a
letter and a picture of herself. When he sees it he falls in love with her
beauty and her pride and, lamenting his former rebellion against love,
immediately sets out to find her although he knows her father is his
family's bitter enemy: Gloriant's father and uncle slew many of the Red
Lion's family.[15]

Gloriant reaches Abelant in the middle of the night so he lies down to
sleep in an orchard. Florentijn sees him from her window and recognises
him. In a rapturous interview in the orchard he puts them both under
the protection of God and the Virgin and swears to marry her and make
her duchess of Brunswick. Unfortunately for them they are seen and
denounced to the Red Lion by his nephew, Floerant. Both are locked up
in separate towers but Florentijn (who has much in common with the
strong-minded heroine – also a pagan king's daughter – of *Aucassin et Nicolete*) persuades Rogier, the jailer, to free her lover.[16] Rogier finally agrees
and arranges with Gloriant to wait in the nearby forest and he, Rogier,
will suggest that Florentijn (who has meanwhile converted to Christianity) should be brought out of her tower and executed. As the headsman is preparing to kill her, Gloriant enters sword in hand and drives
off the Red Lion, Floerant and the headsman. Thus the lovers escape

and return safely to Brunswick where they are welcomed by Gloriant's uncle.[17]

The popularity of this theme in the Low Countries is also attested by the records of a play or plays on the story of Gillion de Trazegnies, the bigamist hero of a historically based but freely adapted romance first recorded in the fourteenth century.[18] Gillion and his wife, Marie, have no children and, desperate for an heir to the family estates, Gillion leaves his wife in Hainault and goes off to the Holy Land. He is made prisoner by the soldan of Babylon but freed by the soldan's daughter Gracienne with whom he falls in love. The plot follows closely the story of *Eliduc*, in the *Lais* of Marie de France but unlike Eliduc, Gillion does not marry Gracienne until he is brought false news (by a would-be suitor of Marie) that his wife is dead. He also insists that Gracienne should become Christian. Many years later, Gillion and Gracienne return to Hainault where they discover that, far from being dead, Marie is alive and the mother of now grown-up twin sons.[19] In contrast to *Eliduc*, the two women both take the veil; Gillion founds an abbey and himself becomes a monk. A performance of the *spel van Stragengijs* is recorded from Audenaard (1373); and a *spel van Tresingis* at Termonde in 1447. The 1532 *Inventaris van Sint Kathelijne ter Hoeyen te Gent* includes: 15. *Item, het spel van den Heere van Trasengijs*.[20] It is possible but, in view of the time span, improbable that all three references are to the same play.

All these versions of the story where the man is the Christian end up with the lovers returning to the husband's country. But in the seventeenth century there is a new development of the theme with the spread of foreign trade to the spice islands. In Fletcher's *The island princess* (1621)[21] the Spanish lover of the Indonesian ruling princess absolutely refuses to give up his religion in order to marry her, fails in his effort to persuade her to abandon her heathen beliefs and is imprisoned for slandering them. However, Quisara, the princess, is so impressed by his declarations of faith that she finally frees him and accepts conversion, though they will of course remain in her island.

The *Floire et Blanchefleur* group of plays reflect the crusades and the increased contact between East and West; later plays are influenced by the spread of the Ottoman empire and some of these plays have a tragic not a happy ending.

The best-known story is that of Soliman and Perside, based on a tale by Jacques Yver in *Le printemps d'Yver*, and used as the brief 'play within a play' in Kyd's *Spanish tragedy*.[22] In *Soliman and Perseda*, a separate play, perhaps by Kyd, the chorus is made up of Love, Fortune and Death.

A Dutch play *Jeronimo* performed in Utrecht by the rhetoricians in 1621 follows the English play closely while Jakob Ayrer's German version of the *Spanish Tragedy is* notable in that it is not set in Spain but in the court of Soliman throughout.[23]

In *Soliman and Perseda*, the lovers, Perseda and Eraste, live in Rhodes but quarrel because he has lost the chain she gave him and Lucina has found it and wears it. Eraste wins it back gaming, is accused of cheating, kills the accuser and has to flee from Rhodes to Constantinople where he takes service with Soliman who is about to attack Rhodes. Eraste refuses to join the attack, so Brusor leads the army which conquers Rhodes and brings back as captives Perseda and Lucina, both mourning their lost love. Soliman wants Perseda for himself but promises to respect her virginity unless he can win her fairly. Eraste arrives, and tells Soliman he is Perseda's lover; Soliman[24] allows them to marry and go to Rhodes. Then he regrets his promise and plots to have Eraste killed, so he can win Perseda. Eraste is called back, falsely accused and strangled, then the false witnesses are all killed. Perseda realises Lucina is involved and kills her. Soliman comes to Rhodes and agrees to fight their 'champion' not knowing 'he' is Perseda in man's attire. Soliman wounds her in the battle and she dies after granting Soliman a kiss; it is poisoned and he dies too. The final chorus agree that death triumphs.[25]

Two French plays on the Soliman and Perseda story were composed in the early seventeenth century when all things Turkish were the rage. Mainfray's *La Rhodienne* follows Yver and is substantially the same as the English play but much less elaborated. The action is all narrated in soliloquies after the event, e.g. the first fall of Rhodes is described by Perseda in the harem, in Act III. Like a Cornelian heroine she declares that if Soliman tries to ravish her she has a dagger and will use it on herself. She accompanies Eraste to Rhodes and in the last act is on the battlements (in man's clothes) when Soliman orders a volley. He enters Rhodes and discovers her dead. Soliman swears he will raise a fine mausoleum to them and executes Brusor who is responsible for the action. Desfontaines' *Perside ou la suitte d'Ibrahim Bassa* (1644) begins at Mainfray's Act III with the death of Eraste but borrows soliloquies from Scudéry's *Ibrahim* (1643) based on the Turkish history of Ibrahim, Soliman's high-ranking Christian slave.[26]

A variant on the theme is found in the two Heywood plays, *The fair maid of the West*, I and II. Bess, the heroine, is a barmaid and subsequently landlady of an inn in Plymouth whence expeditions set out for the Azores. Shown throughout as a model of prudence and virtue she becomes involved in a complex series of adventures as she seeks her lover, Spencer, a gentleman-adventurer, who has been captured by Spaniards and then becomes the prisoner of king Mullisheg of Morocco. Eventually the lovers are reunited and the king provides the wedding feast. At the beginning of Part II, Mullisheg, like Soliman before him, repents of his generosity and tries to separate the lovers and win Bess for himself. The situation turns to farce with Mullisheg pursuing Bess and his wife pursuing Spencer. Bess arranges her escape with Spencer by accepting an assignation with Mullisheg and then sending the queen (who thinks her assignation is with Spencer) to her own husband. After more adventures Bess and Spencer finally are reunited in Florence. The original element in this largely derivative set of plays is the pre-eminence of Bess, the heroine, who arranges everything, maintains her dignity (and her chastity) till married to the man she loves, and all without the help of the Virgin Mary, an angel, a magician or Venus.

There are a number of other plays on this theme with eventually happy endings. Several are based on plays and stories by Cervantes drawing on his experience as a prisoner after Lepanto, for he thriftily re-used his narrative *El trato de Argel* for a *comedia* of the same title, *El trato de Argel*, written in the 1580s but not printed until 1784 (Lope de Vega wrote an adaptation of *El trato de Argel*, called *Los captivos de Argel*, c. 1600, but not printed till 1647). The basic elements of the story include the pursuit of a woman carried into captivity at Algiers; a Moorish princess's love for a nobly born Christian; a captive Christian woman's rejection of a Moorish lover and an escape with the assistance of a repentant renegade.

There are parallels between Massinger's *The Renegado* (1624) and another Cervantes *comedia*, *Los baños de Argel* (The prisons of Algiers).[27] Massinger's heroine, Donusa, combines two of Cervantes' characters: the Lady Zara, courted by king Muley Maluco but in love with Don Lope, a Spanish prisoner, and Halima, wife of Caurali, the captain of Algiers, who actively courts her husband's slave, Don Fernando. Massinger also chooses to show Donusa's conversion on stage (IV. iii), reworking material from a scene in *The Virgin martyr*, in which the heroine Dorothea reconverts two apostate Christians sent to win her from her faith. Paulina corresponds to Don Fernando's young wife Costanza, carried into slavery and vainly courted by Caurali.[28] The English dramatist is as original in developing in Crimaldi a full-scale portrait of a violent man driven to despair and conversion as he is in creating the humane Jesuit, Francisco, from Yzuf's father of the same name in *Los baños de Argel*, or the ebullient Gazet from Don Lope's companion, the shadowy figure Vibanco.[29]

The Jesuit-trained French author, Pichou, composed *Les folies de Cardenio* (1629), based on the story from Don Quixote (Book 3, ch. 9) which had been used in the lost play of the same name, listed in the Stationer's register of 1653 but performed in 1612–13, and generally attributed to Shakespeare and Fletcher. There was also a very successful revised version by Theobald performed in 1723 under the title of *Double falsehood* (Metz, *Sources*, pp. 257ff). Guillen de Castro included these characters in his series of plays *Don Quijote de la Mancha* based on Cervantes' novel and published in 1618.[30]

STAR-CROSSED LOVERS

In contrast to the numerous love stories with a happy ending, there are a number of plays, most of them written post-1500, which end tragically, usually due to the lovers' families. The following examples are chosen because they appear in more than one language. The earliest French play on the classical story of Pyramus and Thisbe appears to be the *Moralité nouvelle de Pyramus et Tisbe, à quatre personnages*, composed about 1535. In this version, based on the popular medieval *Ovide Moralisé*, Pyramus represents Christ, Thisbe, the Christian Soul and the Lion, the Devil.[31] The wall between the lovers is created by the sin of Adam which has cut Mankind off from God. The play opens with two shepherds describing the great love of Pyramus and Thisbe. Throughout the text they act as a sort of chorus.

The story was also dramatised twice in Dutch: once by the Chamber of the Pellicanisten in Haarlem which may date from the early fifteenth century and again, about a century later, in Antwerp. The former is about 500 lines long and includes, as well as the two *sinnekens* Passionate Lust and Sinful Appetite, allegorical figures of Poetic Spirit and Amorous, whose scenes are a framework for the story. In the concluding section Poetic Spirit expounds to Amorous the full meaning of the story in the light of Christ's true love for Mankind, helped by a *tableau vivant* of Christ on the cross with the Virgin and St John standing below. In the much longer Antwerp play (about 1,500 lines) the story of Pyramus and Thisbe is much expanded and includes Thisbe's mother, Pyramus' father and a maid. (Both plays feature the lioness!) The *sinnekens* here are Deceptive Interpretation and Fraudulent Appearance whose role is to cause conflict between the two families and deliberately bring about the tragic ending. In this play too there is an epilogue where the parents of the dead lovers lament their end but see in it that 'This moralising history can be suitably

applied / to the passion of the blessed Christ / interpreted spiritually'
(ll. 1488–90).[32]

Théophile de Viau's *Pirame* (1621), one of the most successful plays
of its day, does not include allegory and moralising. The cast is considerably enlarged to include a royal wooer for Thisbe and the usual
nurse/*confidante*. The final sequence of the tragedy is expressed in three
scenes each consisting of one speech; first Thisbe arrives in the forest, is
frightened by the lion and flees (45 lines). Pyrame then arrives belatedly
and is worried about Thisbe. His long monologue reflects his gradual
discovery of the traces of the lion, the blood stains and Thisbe's scarf.
Convinced of her death he accuses himself of her murder for arriving
late, seizes his sword and stabs himself (150 lines). Thisbe creeps back
timidly and discovers what she first thinks is a sleeping Pyrame and then
her lover's corpse. She accuses herself of timidity in running away, and
prepares to kill herself to join Pyrame, calling on Charon to wait for her
so they can cross Lethe together. Unfortunately at the crucial point of
the scene de Viau tumbles into bathos:

> Ha! voici le poignard qui du sang de son maître
> S'est souillé lachement; il en rougi le traître!
>
> (Ah here is the dagger which with its master's blood
> is cowardly stained; he blushes for it, the traitor!)
> (v:2 vv. 1227–8)[33]

The popularity of the theme of the star-crossed lovers is shown above all
in the many times told tale of Romeo and Juliet. In Luigi da Porto's *Istoria
novellemente ritrovata di due Nobili Amanti* (published c. 1530), the families are
the Montecchi and the Cappelleti; this is also the basis of Bandello's *novella*
translated into English in 1562. The earliest play version is the *Adriana* by
Luigi Groto based on Porto's story and performed in Venice, where Groto
was an actor manager, until his death in 1585. No further performances
are recorded but the text was frequently reprinted.[34] The story is very
similar to Porto's *Istoria* but all the names are different (the lovers are
Adriana and Latino) and it is generally agreed that Bandello's version
was probably the basis of the plays which appeared in three different
languages in the same decade: a lost French play of *Roméo et Juliette* by
Chateauvieux, *valet de chambre du roi*, performed in Neufchatel in 1581;
Lope de Vega's *Castelvines y Monteses* written in 1588 and Shakespeare's
Romeo and Juliet in 1591–7.[35]

In two other well-known stories, the lovers are victims of the heroine's
brothers. Boccaccio's tale of Lisabetta and Lorenzo (Decameron IV:5),

well known in English from Keats' *Isabella or the pot of Basil*, was dramatised by Hans Sachs in his *Tragedi von Lisabetha eines kaufherrn tochter* (VIII, 1546).

Bandello's *novella* (1:26) of the sister who marries the steward and is killed by her brothers (supposed to be based on a true story) was dramatised by Webster as *The duchess of Malfi* in 1612–13 and by Lope de Vega as *El mayordomo de la duquesa de Amalfi* in (1618).[36]

FRIENDS AND RIVALS

A number of plays are based on the stories of devoted friends or kinsmen who either help each other, even to the extent of imprisonment or death on behalf of their friend, or become rivals for the affection of a lady as in the play of the *Two noble kinsmen* based on Chaucer's *Knight's tale*. The oldest play in the first group is that of *Amis et Amile* (Cangé, XXIII).[37] The play opens with Amis searching for Amile because he has been told they are identical in appearance and therefore he believes they are meant to be close friends. The two men meet and swear eternal friendship to each other. They take service with the king of France and are so successful that Amis is married off to the daughter of a great noble while Amile is pursued by the king's daughter. Accused by a jealous courtier, Hardré, of seducing the princess, Amile challenges him to a battle. He explains to Amis his danger, since it is true he had slept with the princess unknowingly. Amis offers to take his place in the battle. Both combatants having sworn they are in the right, Amis / Amile kills Hardré and the king offers him the hand of his daughter and makes him swear to marry her. Amis then sets off to find Amile and God sends Gabriel to tell him his false oath will be punished by his becoming a leper. He takes his farewell of Amile without telling him what God has said but gives him one of a pair of identical goblets as a keepsake. Amile and the princess are married. Amis next appears as a leper who has been thrown out of the house by his wife. Meanwhile, Amile and his wife have two children and return to Paris. God sends Gabriel to Amis and tells him that if Amile will kill his children their blood will cleanse his leprosy.[38] The two friends are reunited when Amile recognises the goblet and Amis is finally forced to tell Amile the price of his cleansing. Amile reluctantly but without hesitation kills his two children and carries the blood to Amis. They wipe it over him on the stage and he is cleansed. Amile tells his wife what he has done but God sends the Virgin, with her escort, to see Amile and tell him his children have been brought back to life. They rejoice and all set off to church to give thanks, Amile promising to give the children's weight in wax as a thank-offering.

The story was very popular in the Middle Ages and *Een spel van Amys ende van Amelis* was performed in Bruges in 1412–13 and a German version of *Amylgus unde Amylcar* in Lübeck in 1469.[39]

The story of Oliver and Artus has many parallels with the Amis story and was dramatised by Sachs in the *Comedi von Olwier und Artus* (1556) based on the *Histoire d'Olivier de Castille et Artus d'Algarbe*, a Burgundian romance composed about 1454–6.[40] Oliver and Artus are stepbrothers and devoted friends. Arthur's mother (who has married Oliver's father the king of Castile) tries to seduce her stepson. He flees the court, having first given Arthur a magic glass that will go black if Oliver is in difficulties. Oliver goes to England accompanied by a knight, Sir John Talbot. They are shipwrecked and Talbot is drowned. As he is heavily in debt he cannot be buried, but Oliver pays the debt and arranges a proper burial. In England, Oliver enters for a tournament whose prize is the king's daughter, Helen. Talbot then returns as a 'spirit or ghost' in the form of a White Knight who promises to help Oliver win the tournament in exchange for half of anything he wins.[41] Having won and married the princess, Oliver becomes involved with a war between the kings of England and Ireland and is eventually taken prisoner by the Irish. Arthur sees that the glass has turned black and the White Knight tells him how to save Oliver, but first sends him to console the distraught Helen in the form of her husband Oliver. He is told he must share her bed for three nights but without any physical contact. Arthur follows his instructions and then the knight takes him to the prison where Oliver is kept and he is freed. When Oliver learns that Arthur has shared a bed with Helen, he is furious and attacks and wounds him, then repents when he learns the truth and prays for help. A voice says he can heal Arthur by killing his two children by Helen and giving Arthur their blood to drink. He regretfully does this and as soon as Arthur has drunk, he drops the crutches he has been using. He asks what is this drink that tastes like blood (no indication of where he learned this taste!) and is horrified to learn that Oliver has slain his children. Helen enters, however, with the children. They have been revived by the White Knight who now returns to demand his half-share of all Oliver has won: one child and half of Helen! After much vain pleading, Oliver accepts the knight's warning of dire consequences if he is forsworn and lifts his sword to cleave Helen in two. The knight then stops him, reveals who he was and his gratitude to Oliver and all ends happily.

Guyon et Tirius[42] is another Marian miracle telling of two English friends at the court of the Soldan. Tirius is falsely accused by a jealous Saracen, and Guyon offers to fight on his behalf. The villain tries to drown Guyon to avoid the battle but the Virgin intervenes and all ends happily for the friends. There is no known direct source for the play.[43]

In the sixteenth century, many plays are based on Boccaccio's *Titus and Gesippe* (*Decameron* x:8) who, like Chaucer's Palamon and Arcite, are both in love with the same woman.[44] Lancashire records performances of a Latin play of *Titus et Gesippus* by John Foxe in 1544, and the *Firmissima amicitia de Titi et Gisippi*, written by Ralph Radcliffe for his scholars to perform in the school hall at Hitchin 1550–7. Other plays include Hans Sachs' *Thitus [vnd] Gisippus zwen getrew* (Sachs, XII, 1546); one by Montanus from Alsace, c. 1560 (Creizenach, III, p. 267); and Hardy's *Gésippe* (Lancaster, I, i, pp. 53–8). Shakespeare uses the theme as the basis for *Two gentlemen of Verona* in which Valentine offers to give up his claim to Sylvia to Proteus, the friend who had betrayed him and caused his banishment.[45] This generosity brings Proteus to his senses and he returns to his original and faithful love, Julia, who has followed him disguised as a boy.

A variant on the faithful friend theme is found in Tasso's tragedy *Torrismondo* (1587). Germondo, king of Sweden, wants to marry Alvida, the daughter of the king of Norway. He refuses to allow the match so Germondo arranges for his friend Torrismondo to woo and wed her on his behalf and then hand her over to Germondo. While the couple are travelling back to Sweden they are shipwrecked on a deserted shore. They share a shelter and believing Torrismondo is her husband Alvida gives herself to him. When Germondo comes to claim his bride, Torrismondo is filled with fear but manages to persuade Germondo to allow him to keep Alvida and accept Torrismondo's sister, Rosmonda, instead, unaware that in fact the one he believes to be his sister was exchanged many years before by the king of Norway and the woman he has married is in fact his sister. The king of Norway dies suddenly, the truth is revealed, and Torrismondo learns he is guilty not only of betraying his friend but of committing incest with his sister. He kills himself, and Alvida, lamenting the sins she has accidentally committed, dies of grief.

CHAPTER 9

Premarital problems

In *Much ado about nothing*, Shakespeare uses as his main plot the false accusation of Hero, who is betrothed to Claudio but apparently seen receiving a lover through her bedroom window. This motif is found in several sixteenth-century narrative sources including Ariosto's *Orlando furioso*, on which Claude Billard de Courgenay based his play, *Genevra*. The subject was later treated in a *novella* of Bandello which is the direct source of Ayrer's *Die schöne phoenicia*. Shakespeare, as is his wont, makes use of both Ariosto and Bandello.[1]

The romanticised story of *Berte au grand pied* (Bertha Bigfoot), a historical figure from Carolingian epic, was told in the fourteenth century by Adenet le Roy. In *Berte, femme du roi Pepin* (Cangé, XXXI, 1373) Berte, the daughter of Floire and Blanchefleur, is sent to France to marry Pepin the Short, accompanied by her maid and the maid's scheming mother. The latter so frightens Berte with tales of the violence she may expect to suffer on her wedding night that she agrees to change places with her maid after the wedding.[2]

When Berte comes to the bedroom later that night, the maid refuses to give up her position, seizes a knife and wounds herself, then cries out and, supported by her mother, declares the supposed 'maid' Berte had tried to kill her and her 'husband'. Like other accused queens, Berte is exiled to the customary pathless forest where she is befriended by a woodcutter. Pepin, hunting in the forest, loses his way and comes across Berte. While she is leading him to shelter in the woodcutter's hut, he tries to rape her, believing her a peasant girl. To prevent him, Berte declares she is really the queen of France. Pepin lets her go. The situation is resolved when Blanchefleur insists on coming to visit her daughter and identifies the supposed queen as Berte's maid. The maid and her mother are executed and the royal couple are reunited. Their son will be Charlemagne.

The theme of the substituted bride is also found in the *Reine de Portugal* (Cangé, IV, 1342).[3] The heroine is the daughter of a *castellain* whose castle is visited one night by the king of Portugal who has been hunting and lost his way. The king is smitten by the girl's beauty and decides to marry her, to the delight of the family. He then tells the girl secretly he wants to sleep with her before the marriage. Afraid of losing such a bridegroom, she gives him a key to the tower where she sleeps. Having arranged a date for the marriage, the king returns to his castle and tells the story to his seneschal who persuades him such a demand was uncourtly. The king repents of his request and confides the key to the seneschal to be returned to the girl. The girl receives the seneschal thinking he is the king but when he has gone to sleep she discovers the deception and, furious and dismayed, cuts off his head with his own dagger. Then she summons a cousin to help her to hide the body down a well. Despite the mysterious absence of the old seneschal, the wedding goes ahead but the girl, to hide the fact she is no longer virgin, persuades the cousin to take her place on the wedding night. All goes well until the girl comes in the night to take her proper place while the king sleeps and the cousin refuses to give up her place as the queen. (It is implied that they look very much alike.) Angry again, the girl ties up the cousin and then sets fire to the bed. When it is ablaze she wakes the king and they flee from the burning room leaving the cousin to the flames. Subsequently the girl repents and confesses her sin to the chaplain who expects her to give in to him in exchange for his silence.[4] She refuses and he betrays the truth to the king. The body of the seneschal is found and she is about to be executed when the Virgin Mary, to whom she has always been devoted, intervenes with her customary idiosyncratic justice: she blames the king for the original idea, the seneschal for his deceitful trick and the chaplain for breaking the seal of the confessional. The last named is executed while the girl is pardoned her two murders but spends the rest of her life in a convent. This, the earliest (performed in 1342) of all the tragi-comedies being discussed, is still more than half a genuine miracle play.

THE THREAT OF THE INCESTUOUS FATHER

The *Historia Apollonii*, the fifth-century Latin story of the father who commits incest with his daughter, was widely known and immensely popular in the Middle Ages. Only three plays, the sixteenth-century English *Dux Moraud*, Shakespeare's *Pericles* (1608) and Bernier de la Brousse's *Les heureuses infortunes d'Apollonie* (1618) dramatise the actual theme of incest, but there are several plays of the father who wants to marry his daughter.[5]

In *La fille du roy de Hongrie* (Cangé, XXIX), *Santa Uliva* (D'Ancona, III) and the *Comedia sine nomine*,[6] the heroine's father, having sworn an oath when his wife dies not to remarry unless he finds someone as beautiful as she is and being urged to marry for the sake of a male heir, decides the only possible candidate is his own daughter.[7] In the first two plays, the daughter cuts off her hand or hands to avoid the proposed marriage.[8] The Cangé play closely follows the fourteenth-century romance of *La manekine*, in which no specific reason is given for the mutilation, but Uliva's father, the emperor, specifically says that no one else has hands as beautiful as she has (p. 253). Both daughters are condemned to death by the angry father but instead the assassins send them off into the blue in a rudderless boat. A variant of the mutilation theme occurs in the Italian play of *Stella*. Here the empress of Rome, jealous of her step-daughter's beauty (an echo of Snow White), orders her henchmen to kidnap and kill Stella and bring back her cut-off hands. They also do not kill Stella but send her off in the usual boat. In the *Comedia*, the heroine (whose father is also emperor of Rome), flees with her attendant and a substantial treasure, otherwise the storyline is the same, though all religious references have been paganised to suit the classical context of the play.

All four heroines find their way to a foreign land where they marry the local lord against his mother's will.[9] Uliva has two intercalated adventures here. In the first she becomes nursemaid to the child of a queen but he is killed when a would-be seducer knocks him out of her stumps. After Uliva's second adventure with a lustful priest, when she has been put to sea in a chest, the Virgin Mary appears and restores her hands. Sachs' *Die vertrieben Keyserin* (1555) combines the two elements. The heroine becomes a nursemaid and is accused of killing the child by a would-be seducer before she is put in the boat for the second time.[10]

A unique version of the incestuous father episode is to be found in the *Yde et Olive* continuation of the cycle of Huon de Bordeaux, dramatised in *La fille d'un roy qui devint soudoyer* (Cangé, XXX). Ysabel, the daughter of the would-be incestuous king, escapes, disguised as a youth, with her attendant. Gabriel is sent by God to help them on their way. He meets them at the port and offers to negotiate their passage, explaining that the shipmaster will not understand their language. He then has a long dialogue with the shipman in Latin. Ysabel takes service as a knight with the emperor of Constantinople and serves him so well that 'he' is made to marry the emperor's daughter. She dare not reveal her true sex because of the jealousy of the emperor's barons but is overheard telling her 'wife' the story and challenged by the emperor who tells the 'knight' that he and his wife must bathe together before witnesses. At the crucial moment, God sends Gabriel in the form of a white stag which immediately distracts the court who set off in pursuit. The 'stag' reappears and tells the girl not to worry about the bath, and lo! when she undresses she is immediately seen by the emperor to be a man! This is obvious comedy since the role, of course, was played by a man so that 'she' can indeed prove her lack of women's breasts simply by removing her coat – as she does. Eventually all is straightened out. Ysabel's penitent father comes to the court and finds her. He marries the emperor's daughter and Ysabel marries the emperor instead.[11]

CHAPTER 10

The falsely accused queen and other suffering wives

PATIENT GRISELDA

The ultimate innocent sufferer must be Patient Griselda,[1] but she is more of a moral example than a falsely accused heroine of romance, for without any true or false accusations of misbehaviour, she suffers much at the hands of her husband, including losing her children and her rank. The story was translated into French (from Petrarch's Latin version of the *Decameron* story) by Philippe de Mézières, as an exemplum in his *Livre sur la vertu du sacrement de mariage* (1384–9) and was dramatised (probably by de Mézières) in the *Estoire de Griseldis* of 1395.[2] Although a popular tale in the Middle Ages, the husband's ill treatment of his wife – forcing her to give up her children, telling her they are dead; and eventually casting her out in nothing but her shift – all apparently as a test of her wifely obedience – was condemned by many, including the author of the *Ménagier de Paris*.

Less moral and more romantic are a wide range of plays in which the lovers, having successfully overcome the barriers that keep them apart, discover that marriage is not the end of a wife's problems: 'they all lived happily ever after' is rarely true of these ill-fated heroines, especially if they are of royal or noble rank. There is so often a would-be seducer or wicked step/mother-in-law to contend with. The significance of the rank of the protagonists is the importance of the succession whose legitimacy would be threatened. Royal adultery was not just sinful, it was treason.[3] There are numerous traditional tales and romances on 'the falsely accused queen' from all over Europe and the Near East,[4] and they fall into two main groups.

THE WICKED MOTHER-IN-LAW

Most of the daughters who escape from their would-be incestuous fathers, then move on to the jeopardy of their in-laws, especially the jealous mother-in-law. While the husband is away at war, a tournament or on pilgrimage, the heroine gives birth to an heir and news is sent to the king but the messenger (thinking it proper to tell the queen mother who has retired to a nearby castle) stops off there en route. She gets the messenger drunk and changes the letters telling the king his wife has borne him a monster (with the implication that she has had intercourse with a devil). The distressed king's reply – to guard mother and child safely till his return – is also changed to an order to kill the queen and child. As usual, the assassin does not obey orders but puts them back in a boat or chest or abandons them in the forest. Stella and her children find shelter in the forest with a hermit and are found by the husband while he is hunting. Uliva and the king of Hungary's daughter both finish up in Rome with their son(s) and are reunited with their husbands (and penitent fathers) when the latter visit Rome on pilgrimage.[5] In *Le roi Thierry et sa femme Osanne* (Cangé, XXXI) based on the fourteenth-century romance of *Théseus de Cologne* the play begins after the marriage and the king's departure: three puppies are put in the cradle by the wicked queen mother, instead of the three new-born children of queen Osanne.[6] The children are abandoned in the forest by the man who was supposed to kill them. They are eventually found, the wife is freed from prison and the wicked queen is punished.

A popular variant of this incident is the late medieval tale of Valentine and Orson which was dramatised in the sixteenth century in a *Fastnachtspiele* of which no text survives but which is illustrated in Breughel's painting of *Carnival and Lent*.[7] The romance is set partly in Constantinople and partly in France. The empress of Constantinople, who is the sister of Pepin king of France, is pursued by the local archbishop. When she rejects him he denounces her and she is exiled. A local merchant who does not believe the archbishop takes care of the queen who is heavily pregnant. In the forest she gives birth to twins, one is carried off by a bear and the other is lost, while the queen is pursuing the animal, but rescued and raised by a forester.[8] In due course Pepin sees the lad, now called Valentine, admires his beauty and adopts him, unaware he is his nephew. Meanwhile the other boy, Orson (or, in early versions of the text, *Nameloos* – nameless), grows up in the forest as a sort of wild man. He is found and succoured by Valentine. Eventually the truth of the story becomes known but only after the young men have fought in many wars and brought about the downfall of the villain in the customary way.

THE WICKED BROTHER-IN-LAW

Where no mother-in-law is involved, a brother-in-law may fill the role of villain. One of the earliest narratives of this kind is a Marian miracle recorded by Gautier de Coinci and dramatised under the title of *L'impératrice de Rome* (Cangé, XVII, 1369). There is also a version by Sachs: *Die unschuldig keyserin von Rom* (1551). A very similar story is told in the Italian play of *Santa Guglielma* by Antonia Pulci, c. 1500.[9] When the emperor leaves Rome, the queen's brother-in-law tries to seduce her during the king's absence.[10] Having failed, he then denounces her as an adulteress on the emperor's return. The husband believes the story without the least hesitation and she is exiled or, in some versions, set adrift in a boat without sails or oars by those ordered to kill her.[11] She suffers shipwreck and is abandoned on a rock but is rescued by the Virgin Mary who gives her a miracle-working herb that cures all those who confess their sins.[12] Meanwhile the wicked brother-in-law contracts leprosy and eventually is brought to this famous healer, confesses his sins and the truth is revealed. In the Cangé and Sachs plays the heroine works as a doctor, in men's clothes, but S. Guglielma enters a nunnery where she performs her healing acts.[13]

Wallensköld in *Le conte de la femme chaste*[14] lists also many narrative versions where the heroine is Hildegard, the second wife of Charlemagne and there is also a sixteenth-century play written in Latin by Nicholas Frischlin and translated into German by his brother Jacob. This is the only play on the subject of the falsely accused queen where the courtiers actually criticise the husband's behaviour, indeed a large part of the play involves scenes of the emperor and an outspoken noble. Hildegard, having been denounced by her brother-in-law, Talandus, is condemned to be exiled after her eyes have been put out. This, of course is avoided by the henchmen who merely send her off into the forest, from which she is rescued by a faithful knight.[15] She goes to Rome, sets up as a healer and in due course heals the brother-in-law who has become blind.[16] The plot is unveiled and the emperor and his wife are reconciled. The Hildegard story has a sort of historical background, at least according to Caspar Brusch in his *Chronologia* of 1682 (pp. 94–5). The story is quoted in the *Acta Sanctorum* for 30 April, the feast day of Hildegardis Beata.

A late Marian miracle play[17] performed by the Confrérie de Notre Dame de Liesse in 1541 uses names from the romance of *Florence de Rome* but makes changes to the story: Florence and Emare are betrothed, not

married, when she is given into the care of Macaire; when they are finally
reconciled and reunited, Florence declares her intention of dedicating
her virginity to the Virgin Mary and enters a nunnery. In Gautier de
Coinci's version of the *Impératrice de Rome*, the queen refuses to return to
her husband and enters a convent; but in the play version of Gautier's
poem (Cangé, XXVII) she goes back to her husband.[18]

Another late addition to the victims in this version of the story is the
historical Genevieve of Brabant, wife of the Palatine count Siegfried.
During Siegfried's absence, the rejected villain, Golo, sends a dwarf to
Genevieve's room and kills him there.[19] In 1638 a very elaborate French
life of 'Ste Geneviève' was published in French by the Jesuit René de
Cérisiers and no fewer than four plays of St Genevieve were performed
in Paris in 1660–70 (Edelman, p. 166). Three subsequent Jesuit plays
from Germany in all of which she is referred to as 'heilige' are recorded
by Szarota (III, 2, p. 2279). Genevieve's sanctification was short-lived,
however.[20]

A variant on the theme of the wicked brother-in-law is that of the
Marquise de Gaudine (Cangé, XII, 1352). Here the would-be seducer is the
queen's uncle and the story is specifically linked to the tale of Susannah
and the Elders.[21] Having got the marquise drunk with the help of a
venial maid, the frustrated old man arranges for a dwarf to be found in
her bed.[22] The dwarf is killed and the marquise condemned to death but
a knight, Anthenor, appears, sent by the Virgin, and challenges the uncle.
They fight and the defeated uncle confesses his sin and is imprisoned.

OTHER JEALOUS HUSBANDS

There are two plays by Shakespeare on the theme of the falsely accused
wife in which someone close to the hero, not a brother-in-law, performs
the same function. In *Othello* he treated the story in tragic vein, with Iago's
diabolical schemes triumphing and no divine intervention. In Cinthio's
story (*Heccatomithi*, III:7) on which Othello is based, Iago is presented
as a vicious version of the traditional brother-in-law, whose desire for
Desdemona turns to hate when she ignores him: 'the love which he had
felt for the Lady now changed to the bitterest hate, and he gave himself
up to studying how to bring it about that . . . if he himself could not enjoy
the Lady then the Moor should not have her either . . . he determined
to accuse her of adultery' (trans. Bullough, VII, p. 244).

A winter's tale is based on Greene's novel *Pandosto*, an accused-queen plot
which omits the character of the would-be seducer and makes the king's

causeless jealousy the motive source in the play.[23] Although the Delphic oracle (replacing the Virgin Mary) declares Bellaria's innocence, there is no Paulina as in Shakespeare to preserve her life – both the queen and her son die and Leontes/Pandosto is left without an heir, having sent his new-born daughter (whom he declares is a bastard) out to sea in a boat. Shakespeare follows Greene closely in the second half of the play until near the end when Pandosto falls in love with his newly discovered daughter, Fawnia, and plans to execute Dorastes (Shakespeare's Florestan) and marry his daughter himself. The would-be incestuous father has come full circle. But when Pandosto learns Fawnia is his daughter, he is so ashamed of what he has nearly done that, after arranging for the couple to be married, he commits suicide.[24] An echo of *A winter's tale* is found in *L'inceste supposé* by La Caze (1640). While the king of Hungary is away fighting the Turks, the queen Alcinée is pursued by her brother-in-law, Clarimène, whom she rejects and threatens to tell the king but as usual the villain gets in first. The story follows generally the usual line (but with no healing element involved). When Clarimène repents and confesses, the king has a fine tomb prepared, with a plaque telling the story. The queen, veiled, poses as a tomb figure and when the king comes there she reveals herself and tells him the truth. Is this an influence from *A winter's tale*? The brother-in-law is pardoned, because the king's sister is in love with him.[25]

An historical example of the unjustly jealous husband which was dramatised many times is the story of Herod the Great and his wife Mariamne. In Sachs' *Herod und Mariamne* she is a very strong figure. Tirso de Molina's *Vida y muerta de Herodes*, based on Josephus, shows Herod as an egoistical tyrant and includes both the death of Mariamne and the slaughter of the Innocents. Hardy's *Mariamne*, written (between 1605 and 1615) for the Hotel de Bourgogne, like most of his plays emphasises action rather than psychology, and *La Mariane* by Francois Tristan L'Hermite (1637) was very highly praised. The subject was also popular with the religious orders especially in Germany, including plays by the Benedictines in Salzburg (Valentin, p. 27) and the Jesuits in Landsberg in 1656 and Landshut 1663 (Szarota, II, 2, p. 2447).[26] La Calprenède wrote a sequel to Tristan's *Mariane* treating of Herod's execution of his sons by Mariane, Alexander and Aristobulos.[27]

CHAPTER II

Domestic dramas

A very high proportion of the plays so far considered in this section deal with royalty or high nobility, as did the epics and romances from which most of their stories are taken. There are a number, however, which deal with problems within a bourgeois family (rural settings are extremely rare), most notably some of the Marian Cangé miracles.

THE GUILTY WIFE

One of the most interesting miracles is a variation on the falsely accused wife in which a bourgeoise kills her brother-in-law because she is afraid everyone will believe he has seduced her. The bailiff, however, is suspicious at this sudden death and makes a careful investigation of the corpse: 'See how black his throat is, someone, whoever it may be, has strangled him.'[1] The wife is arrested and condemned to be burnt but her husband prays to the Virgin and the woman is saved but must spend the rest of her life in a nunnery.

Among the other sinful women who are saved by the intervention of the Virgin Mary are the pregnant abbess (Cangé, v) and the nun who runs away from her convent with a lover (Cangé, VIII) but returns, penitent, some time later to find she has not been missed because the Virgin has taken her place. The same theme is treated by Lope de Vega in *La buena guarda*.[2]

In the domestic tragedies of sixteenth-century Protestant England, there is no divine intervention to protect *Arden of Feversham*, save the *Babes in the Wood*, or to check Calverley in the riotous living which will lead to the *Yorkshire tragedy*. Nor do most of the sinners repent, though an exception is to be found in Thomas Heywood's *A woman killed with kindness*. Having been caught in *flagrante delicto* with her lover, the guilty wife is banished from the house by her husband, though he provides her with all she needs in the way of accommodation, furnishings and servants. Repentant and grief-stricken she goes into a decline. Eventually her servants persuade the husband to visit her. She convinces him of her repentance and in an unusual final scene begs him – not God – to pardon her:

WIFE: 'My fault so heinous is
                   That if you in this world forgive it not,
                   Heaven will not clear it in the world to come.'
HUSBAND: As freely from the low depth of my soul,
                   As my Redeemer has forgiven His death
                   I pardon thee. . . . . .
WIFE: Pardoned on earth, soul, thou in heaven art free.
                                              (Act V, scene 4)

This may be compared to Jean Brétog's 1571 *Tragédie française* in which the servant who seduces his mistress causes the wife to be thrown out of the house and the husband to die of rage and jealousy. He is executed for murder but makes an edifying ending. Although it is, in form, a *moralité*, complete with allegorical figures like *Vénus* and *Chasteté*, Petit de Julleville claims that Jean Bretog, 'avant Diderot a créé la tragédie bourgeoise' (*Répertoire*, p. 33).

CHAPTER 12

The wager

There are plays in English, French, German and Spanish of the story of the 'wager' (*gageure*) probably best known to English readers from Shakespeare's *Cymbeline*. A detailed study of the story was made by Gaston Paris and published just after his death in 1903.[1] In the earliest versions a man guarantees the virtue of a woman (sometimes his sister or his betrothed rather than his wife) against another man who fails to seduce her but by false evidence makes her appear guilty. Many variants are found in medieval narratives, culminating in Boccaccio's story in the *Decameron* (II:9).

Hans Sachs' *Die undultig fraw Genura* (1548) follows Boccaccio very closely: the characters are not royal, and the denouement takes place at the court of the Soldan. On the other hand, Ayrer's *Comedia von zweyen Fürstlichen Rähten* (c. 1600) uses a different story line: two gallants wager with the husband that they will seduce his wife but are tricked by the lady who sends two of her servants instead who do not yield to the gallants but give them a necklace and ring respectively. When the husband returns, the gallants show the jewels to claim their victory but fail to recognise the wife – whom they have never seen – thus proving her innocence. The husband wins the wager.[2]

Another variant, where the heroine is sister not wife of the hero and there is slander but no real wager, is used in Rueda's Spanish play *Eufemia* (1551). Leonardo praises his sister Eufemia as a suitable choice of bride for the king he is serving, but a rival courtier declares he has slept four times with her and produces hairs that she gave him, from a 'seigne' on her left shoulder. The king, furious, has Leonardo imprisoned and condemned to death. Eufemia is warned of the slander by a messenger and goes to court where she manages to convince the king of Pablo's guilt and Leonardo's innocence. Pablo is executed and Eufemia marries the king.[3] Several of these elements are found in the narrative sources especially the all-important 'seigne'.[4]

OSTES D'ESPAGNE

The most important medieval play on this theme, however, is also the earliest. *Ostes d'Espagne* (Cangé, XXVIII) was composed in 1370, before Boccaccio had been translated into French, and shows little resemblance to his version of the story but some fascinating and unexpected similarities to *Cymbeline*.[5] *Ostes* opens in Rome with a claim by the Holy Roman Emperor Lothaire to the crown of Spain.[6] When he learns that Lothaire is about to invade his country, king Alfons abandons his capital Burs (Burgos?) and his daughter, Denise, to the care of the bourgeois of the town and goes to Granada to ask help of his brother, the king. When he learns of Alfons' departure, Lothaire easily persuades the bourgeois to render up the town to escape being sacked, and arranges for Ostes, his nephew, to be married to Denise and given the crown of Spain. After the wedding and the installation of the couple as king and queen of Spain, Ostes returns to Rome with Lothaire, having given his bride a token by which they will always know each other: a bone from one of his toes, which Denise treasures as a precious jewel!

In Rome, Ostes stakes his kingdom in a wager on his wife's virtue with the villain, Berenger, who obtains from Denise's unfaithful maid details of her 'seigne' (never described, except in whispers) and the 'precious jewel' Ostes gave her. Ostes accepts Berenger's evidence and having thereby lost his kingdom (which passes at once to Berenger), goes to Burgos to find and kill Denise. Warned of what has happened by a bourgeois from Rome, the desolate Denise is visited by the Virgin Mary who promises her help and instructs her to flee (like Shakespeare's Imogen) disguised as a boy called Denis, and take service with her father in Granada.[7] When Ostes fails to find her, he threatens to beat God, renounces Christianity and becomes a Muslim.[8]

Unrecognised (by divine intervention), 'Denis' takes service with the king of Granada as one who can fight with lance and sword and also knows much of *eschansonnerie* (the squire's art of waiting at table). Denis becomes a beloved member of the king of Granada's court and persuades the two kings to go to Rome where 'he' will be able to arrange a peaceful settlement with Lothaire. While they are on their way, Ostes repents his apostasy and begs forgiveness. God sends the Virgin and St John to comfort him and send him to Rome to make his confession and find pardon.[9] This brings him back to the imperial court just in time for the grand unravelling of the plot by his disguised wife, who brings peace between Lothaire and Alfons. She then (speaking as the standard-bearer of the king of Granada) challenges Berenger for his treachery. When Ostes hears this he demands the right to defend the honour of himself and his wife and Denis politely yields the battle to him.[10] The combatants appear on stage armed and mounted but Lothaire decides in favour of a battle on foot and the horses are withdrawn. Ostes defeats Berenger who admits his crime. Denise reveals her true identity and draws attention to her feminine figure (but does not strip off as in some narrative forms).[11] She is reunited with Ostes. Berenger is arrested and condemned to death and the rest of the party go off happily to dinner accompanied by a group of 'clers' singing the praises of the Virgin Mary.

The similarities between this text and Cymbeline are obvious and surprising, for, although the wager story was widespread in medieval romance with many examples involving protagonists of high or royal rank, the situation with the marriage uniting warring royal factions of a Roman empire and a rebellious kingdom seems to be peculiar to the Cangé miracle and Cymbeline. There is also the apostasy of Ostes paralleled by Posthumus joining the Roman army against Britain and the consolatory appearance of Jove to him in prison, at roughly the same point in the play as the appearance of the Virgin to the repentant Ostes.[12] Gaston Paris also points out that the villain's report that the husband has been unfaithful to his wife is peculiar to these two plays. The final reconciliation in Rome is of course reminiscent of many of the falsely accused queen stories. There can be no question of a direct link between the Cangé play and Cymbeline but neither play has an indisputable known source for these unique features and it seems possible therefore that such a text existed, and indeed may still do so, somewhere in the libraries of Europe.

THE WIFE'S REVENGE

In contrast to the unjustified trials of all these wives, it is pleasing to discover a triumph over the would-be seducers by a clever woman in Massinger's play The picture (1630). The story derives originally from the Gesta Romanorum (LXI) where a husband who works as a carpenter has to leave home to work on the emperor's palace. He has a shirt which always remains clean and when the emperor comments on this the carpenter explains it was his wife's dowry and will never be soiled or damaged so long as the couple are both faithful.[13] Three knights overhear the story and wager they can seduce the wife. She is ready for them, however, and locks them up one by one in a room on bread and water till her husband comes home.

Massinger's play is set in Hungary and the characters are no longer working class. Despite his wife's efforts to stop him, the knight, Mathias, who has been noted by the king for his valour in battle, goes to court to gain a position which will enable him to keep his wife (who is of noble family) in the style she deserves. Although he claims to trust his wife, Sophia, he admits to a friend that he fears she will not remain faithful. The friend makes for him a picture which will change colour if his wife is unfaithful. At court the queen tries to seduce Mathias, and furious at his refusal and constant praise of his wife, she sends two courtiers who wager they can seduce the wife.[14] Pretending to be ready to yield to them, Sophia tricks the courtiers. One after the other, stripped to their shirts they fall through a trap door into a locked room provided with some straw, women's clothes and the necessary material for spinning and reeling.[15] They are told they must do this women's work or they will not eat. Despite their complaints of cold and hunger they are kept locked up till the husband returns having learned of the wager. Sophia has learned about the picture from the courtiers. Angry at her husband's mistrust she refuses to take him back and asks the king and queen (who have accompanied Mathias) to grant her a 'separation from his bed'. Finally the king and queen persuade her to forgive him and all ends happily – with the queen promising to behave better in future.

CHAPTER 13

Hell hath no fury: the woman scorned

In contrast to the many plays where the would-be seducer is male, there are a number of texts based on the theme of the 'woman scorned' who avenges herself by accusing the young man in question of attempted rape. The structure of the ancient story series of the *Seven sages of Rome*[1] is entirely based on this theme: a queen tries to seduce her stepson, is rejected and denounces him. The young man who has read in the stars that he must not speak a word for seven days will not admit or deny the accusation. The execution is postponed for seven days on each of which the queen tells a story against the youth, while the sages who have been his tutors, in turn, tell one against the falsity of women. On the eighth day the young man tells the truth and the queen is executed.

THE STORY OF JOSEPH

The biblical story of Joseph and Potiphar's wife was dramatised several times in the Middle Ages as part of the Old Testament history,[2] and was a popular subject in the Humanist Latin plays of the sixteenth to seventeenth centuries, culminating in lengthy German versions by Ruf and Hans von Rüte of Bern, in which Potiphar's wife is brought to trial for her false accusation and condemned to a term in prison.[3] There is also an important Jesuit play of Joseph by Bidermann in which 'he traces twenty-three years of Joseph's life from dreamy adolescence and obscurity in the wilderness to worldly wise maturity and fame at Pharaoh's side'. The elaborate drama includes a number of allegorical characters who develop the story but the scene with Potiphar's wife is played off stage as was common in early Jesuit drama with the female characters.[4]

PHEDRE AND OTHER LADIES OF RANK

The other well-known 'woman scorned', the Phaedra of classical drama, did not reappear on stage till the late sixteenth century when she became very popular in France.[5] Instead, there is a Jesuit play by Stefonio (1597) of a parallel historical incident to Phaedra: the story of Crispus, son of Constantine, who, having rejected his step-mother Fausta's advances, is denounced by her and put to death before the truth is discovered (McCabe, p. 182). Other Crispus plays are recorded by Szarota (III, 2, p. 2189), and a performance in Pultusk, Poland, in 1603 by Dabrowka.[6] Plays on this subject are not exclusively Jesuit. Tristan l'Hermite had only limited success on the public stage with his *La mort de Chrispe* in 1645, partly because he altered the more shocking elements making Chrispe's death the result of Fausta's sending poisoned gloves to the princess Chrispe is going to marry. Instead of being executed by Constantine, Fausta then commits suicide.[7]

In Hans Sachs' play of *Die falsche keyserin* (1551)[8] the wife of emperor Otto tries to seduce the count Latron. When he rejects her, she is furious and denounces him to the emperor. Despite his claims of innocence, the count is condemned to death but allowed a last brief meeting with his wife. He tells her he is innocent and how she should go about getting his name cleared and his death avenged. She goes to the emperor and claims the empress lied. When the emperor will not believe her she volunteers to take the test of hot iron. The emperor agrees and when she holds the heated sword and is unharmed, he accepts the evidence. The false empress is burned and the widow is given six castles in compensation for her loss.[9]

The story of the secret mistress, first told in the thirteenth-century *nouvelle* of the *Chastelaine de Vergi*, was revised and retold in the *Heptameron* of Marguerite de Navarre and dramatised by Du Souhait in his *Radégonde* (1599).[10] The duchess of Burgundy is infatuated with one of her husband's knights and to convince the duke that he is innocent of any relationship with the duchess, the knight reveals his secret love for the chastelaine. The duke swears to keep his secret but is tricked by his wife and reveals it. The duchess in her turn lets the chastelaine know she knows, and the chastelaine, distraught, dies. The lover kills himself and the Duke, realising what he has allowed to happen through his weakness, kills his wife, buries all three corpses and sets off on crusade.

In the miracle of *Saint John Chrisostome et sa mere* (Cangé, VI), the saint is falsely accused of rape by a king's pregnant daughter and thrown out into the desert to be killed by wild beasts. The Virgin intervenes, protects him and makes it impossible for the girl to give birth till she has admitted the accusation was false.[11]

In two miracle plays the woman scorned is an innkeeper's daughter. *Théodore, la femme moine* (Cangé, XVIII) tells the story of St Theodora of Alexandria (11 September),[12] a young wife who takes a lover during her husband's absence at the wars, then repents and decides the only place she will be safe from the Devil who tempted her, is in a monastery disguised as a man. Having spent some time there she is sent by the abbot to buy oil for the community and stays overnight at an inn. Urged on by the Devil, the innkeeper's daughter tries to seduce the young 'monk' but in vain, so she settles instead for the stable boy. When she finds herself pregnant, the girl consults her aunt who recommends she accuse the monk of having seduced her. Her father tells her to take the baby to the monastery and present it to its 'father' – she does so and brother Theodore is thrown out, with the child, and goes round begging. After seven years, the Virgin Mary intervenes, saying that by her patient endurance the young wife has atoned for her original sin. The abbot also is moved by Theodore's patience and sends a monk to bring her and the child back to the monastery. Shortly after, the Virgin again visits Theodore to announce her imminent death and salvation. The abbot has a vision of Theodore's death and discovers her true sex. He sends for the innkeeper who takes the child and promises to punish his daughter for her lies. (This detail is not in the *Legenda*.) Theodore's husband reappears, learns her story and says he will remain in the abbey for the rest of his life.

In *Un miracolo di tre pellegrini*,[13] an innkeeper's daughter tries to seduce a young man on his way to Santiago with his parents. When he rejects her, she arranges for him to be found with a valuable goblet in his bag.[14] He is hanged. Through the intervention of St James, he survives, happily swinging in the air, while his parents continue their pilgrimage. When they return and find him alive, they go to the mayor who declares he would as soon believe the boy is alive as that the chicken on his dinner table will get up and crow. It immediately does so. The youth is cut down, the girl is executed and all give glory to St James.[15]

CHAPTER 14

Family feuds

Plays based on an inheritance clash between father and sons or between the sons themselves are well known in the Bible.[1] The earliest medieval version is the *Miracle de Ste Bautheuch* (Cangé, XXXIV) which tells a story of King Clodoveus (Clovis II) and his wife Ste Bathildis (AASS 30 January).[2] According to the play, Clodoveus marries a slave girl, Bautheuch, who bears him two sons. Fifteen years later Clodoveus sets off on crusade leaving his elder son as regent but with instructions to consult his mother before making any decisions. Angry at this order the two sons rebel against their mother and hearing that Clodoveus is on his way home they decide to oppose his return and set off to attack their father's army and seize power for themselves.

Horrified, Bautheuch prays to Jesus and the Virgin and begs that her husband shall be safe and that at least the souls of her sons shall also be saved. The Virgin makes her usual appearance with an escort of angels and promises Bautheuch that her wishes shall be granted. Battle is joined and the princes are defeated and led in chains before their father who consults his barons as to their punishment for this treason. They refuse to pronounce and the king then asks Bautheuch, who recommends that as they have misused their power against their father they should be deprived of 'la force et vertu de leurs corps'. The executioner is summoned and hamstrings the princes with hot irons. Then by order of Jesus, whom Bautheuch has consulted, the crippled princes – who have repented and received their father's blessing – are put in a boat with an attendant and food supplies and sent off down the river Seine. The boat runs aground near the abbey of Jumièges where they are received by the abbot. News of their arrival is sent to the court and the king and queen visit the abbey and endow it very richly.

It is generally accepted that the play has no historical basis and was a legend put out by the monks of Jumièges but there is an echo of the well-known story of the sons of Oedipus, Eteocles and Polynices, who, according to one of the versions of the tale, were cursed by their father to die by each other's hand.[3] When they assumed power after his blinding and deposition, they arranged to reign alternate years, but when the first year ended Eteocles, the elder, refused to give up the throne. His brother then attacked Thebes with troops of his father-in-law leading to the war of the Seven against Thebes, in which both brothers were killed and their sister Antigone was executed for burying her brother.

There is also a certain similarity to the English tragedy of *Gorboduc* where the father, in his life time, divides the country between his two sons, Ferrex and Porrex, who start fighting over it. The younger kills the elder and the mother, who loved her elder son, kills the younger. The people rise in revolt and kill both mother and father and the country is devastated by civil war, and laid waste. The play opens with a dumb show in which six men show that a bundle of six sticks fastened together cannot be broken while the single sticks are easily snapped.[4] In the French morality play of *Les frères de maintenant* (*Répertoire*, p. 34), a version of the story of Joseph, a father stops his sons quarrelling among themselves by the image of one easily broken stick versus the unbreakable bundle.

INHERITANCE PROBLEMS

The father who abdicates in favour of his sons or daughters is a common theme in drama which reaches its apogee in Shakespeare's *King Lear* but is found much earlier in a French morality where the father, having given away all his goods and discovered the greed and unkindness of his sons, is advised by a friend to fill a fine casket with stones and seal it. Then, in the presence of the sons he explains he is leaving this casket with his friend who, when the father has died will give the casket with its valuable contents to the son who has best cared for his father. Thus the father escapes the fate of King Lear, unlike the father in the *Moralité de l'enfant ingrat* (*Répertoire*, 29:2 published 1589). In this play the father is warned by his friend not to spoil his son or he may suffer the fate of the duc de Bretaigne:

Cestuy noble Duc eu trois filles / De droicte generation. / Toutesfois sa succession / A la tierce point ne ordonna, / Pour cause qu'il l'arraisonna / Combien l'aymoit parfaictement. / Et elle dist que seurement / Elle l'aymoit comme son pere, / Ce qu'il print à grant vitupere; / Car les deux autres luy juroyent / Que plus qu'elles ou Dieu l'aymoient. / Parquoy en traictant marïage / Leur donna meuble et heritage, / Duché de toutes les sequelles, / Pensant estre nourry par

elles. / Toutesfois, quant duchesse furent, / Leur propre pere decogneurent /
Et recours qu'à la tierce n'eut, / Qui pour pere le recongneut.

(This noble duke had three legitimate daughters. However he bequeathed nothing to the third because when he questioned her how well she loved him she
told him that indeed she loved him as her father, which he took very badly for
the other two had sworn that they loved him more than themselves or God. So
when they were married they were given furnishings and legacies, dukedoms
and all that went with them, thinking that he would be taken care of by them.
However when they were duchesses they refused to recognise their own father
and his only resource was the third one who acknowledged him as her father.)[5]

The father refuses to believe this story and suffers the consequences,
but the play eventually has a happy and moral ending. Another example
of a test for succession is found in a German play of 1510. Based on a
story from the *Gesta Romanorum* (XLV) it tells of a king who dies leaving
three illegitimate sons and one, the youngest, who is legitimate but whose
mother has been accused of adultery. To decide who should succeed, the
dead body of the father is set up as a target and the sons are invited to
shoot at it in turn. The elder sons all do so and one actually hits the
heart and is convinced he has won. The youngest flatly refuses to treat
his father's body in this shameful way and is declared the new king.[6]

CHAPTER 15

The theatre of cruelty

Although Seneca as a philosopher and scholar was widely known and read in the Middle Ages, his plays, based on Greek and Roman history, were not performed or translated until the beginning of the sixteenth century. Much of their popularity came from the violent and blood-thirsty subject matter. These tragedies were influential in popularising the theatre of cruelty, which also used stories from Boccaccio, Yver and Bandello. As well as plays of sexual violence many of these are plays of vengeance.[1] In an article entitled *Le théâtre de démesure et horreur*, Lebègue discusses in considerable detail the theatre of horror found in many countries in the late sixteenth century, with special reference to England and France.[2] He concludes by a detailed listing of parallels between English and French plays on the same theme: 'On both sides of the channel characters wound and kill each other on stage with swords and daggers. These are the most frequently used stage properties' (Lebègue, p. 364). Having pointed out the development of the horrors as the audience becomes accustomed to them, Lebègue concludes 'certain human remains, faked, of course, are more impressive than a whole corpse. It is difficult to list all the human heads which, either held in the hand, presented on a plate or on the point of a sword, appeared on the French tragic stage between 1580–1640.' The heart is the next most popular remnant. Having mentioned a number of English heads and hearts, Lebègue goes on to list, with examples from both countries, 'the cut off hands, the cut or torn out tongues, and a cut off nose' but decides to pass over in silence 'l'affreuse mutilation de Lavinia' in Titus Andronicus (p. 366).

PLAYS OF RAPE AND SEDUCTION

As with the woman scorned, the stories of rape have both classical and biblical archetypes. The well-known classical tale of Lucrece was frequently dramatised but not before the sixteenth century.[3] The earliest vernacular play with a classical source, *Le viol d'Orgia*, from Lille, is based on a story from Valerius Maximus.[4] Orgia, the beautiful wife of the Galatian king, Ortiago, was taken prisoner by the Romans and held to ransom. She was raped by the centurion who had charge of her so when the ransom money arrived she commanded the Galatians in her native language to kill him. Then she cut off his head and took it to her husband, telling him of her injury and her vengeance.

Of the two biblical tales of rape, that of Dinah, a straightforward tale of seduction and revenge (Genesis 34), has been dramatised only once in Spanish: *Auto del robo de Digna* (Rouanet, I, VIII) and three times in French: *Le viol de Dinah* (*Lille*, 1:7), *Le viel Testament* (ll. 15297–337) and François Perrin's *Tragédie de Sichem ravisseur* (Rouen 1606). The story of Amnon and Tamar, however, a history of rape, incest and revenge (2 Samuel 13), inspired plays in Dutch, French, German, English and Spanish.[5] Tamar is the sister of Absalom and half-sister of another son of David, Amnon, who desperately desires her and eventually succeeds in tricking her into his room by feigning an illness which he claims can only be alleviated if his dear sister will bake him food with her own hands. She does so and he, having got her alone, rapes her. He then turns round completely: 'Then Amnon hated her with very great hatred . . . He called the young man who served him and said, "Put this woman out of my presence and bolt the door after her"' (2 Samuel 13:15–17). The most original play on the subject is *La venganza de Tamar* by Tirso de Molina.[6] In contrast to the Bible story in which Tamar herself is not mentioned after the rape and all the vengeance is planned and carried out by her brother Absalom, Tirso has allowed himself to make Tamar a major character throughout, encouraging the action which culminates in Absalom's murdering his half-brother in a banquet arranged as an occasion of reconciliation.

Elements in the story of Tamar are taken up in the Dutch *abele spel* of *Lanseloet van Danmark*.[7] Lanseloet is desperately in love with the beautiful Sanderijn, a young lady (she is the daughter of a knight, not a shepherdess like Griselda) in his mother's service. His mother considers her quite unworthy of her son and determines to break up the affair but no reason is given. The prologue simply says 'but she was too low for him in wealth and also of birth' (12–13).[8]

Although Lanseloet spends all his time talking of his great *love*, it is clear that he only *desires* Sanderijn, and offers merely a half promise that 'you might still be my wife'(89). But Sanderijn – poor but honest as the Victorian ballad has it – is firmly determined to keep her maidenhood. Lanseloet's mother rebukes him for his unmanly weeping over her and prepares a plot. Lanseloet is to take to his bed and she will tell Sanderijn he is dying and wants to see her. This will give him the opportunity to possess her, but he must swear that he will then reject her with crude and cruel words dictated to him by his mother. In a very uncourtly and unheroic manner, Lanseloet agrees 'I'll do whatever you wish, though it pains me in my heart' (265–6). Sanderijn, who had firmly refused all suggestions of going off to 'play' in the meadows because she knew exactly what would happen, cannot resist the appeal of her apparently dying lover and, like Tamar, agrees to visit him. When Sanderijn next appears on stage she is in despair not only for having been raped but for his rejection and the cruel words he was told to say by his mother: 'And so gorged is my heart as if I had eaten seven sides of bacon'(240–1). So far the story has more in common with the biblical rape stories than with any of the romances, apart from the role of the wicked mother.

In the second part of the text we are in more familiar romance country. Sanderijn runs away and comes to a foreign country where she is befriended by a knight who is hunting in the forest and finds her sitting by a fountain. Although she tells him, in an allegory, of her loss of virginity, he marries her and she finds love and happiness. Lanseloet, on the other hand is driven to despair by the loss of Sanderijn and sends his servant to search for her everywhere (unlike Esmoreit or Gloriant, he does not go in search of her himself). His messenger, learning of Sanderijn's marriage and fearing that Lanseloet might go to war to get her back, returns and tells the disconsolate lover she died of grief. Desolated, Lanseloet turns his face to the wall and dies himself in order that he may meet her in Heaven.

In the *moralité* of the emperor who killed his nephew,[9] an elderly emperor, after discussion with his advisors, abdicates in favour of his nephew and sole heir. The nephew is delighted as this will enable him (without fear of the law) to seize and rape a girl whom he much desires and who is vowed to chastity. He sends his henchmen to bring her to the palace, and despite her prayers, has his pleasure of her, then sends her home to her mother who has been invoking the aid of the Virgin Mary. The mother determines to appeal to the old emperor and when he hears the story he is very angry and summons the nephew. Although his advisors all beg him to forgive the young man, the emperor is adamant – the penalty for rape is death. Knowing his courtiers would never carry out the sentence he produces a sword he has hidden under the cushion of his chair and cuts his nephew's throat. The mother and daughter thank the Virgin for causing justice to be done. The effort is too much for the emperor and, knowing he is dying, he sends for his chaplain to whom he makes his confession but does not include the death of his nephew since that was a proper act of justice. Because he adamantly refuses to concede it is sin, the chaplain refuses him the last sacrament but the emperor prays to God and the consecrated wafer moves of its own volition to his mouth. He takes it with thanks and dies while the chaplain prays forgiveness for having refused it to him.

THE MONSTROUS RANSOM

There are many stories based on the theme of the monstrous ransom in which a woman is offered the choice of rape or death, sometimes her own, but more often that of her husband or other relative.[10] Once again the oldest example is biblical. In the Old Testament apocryphal *Book of Susannah*, the lustful Elders who have sneaked into her garden to watch her bathing, threaten her with death unless she submits to them. She refuses and they denounce her for adultery. Despite her husband's pleading she is condemned by the community led by the Elders who are also the judges, but is rescued by the youthful Daniel's cross-examination as council for the defence. (This story is probably the origin of the 'a Daniel come to judgement' in *Merchant of Venice*.) Numerous plays of Susannah survive in French, English, Dutch, German and Latin.[11]

Ransom stories, however, do not always have a happy ending. Some versions of the story involve a wife who sacrifices herself for her husband's sake and with his permission.[12] The story of Sophronia from Eusebius' *History of the church* is dramatised in the Lucerne play of the *Spil dess heiligen Crützes Erfindung* (Play of the invention of the Holy Cross) compiled by Renward Cysat from various sources. In this version the villain is the Roman emperor Maxentius (c. AD 280) one of the last pagan emperors to persecute the Christians. Among his acts of cruelty, Eusebius tells how he tried to seduce a Christian woman, Sophronia: 'when told that the tyrant's panders were at the door, and that her husband – a Roman prefect at that – through fear had given them leave to seize her and take her away, she begged to be excused a moment, as if to dress herself for the occasion. Then she went into her own room, shut the door, and stabbed herself to the heart, dying instantly.'[13] Cysat's dramatised version of this tale (about 700 lines) forms part of the fourth act of the play. The characters are all developed in some detail but not as part of a saints' play with an emphasis on martyrdom but as subjects of a cruel overlord – a state which was historically not unfamiliar to the Swiss. Maxentius, having bullied the citizens of Rome into giving him all their treasure, sends out his men to collect any beautiful women they find for his bed. When a burgher tries to object, he is killed and his wife taken away by the soldiers. It is against this carefully prepared background that Cysat builds up the story of Sophronia; when the soldiers come and tell her husband their errand he is horrified. He and Sophronia discuss what they can do to escape from this nightmare situation. Finally she says she will go to Maxentius and ask him to change his mind; meanwhile Fabricius, the husband, shall take the children and go away to a family estate outside of Rome. Fabricius agrees and leaves with the children. Sophronia then tells the soldiers she must change her clothes for something suitable to a palace and court and retires into her bedroom. In a long speech she prays for forgiveness for her deed and for her family, and commends her soul to God, then: 'with these words she stabs herself with a knife, falls back, says nothing more and stays there without moving till she is carried away'.[14]

In other sixteenth-century dramatic versions of the 'ransom' plot the wife surrenders to her seducer who then returns her husband – dead. When she complains to a higher authority, the seducer is ordered to marry her. and is then executed. In Rouillet's Latin tragedy of *Philanira* (Paris, 1556; French texts: 1563, 1577)[15] the heroine is left mourning her second husband – since she is married to him she must love him as a husband should be loved – and threatening suicide.[16]

In a number of stories, several from classical times, a virgin is asked by a judge to ransom a father or brother. The English play of *Apius and Virginia*[17] is based on a true incident recorded in Livy, Book 3: Apius is so besotted with the beautiful Virginia that, led on by Haphazard, the Vice, he forces a certain Claudius to accuse her father, Virginius, of having stolen Virginia from him as a child. Apius then orders Virginius to bring her to the court for safe custody. Recognising Apius' intentions, Virginius explains all to his daughter and after much hesitation, at her request, cuts off her head. He presents the head to Apius: 'She sought her fame, thou sought her shame: This arm has smit her dead.' Apius summons Justice and Reward to punish Virginius, but they turn on him instead, and order Virginius to put him in prison awaiting execution. Claudius, who made the false accusation is sentenced to be hanged. Apius kills himself in prison. The story was also dramatised by Sachs: *Virginia die romerin* (III, 1530). Sachs adds to the basic story the character of Cleopatra, a bawd, whom Apius employs to woo and bribe Virginia with jewels.[18]

The French *moralité* of *La pauvre fille villageoise* has a rare happy ending. The local *seigneur* desires a peasant's daughter and is furious when she rejects him, but when the daughter begs her father to cut off her head as otherwise she will kill herself and be damned, the seigneur repents. He makes the father a freeman and governor of his estates.[19]

Cinthio's play of *Epitia* is either based on, or possibly the source of, his own story in *Hecatommithi XIII:5* in which, instead of a husband and wife, the victims are brother and sister.[20] The brother, Vico, is accused of being guilty of fornication – an offence punishable by death. When his sister goes to plead for his life, the judge called Juriste offers her her brother's life in exchange for her body. Eventually, moved by her brother's entreaties and Juriste's promise to return her brother to her and a half-promise of marriage, she surrenders and spends the night with him. The next day her brother is indeed returned to her, but dead. Heart broken, she decides to appeal to the emperor. Having heard her and been moved by her control and careful presentation of the facts, the emperor sends for Juriste and tells him he will be executed for his abuse of power but only after he has married Epitia. But Epitia, feeling that allowing her husband to be executed would be too much like revenge, begs for his life which the emperor concedes and the two live happily ever after. In the play version of *Epitia* a happy ending is arranged when it turns out that Vico was not executed, and he marries the girl he had violated. The story is an obvious probability as a source for the main plot of *Measure for measure* since it includes the punishment of Juriste for abusing his position.[21] In Fletcher's *The queen of Corinth* her son, Theanor, is accused of raping two women and is brought to trial. The queen's advisor quotes from Lycurgus:[22] 'anyone who rapes a virgin shall – according to her absolute choice – either marry her (without a dowry) or be executed'. When the queen offers this choice to Merione and Beliza, the former chooses marriage, the latter Theanor's death. The impasse is resolved when it is revealed that the second rape was of Merione disguised as Beliza. All ends happily with the marriage of Merione and a reformed Theanor.[23]

EDWARD III AND THE COUNTESS OF SALISBURY

A variant of the ransom story is found in the plays of Edward III of England and the countess of Salisbury. The story was popularised by Bandello in a *novella* loosely based on a pseudo-historical story by the chronicler Jean le Bel who claims Edward actually raped her, a claim firmly rejected by Froissart.

The king falls madly in love with the countess and tries to persuade her to be his mistress. She steadfastly refuses despite his entreaties and his threats to her family.[24] Finally he has her brought to the palace but she produces a sharp knife and begs him to kill her either with his sword or the knife. Since the story is not too concerned with history, and makes the king unmarried and the countess a widow, Edward then proposes marriage to her which she accepts, and all ends happily.

Painter's story of *The countess of Salisburie* (1, 46), freely translated from Bandello, provides the basis of the first two acts of *Edward III*, now officially recognised as being mainly by Shakespeare. Painter makes a number of changes to fit in with English history. Both parties are married and Edward is staying in the castle in preparation for an attack on the Scots. He threatens the countess's family and tries to make her father encourage her to yield to him. She tells him she will do so on one condition: he must kill the queen and her husband. He says he will and she then produces two knives – one for him to use against the queen, the other to be plunged into her own breast immediately, unless he swears on oath he will abandon his unseemly suit:

> . . . . . Swear, Edward, swear
> Or I will strike and die before thee, here.
> *Ed.* Even by that power I swear, that gives me now
>   the power to be ashamed of myself.   (II. 2)

Edward keeps his word and turns his attention to the war against the French where the Black Prince will win his spurs.

The story was also dramatised by Ayrer, probably from a version presented in Germany by the English *Commödianten*, with a major role added for the 'Jahn' or clown character. The action closely follows Painter's story, and includes scenes with the king of Scotland laying siege to the castle and the king of France arresting the English ambassadors, which leads to the death of the countess's husband. However, Ayrer, unlike Shakespeare, makes the love-story the main theme of the play, ignores the existence of Edward's wife, Philippa of Hainault and, following Bandello, ends with the bishop on stage preparing to marry Edward and Ellipsa.

La Calprenède's *Edouard* (1639) follows Bandello's tale and omits all the political and historical background. The action begins after the countess is widowed (thus removing any talk of adultery), lasts only the twenty-four hours allowed by this time for a serious play in France and ends with the king marrying the countess. La Calprenède has varied the story by introducing Edward's mother, and her lover, Mortimer (who had both died well before this). La Calprenède mentions briefly the legendary episode of the 'Garter' and the origin of the motto, which is not in Bandello but was well known at the time as can be seen from a verse quoted in a French play of 1624[25] where one of the characters describes the:

> Ordre mis en avant par un roy en dansant:
> D'une comtesse alla la jartiere haussant
> en disant: Honny soit celui qui mal y pense
> Monstrant a ses subjets d'icelle l'innocence.[26]

CHAPTER 16

Le cœur mangé *and other culinary surprises*

The story of the adulterous wife who is fed her lover's heart by her jealous husband is found in a selection of medieval texts, the most important being the romance of the chatelain de Couci and la dame de Fayel.[1] Having discovered his wife's affair with the chatelain, the dame's husband tricks her lover into taking the cross by giving the impression he too is intending to join the crusade and will take the dame de Fayel with him. The chatelain sets off on crusade where, though disappointed of the presence of his lady, he fights valiantly, wearing always a token of his lady's hair on his helmet. When he is mortally wounded he orders his servant, after his death, to cut out his heart, embalm it and take it with the hair and a ring back to the lady. When the servant reaches France he is robbed of the relics by the husband who orders the cook to prepare the heart as a savoury dish. The lady eats of it joyfully and regrets she has never had such delicious meat before. When he tells her what she has eaten she declares she will never eat again, collapses and dies.[2] A *spel van der ridder van Coetchij* is included in the 1532 list of plays belonging to the guild of Saint Kathelijne of Ghent.[3]

The possibility of an embalmed heart being cooked up as a tasty dish, described by Delbouille as 'une invraisemblance flagrante' is avoided in Boccaccio's story of Sir Guillaume de Cabestaing (*Decameron* IV:9) which is closely related to the De Couci story though the characters and background are Provencal rather than from the north. In this version of the legend it is the husband who kills the lover and takes out his heart, which is cooked fresh, not embalmed.

Another recipe for horrors was provided by the story of Atreus and Thyestes where the former avenged himself on his brother, who had seduced his wife, by serving up Thyestes' children at a banquet.[4] Seneca's tragedy was translated into English by Jasper Heywood (1560) and is one of the probable sources of Shakespeare's first (and most blood-thirsty) tragedy of *Titus Andronicus*, who takes revenge for the rape and mutilation of his daughter, Lavinia, by the sons of Tamora, queen of the Goths, by killing them and serving them to Tamora as a dish 'whereof their mother daintily hath fed' (*Titus* V: iii).[5]

Shakespeare also refers in *Titus* to the other classical tale of rape, mutilation and revolting recipes, the tragedy of *Tereus and Progne*. Tereus is married to Progne but rapes Progne's beautiful sister Philomela, cuts out her tongue so she cannot denounce him and hides her in a secret place.[6] She succeeds in making a needlework account of her sorrows which is sent to Progne, who kills her young son Itys and serves him up to Tereus for dinner.

The story was dramatised many times in the sixteenth century: Lebègue mentions a lost French play of *Le ravissement de Philomene par Teréus*, in the repertoire of Valmy's travelling company in 1594 (Lebègue, p. 264), and also lists three Italian versions: *Progne*, by Girolamo Parabosco (Venice 1548); *Progne* (in Latin, anonymous but based on Gregorio Corraro, Venice, 1558) and *Progne* in Italian by Lodovico Domenichi (1561). In all three Philomela never appears, her story is all narrated. In Parabosco's play, Progne addresses the head of Itys before cooking the cut-up corpse.[7]

In Guillen de Castro's *Progne y Filomena* (c. 1590) 'incredibly, although his Progne does serve their son to Tereseo for dinner, he contrives to give the play a happy ending' (McKendrick, p. 128). As Progne discovers that Tereus did not actually rape Filomena and the tongue was only cut and had healed, she is prepared to forgive him, and the still virgin Filomena is able to marry her betrothed, Teosinda. Rohas' seventeenth-century play of *Progne y Philomena* retains the original ending but emphasises the rights of women to avenge their own honour – previously this was the duty of the men in the family.

Compared to these nauseous tales, Boccaccio's story of Ghismondo and Guiscardo (*Decameron* IV:1) is positively bowdlerised. Tancred, the prince of Salerno, does not want his beloved daughter, who has been early widowed, to remarry. Resentful of this curtailment of her life, she takes a lover, Guiscardo the page. Her father discovers the affair and has Guiscardo killed and sends his heart to Ghismunda in a golden cup. She takes poison from the same cup and dies. Her father repents and has them buried together.

The earliest play based on this story, Antonio Cammelli's *Panfila*, was performed in Ferrara with success and published in 1499. The setting is changed to Thebes, moving back towards the classical settings of Seneca, but in other ways retains the medieval form of the *sacra rappresentazione*.

The story was also very popular in the sixteenth century including a *Spiel von der jungfrau sigismunda und tancredi* (1512) and *Ein klegliche tragedi des fürsten Concreti* (1545) by Hans Sachs.[8] A Dutch version, *Sigismunda*, is listed in the plays of the Rhetoricians' chamber of the 'Fiolieren' of 'S-Gravenpolder (*Repertorium* 1U20). The London Inns of Court produced two versions of the story: *Gismond of Salerne* by Robert Wilmot and others (1566) revised by Wilmot as *Tancred and Gismond*, published in 1591.[9]

ALBOIN AND ROSAMUNDA

A popular variant on the 'poisoned cup' story was the legend of Alboin, king of Lombardy and his wife Rosamunda, whom he married after defeating her father and having his skull made into a drinking cup out of which he makes her drink. When she learns that the cup is made from her father's skull, she seduces one of Alboin's generals and orders him to kill Alboin. He refuses, but sends another man to slay Alboin in his bed, Rosamunda having removed his sword so that he cannot defend himself. After his death the couple flee, but Rosamunda sees another man she wants and prepares to free herself by putting poison in her new husband's cup. He notices the bitter taste, guesses what she has done and forces her to drink also from the poisoned cup and both die. The story is told in the *Legenda* (in the *Historica Longbardica*) and was frequently dramatised with variations on the story. Among the earliest plays are Giovanni Rucellai's *Rosmunda* (1515) and Sachs' *Künigin Rosamunda* (1555). Rucellai makes the most of the horrors in his play: 'the decapitation of the corpse of Cunimondo . . . is monstrous, as is the horrible cup which Alboino prepares from the severed head' (Kennard, I, p. 144).[10]

Orbecche was the first tragedy by Giraldi, who also, some years later, included a *novella* on the subject in his *Hecatommithi*. Both the play and the novella have added many details and elements to Boccaccio's story, bringing 'this tissue of monstrosities' closer to the horrors of the Thyestes story dramatised by Seneca.[11] The action is moved to Persia, and the tragedy is shown as divine retribution for the crimes of murder and incest.[12] Orbecche, the daughter of King Sulmone has secretly married Oronte (whom Sulmone had rejected because he was not of sufficiently high birth) and has two children by him. When he discovers the truth, Sulmone has Oronte and the children killed – an episode not shown on stage but narrated by a messenger in much gory detail. The head and lopped-off hands of Oronte are displayed on a silver salver and the bodies of the children are similarly arranged, each with a knife protruding from it. The covered salvers are then brought on stage, Orbecche is summoned and then the covers are removed revealing the 'banquet'. As a strong-minded heroine, Orbecche controls her horror, pretends to regret having married against her father's will and drawing the knives from her children's bodies approaches Sulmone, stabs him and (off stage) hacks off his head and hands and reappears on stage holding them out to the horrified courtiers, then stabs herself. The play ends with the chorus advising the audience to 'fix its gaze on heaven and seek the happiness that is everlasting'.[13]

A play by duke Julius of Brunswick combines elements from all these plays as well as Shakespeare's *Richard III*. The tragedy *Von einen ungerathenen Sohn* (printed 1594) has no known source.[14] It has a strong element of morality play with all the characters having names appropriate to their character; duke Severus and his wife Patientia have two sons, Probus and Nero. The latter, the 'depraved' son of the title, controls all the action as, urged on by his companions, Hypocrita, Seditiosus and Empiricus, and eager to have power to do all he wants, he proceeds to bring about the death of his father, mother, brother, latter's wife, his own illegitimate son and finally the duke's three counsellors, Justus, Verax and Constans. Having had the last three beheaded in a wood, Nero lists with satisfaction all his ill deeds and admits to being tired and ready to rest. He settles down to a feast with his followers and after eating many courses they open three large pots which appear on the table and when opened contain the three counsellors' heads! All cry out in horror and the heads vanish. Nero flees into his own room, the followers attack and kill each other.

In the next scene Nero reappears, having passed a terible night of fear and suffering, and decides to rest in the garden as he is so tired. A series of ghosts then appear, à la *Richard III*, each carrying the weapon or poison by which he died. Each walks three times round Nero who cries out to God and makes the sign of the cross. He wishes he were dead and so out of his agony. The ghosts intone the word *Vindicta!*, *Vindicta! Vindicta!* and remind him of all his ill deeds. Nero's conscience awakes at last as he realises what he has done and laments, while the ghosts intermittently repeat their cry of *Vindicta!* and then the cry *Rache!* (vengeance) for all the innocent blood he has shed. Finally Nero 'bellows like an ox' and falling to the ground summons the devils: 'O ihr Teufel kommt und holet mich, dann ich bin doch euer' (O you devils, come and take me for I am yours). The devils enter with a great outcry and carry him away.

An epilogue reminds the audience of the warning they have received, of the need for all children to honour their parents and trust in God.

6 Esmoreit's wicked uncle steals and sells the baby. His mother is falsely accused of killing him and imprisoned.

(a)

(b)

7 (a) The queen arranges for Stella to be kidnapped and killed. (b) Judith saves the city
by cutting off Holofernes' head.

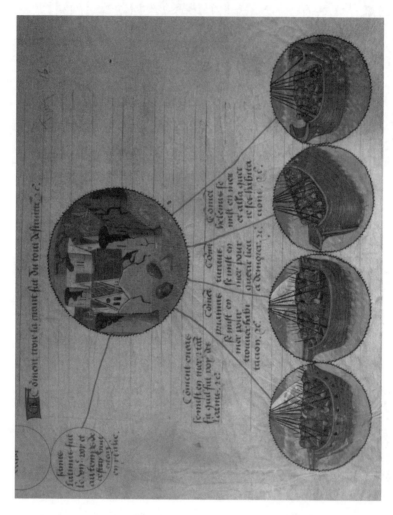

8 Groups of Trojans flee from burning Troy to settle in Europe.

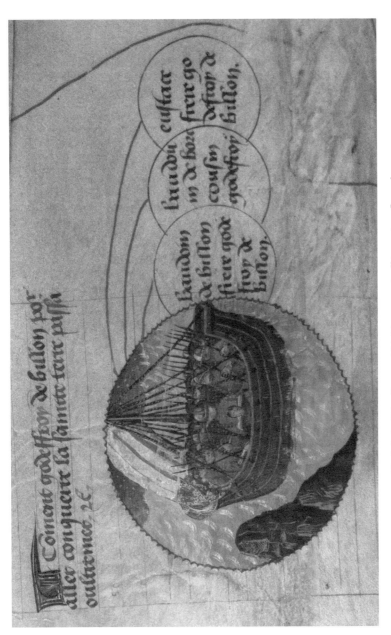

9 Godefroi of Bouillon and his kinsmen set off to capture Jerusalem.

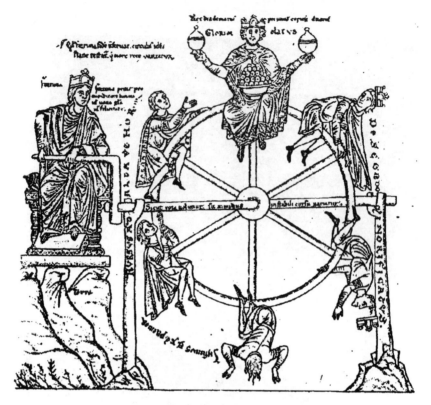

10 Fortune and her wheel.

PART FOUR

Power, politics and patriotism

The plays in this part are neither miracles nor marvellous plays, they are based on legendary and historical events. From the crusading scene of the *Jeu de saint Nicolas* in the twelfth century to the *Siège d'Orleans* and the Hundred Years War in the fifteenth, a considerable number of plays were composed which in contrast to the groups so far considered dealt with conflicts between religions and nations, patriotism rather than sanctity or romance. They include several plays on major sieges, including the siege of Troy, the siege of Jerusalem (AD 70), also known as the *Vengeance Jesus Christ*, and the struggles for Jerusalem during the crusades. There are also biblical plays on sieges from Jewish history.

CHAPTER 17

The siege of Troy

Many classical tales were written up as romances in the twelfth and thirteenth centuries, especially in French, but only the *Roman de Troie* was dramatised before 1500.[1] The earliest reference to a Troy play is found in a letter from Avignon written in 1400 by the factor of the Italian merchant house of Datini describing how many craftsmen (*artieri*) of Avignon at their own expense put on a passion play on the three days of Whitsun; 'fa III mesi ano istriati i questi festa o vero giucho la sembramento di Troia o quella di ducha d'Agioia no fue' (three months ago they acted a play of the siege of Troy, like the one the duke of Anjou attended).[2] There is unfortunately no information about this play though it is probably based on the poem by Benoit de Ste-Maure.[3]

The *Istoire de la destruction de Troie* was translated from Latin *par personnaiges* by 'Maistre Jacques Milet, estudiant en loix en la ville d'Orleans', in the year 1450. In his description of Millet's text, Runnalls mentions that despite the length of the play – 30,000 lines, divided into four days – there exist today no fewer than thirteen fine manuscripts, with splendid illustrations, and thirteen printed editions of which the first, printed in 1484, is the earliest surviving printed text of a *mystère*.[4] All these copies, both printed and manuscript, are identical: 'jusqu'aux moindres détails'. Runnalls suggests that as there is no performance recorded, the text was only intended for reading but the last lines of the prologue clearly indicate that the play was designed for performance: 'si vous prions tres humblement/que recevez d'entente saine / nos ditz, car sans chose villaine / avons joué l'esbatement' (we beg you humbly / to receive with sound understanding / our words, for without anything offensive / we have performed this entertainment) (*Mystères*, II, p. 571). Moreover, Lanson records two performances in the seventeenth century. The first was in 1611 in 'Bordeaux dans l'Hotel de Ville devant le Prince et la Princesse de Condé La destruction de Troye, tragédie jouée par les élèves du Collège de Guyenne.'[5] It was probably also students who in 1613 in Draguignan staged an 'istoyre en deux journées appelée la Destruction de Troye'.[6] Since the title is identical with Millet's text in both cases, and no other French play on Troy is recorded, it is likely that these performances were based on a cut version of the printed text of the *Istoire*.

L'ISTOIRE DE TROIE

The principal source of Millet's play is the twelfth-century narrative poem by Benoit de Ste-Maure,[7] which itself was drawn from two Latin accounts of the siege, one by Dictys of Crete which is pro-Greek and the other, shorter, text by Dares the Phrygian favouring the Trojans.[8] Although they were probably first composed in Greek in the first century AD, both authors claim to have been present at the siege and to present a more accurate picture than that of Homer who wrote a century after the event.

The play begins with king Priam rejoicing over the power and wealth of Troy which has been rebuilt after it was attacked by the Greeks, led by Hercules, because when Jason was returning from Colchis with the golden fleece he had been refused shelter and help by Laomedon, Priam's father and the reigning king of Troy. Priam then sends ambassadors including Antenor to Menelaus to ask for the return of his sister, Hesione, whom the Greeks had carried off. When the Greeks refuse, Priam gives Paris permission to carry off Menelaus' wife Helen in reprisal.

The story of the judgement of Paris and the golden apple is not staged. Instead, Millet follows Benoit in making Paris describe the event as having been a dream in which Mercury brought to him the three goddesses, Juno, Athena and Venus for him to choose who was the worthiest to receive the golden apple. He gave it to Venus who had promised him the most beautiful woman in the world as wife.[9] Paris brings Helen and a great treasure back to Troy and the First Day continues with the Greeks assembling to avenge the insult to Menelaus and their arrival at Troy. The story of the love of Achilles for Agamemnon's daughter, Iphigenia, and his struggle to prevent her being sacrificed by her father for a fair wind for the fleet, although mentioned by Dictys, is not included in Millet or Exeter's *Iliade*.[10]

Day Two consists mainly of battles interspersed with councils and discussion of truces to bury the dead.[11] In addition to general skirmishes they include Hector's killing of Patroclus which Achilles avenges by killing Hector. Since Millet is on the side of the Trojans he presents the Greeks in a very poor light: Achilles kills Hector by stabbing him in the back while he has moved his shield round to protect the front of his body.

'Alors Achille viendra par derriere Hector e le trespercera d'une lance et lors Hector cherra.' Then Achilles will come up behind Hector and will pierce him through with a lance and Hector will fall (p. 214).

In Day Three Millet introduces the love story of Troilus and Briseida which he views in a misogynistic light, foretelling Briseida's infidelity from the start.[12] When Briseida has to leave Troilus she declares 'que jamais ne vous oblieray' (I shall never forget you) (l. 12426). Soon after, having transferred her affections from Troilus the Trojan to the Grecian Diomedes, she hears that the latter has been injured and declares:

Il me fault aller visiter Diomedes, . . . que j'ay esleu pour mon amy / car je scay que je ne pourroye . . . plus veoir celluy / qu'autre fois tant aymer souloye.

(I must go and visit Diomedes . . . whom I have chosen as my lover / for I know that I could . . . no longer see him / whom formerly I loved so much.)

(ll. 16615–22)

A second love story introduced by Dares and Dictys is that of Achilles and Polyxena, daughter of Priam. During the truce on the anniversary of Hector's death, Achilles sees Hector's sister and falls in love with her beauty. Achilles tries to arrange a peace between Greeks and Trojans so he can marry Polyxena but Priam refuses because Achilles had killed Hector. Paris plans an ambush. Achilles is told to go to a certain temple where he will marry Polyxena but instead he is killed treacherously by Paris.[13]

Day Four includes the arrival of Penthesilea, queen of the Amazons who fights on the Trojan side but is killed by Pyrrhus, son of Achilles.[14] Finally, desperate for peace Aeneas and Antenor make a bargain with the Greeks to deliver up the city to them, but explain that first the Greeks must steal the Palladion, a statue of Pallas Athene which protects Troy. Ulysses leads a small group into Troy through a secret tunnel under the temple and escapes with the Palladion. The Trojans are desperate and frightened. Finally Ulysses persuades the Trojans to pull down the walls so that they can bring into Troy the great wooden horse, a peace offering by the Greeks to the offended Pallas Athene. The Greek soldiers hidden inside come out in the night, and open the gates to their army. Troy is sacked and the women carried off as slaves.[15]

OTHER EARLY PLAYS ON THE STORY OF TROY

There were a number of German plays in the fifteenth and sixteenth centuries which made use of various episodes of the medieval versions of the Trojan war, the earliest being two versions of the judgement of Paris by Hans Rosenplut.[16] The *fastnacht spill Troya* (1463) introduces Jupiter and the three goddesses, Juno, Venus and Pallas, talking to Priam. Suddenly a golden apple appears on the table ('da ward ein apfel auf den tysch gebracht'), on which is written that the apple must go to the most worthy ('der aller wurdigsten'). All three goddesses claim the apple and Priam suggests Jupiter should decide the question but he rejects the idea because all three are his relations and proposes, instead, that the decision be made by a certain shepherd called Paris. The goddesses all accept the idea and a messenger is sent to Paris who at first claims he cannot leave his sheep but finally is persuaded. The three goddesses each put their case and Paris rejects Juno's offer of power and Pallas' of wisdom and accepts Venus' offer of the beautiful Helen, because love is the best thing in the world to have.

The second play a *spill mit den dreyen nacketten gottin von Troya* (1468) begins quite differently with a narrator setting the date of the story of Troy – IIIMIX and lxx years after the beginning of the world and 1,131 years before the birth of Christ. Then details are given of the exact size of Troy and its unequalled greatness; finally he describes the names of Priam's five sons who are present. Then the play proper begins, with Priam talking to the citizens ('purgerschaft') of Troy and lamenting the harm that the Greeks had done to the city, which has now been rebuilt and is of unequalled size and power. However, Priam wants the Greeks punished for their attack and especially for having carried off his sister, Exyonam (Dares: Hesione). He tells the citizens to decide if an embassy should be sent to ask for Hesione's return. After discussion the citizens unanimously approve the idea and Antenor is selected as ambassador and accepts the charge. At this point ('legt sich Paris nider und slaft') Paris lies down and goes to sleep. Mercury enters and tells Paris that this apple must go to the most beautiful and the goddesses have chosen him to be the judge. Mercury then explains what each goddess offers him for choosing her: Juno offers wealth and power, Pallas wisdom and fame and Venus the most beautiful woman to be found in the lands of Greece. Mercury then bends over Paris as if listening to him and reports that he is much honoured by their choice of him as judge but cannot tell the most beautiful while they are clothed. Then each in turn takes off her 'Rock' (robe) and goes to Paris and shows herself to him, and offers him a reward for choosing her. Without hesitation Paris gives Venus the apple. Paris then wakes from his sleep and Mercury and the goddesses depart.

Antenor now returns from his embassy and tells Priam that the Greeks have refused to return Exyonam, and threaten him with a worse fate than his father if he should attack Greek lands. Priam consults each of his sons in turn starting with the eldest, Hector, who points out that Priam has the greatest empire in Asia and that Exyonam has been in Greek hands so long she will probably soon be dead from old age ('vielleicht irs alters halben kurtzlich wirt weg genomen duy den todt'). Paris then speaks against Hector and describes his dream and the promise of Venus which shows she is on the side of Troy. Deyphobus supports Paris and suggests he should go to the Greeks; Helenus prefers safety to war for which he is criticised by his brothers and finally Troilus rejects the idea that Paris' dream is surety they will win and insists the only true victory will come from their own courage and sharp swords. Priam approves Troilus' comments and thanks Paris for his offer to go to the Greeks. The narrator finishes the play with a brief speech and a 'Good Night' to the innkeeper ('Wirt'), and a reminder to everyone that what they have played is a true story, not one they have made up.

Hans Sachs' substantial play on the last stages of the Trojan war, *The destruction of the city of Troy*, 1544, is based on Dictys and Dares, and has many similarities to Millet's play.[17] Sachs emphasises throughout the pointlessness and horrors of war expressed through the dialogues between the different groups of characters. He begins part way through the siege, with Priam lamenting the prolonged struggle against the Greeks and his own inability through age and weakness to go out and attack the enemy. Hector immediately declares his intention of fighting, while Cassandra laments that ever Paris brought Helen to Troy. Above all, Sachs' play emphasises the role of Achilles.[18] In a soliloquy Achilles describes his agony of love for Polyxena and sends Patroclus to Hecuba to ask for Polyxena in marriage as a way of bringing an end to the war. Hecuba is hopeful but Hector rejects the idea at once and goes forth to challenge Achilles who, almost reluctantly, kills him. It is Polyxena whose prayer wins Hector's body back from Achilles and she is then forced by Hecuba and her brothers to write to Achilles and arrange a meeting in the wood outside the walls of Troy. When he comes there he is attacked and killed by Paris and his brother 𝔓𝔥𝔩𝔢𝔬𝔴𝔭𝔥𝔢𝔟𝔲𝔰.[19] The body is covered up and left in the wood and the family return to Troy.

Some of the Greeks plan the fall of Troy helped by Aeneas and Antenor who have agreed to open the gates of Troy. There is no mention of the wooden horse as the reason for this.[20] The final lament is given to Polyxena who tells of the end of the siege and of Troy before she is killed.[21]

Georg Gotthart's *Ein schön lustiges Spil oder Tragedi: Von Zerstorung der grossen vnd vesten Koniglichen Statt Troia oder Ilio* was staged in Solothurn in

1598, and printed in 1598/9.[22] It is a substantial two-day play performed by the citizens of Solothurn. The cast lists show that as was usual at this time all the women's roles were played by men. The prelude also makes it clear that Gotthart is writing from a pro-Greek, Catholic view-point. He asks the audience to accept the appearance of 'gods' on the stage since the action of the play is set in 1190 BC. However, a Christian element is introduced by the presence of two devils, Satan and Astaroth, who comment on the trouble caused by women from Eve to Helen.

The first day has nine acts and includes the birth of Paris and the warning that he will bring about the fall of Troy, the scene of the judgement of Paris and his expedition to carry off Helen and much treasure from the Greeks and his return to Troy. The first day ends with the Greek envoys, Ulysses and Menelaus, failing to persuade Paris to return Helen and declaring war on Troy. The herald enters with the epilogue for the day and explains that the Greek trust in their gods is a sort of advance Christianity which will ensure their final victory. The audience are invited to return next day.

Day Two has twelve acts and the prologue mentions all the main combats and incidents to come which include the Greek preparations for the war and Ulysses parting from Penelope. The early episodes are interspersed with announcements by the Herald and the traditional *narrenscene* with the fool commenting on the action. Several battle scenes are also staged. The death of Hector is followed by much mourning and the death of Achilles at the hands of Paris. The love of Achilles for Polyxena is not included. Finally Antenor and then Aeneas go to the Greek camp and prepare for their betrayal of the Trojans. The horse is constructed and brought into the city while comments warn the audience of the forthcoming destruction of Troy. A blind man warns the people to beware Greeks bearing gifts. Troy is destroyed with a blood bath. Priam is killed and the women carried off. Ulysses and Ajax compete for the armour of Achilles. Ulysses wins and Ajax kills himself.[23]

The epilogue stresses the moral lessons of the story and the need to avoid war if possible and show kindness to women and children – a significant comment in the period of the wars of religion – and describes St Ursus the patron saint of Solothurn as the true Christian soldier. The audience and the town council are thanked and the blessings of God, his Mother and St Ursus are invoked on everyone.

The earliest surviving English Troy play, Peele's *The arraignment of Paris*, a pastoral with a strictly classical cast and setting, performed before the queen by the children of the chapel royal and printed in 1558, is only loosely connected with the history of Troy. In the prologue Ate 'condemned soul from lowest hell' shows the golden ball 'the bane of Troy' which it is her task to bring to earth to ensure the fate of Troy which has been condemned by the gods. The play opens with a classic pastoral scene of love and music interrupted by the arrival of Juno, Pallas and Venus. They are welcomed by the shepherds and entertained with stories and songs. A thunderstorm interrupts the festival during which Ate 'having trundled the ball into place, crying *Fatum Trojae*' Juno taketh the ball up (p. 25). They read on it the 'posy' that it must be given to the fairest. All three goddesses claim the apple in turn and finally decide they need a judge, though each is sure she is the fairest. They choose the shepherd Paris 'that must be umpire in this controversy'. The usual scene follows of each goddess putting forward her claim with the help of a 'show' – Juno who promises power and wealth shows 'a Tree of gold with diadems and crowns. Pallas rejects the idea of tempting Paris with 'decaying wealth' and instead offers 'wisdom's worthiness' and 'honour of chivalry'. Nine armed men appear and dance an 'almain' with drum and fife. A footnote suggests they are the Nine Worthies ('or why nine?'). They march off and Venus rejects these 'too hot alarums' and promises she will give the ball to her son Cupid to play with, who will always think of you and 'and bid thee look and choose and he will wound'; her 'show' is Helen who enters escorted by four cupids and sings of her power against the gods of Heaven, Hell or earth. Paris gives her the apple and they exit together. Juno is furious but Pallas is resigned: 'Well Juno whether we be lief or loth / Venus hath got the apple from us both.'

Act III begins with a pastoral scene interrupted by Mercury who has come accompanied by Vulcan's Cyclops to summon Paris before Jove 'to answer matter of great consequence'. Venus goes bail for Paris to appear before the court of Jove since Juno has gone against the arrangement by which they all agreed he should be the judge. The court is held in Diana's bower. After an argument over whether he may be allowed an advocate, it is settled he must answer for himself. Paris then at length describes the scene when the goddesses invoked his aid and therefore the deed 'wherein consists the full of mine offence – I did upon command'. Secondly the accusation of 'partiality' is rejected since beforehand he knows nothing of their appearance or powers. Jupiter sends Venus and Paris out and tries to persuade Juno she has no case against him. She demands a right to appeal. Mercury brings Paris and Venus back and the three goddesses agree that a new judgement should be made, this time by another goddess: Diana. Jupiter dismisses Paris 'Go take thy way to Troy and there abide thy fate.' Diana takes the goddesses and the golden ball apart. She makes them swear to accept her decision and then reveals she is not going to give the ball to any of them, but rather to 'the nymph Eliza' (i.e. Queen Elizabeth) whom Diana then proceeds to describe in most glowing terms as most beautiful, most wise, most powerful and favoured by both the Graces and the Fates who end the play with their songs and speeches of praise.

> So Pallas yields the praise hereof to thee
> For wisdom, princely state and peerless beauty.

The Iron Age I and *II* (1632) are the last in a series of plays on classical subjects, the Golden, Silver and Brazen Age, by Thomas Heywood, who in the prologue to *Iron Age II* commends to the Courteous Reader, 'an intire history from Jupiter and Saturne to the utter subversion of Troy'.[24] A feature of the group is the use of humour – conspicuously lacking in most of the Troy plays. The series of leading events in the saga of Troy, beginning with the judgement of Paris, and the rape of Helen – the only detailed staging of the latter event – are enlivened by the constant interventions and comments of Thersites. Heywood also includes the arrival of Paris and Helen in Troy and the discussion between Priam and his sons as to whether they should keep her or return her. In Acts II–IV, highlights of the siege include the story of Troilus, Cressida, Calchas and Diomedes, but without Pandarus. Council scenes in both camps are interspersed in Troy, with lamentations and pleading against fights by Andromache, unsuccessful, and Helen, always successful. The Greeks' quarrels are mainly between Achilles and Ulysses or Ajax. When Achilles is sulking in his tent Thersites is also there mocking him. In one of the truces a banquet is staged with each Trojan sitting with a Greek, and background musick. Thersites comments: 'See, here's the picture of a politicke state / they all imbrace and hugge, yet deadly hate' (III. 1). Then the Trojan ladies arrive, Achilles sees and falls in love with Polyxena. 'Shee hath done more than Hector and all Troy, Shee hath subdued Achilles.' At this point Cressida makes her final decision to go with Diomedes and her father and 'Troilus shun', for Calchas declares the gods have told him Troy will perish. The post-banquet revels include a 'lofty dance for sixteene princes halfe Troian and halfe Grecian'. When they sit down again Paris and Helen find themselves at table with Menelaus who tries to persuade Helen to return to him but she cannot give up her love for Paris. Menelaus calls the Greek to arms. Hector responds 'then Greece from Troy devide / this difference armes not language must decide'. Achilles swears to Priam he will not fight against Polyxena's family and retires to his tent where he plays the lute despite the mocking and insults from Thersites. The Trojans are dominating the fight and Ulysses begs Achilles to let Patroclus, in his armour, lead the myrmidons on the field. Achilles agrees. All leave except Thersites who taunts Achilles until Diomedes carries the dead Patroclus into the tent. Achilles is moved, but 'love swayes most' until news comes of the Trojans having set fire to the Greek ships and even to the tents of Achilles' myrmidons who are being slaughtered. This finally sends Achilles back into the fight and ends Act III.

Act IV is mainly given to fighting and the battle between Achilles, helped by his myrmidons, and Hector, who is killed by the group, with Achilles only giving the *coup de grâce* and then preparing to drag him round the walls. The Trojans lament the death of Hector, and Paris, aware that Achilles is invulnerable, except in his heel, plans a way to kill him which he shares with Hecuba, knowing Priam would not allow it. Achilles seeks Troilus to kill him, sees him beating Thersites, and will not demean himself by joining in. Troilus returns, challenges Achilles and is killed. Thersites mocks Achilles for killing Troilus 'when he was out of breath. So slewest thou Hector.' Helped by Hecuba, Paris arranges a meeting between the Trojans, who guarantee his safety in writing, and Achilles with the Greek kings for him to marry Polyxena in the temple. When the two parties meet, they go into the sanctuary while Paris fetches his bow and arrows before he follows them. A cry within is followed by the re-entrance of Paris, rejoicing in the death of the murderer of Hector: 'revenge seemes good'. The Greeks re-enter demanding a surgeon but Achilles says it is in vain and describes how his mother held him by the heel when she dipped him in the blood which rendered the rest of him invulnerable. Priam is horrified and denounces Paris but he is unrepentant. Priam allows the Greeks to carry off Achilles' body and declares a truce for the funeral. End of Act IV.

Act V follows Ovid's *Metamorphoses* with the great quarrel between Ulysses and Ajax over who should inherit Achilles' armour. When the kings finally grant them to Ulysses, Ajax goes mad with fury and kills himself. The play ends with a dumb show of the Greeks and Trojans meeting carrying the bodies of Hector and Achilles respectively. They interchange their burdens and both sides depart 'trailing their colours'. Thersites is left on stage to speak the epilogue in which he insists it is better to be alive and a coward than be brave and dead. He foretells what will happen in the sequel with the arrival of Penthesilea and Pyrrhus, son of Achilles.

The first two acts of *Iron Age II* continue the story of Troy. Pyrrhus, son of Achilles, arrives to help the Greeks and avenge his father, while the Amazon queen Penthesilea arrives with 'her train of viragoes' as reinforcements for the Trojans. The groups meet and Pyrrhus insults the Amazons and their queen: 'are you those harlots famous through the world'. Battle begins and in due course Pyrrhus and Penthesilea meet in single combat. Both are wounded before they are forcibly separated by the two armies 'who confusedly come between them'. The battle continues and Paris enters, attacks Pyrrhus and is killed by him. Diomedes enters with Synon who is as critical of the folly of war as Thersites. He meets and falls in love with Cressida who scorns him at first but gives way and is found kissing Synon by Diomedes. She is finally taken in charge by the Amazons while Synon joins forces with Thersites in whom he recognises a kindred spirit. The Greeks enter and are followed by Pyrrhus with Penthesilea's head on his sword. Priam having barricaded himself inside Troy a plan is needed to take the impregnable city. Having learned that Ulysses has in his tent 'the Palladion I brought from Troy' Synon demands 'a horse, a horse'; Pyrrhus replies 'Ten kingdomes for a horse to enter Troy.'[25]

Synon then reveals the whole idea of the way to break the siege by using the horse filled with armed men. Following the main line of the story, the Greeks retire to their ships and depart apparently giving up the fight. The Trojans prepare to bring the horse into Troy. Laocoon hears noise from the warriors inside and tries to warn them against the action, but Neptune sends sea serpents to strangle him and his two sons.[26] Synon succeeds in convincing Priam that the gift of the horse to Pallas Athene will be a better protection for Troy than its walls which are pulled down to allow the horse to enter. Act II ends with vividly presented scenes of the destruction and sack of Troy, bringing in some of the ordinary townsfolk to add to the tragedy of the event and concluding with a wholesale slaughter of Priam and his family. The Greeks prepare to depart with comments on the fact that Aeneas and Antenor have both fled with a good number of ships and men. Pyrrhus has the last word:

> Troy and Troyes people we have burnt in flames,
> and of them both left nothing but their names.

> (p. 395)

Although Heywood only claimed to be going as far as 'the subversion of Troy', he does more. Acts III–V tell the story of the homecoming and death of Agamemnon at the hands of Clitemnestra and Egisthus followed by the revenge of Orestes who is accompanied not only by Pillades but by a certain Cethus who is the brother of the falsely accused and executed Palamides, from early in the story (see p. 248 n. 37). After the on-stage murder of Agamemnon Heywood introduces the strife between Orestes and Pyrrhus for the hand of Helen's daughter Hermione. There is a commentary by the two cowards Synon and Thersites who act as a kind of 'chorus to this history'. Menelaus and his followers arrive and learn of the death of Agamemnon and that Orestes has slain Clitemnestra. The penultimate scene is the wedding of Hermione and Pyrrhus which is interrupted by the arrival, in disguise, of Orestes and Cethus. In a 'confused scuffle' Orestes kills Pyrrhus and Pyrrhus Orestes. Cethus wounds Menelaus and other Greeks. All fall dead save Ulysses who beareth thence Hermione. Cethus and Synon, who have both feigned death now rise and look around. They agree that two arch-villains cannot live within one sphere, fight and kill each other. Helen, Electra and Hermione enter. Helen sends Hermione for a looking glass, then she and Electra depart and Helen looks at her face in the glass, 'a face that has set two parts of the world at warre'.

> Here's that my soul and bodye must divide
> The guerdon of Adultery Lust and Pride. (She strangles herself)

Ulysses as the sole survivor pronounces the epilogue before 'returning to my Kingdom and my dear Penelope'.[27]

The *Destruction of Troy* by John Banks, printed in 1678, begins near the end of the siege but inserts a good deal of earlier material. There is no comedy but a number of battle scenes formally staged.[28]

Act I begins with a council of the Greeks who urged on by Achilles feel it is time to give up the war and go home to their lands and families. Ulysses succeeds in persuading them it is worth continuing as they will surely defeat the Trojans. Afterwards he explains to Diomedes that he has already made a plan with the Trojan lord, Antenor, to steal the Palladion, a statue of Pallas Athene kept in the temple in Troy. So long as the Palladion is in Troy the city cannot be taken. Antenor has promised to lead them by a secret tunnel under the walls to the temple so that they can seize the statue.[29]

Act II is set in Troy where also there are those who want to end the war but Hector is determined they can defeat the Greeks. News suddenly comes of the theft of the Palladion. Antenor has escaped and the Trojans are in despair but Hector declares that he and his brothers Paris and Troilus will challenge three Greek warriors to single combat the following day. The rest of the act consists of a scene between Hector and Andromache as she begs her beloved husband not to risk his life in

this way, and a similar scene between Paris and Helen. The Greek camp
receive and accept the challenge and prepare for battle. Act III begins with
lamentations and prophecies of doom by Cassandra and fond farewells
by the Trojan women, with Polyxena lamenting for her beloved brother
Troilus.

As Cassandra is going off, the SCENE[30] opens and discovers all the Grecian
princes, but Achilles on one side sitting in state. Ulysses, Patroclus and Menelaus
armed for the combat come upon the stage, and meet Andromache, Helen and
Polyxena going to take their seats. Patroclus is in the Armour of Achilles.

(p. 36)

Hector is sorry to see Patroclus, having assumed his foe would be Achilles
himself. After a domestic argument between Menelaus and Helen the
battles begin. Hector swiftly disposes of Patroclus and Paris defeats
Menelaus but is ordered by Helen not to kill him. The SCENE closes
and the Act ends.

The next day the battle is resumed and Achilles, furious at the death of
Patroclus insists on fighting and kills Troilus. Polyxena is distraught and
cannot be separated from Troilus' body which Achilles wants to drag in
triumph round the walls of Troy. Watching her, Achilles is smitten by her
beauty, but she curses him. Hector and Achilles then want to fight but
are put off till the next day.

In Act IV the Greeks meet and Achilles and Ulysses quarrel heatedly
till the former storms out. Then Ulysses reveals his plan to trick the
Trojans by building a huge wooden horse which will be sent as a peace
offering to Pallas Athene but will in fact be full of armed men. The
idea is accepted with enthusiasm. The Trojans attack; Hector rescues
Troilus' mangled body from Achilles' myrmidons; Paris and a group of
soldiers also appear on stage; the Greeks win the battle but Hector beats
off Ulysses and rescues Paris and his men. Achilles appears and he and
Hector fight in single combat, all the soldiers having been ordered not
to interfere. Hector is defeated and after a final speech dies. His body is
removed for dragging but when Diomedes describes Polyxena's agonised
mourning over Troilus, Achilles send Diomedes to rescue Hector's body
and take it to Hecuba telling her he will no longer fight against Troy if
she will give him Polyxena in marriage. When Ulysses brings in Paris
as a prisoner, Achilles frees him and sends him also to Hecuba. Peace is
declared between the two camps.

Act V opens with Andromache mourning over Hector's tomb. Paris
tells her there is peace. The Greek fleet has withdrawn and Achilles is
to marry Polyxena. Andromache curses him for this but Paris explains it

is all a trick to enable them to kill Achilles at the wedding. Andromache is delighted. Ulysses and the Greeks arrive and Ulysses explains that the horse, a peace-offering to Pallas, is too big to go through the gates. Then the SCENE opens showing the horse being brought in. Cassandra has a vision of the end of Troy and sees Aneas carrying Anchises on his shoulders out of burning Troy and Hecuba running mad. The wedding party now enters, Polyxena in tears but Achilles describing at length the depths of his love for her. The scene changes to the Temple with Priam pronouncing the wedding oath. Paris shoots a poisoned dart at Achilles' heel (his only vulnerable spot). When Achilles fears he is dying he begs that Polyxena shall be spared. Paris boasts of what he has done and Ulysses at once sends to summon the Greek fleet back to the shore and to give the signal for the soldiers in the horse. Priam realises at last that Cassandra was speaking the truth. Held upright by Ulysses and Agamemnon, Achilles kills Paris. The SCENE opens showing Troy in flames, and Achilles seated watching, with his feet on Paris' body, declares all the Trojan princes are dead. Agamemnon tells Menelaus he can now go home taking Helen 'the price of all the war'. Diomedes tells how he killed Priam but the women have all been saved except Andromache who went back to the burning temple and died on Hector's grave. Ulysses speaks the final words rejoicing at the end of the ten years of war and the chance now to leave, but mourning the death of Achilles.

> But with glad shouts fill all our empty sails,
> Turning our Joyful Eyes upon the Plain,
> Where the sad Troy in Athens does remain.
>   (Exeunt omnes)[31]

In contrast to these straightforward dramatisations of Dares and Dictys, Jacob Locher's Latin version of the story, the *Judicium Paridis*, composed, before the Reformation, by a professor of rhetoric at the university of Ingolstad and *poeta laureatus*, combines the Greek legend with an allegory of the three states of man; the *vita contemplativa, vita activa* and *vita voluptaria*.[32]

The scene opens with Jupiter inviting the goddesses to celebrate the wedding of Peleus and Thetis, whose son, Achilles, will play such an important role in the story of Troy.[33] Discordia enters and casts among them the golden apple to be given to the most worthy. Jupiter then summons Paris to leave his peaceful shepherd's life and come to judge between the three goddesses.

In Act II Paris appears before Jupiter to make his judgement – the core of the play consists of the bribes the three goddesses offer to Paris: Pallas offers wisdom and knowledge as the most worthy things in life – the *vita contemplativa.* Juno offers fame, many possessions, wealth and status – the goods of the *vita activa.* 'This is the life led by some tyrants of old, in ours it is the life of the whole world.'[34] Finally Venus offers the delights of the life of pleasure (*voluptaria*), which values nothing that is good, only the satisfaction of the senses. Paris awards her the apple. The other goddesses warn Paris of the forthcoming catastrophe for Troy but Venus tells him not to worry and sends him to find Helen.

In Act III Paris tries to persuade Helen to come with him. At first she hesitates but Cupid's arrow pierces her and she goes off with Paris. Act IV presents a debate between Menelaus and Agamemnon and preparations for war against Troy. In Act V representatives of the three lifestyles each speaks in favour of her preferred choice and the play ends with a chorus of the actors and the author.

Locher's play was acted in Ingolstadt and Freiburg and was also well received in Poland where in February 1522 it was performed in Cracow castle before king Sigismund by students of the university – the first recorded performance there of a Humanist play whose text has survived. It probably influenced the first Polish tragedy – Jan Kochanowski's *The dismissal of the Greek envoys*, performed in 1577.[35] This play deals with the Greeks preparing a fleet to attack Troy after the kidnapping of Helen by Paris Alexander, son of Priam.[36] The play is quite short, only 503 lines, and the action all takes place outside Priam's palace as Ulysses and Menelaus, the chosen envoys of the Greeks, demand the return of Helen and warn that failure to do so will lead to war immediately. Many of the Trojans led by Antenor want Helen to be returned and are very critical of Paris' action. Helen herself laments her folly in going off with Paris and complains she is now a slave in Troy to his every whim. Despite the warnings of Cassandra and the strong arguments in favour of returning Helen, Paris succeeds, partly by bribery and threats, in getting a majority of the Trojans on his side and forcing Priam to send Ulysses and Menelaus off empty handed. The epilogue is spoken by a Trojan captain reporting to Priam about a small Greek force of five ships which has attacked Trojan territory and carried off the cattle. He has taken a prisoner who tells him a thousand Greek ships are now sailing towards Troy. Priam orders preparations for the defence of Troy but Antenor has the last word: 'Better to hold a council supporting war rather than defence. Let us proceed to war and not await it.'[37]

Of all these versions, Millet's great *Istoire* and Gotthard's *Lustige spiel o tragedi* remain the only attempts to stage the whole story with the actual battles and destruction, until the dubious efforts of Hollywood in the twenty-first century.

Plays based on the events which followed the destruction of Troy are found in many languages from 1600 onwards, by far the most popular being the story of Dido and Aeneas from Virgil's *Aeneid*. 'Next to Sophonisba (see p. 186) Dido gave her name to more humanist tragedies than any other heroine.'[38] Two Rhetoricians' plays on the story of Dido and Aeneas, both by Cornelis van Ghistele, of the Chamber of the Goudbloem in Antwerp, are among the large number of plays on the theme from the sixteenth century. Although the Dutch plays still include the traditional medieval Sinnekens or Vice figures, their role is reduced and *Van Eneas en Dido* 1 is primarily concerned with Aeneas' political mission while in *Van Aeneas en Dido* 2 the stress is on Aeneas' betrayal and Dido's tragedy.[39] In the early French version by Jodelle, *Didon se sacrifiant* (c. 1560) there is still a medieval flavour combined with the classical forms, as when the Trojan Chorus at the end of Act I speaks of 'Ceste inevitable Fortune / qui renversa nostre cité' and later pities poor Dido: 'Comment la Fortune se jouë / D'une grande reine sur sa rouë.'[40] Marlowe's *Dido*, the best known of the seven English Dido plays listed by Harbage, follows the *Aeneid* closely with long speeches and little action.

THE TROJAN WAR AND EUROPEAN HISTORY

In his prologue, Millet explains that his unusual choice of subject matter was inspired by his discovery of some buried 'armes des Troyens / Dont 'l'ost de France est descendu.'[41] According to the Merovingian chronicles of Fredegarius, the French dynasty was said to go back to Hector's son, Francus, ancestor of the Frankish kings, who named Paris after his uncle.[42] In 1454, Georges Chastelain, historiographer of the Burgundian dukes composed a play of *Les épitaphes d'Hector* as part of the festivities for the meeting of the rival Valois and Burgundian dynasties to arrange a marriage which, it was hoped, would end the civil war in France. The play describes how Alexander the Great goes to Hades to see the tombs of Achilles and Hector, and challenge the former for having slain Hector treacherously. (This seems to refer to the killing of duke Jean sans Peur by the Armagnacs.) The play may have been successful but the marriage arrangements fell through.[43]

Other medieval dynasties also claimed descent from Trojan heroes. MS 100 in the Brotherton Library, Leeds, is a fifteenth-century scroll MS which narrates the history of the world in a series of parallel columns with roundel illustrations. The prologue describes the beginning of the world up to the Flood, after which all the peoples of the world are descended from one of the three sons of Noah. 'Comment les troyens descendirent de la lignee japhet et puis monstre par signes comment quatre maniere de gens se partirent de troye la grant apres la destruction dicelle lesquelx habiterent et peuplerent pais . . . et terres et fonderent plusieurs cites villes et chasteaulx par espicial romme, paris, londres'.[44] In the French history column there are four roundels showing the Trojans fleeing from Troy, each followed by a description of their adventures.[45] The Aeneas story follows Virgil, another roundel is said to represent Priam escaping and a third has a group finishing up on the Italian coast where they construct the city of Venice and install Antenor as king.[46]

The English claim to Trojan descent depends on Aeneas, whose grandson Brutus gave his name to the realm of Britain.[47] There is a reference to the Trojan origin of Britain at the beginning of *Sir Gawain and the green knight* which reflects Dares' claim that the fall of Troy was due to the treachery of the Trojans, Aeneas and Antenor: 'The wight that the trains of treason there laid / was tried for his treachery, the truest on earth / It was Aeneas the Athel and his high kindred' (ll. 6).[48] Peele's play of Edward the First is rich in references to the Trojan origin of Britain especially in the scenes set in Wales: 'Follow the man that means to make you great; / Follow Lluellen, rightful Prince of Wales, / Sprung from the loins of great Cadwallader / Descended from the loins of Trojan Brute'.[49]

There is also a Dutch play which links Troy with a modern conflict and leaders.[50] *Hertoge Karle*, a *spel van sinne* from a sixteenth-century Brussels collection is a celebration of the birth of 'our emperor' Charles V. The play starts with a complaint by Venus of the condition of the world under the rule of Mars and Vulcan, then Prometheus and Cupid announce the news of the birth of Charles, the offspring of Jupiter's son Philip the Fair (son of Maximilian and Mary of Burgundy) and the Paladijnne Joanna la Loca (queen of Castile). From these he has inherited both divine and warrior qualities and he himself is the light of grace (Catholicism). Mercury then arrives and in a scene reminiscent of the christening of Sleeping Beauty they summon gift-bringers, four Goddesses whose gifts are linked with the four elements: fire (fear of wrongdoing); water (humble self-knowledge); earth (charity); and air (discretion). To find out more about the paragon who has received all these qualities they go to *Het Ylyon van Troyen* (the citadel of Troy) where they meet Ylus and Ganimedes who explain the significance of the gifts. (Hummelen adds a note here that *Ylion of Troy* signifies Brussels, but gives no other details.)[51]

CHAPTER 18

The siege and destruction of Jerusalem in AD 70

As in the case of the Troy plays, the second of the great siege plays, the *Destruction of Jerusalem* by Titus and Vespasian, is based not only on historical works like Josephus' *The Jewish war* but on medieval narrative versions, especially the *Vindicta salvatoris*, a Latin prose text from about 800.[1] There is also a special version of the story in the *Legenda* under the entry on St James the Less, the brother of the Lord (1 May).[2]

THE *VENGEANCE JÉSUS CHRIST*

The oldest and longest of the plays, the *Mystère de la vengeance* by Eustache Marcadé, has survived in two fifteenth-century manuscripts and six editions printed between 1491 and 1539.[3] In the earlier MS (pre-1468 and now in the duke of Devonshire's library in Chatsworth House, Derbyshire) the play is just under 15,000 lines and arranged for performance over four days. The second MS, in the Bibliothèque Municipale at Arras (1491) is slightly shorter and is linked with a four-day passion play (the *Passion d'Arras*). There is no complete modern edition of the *Vengeance* play but Wright refers to some partial editions in theses (p. 96 n. 1).[4]

The first day of Marcadé's *Vengeance* is set in Jerusalem where the Jews are celebrating the Passover with joyful dancing and singing. A scene in Heaven follows with the well-known debate of the four Virtues, Justice, Mercy, Peace and Truth. Justice, supported by Truth, demands that God should take vengeance on the Jews for having crucified Christ. Mercy and Peace intercede in vain but God promises to send the Jews plenty of warnings of what will happen if they do not repent of what they have done. Thunder and earthquakes, fountains running with blood – all the signs are ignored by the Jews but Pilate is afraid, and having questioned the guards from the tomb and Joseph of Arimathea, he decides to write to the emperor Tiberius and place all the blame for the crucifixion on the Jews. Meanwhile, Vespasian, the Roman governor in Spain is suffering from leprosy, and God sends the angel Uriel, disguised as a pilgrim, to his doctors to advise them that they should send to Jerusalem for the miracle-working *Sainte-face*, the cloth with which Veronica wiped Jesus' face on the way to the cross and which retains an imprint of the face. Vespasian sends off his messengers at once. Meanwhile Caiphas has denounced Pilate to Rome and put all the blame for the trouble in Jerusalem on his shoulders. Pilate in return denounces Caiphas and the first day ends with all the messengers setting off for Rome.

The second day opens with Tiberius listening to the letter sent him by Pilate which is based on the original letter quoted in the apocryphal *Acts of Pilate*.[5] The emperor is so impressed by the details of the miracles attributed to Jesus that he wants the Senate to declare that Jesus is indeed God. They refuse. Meanwhile Veronica travels to Spain with the *Sainte-face* and, despite all the devil's efforts, arrives safely. One sight of the relic cures Vespasian immediately.[6] When Tiberius hears this news he is even more angry with Pilate for killing such a mighty prophet and sends orders for him to come to Rome. Pilate obeys but takes with him Jesus' seamless robe which he has acquired and is wearing under his clothes.[7] Miraculously the robe protects him. When face to face with the emperor, Tiberius fawns over him; immediately he has left the room Tiberius' anger returns. Eventually the cause of this phenomenon is discovered and Pilate is forced to take off the robe. He is condemned to prison and there gives way to despair and kills himself. The devils carry off his soul.[8] In a brief time sequence, Tiberius dies and is succeeded by six emperors including Caligula, Claudius, Nero and Galba whose death in January AD 69 will finally brings Vespasian to the imperial crown.[9] Meanwhile, during the reign of Nero the Jews revolt because Nero wishes to erect a statue of himself in the temple in Jerusalem. Nero sends Vespasian and his son Titus to punish the Jews and the act ends with the Roman army's first victory: the city of Jonaspare is taken and handed over to the soldiers.

Day three begins with a prologue in which the 'meneur de jeu' announces and approves God's imminent vengeance on the Jews. The first episode shows the siege of another city, Jotapate, ruled by Josephus (the historian). Alternate scenes show the stages of the siege and events in Rome:

The besieged town of Jotapate is running out of water.

In Rome, Nero kills Seneca, his own mother and many others as well as setting fire to Rome. Nero is eventually killed by the Romans and the devils carry off his soul.

Jotapate is taken and sacked but Josephus' life is spared and he becomes
an ally of the Romans against his fellow countrymen.

Galba, Otho and Vitellius fight over the empire. When all are dead,
Vespasian is chosen emperor by the army and the Senate.

The rest of Day three is devoted to the sacking of Jerusalem with numerous scenes of horrific violence including the skinning alive of the sons of
Annas and Caiphas and the disembowling of a number of Jews who had
tried to save the Temple gold by swallowing it.

Petit de Julleville expresses surprise that the audience could accept
this cruelty (*Mystères*, II, p. 459) but the play was in fact very popular,
with a large number of performances recorded in the fifteenth century,
many of them for the dukes of Burgundy who were frequently talking of
a new crusade against the Muslim rulers of Jerusalem, though they never
actually fulfilled their half promises.

In the Burgundian Netherlands these performances often combined
the Passion and the Vengeance:

The combined *Passion* and *Vengeance* was also performed in Lille in 1484, when
the proceedings extended over ten days . . . The town of Malines organised its
own performance in 1494 of the *Passion / Vengeance*, in the presence of Philippe
le Beau, and its *échevins* imported six actors from Lille to play the main roles.
The *échevins* of Lille had to pay their expenses: 'XVIII s. pour les despens de
VI compaignons ordonnés d'aller en la ville de Malines pour juer la *Passion,
Resurrection et Vengeance de Nostre Seigneur Jhesucrist* devant la personne de l'archiduc
(Philippe le Beau).' Malines also seem to have used the Lille text, the thirteeen
volumes of which had been entrusted to the possession of a priest: 'Item, a sire
Thurien Blouet, prestre, IIII livres pour les Jeux de la *Passion* en XIII volumes.'[10]

Other performances after 1491 may well be based on the first printed
edition of the play, in 1491, which has several hundred additional lines
and is preceded by a *ballade* by the printer Verard in honour of Charles
VIII praising him especially for his attitude to the Jews 'qui de son pays
les juifs a hors boutés'. He is hailed as the new Vespasian to avenge the
death of Christ (*Mystères*, II, p. 453). Wright lists a considerable number
of performances in the sixteenth century, the last in France being at St
Jean d'Arves in 1539 and Plesset -Piquet in 1541 (Wright, p. 112).

VENGEANCE PLAYS IN THE SIXTEENTH CENTURY

Sainte Venice[11] is a French play of 875 octosyllabic lines, based on the
apocryphal legend of St Veronica and written for seven characters. It
was printed in the early sixteenth century and survives in a single copy.

Vespasian, the Roman governor in Spain, is gravely ill with leprosy. His son, Titus, and his advisors are informed by his doctors that they can do nothing to cure him. However, God has other plans, and intends to use Vespasian as a means of wreaking vengeance against his enemies. He instructs Gabriel to go in disguise as a pilgrim to Vespasian and tell him that he will be cured if he can touch something belonging to a Jewish prophet, now crucified. Vespasian sends two knights to Pilate in Jerusalem, to ask for such an object. In the meantime, God, in a dream, has informed Veronica (who is also in Jerusalem) that she will soon be approached by the two men; she must intercept them before they reach Pilate and tell them about 'la Véronique', the piece of cloth bearing Jesus' image. Veronica meets the two knights at the Golden Gate, and they escort her to Vespasian in Spain. She tells him that he can be cured by touching the miraculous object but only if he abjures his pagan religion. Vespasian eagerly agrees, is cured and the play ends with his swearing to destroy those who killed Jesus.

The only extant Spanish play is the *Aucto de la destruición de Jerusalén* included in the collection of sixteenth-century plays published by Rouanet.[12] The story (700 lines) is presented in a continuous sequence of brief scenes probably performed on wagons for the Corpus Christi procession. The play opens in an unidentified place with the unnamed emperor lamenting his continuous illness and suffering (he is later identifiable as Vespasian and the location as Rome). The seneschal mentions that in the time of his predecessor (Tiberias) there was a prophet in Jerusalem who worked miracles and cured many people. He was put to death by the jealous Sanhedrin, buried, but rose again in glory. Surviving relics of him have healed many people. Vespasian declares his faith in these miracles and sends the seneschal to Jerusalem, promising that if a relic can heal him he will avenge the prophet on the perfidious Jews. He orders the seneschal also to see Pilate and ask him why he has not sent the tribute owed to Rome. Arriving in Jerusalem, the seneschal greets a Jew and asks him for somewhere to stay – he will be well rewarded. He is welcomed and looked after, then confides to his host his search for a relic to heal the emperor. The Jew recounts the miracle of the *panyo imprimida* of Veronica and its healing powers. Veronica is brought to the seneschal and on his promise of secrecy says she can cure the emperor if he believes 'en la catolica fee'. The seneschal sends most of the party on their way but he goes with king Archelaus to visit Pilate and give him the emperor's message. Pilate insists he protects the city as his own. Fearing he will not allow the seneschal and his party to depart, Archelaus urges immediate and secret escape before the Jews reach their boats. They return to Vespasian with Veronica and Clemente (probably meant to be pope Clement I c. 91–c. 101) who instructs Vespasian in the doctrine of the Trinity and prepares to heals him. Vespasian first insists on having his crown and sword brought and swears that if he is healed he will avenge Jesus on the Jews. When the 'Veronica' touches him 'se le cae la lepra' (the leprosy falls off him). Vespasian rewards Clement with many castles which are accepted on condition he and all his people are baptised.

Vespasian then sets out with his army against Pilate whom he orders to surrender the town which has belonged to Rome since the days of Caesar, but Pilate has withheld the tribute for six years. Pilate insists the city is his and the battle begins. Two well-known incidents follow. In the first, women cook and eat their own dead children. In the French prose version of the Vengeance (which includes the Veronica story and the death of Pilate) there are two mothers, called Mary and Clarice, who are Christians and cook their children to fulfil Jesus's prophecy on Palm Sunday of the desolation of Jerusalem.[13] In the Portuguese *Vespesiano*, the two women are Clarice and the queen of Africa who kill and eat their children at the instigation of an angel.[14] The city is forced to surrender from starvation and the Jews who had swallowed gold to keep it from the enemy are disembowelled by the triumphant Romans.[15] The disembowelling is the subject of an illustration from the *Libro y storia del noble Vespesiano* reproduced in the new edition of the *Aucto* included in the *Códice de autos viejos*.[16]

GERMAN PLAYS OF THE DESTRUCTION OF JERUSALEM

There are three very varied German plays on the destruction of Jerusalem, the earliest version being found as the last part of the *Ludus de assumptione beatae Mariae*, a Latin play from Thuringia performed in 1391, and closely connected with the liturgical readings on the history of the early church.[17] The first part of this play of more than 3,000 lines, with a multiple stage of many locations, describes the missionary work of the apostles; in part two they assemble in Jerusalem for the funeral and Assumption of the Virgin which involves many actors and singers. Only the final 700 lines describe the attack on Jerusalem when the Jews, learning that the (un-named) king and his wife have been converted to Christianity and baptised by SS. John, Peter and Paul prepare to rebel. The king establishes his soldiers as a Christian order of knights and prepares to attack the Jews who have barricaded themselves in Jerusalem.

When the attack fails the king withdraws his forces to regroup; the Jews think they are beaten and come out of the city. The king rallies his forces – and the play breaks off here with a simple 'et cetera' which Wright (p. 49) suggests is intended to leave the staging of the final battle to the producer.

The second play is the fragmentary *Gothaer Botenrolle*, composed in the early fifteenth century. Like the *Ludus de assumptione*, this two-page fragment of an actor's role, containing lines and cues for a herald in a two-day play, includes a number of episodes connected with the history of the Jews in the period following the death of Christ and the beginning of the preaching of Christianity, especially the work of Peter and Paul in Rome. The early speeches suggest the story of the messenger sent to Pilate by Tiberius seeking healing for the emperor's leprosy. The only reference in the fragment which may refer to the staging of the destruction of Jerusalem is at the end of day one when the herald refers to the triumphal entry of Titus and Vespasian into Rome after they have 'with great might destroyed the insolent wicked city (*snode bosse stat*)'.[18] Wright also draws attention to records in the Thuringian chronicle of performances of a vengeance play in Schmalkalden between 1514 and 1603 (p. 69).

An interesting and original play by the Zurich playwright, Jakob Ruf, *Ein huipsch nuiw spil von dess Herren wingartten*, was staged in Zurich, on Easter Monday 1539.[19] The MS included many *federzeichnungen* (pen and ink drawings) which provide details of the costumes and characters but they are only described, not shown in the printed edition. The play has five acts (4,301 verses) and is a conflation of two parables: the tenants (Matthew 21) and the labourers in the vineyard (Matthew 20). Scene shifts are indicated by the direction MUSICA.

In this summary information from the *federzeichnungen* is enclosed in parentheses.

Act I. God the Father tells the Son (both wearing halos and the Son girt with a sword) he has built a vineyard and shows it to him (a drawing of the vineyard). The Son puts Moses and Aaron in charge of the vineyard and tells them to take on workmen. Enter Batt (dressed as the pope) and Carly (a cardinal in a red hat) lamenting the changed times which might even mean their having to earn a living by labouring in the fields. Moses and Aaron arrive, seeking suitable tenants (*leeliute*) to look after the householder's – God's – vineyard, they are impressed by Batt and Carly and agree to take them on. Sc. 3: God the Father and the Son agree to accept Batt and Carly as tenants, and tell them now to recruit labourers. The head gardener (*baumeister*) leads Batt and Carly to the vineyard.

Act II. In Hell, Lucifer decides that God's plans must be defeated, so Satan (along with three other devils) dresses up as a peasant, using the name Harms Ok and mingles with the crowd of men and women waiting for someone to employ them. Batt and Carly commission the steward (*Hufknecht*) to engage some workmen (*buliute*) and amongst the five he recruits is Satan. They all work well in the vineyard. However, Batt and Carly so enjoy the fruits of this labour that they resolve not to send the Father his dues. They drive out the steward who goes off to complain to God the Father. Carly meanwhile encourages the labourers to dress as clergy.

Act III. After the steward has reported what happened, God the Father sends one group of three prophets and another group of four to remonstrate with Batt and Carly but in vain. They get thoroughly beaten up several by a cook with a big ladle (the standard comic villain) but not killed. Satan reappears during this in the dress of a bishop. The Act ends with a final group of prophets (Abdias, Zephanaiah, Jeremiah and Joel) being beaten and driven off. The prophets report their trouble to the Father and Son.

Act IV. The Son foresees what wll happen and laments his coming suffering. God summons five more prophets and sends them to demand the wine be sent to him as planned. Urged on by the devil, the peasants and warriors agree to resist – they will work the vineyard but keep the wine for themselves. When the Father hears this he tells the Son he is going to send him to the vineyard – the workers must respect him. The Son laments that he is being sent like a lamb to the wolves. He asks that the chalice pass from him (as in Jesus' prayer in Gethsemene) and reminds the Father he is his only Son. The Father stresses the need to save the remaining innocent people in the world or it will all be destroyed. The Son accepts the task and the suffering to come. The Son meets Batt and Carly who rejoice because with the heir dead the vineyard will be theirs. (Satan slips quietly away from the crowd he has been urging on.) The *kriegsman* (warrior) sees the Son and strikes him. The Son kneels and prays 'Father forgive them they know not what they do.' Carly engages two *Buchsenschutzen* (marksmen) to help them keep the vineyard. They seize the Son and bind him. Hell opens and the devils rejoice. A young devil sees angels coming – Gabriel and Raphael enter and tell the devil he is damned for all eternity and has lost his power over the penitent.

Act V. A *nachbar* (neighbour) talks to the Father and commiserates with him. They discuss what should be the punishment for those who have so ill-treated the Son.[20] The neighbour offers advice: he has two men who will do the task well; he brings forward Vespasian and Titus in full armour. The Father explains that his vineyard has been seized by wicked men who have beaten and killed all his messengers including his only

Son. They agree willingly to undertake the task. The army assembles with heralds and soldiers. There is a band of drums and pipers and the army attack the enemy while devils with hand carts rush around the stage carrying off the corpses. Batt and Carly do not appear in this Act but there is a clever irony in having the two marksmen *dressed* as Batt and Carly: so did the real Batt and Carly slip away unpunished?

The Father rejoices that the wicked have been punished, and he decides to send messengers out to teach the people about the story and the truth. All the apostles enter, each with his emblem and promise to serve the Father faithfully. The play ends with the usual Herald's concluding address to the audience. (He also does not mention Batt and Carly.) He thanks the audience, then he sends the actors away: 'es hatt ein end'.

Wright cites a record by Pierrefleur of a performance in the Pays de Vaud, Switzerland, in 1549: 'what may have been a farcical rendition of the Vengeance of Our Lord was staged by a group of Swiss calvinists . . . a version of "la destruction de Jerusalem" which ridiculed the Roman church and its priests'.[21] The play also apparently included a prophecy of Jeremiah which leads Wright to consider a play on the Babylonian conquest of 587 BC. However the existence of Ruf's play, written in 1539, performed on Whitmonday in Calvinist Zurich, containing mockery of Catholic priests and prophecies by Jeremiah, and ending with the siege of Jerusalem by Vespasian and Titus, surely makes it probable that Pierrefleur is in fact describing a performance of the *Weingarten*.

THE SIEGE OF JERUSALEM IN ENGLAND

Harbage notes two lost plays on the *Destruction of Jerusalem* in England, the lost Latin play by Thomas Legge (better known for his *Ricardus tertius*) and an English text by John Smythe, both from 1584. The latter was specially composed as a waggon play to replace the banned Corpus Christi plays and was first performed in Coventry in 1584: 'This year the new play of the Destruction of Jerusalem was first played.'[22] There is some information about the play including a list of named characters in the Smiths' accounts for two of the episodes.[23] Thomas Sharp's *Dramatic mysteries of Coventry* (1825) includes a list of the characters' names and roles which can be usefully compared with Josephus' *Jewish war* chapters 14 and 15, which describe the factions and internal fighting in Jerusalem before the Romans finally intervene:

SYMON.   – Simon of Gerasa, leader of one of the factions.
PHYNEA.   – Phineas Son of Clusothus, an Idumean Commander.
ANANUS.   – The eldest High Priest, slain by the faction of John.
ELIAZER. – Eleazer, Son of Simon.
JOHANNES. – John of Gischala, leader of another faction.
JACOBUS.   – Jacob, Son of Sosus, a Commander in the service of Simon. Hippenus.
JESUS.   – Another High Priest, slain by the faction of John. [Josephus has Jeshua]
ZACHARYUS.   – Zachariah, Son of Baruch, slain by the same faction.
PRISCUS.   – Priscus, a Roman Centurion, who slew Jonathan the boaster.
MATHIAS.   – An High Priest, sent to invite Simon into Jerusalem.
ESRON.   – There is Simon, Son of Esron, named as a principal Jew.[24]

Wright cites an entry in Henslowe's diary of a new play of *Titus and Vespasian* in the Rose Theatre in 1591, the year of the last performance of the Coventry play, and suggests it might be a reworking of the latter (p. 204), but the only surviving later play is that by John Crowne, whose two-part play of the destruction of Jerusalem was first performed in 1670. Wright dismisses Crowne's play as being linked with the medieval Vengeance plays 'only by virtue of the fact that its story of forbidden love and political intrigue is acted out against the familiar backdrop of the Roman siege of Jerusalem' (p. 206). It is worth noting, however, that much of Crowne's play is based on Josephus and includes many of the characters listed in the Coventry play. Moreover, one of the love stories mentioned is that of Titus and Berenice which had already been added to the dramatic treatment of the destruction by French dramatists.[25]

The real interest here is the revival in the 1670s of material from the two major medieval themes of Troy and Jerusalem, which had been printed well into the middle of the sixteenth century before undergoing a revision of emphasis as the psychological stress of classical drama gradually began to overwhelm the violence and warfare of the earlier popular theatre.

An entirely new ending to the story is introduced in Gaspar de Aguilar's Spanish play of *La gitana melancolica*, which begins with a scene taken from the biblical account of Judith and Holofernes.[26] A young woman, Aber, is chosen by lot to save Jerusalem from the Romans by seducing the emperor Tito and then killing him – in explicit imitation of the famous biblical widow. But the plan misfires and she kills the wrong man. When she realises what she has done she begs Tito to kill her, and when he refuses, she resolves to do the deed herself but then humbly accepts Tito's offer of peace, content in the knowledge that she has helped to achieve it.[27]

CHAPTER 19

Early Christian Europe: Constantine to the crusades

A number of plays treat of the conversion and baptism of Constantine, and the stories of the Invention (discovery) and Exaltation of the Holy Cross.[1] As the plays vary greatly in what they include or omit it seems preferable to describe the individual texts in chronological order rather than try to group them by separate elements. The major source is the *Legenda*, under the entries for St Sylvester (14 December), the Invention of the Holy Cross (3 May) and Exaltation of the Holy Cross (14 September).

THE CONVERSION AND BAPTISM OF CONSTANTINE

The oldest play is the *Miracle de Saint Sevestre* (Cangé, XX, 1,450 lines) which uses mainly the *Legenda* entry for St Sylvester and begins with the accession of Constantine as emperor and his persecution of the Christians. Sylvester sends one of his *clercs* to preach to the people. The sermon is apparently a well-known one since only the opening and closing biblical quotations are given: *et se finist par in secula seculorum*. The action then moves to Constantine who has developed leprosy. He sends for his wise men and one of them declares the only known cure is bathing in the blood of small children. Constantine sends his knights to collect the children, which they do in scenes reminiscent of the slaughter of the innocents. They tell Constantine they have collected 3,000 and are prepared to slaughter them all to provide the emperor's bath. The mothers lament and complain and Constantine suddenly realises he cannot do this because it is Roman law that anyone of the ruling family who kills a child in battle shall be executed. How then can he have 3,000 slaughtered – especially as the cure is not guaranteed? The children and their mothers are rewarded with money and jewels and sent home. Constantine goes to rest and the knights and clerks to have dinner.

In Heaven, God summons Gabriel, Peter and Paul and tells them to go to Constantine and tell him if he will become Christian and be baptised he will be cured. They descend (with the customary angelic music) and tell Constantine that his refusal to kill the children will be rewarded: his leprosy will be cured if he becomes a Christian. Then they return to Heaven. Constantine tells the knights to summon Sylvester, the Christian pope. When Sylvester sees them coming he tells his followers they will probably be put to death and gives them a final blessing. The knights ask him to come to the emperor and he follows them. Constantine says he has been lying down too long and must sit up, then he greets Sylvester as 'Amis' and describes his vision of two gods and their promise. Sylvester says they were not gods but apostles of the one and only God. Constantine receives instruction in Christianity and is then led to an on-stage bath where he strips and enters it and is baptised. He tells Sylvester that he saw Jesus Christ, who made a sign with his hand and the leprosy fell from his skin.

The second part of the play now begins with Constantine send-ing messengers to his mother Helena who is in Bethany. When she hears the news of his recovery she is delighted but questions why he should believe in a god who was a criminal executed by the Jews. On Sylvester's advice a meeting is arranged with the emperor, his mother and a group of Jewish sages to discuss the matter. Sylvester goes to church and prays to the Virgin Mary, who makes her statutory descent with angelic accompaniment and assures him all will go well. She departs and Helena and her companions have arrived. Two pagans are appointed to judge the arguments of the two sides. Three points only are argued – the *Legenda* version has twelve – the nature of the Trin-ity, the Virgin birth and the reasons for Christ's sufferings.[2] The pagan judges and the Jews all declare themselves convinced and converted. They go off for a mass baptism, led by Sylvester and singing *Ave regina celorum*.

The Cornish play of St Meriasek[3] has two scenes interpolated from the life of St Sylvester (Part I, pp. 45–59) which follow the *Legenda*, beginning with Constantine sending out soldiers to kill the villainous Christians. There is killing on stage and then Sylvester prays to God and the Virgin, and Michael and angels come down and take the souls to Heaven. The martyrs' bodies are buried. Sylvester and his followers retire to Mt Soracte and Constantine is stricken with leprosy. A typical comic doctor scene follows complete with urinal. The doctor is given ten pounds to go and buy the necessary books. A pagan bishop suggests the bath of blood and the children are collected and then spared because 'in Rome the moral obligations of the blood royal are quite explicit' (referring to the law against killing a child in battle). The rest of the episode includes the sending of Peter and Paul by Jesus. Constantine is cured and baptised by Sylvester and declares his intention of spreading Christianity all over the empire.

Part II (pp. 107–44) stages an episode, also from *Legenda*, in which a dragon is terrorising the land. The stage directions require 'Here a gun ready in the dragon's mouth and fire' and 'some of the soldiers swallowed' (p. 109). The knights blame Constantine's conversion for the dragon's appearance. Sylvester tames the dragon and banishes it to a desert and all the court are converted.[4]

The *Rappresentazione di Constantino Imperatore, San Silvestro Papa, e Sant' Elena* (D'Ancona, II) survives in nine sixteenth-century printed editions. It is made up of two plays combined, and uses not only the *Legenda* but also Eusebius' *History of the church*, especially at the beginning. The play is long and involves many different episodes with abrupt scene changes. It opens with the ambassador, Quirino, travelling from Rome to France[5] on behalf of the Roman Senate to summon Constantine to Rome to become emperor and expel Massenzio (Maxentius) who has seized the throne on the death of Constantino, Constantine's father, who had been friendly towards the Christians.[6] While Constantine is collecting his legions for the journey, Massenzio learns of his advance and sends his men to gather all the men he can from farms and villages and promise them great rewards if they will support him. Before the two armies meet an angel appears to Constantine in a dream and gives him a cross telling him that in this symbol he will triumph.[7] Constantine thinks the cross is from Jove but his captain corrects him, and is given the honour of carrying the symbol into battle. The two armies meet on each side of a bridge. When Massenzio's armies try to cross the bridge it breaks apart and many are cast down into the flooded river and drowned. The remainder swear loyalty to Constantine and accompany him on his triumphal entry into Rome. The action now goes back in time to the story of St Timothy (24 January), a Christian who had known St Paul and then worked in Rome with St Sylvester before the latter became pope. Timothy preaches and is arrested, tortured and martyred. Because he had been a disciple of St Paul he is buried next to the great saint's grave. One of the knights tells the prefect that Timothy had spoken of great treasure he had possessed. They send for Sylvester and ask him about the treasure; he explains it was all given to the poor and needy. He warns the prefect that he will die this night. Sylvester is imprisoned because it is dinnertime. The prefect is served with a fine meal of fish but a bone sticks in his throat and he dies. His follower is impressed and frees Sylvester and declares himself converted.

The next scene returns to Constantine who laments that despite his rank and possessions he is cursed with leprosy. The High Priest sacrifices an offering for the emperor but the gods do not cure him. Everyone is ordered to pray and honour the gods on behalf of the emperor. To avoid this Sylvester and his followers retire to Mt Siratti. The children are collected for the bath of blood and Constantine drives out to see them but is moved to pity and orders their return to their families. The mothers thank him and promise their prayers for him. During the night Constantine has the vision of Peter and Paul who tell him to summon Sylvester who is on Mt Siratti, and will tell him how he can be cured. When Sylvester explains who the apostles are, Constantine wants to see a picture of them and the deacon shows him images of them which he always carries with him. Constantine recognises the saints and declares his conversion. He is baptised by Sylvester and the first play ends with a youth sending the audience away and bidding them return tomorrow.

THE INVENTION OF THE HOLY CROSS

The second play opens with the youth with a citar telling of the peace and joy in Rome now the emperor is converted and Christianity the official religion. He also narrates briefly the story of Sylvester and the dragon. Then a messenger rides up with a letter from St Helena who rejoices her son is no more an idolater but regrets he worships a man who was executed and insists the only true religion is that of the Hebrews. Constantine sends a message back insisting Christ is the true God and Helena should come at once to Rome with Jewish priests to learn the truth. While waiting for her, Constantine begins to build a great palace: 'which I will dedicate to God, and it will be the *tempio Laterano*'.[8] While they are building, the messenger reaches Helena and gives her Constantine's letter. She and the Jews set off for Rome. The assembly held to debate the question follows at first the same lines as in the *Cangé* play but then introduces a new story from the *Legenda*. Zambri, the twelfth Jewish doctor claims that the name of God is so powerful that no one can hear it and live. He tells them to bring in a powerful bull and he will speak the name of God in its ear and it will die. Sylvester asks how he can speak the name of God and survive but the Jew says a Christian is not fit to understand this mystery. The wild bull is brought in and when Zambri murmurs in its ear it gives one bellow and falls dead. Sylvester points out a greater

miracle would be to bring it back to life. Zambri admits that and says he
will believe Sylvester if he can restore the bull to life. Jews and pagans
all promise to become Christians if Sylvester can do it. Sylvester turns to
the bull and orders him by the power of him who died upon the cross to
rise up and live. The bull is resuscitated and everyone is converted and
baptised. Helena announces her intention of returning to Jerusalem to
find that most holy wood – the cross of Christ.

In Jerusalem Helena finds Judah who knows where the crosses were
buried but refuses to tell her. He is put into a dry well without food
and eventually gives in and directs her to the place. A devil appears and
rebukes him for giving away the secret but Judah declares his conversion
to Christianity. (In the *Legenda* we are told he was baptised as Quiriacus
and became bishop of Jerusalem.) When they dig they find all three
crosses but Christ's is identified by putting all three in turn on a corpse
– when the true cross touches him he is brought back to life. They also
find the four nails. The sacred relics are venerated and all sing the hymn
Pange lingua gloriosi.

Helena sends a messenger to Constantine with two of the four nails
they have found and a part of the wooden cross. Constantine declares his
intention of putting one nail on his helmet and one on his horse's bridle so
that the enemy will be aware of them when he rides into battle. Licinius,
formerly a friend of Constantine, tries to seize the empire but Constantine
defeats him in battle and makes him walk behind the emperor's chariot
in the triumph in Rome. Then he is beheaded.

News comes of a dragon that is wasting the land. The pagan priests
complain to Constantine but Sylvester appears and tames the dragon by
the power of the cross. The pagans are converted and the play ends with
Constantine rejoicing in the conversion of the city. All sing together a Te
deum.[9]

THE EXALTATION OF THE HOLY CROSS

The story of the exaltation of the Holy Cross is dramatised separately
in Cecchi's *commedia spirituale L'Esaltazione della Cruce* (D'Ancona, III). The
play was written at the very end of his life and was first performed, after
his death, by the boys of the Company of St John the Evangelist, on the
occasion of the marriage of the grand duke of Tuscany in 1589.[10] Most
of the play is made up of dialogue between minor characters (Cecchi's
son explains that much of the main text is his father's own invention) and
descriptions of the actions of the Persian king, Chosroes, who had carried

off the cross from Jerusalem. Heraclius appears briefly at the end of Act II declaring his intention of attacking Chosroes and winning back the Holy Cross. Only in Act V does the play enact a scene from the *Legenda* account of the exaltation: when the crowd gathers to welcome back to Jerusalem the triumphant emperor who has defeated Chosroes and is restoring the Holy Cross. A long stage direction specifies a magnificent entry of Heraclius with the cross on the triumphal chariot with Chosroes' son Arete at his feet and an escort of soldiers, as many as possible; 'and when they reach the gate let the artillery let off a salvo, although there was none at that time, this will add pomp and glory to the occasion, and let all the characters who have been in the play also take part in the procession'. They are greeted at the gate of Jerusalem by the pope and prepare to enter but the gates close and an angel appears and reminds the emperor that Christ entered Jerusalem in a lowly form, not as a great king. He gives the pope the crown of thorns and two red garments which recall the 'purple' (i.e. red) robe Herod put on Jesus in mockery. Heraclius leaves the chariot, takes off his royal garments and his shoes and puts on one of the red robes (the pope puts on the other). Heraclius touches the closed gates with the base of the cross and they open. All pass through in order honouring the cross as they pass. Trumpets and trombones are sounded and more artillery is heard. One of the minor characters speaks the *licenzia* and thanks the audience for their attention and reminds them there is one more interlude.

A detailed account of the interludes by Cecchi's son follows the play in the printed text. The six interludes, one as a prologue and one after each of the five acts, involve elaborate scenery, tableaux and music. The first shows the glorification of the cross. After Act I the second interlude is built round the story of Jacob, then the third shows scenes of the life of Moses and his becoming the leader of the Israelites, the establishment of the Twelve tribes and Aaron's flowering rod which is the forerunner of the cross (Numbers 17). The fourth shows the rebellious Israelites in the wilderness being punished by the plague and Moses' construction of the brazen serpent (also an anti-type of the cross), the fifth and most magnificent shows a great walled city – Jerusalem the city of David. The last interlude shows the spread of the Church and the founding of all the religious orders, such as the Knights of St John, Malta, the Teutonic Knights and Knights of Santiago. When all are gathered, filling the stage, the pope appears in magnificent robes and the papal tiara, holding a jewelled cross. All the company kneel and venerate the cross. Angels appear and foretell the last judgement and the triumph of the faithful.

SIXTEENTH-CENTURY GERMAN PLAYS OF
CONSTANTINE AND THE CROSS

Three sixteenth-century German plays of Constantine and the Holy Cross survive, one from South Tyrol (c. 1490s) preserved in Augsburg, and two from Switzerland, one by Renward Cysat of Lucerne (1575) and one by Wilhelm Stapfer of Solothurn (1598).[11] All three are described as Holy Cross plays and treat mainly of the discovery of the cross by Helena and its later exaltation by the Roman emperor Heraclius. As there is much overlap I shall summarise briefly the episodes included in each with indication of the most important variants.

The Augsburg play begins with the battle between Constantine and Maxentius. God sends the angel to announce to Constantine the 'sign' by which he will conquer. Having defeated Maxentius he tells Helena what has happened and she sets off for Jerusalem. After much discussion with the Jews she finds the old Juda who knows where the crosses were buried but refuses to tell her until he has been imprisoned in a dry well without food for several days, He finally takes her to the burial place upon which a tree was planted which is now very large. The tree is felled and the crosses dug up. The true cross is identified by the resurrection of a corpse which it touches. Juda is converted to Christianity and made bishop of Jerusalem. Helena takes him back to Rome with her and Part One ends with general rejoicing there. Part Two begins with the devils determined to have the cross lost again. The story moves from the invention to the exaltation of the cross. Contras (Chosroes of Persia) attacks and captures Jerusalem. He puts his son in charge there and carries off the part of the cross left there by Helena together with much treasure with which he builds a magnificent tower and claims he is now the equal of the Trinity.[12] Christian knights tell Heraclius, the Roman emperor, what has happened and he sets out with a great army and meets Chosroes' son at the Danube. They agree to a single combat on the bridge and Heraclius triumphs and beheads his opponent. The Persian soldiers all accept Christianity. Heraclius then goes to Chosroes' palace and beheads him when he refuses to accept Christianity. Chosroes' younger son is converted. Heraclius takes the cross and all the stolen treasure back to Jerusalem to the fury of the devils.

Acts I–II of Stapler's *Tragedia von Erfindung dess heiligen fron creützes wie ouch dessen Erhöchung* present a dramatisation of the legend of the cross beginning with the visit to Paradise by Adam's son Seth who brings his dying father a seed from the tree of life, which is buried with him and grows to a great tree. During the visit of the queen of Sheba, Solomon has it cut down to use in building the temple but its length keeps changing and it is thrown aside into the pool of Siloam.[13]

Act IV. During the life of Christ a lame man and a blind are healed when the angel troubles the pool. In Acts V and VI the story has reached the time of Constantine[14] and stages the scene of the angel giving Constantine a cross before the battle with Maxentius and the *In hoc signum vinces* promise. The leprosy story is omitted and Constantine is converted by Christians. He is baptised by Sylvester. In Act VII Constantine asks his mother to go to Jerusalem and look for the cross of Christ. She sets off quickly and comes to Jerusalem where she is welcomed by the king of Jerusalem who promises her help. The Jews are threatened with burning and Helena also summons an executioner. Finally Judas gives in and shows the place where the crosses are buried. They are dug up and the true cross is found by the raising of a dead man. After a lengthy scene with the devils, Judas appears with Sylvester who is to baptise him, after which Sylvester makes him Crocus, bishop of Jerusalem. He finds the nails for Helena who takes one and the cross back to Constantine and there is much rejoicing as Part One ends.

Part Two begins with the Argumentation giving an outline of the next part of the play which begins with Cyriacus being martyred by Julian the Apostate who succeeds Constantine as emperor of Rome (*Legenda*, invention, pp. 274–5). This is followed by an episode taken from the life of St Justina (26 September) who converts Cyprian and is martyred with him. Other interpolations include miracles of the Holy Cross. In Act XIV, the story of the exaltation of the Holy Cross (14 September) begins with the conquest of Jerusalem by the Persian emperor Chosroes in 615. He carries off the piece of the wood of the cross left there by St Helena. He then sets himself up as a supreme god and ruler. Heraclius the Christian Roman emperor raises an army and prepares to win the cross back. He defeats Chosroes and offers him the choice of baptism or death. Chosroes chooses the latter and Heraclius has his son baptised by pope Sylvester and establishes him as Chosroes' successor.[15] Heraclius then returns the cross in triumph to Jerusalem. The play ends in Act XVI, with the devils in Hell setting out to attack the Christians in different parts of the world.

Cysat's *Spil dess heiligen Crutzes Erfindung* was prepared for a performance in 1575 which was abandoned because of an outbreak of plague. Only a partial, later copy has survived, four out of the original seven acts. The survival of several cast lists makes it possible to follow the rest of the proposed action. The first two Acts are a series of scenes in different cities and involving different characters.[16] The action is based on Josephus and Eusebius and begins just after the Resurrection with arguments between Cayphas and other Jews against Joseph of Arimathea. Annas and Cayphas die suddenly. Herod and Herodias go to Rome and denounce Pilate to the emperor (Caius Caligula). Pilate has a scene in prison where he kills himself and is taken by the devils. A new episode, introduced by music, shows Mary Magdalen in Rome telling the story of Christ's life and death.

In Act III the action has moved on to the tyrannous reign of the general Maxentius and Act IV consists mainly of the story of Sophronia who killed herself rather than submit to the emperor.[17] The actual story of the finding of the cross begins in the lost Act V when the cast list includes St Sylvester, and the other characters are all described as 'in hungers not' (starving). In Act VI Constantine appears for the first time, also Peter and Paul, the apostles, and a doctor. Helena, bishop Macharius and Juda the Jew are also listed with many minor roles. This indicates the story of Constantine's conversion and Helena's visit to Jerusalem which is supported by the inclusion of a stage location for Helen among the Jerusalem group.[18]

The theme of the exaltation of the cross was very popular with the Jesuits. The English Jesuit College of St Omers performed a play of the triumph of the cross in English (*Omnia anglice*) in 1613. The college records tell us that it included the consecration and inauguration of emperor Heraclius, Chosroes' capture of Jerusalem, the war between the two emperors and the restoration of the cross to its original place. A Latin play on the subject was performed at St Omers in 1671 (McCabe, pp. 82 and 99).[19]

CHAPTER 20

Christianity goes west

There is little dramatisation of the period – between the conversion of Constantine and the events of the reign of Heraclius – which saw the spread of Christianity into Western Europe, except in France, where the conversion and baptism of the pagan Frankish king, Clovis, is dramatised in *Le miracle de Clovis* (Cangé, XXXIX) and forms one section of the *Vie de St Rémi*. The full title of the Cangé play refers to the historical event which took place at Rheims on Christmas day 496: 'how king Clovis was baptised at the request of his wife Clotilde because he was going to fight the Alemans et Senes'.

The play, like many of the other Cangé texts presents a sequence of short scenes often involving messengers and ambassadors moving from place to place. Clovis wants to marry the niece of the pagan king Gondebaut of Burgundy. She is reluctant to marry him because he is a pagan but finally consents. Scenes of battles against the invading Alemans alternate with Clotilde in labour and giving birth to a son whom she has baptised immediately. He dies soon after and Clovis is certain this is the result of the baptism. Much diplomatic activity between Clovis and Gondebaut succeeds eventually in regaining the treasure which he had stolen from Clotilde's parents. Clotilde has another son and has him christened also. Clovis is angry that the child seems to be a weakling and again blames the baptism. Clotilde prays to God and the Virgin whose customary visit accompanied by singing angels assures the child's health. At length Clovis finds himself outnumbered four to one in a battle against the Alemans and decides to invoke his wife's Christian god, promising that if he wins the battle he will believe in God and be baptised. He swiftly disposes of all the enemy soldiers. When Clotilde hears of his promise to be baptised she sends for St Rémi the archbishop of Rheims who gives Clovis a quick course in Christianity with emphasis (as with Constantine) on the doctrine of the Trinity. At the baptism, after Clovis has been immersed in the font a dove appears from Heaven holding a flask containg a sweet-smelling balm. This is the chrism, Rémi explains, and anoints Clovis with it. He is then robed in fresh garments and carried out by his knights for the celebratory feast.

The *Mystère de Saint Rémi* includes a version of the same historical events (including the birth and death of the first son) inserted among episodes of the life of Rémi and his miracles, and the customary *diableries*. The editor suggests the play may be an amalgum of several separate short plays performed in Rheims on appropriate occasions such as the coronation of Charles VIII.[1] The 'play' of Clovis[2] begins after the marriage of Clovis and the unnamed 'royne', who was herself converted by St Rémi and venerates him highly. When Clovis decides he needs God's help against the Alemans, he then encourages his soldiers with a speech that Henry V would have approved, for he tells his men they must have the heart of a lion, the sting of a scorpion, the leap of a leopard, the cunning of a fox, the aspect and glance of a tiger and the bold courage of a bull (ll. 8232–9).

The scene of the baptism of Clovis includes a speech by God who tells St Michael that the clerk with the chrism cannot get through the crowds in the church. Michael is to take 'celle ampoule belle et sainte' full of chrism which was made in Paradise and put it in Rémi's hands.[3]

ST GENEVIEVE, PATRON SAINT OF PARIS

The unusually nationalistic nature of the *Vie de St Rémi* play, with its emphasis on the formation of the kingdom of France, links it with a few other saints plays, including St Didier of Langres and, especially, St Genevieve, patron of Paris and contemporary of St Rémi.[4]

The first of the St Genevieve plays tells 'How the angels rejoiced when Madame St Genevieve was born.' It begins with a brief scene featuring the mother and the *chambrière* with the angels singing 'without budging from Paradise' one of the hymns for the feast of a Virgin. This Nativity is followed by the identification of Genevieve's sainthood. The scene begins with St Germain of Auxerre being dispatched by St Rémi and St Lou to deal with the pelagian heresy in Britain. (Mention of the British and their *erreur perverse* would no doubt be pleasing to a French audience of the 1380s!) While passing through Paris, Germain sees the young girl and in an echo of John the Baptist's *Ecce agnus dei*, he declares: 'there I see a maiden, holy, devout and good and beautiful, filled with the grace of God'. He speaks to Genevieve urging her to devote her life to God and live in chastity. The rest of this play contains Genevieve's first actual miracle: her mother, who has been inflicted with blindness because she struck the girl for wanting to go to church with her, is cured by Genevieve's prayers.

The fifth play in the sequence, one of the longer pieces (more than 600 lines) shows Genevieve as the patron saint of Paris. A messenger, called with great originality Trottemenu, brings word that Attila and the Huns are on their way to attack Paris. As the bourgeois decide to send their families and their goods out of the city, Genevieve kneels down and prays to God to take Paris under his protection. She also invokes the aid of the Virgin, Peter, Paul, Denis and all the saints, both men and women, to appease God's just wrath. The saints in full canonicals stand up and an intriguing pre-trial in Heaven follows. Peter appeals to the Virgin, as Man's supreme advocate towards God, to hear the intercession of this maiden for the people of France and especially of Paris. He mentions the church that a king will build on the site of Mont Parloeir (later Mont Ste Geneviève).[5]

St Paul adds that Genevieve deserves to be heard, for in Paris there will be a university filled with scholars who will preach the faith. Finally St Denis has his say, pleading for the France he had converted and missionised. He then asks the Virgin why God should have been born of her if it was not that he had compassion on sinners? He offers himself to die again if it were possible to help France and 'Paris qu'on dit Lutece' (a pleasant bit of linguistic detail) and especially because 'vostre amie Genevieve' asks it of God. The Virgin then questions whether such a request to God would be 'bonne, juste et honneste', for although God is pitiful he is also just and unchanging – if he has already sentenced France to destruction their efforts will be wasted. St John Evangelist now intervenes and points out that even if there is iniquity on earth, God's grace is not insufficient, and he does not punish those who repent, for his Mercy tempers his Justice. They all go to God, and the next part of the scene is a mixture of the trial in Heaven and the last judgement with Jesus rejecting their pleas on the grounds of man's continuous iniquity. The familiar motif of the Virgin showing her breasts and pleading her maternity follows, but whereas in doom-plays the Virgin's intercession is vain, here as in the miracles of Our Lady she is ultimately successful. Gabriel is sent to tell Genevieve the good news. So far in this play the emphasis has been more on the Virgin Mary than the Virgin Genevieve but now the action moves back to earth. Genevieve exhorts the people to repent, appealing particularly to the women and reminding them of two women saviours in the Bible, Judith and Esther, and asking them to urge their husbands not to abandon Paris.

Because Genevieve claims to *know* that Paris will be saved, a group of bourgeois decide that she is a sorceress, one pointing out that Isaiah says only God knows the future. He suggests drowning her in the Seine, the second prefers stoning, the third points out that these are risky for them – they would be accused of murder. 'Let's find a ditch and bury her alive.' At this point, Trottemenu conveniently arrives, with the archdeacon of Auxerre. He explains to the bourgeois the exceptional status and holiness of Genevieve, so that she is no sorceress. After his long disquisition on her sanctity, they are convinced and agree they were 'going the wrong way until God sent him to them'. The last couplet ends the play neatly: the archdeacon declares 'je vais diner a Saint Fiacre', they reply 'adieu donc Sire archediacre'.[6]

BALDWIN, ST LOUIS AND THE CRUSADES

There are no plays on the crusaders at Jerusalem, but on Epiphany 1378 Charles V held a banquet in the Palais de Justice for his uncle the emperor Charles IV. Among the entertainments was a presentation of the conquest of Jerusalem by Godefroy de Bouillon. A great ship with forecastle filled with Christian warriors among whom could be seen the monk, Peter the Hermit, travelled across the hall (with the help of wheels skilfully installed inside it) to the other side where there was a structure of Jerusalem with its tower and the temple and the walls manned by many Saracens. The Christians then scaled the walls with ladders and won the city.[7]

Philip the Good of Burgundy was sworn in as count of Hainault in Mons in 1433 and when he revisited the town in 1455, preparations were made for the customary greetings tableaux, including one portraying 'par personnaiges' *Le conqueste et prise de Constantinople* by Baldwin count of Flanders and Hainault in 1204. A second stage on the market place showed the crowning of the said count Baldwin, following history as closely as possible (Cohen, *Mons*, p. xii). The popularity of the story of Baldwin in his native country is emphasised by a Latin school play performed in 1616 of the 'pseudo-Baldwin' – a man who in 1225 claimed he was Baldwin, count of Flanders. He was unmasked and hanged (Worp, I, p. 230).

The only full-scale plays on the crusades, however, are those featuring the saintly Louis IX of France, who is the subject of two major plays, a *mystère* from about 1460 composed for the *Confrérie de la passion* and a *Vie* from about 1515, written by the nearest thing to a medieval forerunner of Molière, the notable poet, playwright, director and actor Pierre Gringore.

The *mystère* has a cast of more than 250 and is divided into three days.[8] The play begins with Louis' coronation and marriage. Then follows a rebellion by the *comte de la marche* followed by the war with England by which Henry III lost much of the territory won or inherited by his father, including Aquitaine. The birth of Louis' son then introduces preparations for a crusade which is to be the main theme of the rest of the Act culminating in the crusaders attacking Cyprus and conquering Damietta. Act II begins with a council in Hell followed by the battle of Massoure. Louis is taken prisoner but set free. After a pilgrimage to Syria, Louis returns to France where he publishes 'ordonnances' which Etienne Boileau, the provost of Paris, enforces with great severity. The act ends with an emphasis on Louis' acts of charity. The third Act begins with disaster for the Christians in the Holy Land and Louis' preparations for another crusade. He arrives in Tunis and is successful for a time but becomes ill with fever and dies there.[9] The author quotes the king's last advice to his son Philip. His body is taken back to France and he is canonised very quickly. Many miracles are worked on pilgrims to his shrine.

Gringore's play is specifically called a *vie*, not a *mystère* and is one of the first truly historical plays in French. It was composed c. 1513 for the important guild of Masons and Carpenters for performance on the feast of their guild patron (25 August). The play is in nine 'livres' with a total of 1,672 lines, which were performed, one or two at a time, in successive years as is indicated in the MS with such closing words as: 'suffise vous a cette année' at the end of livre V. The cast is much smaller than in the *mystère* and includes a number of rhetorical figures such as are found also in Gringore's many morality plays. Book I begins at the death of Louis' father when he is only twelve. His mother, queen Blanche, becomes regent against the wishes of the great vassals who try to gain power. Louis is shown giving alms to the poor and in scenes with his confessor. In Book II the vassals rebel against their young king but the people support him. Book III shows the emperor Frederic II preparing, with the help of *Outrage*, to attack or murder the young king whom he sees as a rival in the politics of Europe. When the plan fails he attacks the pope and is excommunicated. In Book IV, Louis falls ill and when he recovers vows to take the cross and join the crusaders in Jerusalem. In Book v the English prepare to attack France in Louis' absence, but he returns because of his mother's death and they withdraw. In Book vi Louis makes Etienne Boileau provost of Paris. He carries out his duties with great severity even condemning to death his own son. In Book vii Louis also rules with strictness but with justice for the poor against the nobility. In Book viii, Louis again sets off to fight the Saracens, falls ill and dies (in 1270) after giving good advice to his son. His body is taken back to France and mourned by all his subjects. Book ix records miracles performed at his tomb and the process of his canonisation which was completed in 1297.[10]

In addition to Louis there are examples in other plays of the concept of what has been called a secular or state saint play. The principal example cited is Shakespeare's *Henry V* which is described by Wasson as an example of the transfer of 'the theme and structure of these saint plays to secular subjects'.[11]

CHAPTER 21

The worthy, the proud and the popular

A substantial number of plays deal with the exploits of individuals as well as national or religious conflicts. They have been arranged for convenience under three main headings.

THE WORTHIES

A number of heroes were grouped together in the Middle Ages under the title of The Nine Worthies (in French, *Les neuf preux*), three Old Testament – Joshua, David and Judas Maccabaeus – three classical – Hector, Alexander and Julius Caesar – three Christian – Arthur, Charlemagne and Godfrey of Bouillon.

These Worthies sometimes appeared as a group in processions or other semi-dramatic works and they are perhaps best known today from Shakespeare's comic play in *Love's labours lost.*[1] There were also attempts to establish nine female worthies, especially in France, where the *Neuf preuses* are as well attested as the *Neuf preux* though their membership varies from time to time.

Taking the *Preux* in their chronological order we find that Hector is the only classical Worthy to have a major medieval dramatic role, as the hero of the Trojan war, but Alexander appears in a number of sixteenth-century plays including one by Hans Sachs, *Alexander magnus*, 1553, and a trilogy by Hardy influenced by the *Alexandre* of Jean de la Taille published in 1573 (Lancaster, I, i, p. 46).[2] Julius Caesar features not only in Shakespeare's historical play and Lope de Vega's *Cesar y Pompeyo* but in an unusual Latin play by the German Humanist Frischlin. In *Julius Redivivus* two men, Hessus and Hermannus, conjure up both Julius Caesar and Cicero and take them on a tour of the new Holy Roman Empire. Cicero is very favourably impressed by the printing works, but other aspects of Renaissance culture are differently viewed, especially the visit to a gun-maker's shop. When Hermannus fires off a rifle to demonstrate the power of his weapon, both Romans fall on their knees and worship him as Jupiter the Thunderer. When they learn it is a creation of man, Caesar is impressed but Cicero is terrified; 'If Caesar had been armed with those things when he prepared for the civil war, nothing of ancient Italy would have remained for this age.'[3]

Many of the Old Testament plays involving the Jewish Worthies have already been described in *Biblical drama*, but there are also a number from the end of the Middle Ages which emphasise Joshua, David and the Maccabees not as forerunners and types, but as warriors, with descriptions of their battles. The most important of these plays are the newly published ones from the *Mystères de la procession de Lille*.[4] *De la prinse et destruction de la cyté de Hay* is based on a story from Joshua 8. It includes battle scenes and the stoning of the Jew who has disobeyed the order not to take booty from the city. *Coment Josué sauva ceulx de Gabaon du siege des cinq rois* (Joshua 10), also includes battle scenes and terminates with the hanging of the five kings who seized the city to prevent the inhabitants joining Joshua and the Israelites.

There are several plays based on incidents from the reign of David including a battle against Saul and one against David's son Absalom. There is also a particularly blood-thirsty and spectacular play *De la glorieuse concqueste que fist Judas Machabeus contre Nichanor* based partly on Maccabees I:5 but mostly on Maccabees II:7. Knight (*Lille*, II p. 63) points out that these plays, presented for the annual procession of the Virgin Mary, were competing for prizes and therefore they needed 'des sujets spectaculaires' which also had to be original.[5]

Of the three Christian Worthies, Godfroi de Bouillon, elected king of Jerusalem by the victorious crusaders in 1121, first appears on stage in a Jesuit play: *Godfrey von Bouillon* which was performed in Germany in 1596.[6] Charlemagne appears in Frischlin's play of *Hilda Beata*, a falsely accused queen (see p. 97). Both Arthur and Charlemagne are listed among the subjects of plays by Lope de Vega in Book III of the *Arcadia*, but neither play has survived.[7] In 1684, the students of the Jesuit college of Louis-le-Grand presented a play of *Carolus magnus*. The accompanying ballet linked Charlemagne's victories with those of Louis XIV (Boysse, p. 187).[8]

King Arthur's importance in British legendary history did not convince continental writers of his authenticity – he belonged to romance not history. It is significant that Dante excludes him from the *Divine comedy*, whereas Tristan, who was believed to be a historical figure, was duly condemned to Hell for his adultery (*Inferno* v. v, 67).[9] The only extant early play of Arthur, *The misfortunes of Arthur*, was presented before Queen Elizabeth at Greys Inn in February 1588. The play is based on Geoffrey of Monmouth and has no connection with the Arthur of romance.[10]

A rare and intriguing three-act play from English history was performed at St Omers in 1624. *Innocentia Purpurata seu Rosa Candida et Rubicunda* (McCabe, p. 85). The cast list is divided into two groups of men. No women are included except the river goddess *Floris, dea fluvorum*. The Lancastrians are headed by *Henricus Plantagenata, Dux Lancastreiae* (Rex Angliae, Henry IV) and the Yorkists by *Odoardus Plantageneta* (Rex Angliae, Edward IV). The lists also include kings Henry VI and Richard III, so it is obviously a play on the Wars of the Roses covering a considerable period of time. It is tempting to postulate a possible borrowing from Shakespeare's *Henry VI* which had been published with all three parts together in the first folio of 1623.

LES NEUF PREUSES AND OTHER WOMEN WARRIORS

In Eustace Deschamps' fourteenth-century list of the *Neuf preuses*, all of them are Amazons but only one appears in a pre-1500 play, the Amazon queen Penthesilea in the *Istoire de Troy*.[11] In a verse in Lope de Vega's *Arcadia* (referring to a lost play), Pantasilea declares that she came to Troy not to defend Helen, who was guilty and bad, but for her own honour.[12]

In the fifteenth century the *Preuses* were often portrayed in tapestry and other works of art and began to include Jewish and Christian heroines such as Judith and Jael and the most popular of all, Joan of Arc.[13] Christine de Pisan in her *Ditie de Jeanne d'Arc* (1430) compares Joan favourably to Joshua, Hector and Achilles and then tells how she excels the biblical *Preuses* such as Judith and Esther.[14]

The earliest Judith play *Comment Judich tua Holoferne* was performed in fifteenth-century Lille, possibly on two waggons since the miniature for the play shows two locations, the Jewish town of Bethulia and the camp of the attacking Assyrians. Nebuchadnezzar having ordered his subjects to worship him as a god learns that the Jews have refused to do so and he sent an army, led by Holofernes, to attack the city of Bethulia. The play opens with a soldier assuring Holofernes that the besieged town will soon have to surrender as they have no water supply.[15] The Jews decide to try to hold out for five days after which they will surrender.

When the widow Judith hears this from her maid, Abra, she prays to God for guidance and then plans to gain access to Holofernes by going to plead with him and counting on her beauty to give her an opportunity to kill him. Having asked the priests to pray for her success, she takes off her hairshirt and her widow's weeds, anoints her body and dresses in her finest clothes. Then she loads her maid with food and drink (bread, cheese, wine and oil). By the fourth day of her stay in the camp Holofernes, seduced by her beauty, has promised not to attack Bethulia if Judith will sleep with him; she feasts with him and his followers and they then retire, leaving her with Holofernes. She prays to God for help and then returns to Holofernes' tent. She cuts off the head of the sleeping Holofernes (apparently in full view of the audience) and takes her leave of the camp and returns to Bethulia. Meanwhile in the camp the soldiers discover the corpse and lament the catastrophe.

A very similar play is found in the *Viel Testament*, a collection of Old Testament plays first printed in 1508.[16] In this play which has a good deal of humour in it, Judith has a nightcap tucked in the luggage and when she leaves the camp she carries the head past the guards in this nightcap.[17]

The story was one of the most popular in the sixteenth century with performances recorded from all parts of Europe. There are several Protestant plays since Luther in his translation of the Bible discussed the possibility that the Book of Judith was not history but fiction intended to teach the readers, possibly even by dramatic representations.[18] Hans Sachs treated the subject in 1551, following closely the biblical story and including the well-known tableau of Judith holding up the head of Holofernes in one hand and a still dripping sword in the other (Sachs, VI, p. 76). Hummelen lists two Dutch plays on Judith, *Judich ende Holofernes* by Robert Lawet (1571, *Repertorium* 1M8) and *Judith* from Hasselt (1642 1S7).

Adrien d'Amboise's *Holoferne* was printed in Paris in 1580 and there are also a number of performances recorded from Benedictine and Jesuit colleges.[19] The school plays not surprisingly do not include the humour and underplay the sexual innuendos of the original story. Sometimes in the school plays the story is seen as allegorical. The Benedictine teacher Schmeltzl in his *Judith* of 1542, the first Catholic play performed in Austria, presented the threat of Holofernes to Bethulia as parallel to that of the Turkish invasions of Vienna, while the text by Tuccio performed in Messina in 1564 presented the play as an allegory of the Redemption with the widow Judith as the Virgin Mary. A form of Annunciation is shown as the archangel Raphael goes to Judith/Mary to tell her she will save the people of Bethulia from the Devil in the form of Holofernes.[20]

A late French play on Judith by the abbé Boyer staged in 1695 in Paris had a remarkable success with the ladies. There was a scene in the fourth Act where it was the tradition to burst into tears and which, for that reason, was known as 'la scène des mouchoirs' (the handkerchief scene).[21]

JOAN OF ARC AND THE SIEGE OF ORLEANS

The oldest play on Joan, the *Mistere du siège d'Orleans*, copied in the early sixteenth century, closely follows the chronicles, which record the 'fetes commemoratives' staged every year in Orleans from the date of the French victory in 1429.[22] Unfortunately, the author of the play though a painstaking chronicler was an execrable poet, his verse not being improved by the number of English characters in the play and his finding it necessary to try to rhyme Gordons and *raison*.

The bulk of the play is dialogue with minimal action, merely the normal movement from place to place. From time to time, however, there is an extended stage direction for what can only be described as a set-piece. Thus part of the all-important struggle for the towers, or Tourelles, which were the key to the raising of the siege, consists of a discussion by the French on the damage done by the English artillery set up there and a decision to try to dislodge them with their bombard. A stage direction follows:

> Then there is a *pausa* and the big bombarde called the Bergere shall be fired and all the top of the Tourelles shall fall down at the shot and a good quarter of the tower, and six English must fall down headfirst killed by the shot from the Bergere from the ramparts of the Belle croix, then all the French will make a great noise of trumpets and clarions.

Then the dialogue recommences. It is tempting to see here a description of one of the *mystères* staged annually on 8 May for a number of years, to commemorate the end of the siege in 1429. In 1435, for example, it is recorded that *eschaffaulx* for these *mystères* were erected on the ramparts above the bridge, while in 1439 a painter was paid for making armour, *fleur de lys* and two 'godons' (i.e. *goddams* the general French word for the English) for the celebration of the recapture of the Tourelles.

Another longer direction describes a joust between two English and two Gascon soldiers who challenge them to single combat. It is possible that this was also an original 'mystère'. The preliminaries are arranged through the usual ubiquitous messenger who collects information then goes off; there is music, then he returns and says 'Lord Talbot agrees' or

similar words. No such vagueness attends the actual joust. 'Then all the English princes will jump up (*sauldront*) and come in proper array all on one side. And similarly La Hire and all the lords of Orleans will come, each properly armed, and will all stand on the other side.' The actual joust is described blow by blow like a chronicle of a tournament with every weapon and piece of armour noted. One of the Gascons kills his opponent; then the other pair fight until the trumpets sound a retreat. Each party retires in order and the English remove their dead man into their tent.

Such a scene could perhaps not have been done on the ramparts (though the numbers of people involved are not great) but the procession could well have also passed by a larger open space where it would be easy.

In addition to these two strands, the dialogued chronicle and the set battle pieces, there is a third: the story of Joan herself. Although Joan was not canonised till 1920, there was a strong popular cult for her in the Middle Ages even before a new enquiry declared her innocent of heresy in 1456. Soon after her death in Rouen in 1431, rumours spread that she was still alive, having either miraculously escaped while someone else was burned in her place or, the more popular view, she had died and risen again. It is not surprising therefore to find inserted in the story of the siege, scenes consonant with this hagiographic approach, beginning round about l. 7000.

A group of French captains arrive at Chinon to tell the king (Charles VII) that the people of Orleans are hard pressed by the English. Charles promises immediate aid and names the leaders he will send. A stage direction follows: 'Here there is a long *pause*. Then the king of France kneels down facing Paradise and speaks.' (Have we here yet another of the processional set-pieces?) In a forty-line speech of rather better verse than usual, the king appeals to God for help for France and for Orleans which is his only hope. He offers to abdicate or be deposed (*desmis*) if that is God's pleasure. The Virgin Mary is the first to speak and appeals to her son. It is wrong, she says, 'that the King of the *fleurs de lis* whom you raised to the dignity of ruler of France should have to submit to foreigners'. She goes on to claim that France is the country which supports and maintains Christianity and that no one else has a right there but Charles the true heir of France. St Euvertius and St Aignan, the patrons of Orleans, take up the appeal on behalf of their people. God replies by condemning out of hand all the people of France from 'haulz prince' to 'laboureur' for their wickedness. All behave badly and take no heed of God. He cannot accede to his mother's request for the atmosphere stinks of their vile and ignoble behaviour. Their suffering is a just sentence for their deeds.

Each suppliant pleads again, emphasising the king's humility and acknowledgement of his sins. God finally agrees that the realm shall be saved because of the king's prayer but in such a way that 'the Frenchmen shall not have the honour of regaining it themselves, nor shall I give them the victory'. So far then the emphasis is on the merits of Charles, not of Joan but now the stress shifts, for God summons Michael and sends him to a small village called Domremy on the estate of Vaucouleurs, where he will find a girl: 'bonne, juste et innocente / honneste, sage et bien prudente'.

Michael is to tell her that God's power will be in her 'qu'en elle sera ma vertue'. It is she who, dressed in man's clothing (a specific instruction from God), will raise the siege of Orleans. Michael is to send her to Robert de Baudricourt who will take her to the king and his court. A *pause d'orgues* follows the usual indication of a supernatural journey, and Michael comes to the Pucelle who is keeping her father's sheep and sewing her linen. The Annunciation play (for that is certainly what we have here) ends with Joan accepting her mission, and in a lyrical farewell, Michael several times refers to her as the shepherdess of God ('sa pastorelle') (v. 7168).

Michael reports on his mission, and God promises the *pucelle* shall be emboldened to defeat her enemies. Joan sets off to find de Baudricourt who refuses to help her. The military action then continues for another 1,800 lines followed by another scene in Heaven. Michael again sends Joan to de Baudricourt who does not refuse her this time.

When Joan comes to Chinon, the scene closely follows the official version of her recognition of the king and his eventual acceptance of her divinely inspired mission. A sword is found for her in a monastery with five crosses on it. The way this scene is written suggests it might be another set-piece.

For the last half of the play, some 9,000 lines, we are back to the siege and as the end of it approaches the detail of the sequence of events becomes ever more minute. Joan is wounded outside Orleans but insists that the assault should continue and the Tourelles are attacked and seized. Joan enters Orleans in triumph. Further battles follow as they clear the way between Chinon and Rheims so Charles can ride to his coronation. This addition is apparently only for the purpose of showing Joan involved in a miracle: outside the town of Jargeau there is again a siege situation with presumably the same set of walls, artillery etc. Joan is alone under the wall and the direction then says 'an Englishman shall pick up a great stone, large, broad and thick and throw it on the head of the *Pucelle* and she shall fall on her hands and knees and the stone shall break in pieces although it was a large and heavy stone and everyone must see it fall on the *Pucelle's* head'. In the following scene, the soldiers discover she is miraculously unhurt, and La Hire declares the Englishman thought it would smash her brains but it fell to pieces 'come paste' (p. 644).[23] Finally the English are defeated and their leaders, including Talbot, taken prisoner. The play ends with Joan's triumphant return to Orleans where she instructs the inhabitants to hold processions and praise God and the Virgin Mary and make preparations for the coronation in Rheims.

The story of the Maid of Orleans has attracted many authors from Shakespeare's *Henry VI*, Part I, to Schiller and Bernard Shaw. An anonymous *Tragedie de Jeanne d'Arques dite la pucelle d'Orleans* was printed in Rouen in 1600. One of the most important early plays, Vernulaeus' *Joanna d'Arca* (1629), was translated into French by Antoine de Latour in the late nineteenth century. A eulogy of Vernulaeus' depiction of Joan was read at the glorification of the newly canonised saint in Orleans cathedral in 1921.[24]

Vernulaeus' play is in five ACTS:

I. The play opens with laments by the French and news that besieged Orleans is starving. The Act ends with a chorus of Virgins.

II. Shows the arrival at court of the saviour of France as Poulengy brings Joan to king Charles VII who is doubtful of her story. He calls a council and is advised to believe her. The English learn of her arrival and a sword is found for Joan at Tours. Again a final chorus of Virgins.

III. After a battle scene the English soldiers describe Joan as a plague, a furie, a lion. They flee the *Puella* and Orleans is free. A chorus of soldiers rejoice: Viva Joanna D'Arca! jam libera est Aurelia (Orleans).

IV. After a dialogue between Charles and the English leader Talbot in which Charles describes the English action as 'stealing', the French set off for Rheims for the coronation which is staged with music and much liturgical detail described in one of the few stage directions in Vernulaeus' plays.

V. Joan is captured and condemned but the play does not show her martyrdom.

In addition to school productions such as that at the Jesuit college of Plombières in September 1580, when the *Histoire tragique de la pucelle de Domrémy autrement d'Orleans* by P. Fronton du Duc was performed,[25] other French plays are recorded and there are many pageants of the seventeenth century which introduce references to Jeanne d'Arc.[26]

CHAPTER 22

Pride and the wheel of Fortune

Fortune with her wheel first appeared on the medieval stage in the thirteenth century in Adam de la Halle's comedy *Le jeu de la feuillée*, which also sees the stage debut of those notable romance figures the *fées* (see p. 203). In Adam's play, Fortune is shown holding her wheel on which are many figures rising and falling. The senior *fée*, Morgan, explains that 'celle qui tient la roue . . . est de naissance muette, sourde et aveugle (she who holds the wheel . . . is from birth, dumb deaf and blind).[1] The fifteenth-century *Moralité de bien avisé et mal avisé*[2] includes a scene of Fortune with her wheel on which are four figures: *Regnabo, regno, regnavi, sum sine regno* (I shall reign, I reign, I have reigned, I am without kingdom). As the figures climb and fall at the turning of the wheel they beg Fortune to favour them, but in vain. *Bien avisé*, guided by Prudence, refuses to consider trying to climb the wheel. It is clear, therefore, that Fortune is a matter of chance, but also of choice.[3]

In the seventeenth century, Fortune appears in person on the stage not only in classical plays but also in the Christian drama,[4] since, as Jesuit -educated Pierre Corneille makes it clear, neither saints nor angels are acceptable on the serious French stage in the 1650s:

If I had brought Jupiter down to reconcile Nicomede with his father or Mercury to reveal Cinna's plot to Augustus, my audience would have rebelled and this 'marvel' would have destroyed all belief in the rest of the action. You may say that these apparitions do not please us because we know they are manifestly false and contrary to our religious belief which was not the case with the Greeks . . . but we have at least as much faith in the appearance of angels or saints as the ancients had in their Apollo and Mercury; however what would be the reaction if [in the play of Heraclius] I had used an angel to reconcile Heraclius and Martian after the death of Phocas? This play is about Christians and such an appearance would have been as justified as that of the classical Greek gods, nevertheless it would have been an infallible way of making the play ridiculous and only a little common sense is needed to make this obvious.　　　　(pp. lx–xi)[5]

However, religious subjects such as saints' lives and miracles are still allowed in college and school plays with occasional appearances of angels even up to the end of the century.

HE SHALL PUT DOWN THE MIGHTY

Sudden changes of Fortune are used as the theme of many poems and several plays based on story LIX of the *Gesta Romanorum* in which the emperor Jovinian, thinking of the extent of his dominions 'impiously asked, "Is there any other god than me?"'[6] Next day, while out hunting, he is overcome with heat and decides only a cold bath will cure him. Leaving his attendants he goes to a lake, strips and goes into the water. While he is enjoying his bathe, an angel who looks exactly like Jovinian takes his horse and clothes and returns to the hunting party who accept him as their emperor. Jovinian finds himself abandoned and naked and when he manages to reach a neighbouring castle and claims he is the emperor, he is driven away as a madman because the emperor and his suite have recently passed by. In turn, Jovinian is rejected by his court, his dogs and falcons and even the empress. At length he remembers his rash words, confesses his sin to the priest and is immediately recognised. The angel then reveals himself as Jovinian's guardian angel, explains what has happened and why, then disappears. Jovinian 'gave thanks to God, and lived happily and finished his days in peace'.[7]

The fifteenth-century French *Moralité de l'orgueil et presomption de l'empereur Jovinien* was printed in Lyons in 1584. Petit de Julleville lists the latter as a lost text (*Répertoire*, p. 308) but a copy turned up in a sale in 1912 and was edited by Emile Picot.[8] This long *Moralité* (2,000 lines) follows the *Gesta* closely but adds a number of details – the angel is Raphael and the series of rejections are emphasised by a series of beatings by the servants of the different lords approached. In one instance he is flogged by three *tyrans* in a scene reminiscent of the flagellation of Jesus scenes. There are also interpolated episodes of peasants singing and rejoicing.[9] They take pity on the outcast and give him food. Eventually Jovinian recognises his sin and, penitent, makes his way to a hermit who hears his confession, acknowledges his genuine repentance and gives him absolution. At once he becomes himself again and the play ends happily with Jovinian repentant and humbled.

A detailed account of the origin of this story, going back to early Jewish or Persian sources is given by D'Ancona in the preface to his edition of the Italian play of the *Re Superbo*[10] which adds to the *Gesta* an account of the (unnamed) Signore going to vespers and hearing the choir singing the Magnificat. He takes offence at the verse: *Deposuit potentes de sede, et exultavit humiles*[11] and declares there is no one able to upset his position as lord. He gives orders that no one, on pain of death, is to say or sing these words again. There is no hunting party but the lord is immediately taken ill and advised to have a cold bath to reduce his temperature. The rest of the play follows the *Gesta* fairly closely. Hans Sachs uses the story for the *Comoedia Kaiser Julianus im bad*, thus emphasising the bathing scene. Sachs does not mention the Magnificat but emphasises the emperor's attacks on Christianity. He allows himself a good deal of humour without treating the subject too lightly (Sachs, XIII).[12]

A variation of the story with the same subject but a different protagonist was popular in England. Narrative poems of *Robert of Cisyle* are found from the fourteenth century but the story, which includes the verse from the Magnificat but not the bath scene, is probably best known today from Longfellow's poem in *Tales of a wayside inn*.[13] There is no English play extant but Lancashire records performances of 'Robert of Sicily' in Lincoln (1452–3) and Chester (1529). The incomplete play *Pride of life* opens with the king boasting of his invincible power but he challenges not Heaven but Death. The play almost certainly ends with his losing his duel with death (Davis, *Non-cycle plays*, pp. 90–105).

The Spanish *Aucto del emperador Juveniano* (Rouanet, XXIII) is short and follows the *Gesta*, but in Rodrigo de Herrera's *Del cielo viene el buen rey*, the protagonist is a Sicilian: *Federico, re di Sicilia*. The Spanish text includes the bath scene, which is absent from all the English versions, but there is no Magnificat sequence. The long (4,000 lines) play begins with a lengthy speech by the king who describes a dream he has had of an angel coming from Heaven and taking away his crown. There are several Old Testament stories on this theme, most notably that of Nebuchadnezzar who also dreamed that 'a holy one came down from Heaven' (Daniel 4:10) and foretold his downfall. Daniel explains it is the punishment for his pride. Soon after Nebuchadnezzar 'was driven away from among men and did eat grass like an ox'. He is finally restored to his greatness. Herrera's play, which is in three *jornadas* (days), is much padded out with minor characters, a love interest and comic scenes with the *gracioso* but the end is very effective.

Federico, now called a madman, challenges the angel to a duel. To the court's surprise the angel-king accepts the challenge and is armed. In an aside he prays to God that this *Luzbel* shall ask forgiveness.[14] Federico rides on to the stage but is told by the angel to dismount. They fight and the angel forces Federico to the ground, sets his foot on the king's neck and waves his sword over him. Federico repents his pride and confesses his sins, declaring that he feels the angel's power as being the 'arm of God'. The angel believes him and, explaining he is the archangel Michael, he changes his appearance and presents Federico to the assembled court as being indeed the king, then vanishes.

FORTUNES OF WAR

In the seventeenth century, Fortune appears in person on the stage not only in classical plays but also in the Christian drama.[15] Among the proud warriors in whose life Fortuna plays a major role is the Byzantine general, Belisarius.[16] In the Latin play by the German Jesuit writer, Jacob Bidermann, first performed in 1607, the rise and fall of Belisarius is attributed to the turning wheel of Fortune.[17] We are shown his rise to great fame and glory as successful leader of the Christian Byzantine army against the Persians, Vandals and Ostrogoths. But the appearance of Fortune in a chariot reminds us that her favours never last,[18] and as the play proceeds, Envy and Calamity, her constant followers, are seen more frequently on stage. In Act IV the final decision has to be made: emperor Justinian's wife, the former actress Theodora, is determined to dispose of pope Silverius who has opposed and criticised her way of life,[19] and orders Belisarius to do the deed. This is the critical moment of the play as Bidermann shows how the general who can defeat armies on the field cannot withstand the power of a wicked woman. He disposes of the pope on a trumped-up charge and returns to Constantinople. Fortuna now forsakes him and Envy is allowed full sway. Belisarius is wrongfully accused of being involved in a plot against the emperor and blinded in punishment. Accompanied (like Shakespeare's Gloucester) by his son, Belisarius leaves the city for which he fought so much.[20] There is, however, a hint at the end that God may eventually relent to a man who was weak rather than wicked.[21] Plays on the subject of Belisarius for the public theatre are also extant from France and Spain.

Mira de Amescua's *El ejemplo major de la desdicha* (The great example of misfortune) (1625) based mainly on the secret history of Byzantium by Procopius, was used by Nicholas Desfontaines for his *Belisaire* (1641) which in turn inspired Rotrou's play of *Belissaire* (1643), though the latter made much greater use of the Spanish source. A detailed analysis of the Rotrou and de Amescua's plays in parallel shows how closely he followed his source, and the changes made to appeal to a more popular audience.

Belisarius is involved by Theodora in a web of intrigue and murder. The plays include love interests and the themes of the 'woman scorned' and the innocent victim[22] but they also both introduce the concept of Fortune. At the end of Act III Belisarius is at the height of his fame and invokes Fortune: 'Arrete ici, Fortune, Arrete ici ta roue'.[23] Not long after, the emperor, convinced by Theodora that Belisarius is a threat to his throne, has him arrested and blinded. Act IV ends as Belisarius laments his fate but accepts that Fortune has changes:

> . . . . enfin la Fortune se lasse;
> . . . . il est de son ordre inconstant
> De rebuter enfin ce qu'elle obligea tant,
> Et n'élever personne au plus haut de sa roue,
> Que la fin de son tour ne jette dans la boue.

> (At last Fortune grows weary . . . it is part of her inconstancy to reject those whom she has favoured; no man is raised to the top of her wheel who will not be cast down in the mud by its final turn.)[24]

Another victim of Fortune and of pride is the Roman general Coriolanus (Livy Bk 2). Though best known from Shakespeare's play of 1607, the story was most frequently dramatised in French. The earliest version, the *Coriolan* by Alexandre Hardy (c. 1625), is interesting for its inclusion of invocations to the classical gods: the play opens with a long speech by Coriolanus to Jupiter demanding that he should punish the criminal ingratitude of the Roman people after all he has done to bring them peace and victory, including his achievement at Corioli where he won his name. In the seventy-four-line speech he blames everything on envy. Volumnia urges him to be humble and satisfy his enemies; when he declines, she begs him by the shades of his father and by the breasts he sucked – an interesting survival of the medieval motif of the Virgin interceding with Christ.[25] When Coriolanus is again attacked and threatened, he accepts banishment with relief. Basically, for Hardy, it is a vengeance play in classical form, with the women well represented by Valerie, a noble roman lady and a chorus of women as well as Volumnia and Virginia. Coriolanus' death is described by a messenger to Volumnia and the play ends with her lament.

The popularity of the story is shown by two other French plays, from the 1630s. *Le véritable Coriolan*, written for the Hotel de Bourgogne by Chapoton, follows Plutarch and Hardy. There are many directions for elaborate staging and the death of Coriolanus is shown on stage.

Chevreaus' *Coriolan* of the same period was probably written for the rival
Marais theatre. It cuts much of the earlier material and emphasises the
conversion of Coriolanus by his wife and Volumnia. The death scene is
again showed on stage which is unusual at this period (Lancaster, II, i,
pp. 160–2). A play of Coriolanus was also presented at the Jesuit college
in Paris in 1683, the year it took the name of Collège Louis-le-Grand
(Boysse, p. 185). There are no details preserved, but it may have been the
same play as the *Marcii Coriolani pietas in matrem*, staged in Mechelen in
1699, which emphasises Coriolanus' filial respect for his mother's wishes
(Szarota, III, 2, pp. 2258–9).

In *Sejanus his fall*,[26] Ben Jonson shows how Fortune's wheel can be
turned by deliberate action of a man: Tiberius, having raised up Sejanus
to great heights, begins to fear Sejanus may be a threat to the emperor
and prepares to have him brought lower. Macro is instructed: 'both to
spy / inform and chastise'. Macro rejoices in this charge as he prepares
his own rise to Fortune: 'The way to rise is to obey and please' (Act III,
scene 2).

CHAPTER 23

Affairs of state

Whereas the men caught on Fortune's wheel are usually involved in war, stories on the rise and fall of queens are more often linked with the problems of combining government with romance. Semiramis, who became the ruler of the Assyrians after her husband's death by dressing as her own son and ruling in his name, was a popular subject in the drama in both France and Spain. After adding Ethiopia to the empire and restoring the walls of the great city of Babylon, she eventually succumbed to her sexual lusts and tried to seduce her own son who then killed her. Calderon's *Semiramis* omits much of the traditional story and paints instead a simple portrait of an ambitious woman.[1]

Another woman who rose high on Fortune's wheel but fell through her own weaknesses was Mary, queen of Scots. Her dramatic rise can be held to have begun in France where in 1556 at the age of '13 ans et 4 mois' the queen of Scots played the leading role in a court production of a French translation of Trissino's *Sophonisba*, staged by queen Catherine de Medici on the occasion of the marriages of four members of the court.[2] According to a chronicler the queen later believed this performance had brought bad luck and never staged another play. Lebègue admits almost to accepting this superstitious belief, since of the two young princesses, Claude died in childbed and Elizabeth, who was the second wife of Philip II of Spain, also died young, 'et surtout Marie Stuart, dont les mariages ne lui valurent que tristesses et déboires' (and especially Mary Stuart whose marriages only brought her grief and heartbreak).

Whatever the cause, the 'Ecossaise' as she is often called in French plays, beginning with one by Montchrestien performed in Orleans in 1603, was usually shown as a victim of Elizabeth's jealousy and a political martyr – a role she maintained well into the eighteenth century in Schiller's play.[3] Whereas Montchrestien shows some sympathy for both queens (they are not called by their first names in the play) who are to some extent the victims of their advisors, Regnault, writing thirty years later when the tension between Catholic and Protestant had greatly increased, makes clear his sympathy for Mary whom he treats as a martyr. The Dutch Catholic writer, Vondel, almost deified her in his *Maria Stuart of gemartelde maiesteit* of 1646.[4] Much disturbed by the execution of Charles I – whose fate he dramatised in *Carolus Stuardus* – and the rise in power of Cromwell, the Puritan usurper, Vondel went as far as to compare Mary's fate to the Passion of Christ: 'She celebrated a "Last Supper" with her handmaidens, forgave her oppressors and commended her soul to God before her death.'[5] Above all Vondel emphasised Mary's innocence, a theme repeated in Jesuit plays, most notably in *Maria Stuarta, Scotia Regina, tragoedia*, performed in two different colleges on 4 and 6 September in 1702 and 1709. The title page of the *periochies* describe her as 'Queenly innocence through royal falsity brought to death by the sword' (Szarota, III, 2, p. 2203).

Boursault, on the other hand, who was a Huguenot, and writing about the time of the revocation of the edict of Nantes, is on Elizabeth's side and when Mary entered Edinburgh as queen of Scotland in 1561, the tableaux which helped line the streets for the festivities included one on Abiron and Dathan (Numbers 16:17–23) who were swallowed up by the earth for idolatry. This was evidently an attack on popery and Mary 'was not amused'.

Mary's fall from the wheel of Fortune was not only due to her Catholicism, however. Some writers classified her with Clytemnestra and Hamlet's mother as a wicked woman who killed her husband and married her accomplice.[6]

SOPHONISBA

Not all the plays about ambition involve simple political conflicts, There are also instances of a clash between love and affaires of state including the many plays on Dido and Aeneas (see p. 145) and, the most popular subject of all, the story of Sophonisba, which is dramatised in plays in Italian, French, German and English.[7]

According to Livy XXX, 12, Sophonisba was the daughter of the great Carthaginian Hasdrubal who was at war with Rome. When she reached marriageable age he married her to Syphax, the elderly king of Numidia, who was friendly towards Rome, in the hope it would win him over to the Carthaginian cause. As Sophonisba was very beautiful the plan succeeded and Syphax allied himself with the Carthaginians. The Romans, led by Scipio Africanus, retaliated by landing near Carthage and defeating Syphax with the help of his old enemy, king Masinissa, who was sent by Scipio to take over Numidia and take the queen prisoner. Masinissa fell in love with Sophonisba as soon as he saw her and promised to save her from the Roman general's triumph if she would marry him, which she did. She thus had two living husbands. Scipio rebuked Masinissa for marrying an enemy and, not wishing to lose the Roman general's favour, Masinissa sent to Sophonisba a draught of poison as the only way to save her from the triumph and himself from Scipio. She sent a message to Masinissa thanking him for his gift, drained the cup (a subject frequently portrayed in Italian art) and fell to the ground dead.[8]

Livy does not attempt to justify the marriage between Sophonisba and Masinissa, but Appien of Alexandria introduces a previous betrothal between Masinissa and Sophonisba, before the former went to war against the Romans in Spain with Hannibal. During their absence, Syphax who had also wanted Sophonisba, began plundering her estates and the Carthaginian Senate forced her to renegue on her first vows and marry the elderly Syphax. The details of this complex interweaving of motives and emotions allows for great variety in the treatment of the subject.

C. Ricci in *Sophonisbe dans la Tragedie classique Italienne et française* (Grenoble, 1904), studies the theme from Petrarch's elaborate treatment in his *Trionfo amore* to the earliest play, the *Sofonisba* of Galeotto del Carretto, composed c. 1500, and inspired by the sad conditions in Italy, torn by war as France and Spain struggled to conquer it. (p. 49). The most influential Italian play, by Trissino, was composed in 1515 in Rome at the court of Leo X at the height of the Renaissance, printed in 1524 and first performed in a magnificent production in Vicenza in 1562 (p. 55). Trissino's play is modelled on the dramas of Euripides, especially the Alcestis. Unusually the heroine has a son (a fact never mentioned in the sources). Moreover at the end Masinissa comes to help Sophonisba but finds she has already drunk the poison, so he tells her people to prepare a worthy funeral.[9]

Trissino's play was translated into French by Mellin de Sainct Gelays and published posthumously in 1559. The play is in prose except for the chorus of women 'qui parle en vers de plusieurs genres', as the publisher explains.[10] *La Cartaginoise* by Montchrestien, which followed Livy closely, was published in 1596, and Montreux's *La Sophonisbe*, which followed Appian and Plutarch's life of Scipio Africanus, was published in 1601. In the Argument which precedes Montreux's play, he introduces one of the important themes of the story – the importance of keeping one's word: 'Massinisse forcé d'obéir à Scipion et a la foy qu'il avait donné à Sophonisbe, executa l'un et l'autre' (Forced to obey Scipio and to keep his promise made to Sophonisba, did both). Jean Mairet's *Sophonisbe*, published in 1634, is the first French tragedy to observe exactly the three unities of time, place and action. The place is the besieged city of Syphax who has defied the Romans for Sophonisba's sake and now finds a secret letter she has written to her earliest love, Massinissa, who leads the enemy forces. A battle follows in which Syphax is killed and Massinissa captures the city, and gives orders to take prisoner the queen who will ornament the triumph in Rome. Sophonisba, having feigned a desire for death, proceeds to seduce Massinissa and accepts his offer of marriage without hesitation when he promises to save her from the Romans. Scipio arrives and Massinissa finally realises he can only save Sophonisba from the Roman triumph at the cost of her life. He sends her the poison, promising not to outlive her and duly stabs himself on the body of his wife in front of Scipio.

Mairet's play was very successful as Corneille explains in the preface to his own play on the subject in 1663, for which unfortunately he cannot make a similar claim, his Sophonisba being one of his worst plays, partly because he is so careful to make it clear he is not imitating Montreux that he finishes up with a complex and unconvincing plot line which includes an extra candidate for Massinissa's love, the captive princess Eryke. The play ends when Massinissa, having been forbidden by Lelius, the Roman leader, to see Sophonisba, keeps his word by sending her the poison by messenger but she prefers to use her own! Lelius consoles Eryke with a remark very similar to the tag from the Cid: 'laissons en faire au temps (leave it to time).

The earliest English play, Marston's *Sophonisba* of 1606, presents the story as a struggle between Massinissa and Syphax to get Sophonisba into their bed. Act I opens with Sophonisba being settled in the bridal bed and the entrance of Massinissa to join her during a musical interlude and song to Hymen. It is interrupted by the arrival of a wounded Carthaginian soldier with the news that Carthage is under attack from Rome. Massinissa changes his bed-gown for his armour and abandons his grief-stricken bride. In Act II the Senate of Carthage decides to save their city by handing Sophonisba over to the king of Numidia, Syphax, who is desperately enamoured of her. She reluctantly accepts the need to save her country. In Act III, Sophonisba goes to Cyrta, Syphax's palace. He comes to claim her with indecent haste but she manages (with

difficulty) to keep him at arms length by pretending she is quite willing
to submit to his lust, provided she can first make a sacrifice to the gods.
Syphax believes her and leaves the apartment. Sophonisba arranges the
sacrifice and then sneaks out of the palace through a secret passage leading right outside the walls into a wood. However, her attendant reveals
the passage to the frantic Syphax who pursues her into the forest. When
he fails to catch her he appeals to a hideous witch, Erictho, who says she
can bring Sophonisba to him by magic. In fact, after a passionate scene
with – as he thinks – his desired bride, he finds he is holding the witch
instead, who mocks the old king before she disappears.

The ghost of Sophonisba's father, Asdrubal, appears and tells Syphax
the Romans and Massinissa are advancing on Cyrta. Massinissa begs
Scipio to allow him the battle against Syphax, whom he defeats and
brings to Scipio's feet. Syphax is now shown as even more vile. He declares
all the anti-Roman activity was Sophonisba's doing and he was helpless
against her. Scipio sends Lelius to make sure that Massinissa hands over
Sophonisba as a prisoner of Rome. Massinissa comes to Cyta wearing a
closed helmet. Sophonisba does not recognise him but begs her captor
not to give her to Rome. He reveals himself and they have a brief moment
of joy together before Lelius comes to collect the prisoner. Sophonisba
decides to solve Massinissa's dilemma by committing suicide, which she
does with dignity. In the final scene at the Roman camp, Massinissa brings
the corpse to Scipio, and bids farewell to his beloved before rejoining the
forces of Rome.

Axelrad calls the description of Erictho 'impardonable' with Marston
aiming at horror but almost certainly achieving a roar of laughter![11],
and declares Nathaniel Lee (1676) succumbs to bathos by overdoing the
bombast:

> When all with crimson slaughter cover'd o're,
> We urged our horses through a flood of gore;
> While from the battlements of Heaven's high wall
> Each god look'd down, and shook his awful head,
> Mourning to see so many thousands fall,
> And then look'd pale, to see us look so red.[12]

At the other extreme, the nuptials of Massinissa and Sophonisba in
Lowenstein's German play of 1682 are graced by the presence of 'twelve
naked Cupids'.[13] Axelrad also analyses a series of French and German 'Sophonisba' plays in the eighteenth and ninetenth centuries. His
final conclusion is that in four centuries of plays not one of them is a

masterpiece and the general standard is very low. He finally concludes: 'Sophonisbe est impossible sur la scène tragique'.[14]

Ricci views the plays in a similar light, and blames it on the influence of 'cette fatalité qui pesa si lourdement sur sa triste et glorieuse existence' (that fatality which dominated her sad and glorious life).[15]

ELIZABETH AND ESSEX

A much smaller but very interesting group of plays were published between 1603 and 1761 on the subject of the relationship between Elizabeth I of England and Robert Devereux, earl of Essex. All the plays begin near the end of Essex's career and terminate in his execution in 1601 on an accusation of high treason over his behaviour when sent to subdue the count of Tyrone in Ireland.

The earliest of them, a Dutch Rhetoricians' play of c. 1603, treats the subject primarily as a question of politics. The following account is based on the detailed analysis of the play given by Wim Hüsken in *Queen Elizabeth and Essex: a Dutch Rhetoricians play.*[16] This aspect is developed mainly through the two 'sinnekens', the traditional Dutch allegorical figures of Evil, which here are a woman called *Jaloers Bedryf* (Jealous Affair), and a man called *Schyn van recht* (Semblance of Justice). Their introductory dialogue makes it clear that they will be present in the legal battles, when the critics of Essex will be more concerned with winning their case than doing justice.

The play is set in 1601, two years before Elizabeth's death. Essex, having reached great heights as a general and been made earl marshal of England, has also made many enemies, especially Robert Cecil, son of Lord Burleigh, Elizabeth's chief minister for many years, and Walter Raleigh. Essex learns of the criticisms urged against him and although commanded by the queen to remain in Ireland where he has been sent to deal with the rebellious earl of Tyrone, disobeys her orders and returns to England, hoping that his long success as Elizabeth's favourite will enable him to win back her support against his enemies. She refuses to see him, and angry and frustrated, Essex raises a mob among the citizens of London against Cecil and his other enemies, and as a result is arrested and imprisoned. *Jaloers Bedryf* concentrates on encouraging this behaviour while her fellow sinneken is busy making sure that his trial (on a charge of supporting rather than subduing Tyrone) will be a true example of false justice. Urged on by his only faithful friend, the earl of Southampton, Essex eventually succeeds in getting an interview with the queen, who still cares for him but is angry at his arrogance and pride. She accepts the court's verdict of guilty and a death sentence. The sinnekens comment on the preparations for the execution on the stage. 'They notice that the scaffold has been made out of the timber used to support the cannons in one of Essex biggest victories, the battle of Cadiz.'[17] A messenger arrives from the palace with a letter from the queen, and her ring as an extra token of credibility, to save the earl's life, but is told it is too late. Essex has already been beheaded.[18] The sinnekens rejoice at their success – they are now hated by everyone. When the queen hears the news she bursts into tears and leaves the stage, while the messengers talk of the downfall of the proud 'when Lady Fortune turns her wheel'.[19]

The seventeenth-century French and eighteenth-century English plays exclude the trial and riot scenes and deal mainly with the relationship between the queen and the courtier. The dedication of La Calprenède's *Le comte d'Essex* to Madame la princesse de Guiméné begins: 'J'offre une excellente reine à une excellente princesse.' He hastily qualifies this praise of Elizabeth's behaviour by classing her with Herod and Tiberius, but concludes that for many she represents 'la plus grande princesse qui fut jamais'. It is clear that, despite the title, the queen in this play is as important as the Comte.[20]

The cast is substantially the same as in the Dutch play (except of course for the sinnekens) but there is one important addition: Madame Cécile, wife of the secretary of state. The play opens with a scene between Essex and the queen who tells him he is accused of conspiring against her life. He hotly denies any such intention and claims he wishes only to have the opportunity to convince her of his loyalty and devotion. He then attacks Cecil and the other lords for their treachery and falseness and denounces them as: 'Inutiles en paix, inutiles en guerre . . . Bref qui vous servent mal comme je vous sers bien.' Elizabeth's response is anger tempered with a hint that she still cares for him, as she produces documents which seem to impeach his good faith in dealing with Tyrone. Furious, Essex declares it is a forgery and tears it up. The queen promises he shall have his chance to defend himself when he is tried by the council. Then she dismisses him, and after a soliloquy in which she declares her feelings for him but her need also to rule well, the captain of the guard is ordered to arrest both Essex and his friend Southampton and imprison them together in the Tower. The queen's attendant comments on her apparent distress: 'Que son cœur est pressé d'étranges passions!' While he is in prison, Essex receives a visit from Lady Cecil and the conversation makes it clear they have been lovers and she resents his change of heart. However, she has been sent by the queen to persuade him to behave with less pride and arrogance and to know that the queen is still on his side. The play continues in a series of meetings and clashes of will with the emphasis most of the time on the emotional clashes between Essex, the queen and Lady Cecil, and only one of the legal scenes found in the Dutch play where Essex is tried and found guilty and condemned. Learning of this, Elizabeth reveals to Lady Cecil the story of the ring she gave Essex with a promise that if he sent it to her she would always pardon him whatever the crime. She tells Lady Cecil to go to Essex and discreetly and indirectly remind him of the ring. Reluctantly she does so, but bitterly jealous because she knows Essex does not love her as he said he did, she takes the ring from him but does not give it to the queen, who learns with shock that Essex has been executed. While she is alternately criticising and lamenting Essex, an attendant arrives with news that Lady Cecil is dying, having collapsed on learning that Essex was dead and wants to see the queen. Elizabeth goes to her and tries to comfort her. Then, having sent everyone away, Lady Cecil tells the queen she lied about Essex not giving her the ring. Elizabeth faints and Lady Cecil is carried away leaving Elizabeth with her faithful attendant, Alix, lamenting the death of Essex and the difficulties of being a queen.

In 1678, Thomas Corneille chose to dramatise the subject in his *Le comte d'Essex*. In the *Au lecteur*, he mentions the success of La Calprenède's play and refers to the kind reception his own play has also received.[21] Corneille claims he has followed history closely and complains he has been accused of falsifying it because he has omitted the episode of the ring Elizabeth was said to have given to Essex. He points out that there is no historical evidence for this episode which he believes was entirely the invention of La Calprenède. But Corneille did not know of the Dutch play already mentioned, in which a version of the story appears long before La Calprenède wrote his play. Since the Dutch text follows the historical account by Camden very closely, according to Hüsken, it is tempting to see the reference to Elizabeth's sending her ring with the letter, to authenticate her change of mind, as being true and perhaps the origin of the more romantic versions created by all the later authors.

Corneille changes the 'woman in the case' from Lady Cecil to the imaginary duchesse d'Irton who plays a major role in the early part of the play as she tries to persuade Essex to make his peace with the queen before he is arrested. Then follows a scene with Cecil in which the image of the rise and fall is emphasised: 'Mais dans quelque haut rang que vous soyez placé / souvent le plus heureux s'y trouve renversé.' Thomas Corneille follows the family tradition in presenting both Elizabeth and the duchess as strong women, well able to control their passions and act energetically when need arises – a marked contrast to the emotional scenes and fainting fits found in La Calprenède. This Elizabeth refuses to commute the death sentence unless Essex himself asks for it. His obstinate pride must yield to the queen's superior power but he will not do so despite the prayers of the duchess, who finally goes to tell the queen he is on his way to execution. Elizabeth tells her attendant, Tilney, to 'cours, vole et fait qu'on le ramène' acknowledging that her pride has conceded the struggle. Cecil enters and the queen tells him that if Essex is killed his own head will pay for it but Cecil is unmoved and Tilney brings the news that Essex is already dead. Salisbury arrives and describes the scene on the scaffold and the last words of Essex. Elizabeth declares herelf ready to die for what she has lost, but meanwhile tells Salisbury to accompany her to see that Essex is buried with full honours.[22]

The source of the first English play of Elizabeth and Essex, John Banks' *The unhappy favourite or, the earl of Essex*, published in 1682, is an anonymous 'romance' published in 1650.[23] Both texts have the same principal characters including Lord Burleigh, the chancellor (who had died in 1598) rather than his son, Cecil, and, in the role of the jealous woman, the countess of Nottingham.[24] In contrast to the French plays there is also a second woman who is the secret wife of Essex and a main cause of the queen's jealousy.

In contrast to the French versions, the English play emphasises the enmity between Spain and England especially in Burleigh's speech in the first act:

> What truth can we expect from such a Race
> Of Mungrells, jews, Mahumetans, Gothes, Moors,
> And indians with a few of Old Castilians,
> Shuffled in Natures mould together?   (p. 7)

The scene continues with the queen and courtiers recalling with delight the defeat of the Papist Armada with the pope having to bless so many people 'it gave his arms the gout'. This scene of rejoicing is then gradually guided by Burleigh into a discussion of the Irish rebellion and the behaviour of Essex who, Burleigh tells the queen, has just returned to London, against her orders. The queen is furious but when news is brought to the queen that Essex has been impeached she turns against Burleigh.

In Act II the queen gives order Essex be admitted and then soliloquises on the pain of queenship and the pleasures of the simple country girl with the flowers and birds. Essex enters and kneels and speaks to the queen who pretends to ignore him and talks to Lady Nottingham, then departs without speaking to him. Burleigh and Raleigh enter and tell Essex he is stripped of all his offices, is to surrender his earl marshal's staff and confine himself to his house till further orders. The countess of Rutland, who is Essex's secretly married wife, enters and the two lament together over the problems caused by Burleigh and the other enemies of Essex, and reaffirm their love for each other.

In Act III Rutland has an audience with the queen and tells her that Nottingham is working with Burleigh against Essex. Elizabeth agrees to see Essex and let him defend himself to her. The meeting takes place but Essex reacts too proudly against the queen and receives a box on the ear (a known historical event). In Act IV Essex is arrested by order of the council but manages to have another private meeting on his way to prison, during which Elizabeth gives him a ring:

> Here's a pledge
> I give it from my Finger with this Promise,
> That whensoever you return this Ring (Gives him a Ring).
> To grant in lieu of it what e're you ask.   (p. 52)

Essex is led away by the guards for his trial. Rutland pleads with the queen who discovers her secret marriage to Essex. Furious she condemns him, but soon after repents and sends Nottingham to remind Essex of the ring. He hands it over, with an explanation of what it means. Nottingham, however, tells the queen he is unrepentant and too proud to beg anything since he is innocent. She recommends the queen to send Rutland to join her husband in prison. They lament together and Essex gives his wife a letter for the queen. He is led away to execution but when the queen sees Rutland she receives the letter which shows up Nottingham's treachery. Elizabeth sends Burleigh orders to stop the execution and then turns on Nottingham:

> Repentance, horrors, Plagues, and deadly Poysons,
> Worse than a thousand deaths torment thy soul . . .
>   (p. 76)

She then curses Nottingham and orders her to be taken away 'For she and I must never meet again.' Burleigh then enters and tells the queen he was too late and Essex is dead. The queen tells Rutland, 'thou choice relickt of lamented Essex', that Essex's death shall be avenged, but asks Rutland not to blame her 'Since 'tis th'almighty's Pleasure, though severe / To punish thus his Faithful regents here.'

Plays by Henry Jones and Henry Brooke, both called *The earl of Essex*, were performed at Drury Lane theatre in the eighteenth century. The cast and general form of the plays are copied from Banks, though each text is verbally unique and each has a slightly different ending. In Jones' play, when the queen receives the letter she immediately dispatches a messenger to stop the execution, then turns on Nottingham and orders her to be taken to a dungeon 'deep sunk from day . . . and from the torments of thy conscious guilt / may hell be all thy refuge'. When Cecil (not Burleigh in this play) brings the news Essex is dead, the queen declares he has 'Pronounc'd sentence of death upon thy Queen' who will never eat or sleep again 'Mark me – You hear Elizabeth's last words'.

Brooke's play ends with Burleigh telling the queen of Nottingham's deceit: 'in this she murdered Essex!'. Elizabeth has the last word: 'but Heav'n alone can view my breaking heart; / then let it's Will be done.'

Banks' play was translated into German and there are several other German plays on the same subject from the eighteenth century.[25] A popular Spanish play by Antonia Coello y Ochoa, *Le conde de sex* was published in 1638 and frequently reprinted in later centuries. It ignores completely the historical facts, starting with the coming of the Armada in 1588 and Essex being appointed admiral of England after leading the English fleet to victory. The cast includes the duc d'Alençon, the French prince who wanted to marry Elizabeth. The execution of Mary, queen of Scots, inspires Blanca, Essex's beloved, into plotting against the queen. He tries to trap the conspirators without involving Blanca but a letter falls into the queen's hands and it is this which condemns Essex. The 'ring' is not mentioned but the end scene is not unlike the other plays with Elizabeth arriving to save Essex and asking 'Donde esta el conde?' The Alcaide replies: 'Here he is as you had ordered' and discloses the headless Essex. The play ends with Elizabeth's speech of lamentation.[26]

CHAPTER 24

Patriots and popular heroes

Two Roman patriots, Mucius Scaevola and Regulus, are included in the subjects of plays in the Lille collection where the heroes are treated as Christian martyrs.[1] These are probably the oldest extant vernacular plays on Roman history. The Lille play of *Mucius Scaevola* is based on the account in Livy (Book II 12–13) of the vow taken by many young Romans to assassinate the Etruscan general Lars Porsenna who is besieging Rome. Mucius makes his way secretly into the Etruscan camp but cannot tell which of two richly robed men is the king and which his secretary. Unfortunately he kills the secretary.[2] He is captured and when Porsenna orders him to be burnt on the sacrificial altar like an ox or heifer, Mucius thrusts his right hand into the brasier and holds it there till it is consumed, saying: 'ceulx qui considèrent gloire / repute le corps . . . vile chose ('those who aspire to glory consider the body to be worthless').[3] Seeing his bravery Porsenna frees him and having learned from Mucius that he is one of three hundred Romans sworn to assassinate him, Porsenna lifts the siege and makes peace with Rome.[4]

REGULUS

The story of Regulus has been dramatised a number of times.[5] The Lille play begins when Attilius Regulus has already been a prisoner of the Carthaginians for five years. In an endeavour to end the war the Carthaginians plan an embassy to the Romans asking for a peace treaty and the return of the very large number of prisoners held by the Romans in exchange for Regulus himself. Thinking that the Romans will want to rescue Regulus 'qu'ils aiment parfaitement' (whom they truly love), they decide to send him with the embassy on the understanding that if he fails to achieve peace he will return to Carthage and certain, painful death. The jailer brings in Regulus who agrees to the terms and the embassy sets out for Rome. A narrator describes their journey – in order not to make the play too long – and apologises for them to be seen travelling on foot, since no one knows how they travelled.

The second scene begins as they approach Rome with Regulus rejoicing at the sight of the city for which he has suffered so much. He suggests they should go straight to the Senate as the proper place to meet the Romans. He is greeted with joy by many of the citizens. Hasdrubal explains their mission and the Senate then asks them to withdraw, leaving Regulus with the Senate to discuss the matter. They then ask Regulus for his opinion and he advises against the treaty because the Carthaginians are so exhausted that they can finally be defeated, especially if the prisoners are not returned to enhance their numbers of fighting men. One of them advises Regulus not to return to Carthage as they will be very angry with him. He insists he has never broken his word and will not now. Another Roman suggests he should at least see his wife and children first but he rejects the idea as abhorrent when he is still a prisoner. The Carthaginians are recalled and when they hear the verdict are angry. Hasdrubal tells Regulus he will regret it and Regulus knows he is going to suffer at the hands of tyrants, but nothing will make him break his word. The return journey is again described by the narrator.

Back in Carthage the embassy reports their failure which is probably due to Regulus. Avulcar (Hamilcar) declares he will be furious if Romulus is not put to death and all agree. With the help of the jailer, Avulcar prepares the torments of Regulus: his eyelids are to be slit and he is to be put in a narrow place surrounded by pointed nails so that he cannot avoid being pierced by them and will die slowly of hunger and in agony. The jailer agrees enthusiastically. He is shut in the prison and alone on the stage has a final speech in which he mentions his sufferings and his regret at not seeing his wife and friends again but he is resigned. What Fortune has chosen for him, has to be accepted. There is nothing more he can do except cease his lamentations.

The story of Regulus was very popular in the sixteenth and seventeenth centuries with plays in English, French and German. Jehan Beaubreuil's *Regulus* was published in Limoges in 1582. This play follows the Latin account closely. At the end, Regulus declares his intention of sacrificing himself for Rome as Mettus Curtius had done:

> Croyant qu'en ce faisant, si je souffre du mal
> J'auray loyer au Ciel a ma vertu egal.
>
> (Believing that if I suffer harm for acting thus, / I shall receive
>   in heaven a reward that equals my deed.)

The description of Regulus' death is given by a messenger in Rome: 'They sewed his eyelids so wide open that his eyelashes almost touched his hair.' As a result he could not sleep and died of exhaustion.

There is considerable difference between these first two plays and their later successors, all entitled *Regulus*. In the dedication of Pradon's tragedy of 1688 he explicitly declares his debt to '*le grand* Corneille', who had died in 1684 and refers to Louis' victories. The characters are all Roman and include Regulus' betrothed, Fulvie, as well as his son by his first marriage. The action is set in the Roman camp outside Carthage where Regulus has just been taken prisoner. A secondary plot involves a treacherous Roman, believed to be a friend of Regulus but actually his rival for the hand of Fulvie. The first three Acts are concerned with these plottings and Regulus does not appear till the fourth Act. He explains that he is so afraid the Romans would give way to the Carthaginians that he has come himself to ensure they do not, though he knows he will suffer for this. Regulus points out that if they exchange prisoners Carthage would benefit from a large number of fine soldiers. The Roman pro-consul and father of Fulvie tells Regulus he recognises in him 'un vray Romain'. They try to persuade Regulus not to return to Carthage but he insists that a man should prefer death to life as soon as that proves useful 'a la patrie'.

The ending is not historical: Regulus is taken back to Carthage by the pro-consul, who, as soon as Regulus is handed over (thus keeping his word), orders the Romans to attack. They mount the walls on ladders, pressing home their advantage when the dying Regulus is brought out, covered with blood from numerous wounds. The sight spurs them on and Regulus 'Meurt tranquillement pour sa chere patrie' (dies peacefully for his beloved country). Fulvie has the last word as she prepares to find death on the walls of Carthage.

John Crown's *Regulus* of 1694 also has a background of contemporary patriotism with references to the English naval victories against the French in the Mediterranean. Crown has followed Pradon in setting the play outside the walls of Carthage and he also includes the characters of Fulvie and her father. But he does not limit the cast to Romans but has a number of Carthaginians including Harbias, a luxurious priest, and Batto, a rich treacherous citizen who trades secretly with the Romans and flatters all sides for profit. That the Carthaginians are meant to represent the French is clear from a remark made by Regulus towards the end of the play when his friends are blocking his path to prevent him returning to Carthage and death. They finally give way and prepare to avenge him instead and Regulus says 'I was afraid that I had lost all my friends / . . . and that you slighted faith; which I believe / No *Roman* ever does, *except a Roman priest!*' (my italics) (This play on words is surely an attack on the Catholics.)

Crown also introduces a Spartan general, Xantippus, who has been appointed leader by the Carthaginians, who then turn on him when he condemns their treatment of Regulus. Regulus has great difficulty in keeping his word in this play, when Fulvia attacks him for giving himself up and swears he does not love her. She has a long scene of recriminations and laments which cause Regulus more pain than the prospects of the Carthaginians' tortures. Eventually she swoons which gives him a chance to return to Carthage. The Romans attack the city and led by Fulvie succeed in recovering the tortured Regulus: 'The SCENE is drawn and Regulus is discovered sitting in a chair, bloody.' He survives long enough to bid a fond farewell to Fulvia with a promise they will meet again in Elizium. Then he dies. Xantippus declares he will take his body to the Roman camp before leaving Carthage to return to Sparta.

It is notable that all these Regulus plays are performed in times of threat to the country and this is also seen in the German play of *Regulus* by Collin (1802). The action takes place in the Senate in Rome when Regulus has come with his embassy. Instead of pressing for peace as the Carthaginian ambassador hopes, he insists on the importance of continuing the attack on Carthage though he knows it will be his death. There is a moving scene of Regulus with his wife and young children but generally the play, performed in the middle of the Napoleonic wars, lays all its stress on the fatherland and the need for patriotism.

WILLIAM TELL

The popular hero is also a patriot but not usually a tragic one, as can be seen in the plays of the Swiss hero, Wilhelm Tell. Two sixteenth-century plays, one anonymous, known as the *Urner Tellspiel* (1520–4) and the second *Das neuer Tellenspiel* by Jakob Ruf (1545) present very similar versions of the well-known story of Tell's failure to salute the hat of the Austrian overlord and being made to shoot an apple off his son's head.[6] In both cases Tell then escapes from the boat which is carrying him to prison and kills the overlord. The *Urner Tellspiel* is only 800 lines long and presented without scene breaks. After Tell's escape about half way through the play, the author uses single narrators to describe the meeting of the Swiss at the *grütli* meadow where they all swear an oath to fight together against tyranny. Ruf's play is more than 2,000 lines, divided into five Acts, with the episode of the hat and the apple divided between Acts II and III, which breaks the tension. Act III also includes Tell's arrest and escape by leaping out of the boat. Acts IV and V then dramatise in some detail the meeting and discussion at the Grütli and the swearing of the oath. A Zürich play of 1514 had already presented a strictly political treatment of the forming of the Swiss confederation – die Eidgenossenschaft – in which a number of famous Roman patriots including Horatius Cocles and Mucius Scaevola praise the efforts of the Swiss to achieve their independence and freedom from foreign domination.[7] The defence against foreign powers is also seen in the story of the English Guy of Warwick, who fought and defeated the Danish Champion, and was the hero of a Latin Jesuit play performed at St Omer's in 1623 (McCabe, p. 84).

ROBIN HOOD

Robin Hood, however, the most popular of English heroes, is fighting for the people against the tyranny of native rulers. In the Middle Ages many festive events were linked with his name, including church ales and other fund-raising events.[8] There are also a few actual plays including the fifteenth century *Robin Hood and the sheriff of Nottingham*, the May game plays printed by William Copland in c. 1560 in two parts, *RH and the friar*, followed by *RH and the potter*. *Robin Hood and Little John*, a pastoral comedy, is recorded from 1594.[9] George Peele's *Famous chronicle history of king Edward the First* (1593) is mainly set in Wales. A group of Welsh rebels take on the names of Robin and his band. Friar David ap Tuck introduces to the king: 'Our thrice renowned Lluellen, Prince of Wales and Robin Hood of the great mountain.'[10] Edward takes the opportunity to try to settle the warfare between the Welsh and the English by creating the first prince of Wales.

Two Robin Hood plays by Anthony Munday were staged in 1598. *The downfall of Robert earl of Huntingdon* and *The death of Robert earl of Huntingdon*.[11] In the first play, the earl earns the enmity of prince John by supporting the cause of those oppressed by John when he is ruling during Richard's absence from England. He becomes the famous outlaw, Robin Hood, with his followers, including Little John, Much the miller's son, Scarlet and Friar Tuck. Marian, his betrothed, also appears for the first time (later in the play she is renamed Matilda). John tries to win Marian but she rejects him. At the end of the play king Richard returns and, at the earl's request, pardons John for his attempt to seize the crown. In *The death of the earl of Huntingdon*, John, still smarting from the earl's behaviour to him and still desperate to win Matilda, manages to arrange for the earl to be poisoned on the eve of his marriage. Soon after news comes of Richard's death in Austria and John becomes king. Despite the presence of his queen, Isobel of France, John still pursues Matilda, who defeats him eventually by taking the veil and when he threatens the nunnery, she takes poison.[12]

FROM MARTYR TO CHAMPION: ST GEORGE OF ENGLAND: A UNIQUE CASE

Patriotism in English drama is represented above all by Shakespeare's Henry V, with his battle cry: 'God for Harry, England and St George.' There are lost plays of St George recorded by Harbage from the fifteenth and early sixteenth centuries which are probably all concerned with dragon slaying as is suggested from the cast list for a York play which includes a king and queen, a daughter and a dragon.[13] However, in the 1530s pope Clement VII ordered 'the excision of the dragon-story from the office-books of the Church, and pronounced that George was thenceforth to be venerated for his martyrdom alone'.[14] This seems to have been the cue for the development of a revised St George, who from being a Byzantine martyr became not merely a champion of England but a true Englishman, born in Coventry, who has a long and successful career as a knight errant.

The inventor of this new St George seems to be Richard Johnson, the author of *The seven champions of Christendom* first published in 1596–7.[15] Accompanied by six other patron saints – Andrew, Patrick, David, Denis of France, James of Compostella and Anthony of Padua – he travels round Europe and the Mediterranean, freeing prisoners, taking part in tournaments and killing magicians and dragons. He also rescues and marries the princess Sabra of Egypt. They have three sons. At the end of Part I of *Seven champions*, George invites the other six saints to return with him 'home to his countrie of England'.[16] At the beginning of Book II, Sabra is killed in a hunting accident. The rest of the book describes the adventures of George's sons. There's no account of George's death, as the result of a battle with another dragon, until the end of the 1611 edition of Part II.

One possible answer to the inevitable question 'Why Coventry'? may be the existence of the Coventry St George:

The Coventry St George is polychromed oak and mid-to late fifteenth century. This figure formerly stood in a gate chapel on the city walls of Coventry, where it probably reflected the contemporary identification of St George as a figure of authority and urban government, crushing the threat of chaos and disorder embodied by the dragon. It is a rare survival of an English image of a saint carved in wood.'[17]

The story of St George the dragon-slayer, as told by Johnson, is the basis of many of the English mumming plays which include some of the other patron saints and the princess Sabra. There is no certain evidence of these folk plays before the eighteenth century but they still survive today.[18] St George remained a popular saint on the continent as well. In Mons, the capital of Hainault, an annual celebration, held on Trinity Sunday and dating back to the fourteenth century, was revived in the nineteenth century. Nowadays the 'Ducasse' starts with a procession of the reliquary of St Waudrue, patroness of Mons, which is followed by a battle of St George against the dragon (called the 'lumeçon') on the Grand Place where so many medieval plays were performed. He finally dispatches the dragon with a pistol shot (Cohen, *Mons*, p. x). A recent postcard shows St George on horseback, dressed in a uniform similar to the English Lifeguards.

Conclusion: from Queen of Heaven to Fairy Queen

CHANGING FORTUNES OF THE VIRGIN MARY

The changes in the legend of St George from saint and martyr in the eighth century, to knight errant and champion of the weak in the sixteenth and folk hero in the twentieth encapsulates the evolution of the dramatic presentation of the triumph of good over evil. The former, whether represented by saints, angels or the Virgin Mary, must triumph over the pagan tyrant, wicked step-mother or the Devil.

In the seventeenth and eighteenth centuries, European drama passed through many changes of subject matter and treatment. One important development was the almost total disappearance of the miraculous Christian element. The Virgin Mary disappeared at the end of the sixteenth century because the Protestants rejected her, the Catholics thought her too important to put on the public stage and the growing secularisation of society found her irrelevant. Her fellow miracle worker, St Nicholas, found a new role as the patron saint of children to whom he gave gifts, and eventually Santa Claus became Father Christmas. The other saints and martyrs rarely appeared on the stage especially after the papal suppression of the Society of Jesus in 1773.[1]

However, the revival of interest in traditional stories and medieval romance and the growing cult of the fairy story in France in the seventeenth century reintroduced the concept of the supernatural and the importance of magical interference in human affairs. The result was the appearance of that unique combination of Christian and secular helper-in-need, the Fairy Godmother.[2] The *fée* had of course already appeared on stage many centuries earlier in the thirteenth-century *Jeu de la feuillée* which features Morgan Le Fay of Arthurian romance in a scene reminiscent of Sleeping Beauty. Adam de la Halle's play (c. 1270) has some claim to be considered the oldest extant romance drama. After scenes of mingled comedy and satire there is a change of mood: three fées, Morgan le fay, Morgue and Arsile, represented as 'de belles *dames*, *richement parees*', visit the town of Arras and find a meal waiting for them, prepared by Adam and his friend. They decide to reward their benefactors with favours. But unfortunately one of them has no knife. The table-setting or *couvert* was always the cause of the wicked fairy's ill-wishing of the heroine in the French versions of Sleeping Beauty. As a result, when the other two *fées* give favours to their hosts, the disappointed one gives only what may amount to a curse.[3] The addition of the Christian title 'Godmother' was new and was used alternately with the simpler title.

It is the plot structure which made the stories work in the first place and allowed the dramatised versions to hold their popularity for so many centuries. Under a variety of different forms – from miracle plays to opera and ballet, pantomimes and Disney cartoons, the folk-cum-fairy tale with its happy ending retains its popularity with the public.[4] A good plot where justice and innocence triumph at the end of a series of diversions and complications, can carry a play with an audience even if the characters and dialogue are familiar: Agatha Christie's *The mouse trap* has been running in London for more than fifty years.

The classical deities who dominated court masques and ballets in the reign of Louis XIV were replaced in the eighteenth century by fairy tale characters for ballets and, in the time of the Romantics, in opera. It is interesting that in *Cenerentola*, Rossini replaces Cinderella's traditional godmother by a man, but his support of the heroine is still based on her goodness, implying a moral element in the plot which links it to the persecuted innocents of the medieval romances. The final evolution of the *fée* occurred in the nineteenth century when Planché introduced his fairy tale extravaganzas from which the modern English Christmas pantomime has developed, complete with those warring monarchs, the Fairy Queen and the Demon King. The Devil was never barred from the stage as can be seen in the Faust plays, and operas, but his conqueror has passed through a number of transformations.

'Last stage of all' in the dramatisation of these tales took place in the twentieth century when first the cinema, then television, stressed the importance of spectacle to accompany the ancient role of the story-teller. The romances were illustrated and the epics restaged. Fairy tales were animated and animals talked. The ancient battle of good and evil was reinterpreted. Graham Greene once suggested that the detective story is the modern fairy tale, in which case we may wonder if there is any significance in the fact that the most frequently dramatised of female detectives, Agatha Christie's Miss Marple, happens to live in a village called St Mary Mead.

Notes

INTRODUCTION: STAGING THE STORIES

1. I am grateful to Alan Knight for sending me advance copies of relevant plays from the not yet published 4th and 5th volumes of the *Mystères de Lille*.
2. Peter Meredith, 'A tale of two plays', in *Mainte belle œuvre faite*, p. 407.
3. Graham Runnalls, 'Le dernier mystère originale', in *Mémoire en temps advenir. Hommage à Theo Venckeleer* (Leuven, 2003), p. 153.
4. In a few examples the story is followed through even to the eighteenth century.
5. See the table on p. 91 of Alan Knight, *Aspects of genre* (Manchester, 1983).
6. Only in farces and other similar play types was the author free to 'make up' the story from scratch and even then the basic material is often recognisable. Whether the transmisison of these stories was verbal or written is a subject beyond the scope of this book.
7. For details of the Paris Goldsmith's guild's Confraternity of Notre-Dame-de-l'Annonciation, see R. Clark, 'The "Miracles de Nostre Dame par personnages" of the Cangé manuscript and the sociocultural function of confraternity drama', UMI dissertation services, 1994, pp. 113–15. The Cangé miracles are based on well-known stories whose sources Clark lists in Appendix I, pp. 222–5.
8. The largest French collection of Marian miracles is the work of the twelfth-century poet, Gautier de Coinci, but there are many other extant versions of these stories. An important group of sixteenth-century miracle plays are those by Louvet (see p. 233 n. 42).
9. See Black.
10. For a survey and list of extant French saints' plays see Lynette R. Muir, 'The saint play in medieval France', in *The saint play in medieval Europe*, ed. C. David son, EDAM monograph series, 8 (Kalamazoo, 1986), pp. 123–80. There are only two extant English saints' plays but for details of many of the lost texts see Davidson's 'The Middle English saint play and its iconography' in ibid., pp. 31–122. The very large numbers of surviving MSS and early printed texts of Italian plays are listed in Cioni, *Bibliografia delle sacre rappresentazioni*, Biblioteca bibliografia Italica, 22 (Florence, 1961). The half-dozen surviving saints' plays in German are printed in Ukena, and records of lost texts are

included in Von Bernd Neumann's *Geistliche Schauspiele im Zeugnis der Zeit. Zur Aufführung Mitteralterlicher religiöser Dramen im deutschen Sprachgebiet*, 2 vols. (Munich, 1987), and R. Bergmann's *Katalog der deutschsprachigen geistlichen spiele und Marienklagen des Mittelalters* (Munich, 1986). Hansjürgen Linke's article 'A survey of medieval drama and theater in Germany', in *Medieval drama on the continent of Europe*, ed. Clifford Davidson and John Stroupe, Medieval Institute Publications (Kalamazoo, 1993), n. 81, gives a list of performances of saints' plays including some from the sixteenth century. There is no single source for the quite substantial number of extant Spanish texts, but information about staging and performance is in N. D. Shergold, *A history of the Spanish stage from medieval times until the end of the seventeenth century* (Oxford and London, 1967) and McKendrick.

11. This is the earliest recorded occasion when a girl took the lead in a public play. A gentleman in the audience was so impressed by her performance that he married her. See TIE *Medieval*, E.104. In France, women acted in travelling companies and civic plays from the beginning of the sixteenth century.

12. See Helen Cooper in *Sources and analogues of the Canterbury tales*, ed. R. M. Correale 2 vols. (Cambridge, 2002–5), p. 19.

13. Published in *Musique et arts plastiques*, PUPS (Paris, 2005). I am grateful to Elsa Strietman for bringing this article to my attention.

14. For details of the Rhetoricians and their play contests see TIE *Medieval*, G. (the Low Countries), and Lynette R. Muir, 'Rhetoricians and the francophone tradition', in *Urban theatre in the Low Countries 1400–1625*, ed. Elsa Strietman and Peter Happe (Brepols, 2006).

15. E. B. Weaver, *Convent theatre in early modern Italy, spiritual fun and learning for women* (Cambridge, 2002).

16. John L. Flood, 'Hans Sachs and Boccaccio' (p. 152), in *Hans Sachs and folk theatre in the late Middle Ages. Studies in the history of popular culture*, ed. R. Aylett and P. Skrine (Lampeter, 1995). These latter plays were performed in St Martha's church in Nuremburg (then secularised) as a way of raising money for the School of Mastersingers.

17. The audiences of the Madrid theatres demanded two new plays a week and Lope alone claimed to have written 1,500 plays, of which more than 400 have survived. For the development of the theatre in Madrid see H. A. Rennert, *The life of Lope de Vega* (Glasgow, 1904; repr. 1937), ch. 6. Rennert mentions that although women's roles were at first played by boys as in England, from 1587 onwards married women were allowed on the stage in the same company as their husband (ibid., p. 127).

18. McCabe, p. 47. McCabe discusses many aspects of the drama, from choice of subject to the elaborate staging. He also gives particular details of the performances at the English college of St Omers, situated in the town of St-Omer in north-west France (which had also a normal local Jesuit college). St Omers was intended for English Catholic boys and also accepted 'heretics'. It was well known in the early sixteenth century and some of its play-texts,

based on specifically English subjects like Guy of Warwick, are preserved in the modern Jesuit college of Stonyhurst. (See Lynette R. Muir, *The biblical drama of medieval Europe* (Cambridge, 1995), p. 213.)

19. The plot is summarised Act by Act and scene by scene in parallel lines of Latin and German. Some 600 of these programme notes are printed and discussed by Szarota in her six-volume work on *Jesuitendrama*.

20. A general study of the plays from German-speaking countries is made by Valentin. The third volume of this wide-ranging work includes 200 pages of bibliographies both on Jesuit matters and on the stories used by them.

21. Boysse, pp. 79ff.

22. For the French drama see Clarence D. Brenner, *L'histoire nationale dans la tragédie française du dixhuitième siècle* (Berkeley, 1929).

PART ONE: INTRODUCTORY SECTION

1. Throughout this book I have used the English forms of saints' names except for specific quotations or titles. For the present state of hagiography, unless otherwise stated I have used the latest edition of *The book of Saints*, compiled by the Benedictines of Ramsgate (London, 1989). It is notable that many of the more interesting legends of the saints which feature in the plays were rejected by the Church in the 1969 revisions.

2. Plays of the Acts of the Apostles treated in Muir, *Biblical drama*, will be omitted here, though there are substantial additions to the group in Henrard, especially a *Mystère de St Barthelemy* which includes a number of elements from the traditional stories, such as his mother being falsely accused of adultery (p. 381). For a detailed treatment of this theme see Part Three. An elaborate *festa* of S. Bartelemeo was performed in Florence in 1471 (Newbigin, p. 139).

3. The play includes episodes of Meriasek's life in Cornwall and Brittany and some separate miracles (see p. 43). Plays on the early spread of Christianity after the conversions of Constantine are considered in Part Three.

1 THE NOBLE ARMY OF MARTYRS

1. The abbey of Gandersheim was directly held from the king and the abbess had the status and role of a feudal baron. In Hrotsvitha's time the position was held by a niece of emperor Otho I. Although the nuns kept the rule of St Benedict, they were members of the nobility and highly educated. Hrotsvitha specifically claims Terence as the inspiration for her plays.

2. The Latin text of Hrotsvitha's plays was published with great success by Conrad Celtes in 1501. All quotations are taken from Christopher St John's *The plays of Roswitha* (New York, 1966), translated (and some of them performed) before World War I, but not published till after World War II. The translator refers to several performances of the plays and also lists published editions in Latin and French. *Dulcitius* was performed, in Latin, at the Leeds SITM foundation meeting in 1974.

3. For the hermit plays see pp. 22–6.
4. This episode is reminiscent of the story of Jovinianus, see pp. 180–2.
5. For the *perioche* of three Jesuit plays on the story of Gallicanus see Szarota, I, 1, pp. 135–66. In 1969 the cult of Giovanni and Paolo was limited to their local church.
6. For the legend of St Sapientia (more usually called by her Greek name, Sophia) and her three daughters Faith, Hope and Charity see *Legenda* (30 September).
7. The explanation of uneven and even numbers, diminished, etc., occupies four pages in the translation.
8. In her article 'Agata, Appollonia and other martyred virgins', *EMD*, 1 (1997), pp. 175–97, Nerida Newbigin discusses the likelihood that the many Italian plays of the torture of virgin martyrs were designed for reading rather than performance.
9. The stage directions for this scene are translated in TIE *Medieval*, p. 172. Here and in other 'brothel' plays, the heroine converts the prostitutes and/or the men who come there. Shakespeare's Marina in *Pericles* has a similar effect on her 'clients'. See Bullough, VI, *Pericles*, for the various texts on the subject.
10. Ciono lists fifteen editions through to the seventeenth century. *Théodore vierge et martyr* by Pierre Corneille was published in Paris in 1646. The Cangé *Ste Theodore* is a different story altogether; see p. 108.
11. She is not mentioned in England but her 'castle' was part of a Corpus Christi procession in Dumfries, Scotland, in 1450 (Lancashire, 1653).
12. The French plays (*Mystères*, II, pp. 478–88) are not yet published, but partial texts and details are available in Mario Longtin's thesis: 'Edition critique de la cinquième journée du mystère de sainte Barbe' (doctoral thesis, Edinburgh, 2001). There is an Italian play (D'Ancona, II, and twelve editions listed by Cioni, *Bibliografia*) and a Spanish *Auto del martyrio de sancta Barbara* (Rouanet, II, pp. 79–90). For conversion in a tower, see p. 26.
13. Not surprisingly, there are few school or Jesuit plays on female saints but an interesting series of references to such plays is to be found in Weaver.
14. The brothers were the patron saints of shoemakers and their plays are usually staged by a shoemakers guild.
15. References to special effects for these plays are in Meredith and Tailby. A number of plays are also mentioned in the different language section of TIE *Medieval*. A number of little-known saints were specially honoured in their native cities, such as the *Trois Doms* at Romans in 1515 whose play is more famous for having one of the most detailed and complete sets of surviving accounts than for the names of the saints. For English summaries of a number of Italian saints' plays see Kathleen Falvi 'The Italian saint play', in *The saint play in medieval Europe* ed. Davidson.
16. In the French play of St Laurent, his companion, St Hippolyte, is torn apart by wild horses see TIE *Medieval*, E.58.
17. Lion skins for these roles were freely available because great men often kept menageries. See Lynette R. Muir, 'René d'Anjou and the theatre in

Provence', *EMD*, 3 (1999). Bears are more common in the romances like Valentine and Orson. See p. 96.

18. *S. Venanzio* is an unusual saints' play for although Venanzio resists all efforts to make him renounce Christ, he allows himself to complain of the suffering he is enduring and finally begs Christ to spare him more torture (Castellani Castellano, ed. *La rappresentazione di San Venanzio*, Nerida Newbigin (Camerino, 2000), p. 54).

19. David Scott Fox, *Saint George. The saint with three faces* (Windsor Forest, Berkshire, 1983), provides a useful outline of the history of the cult of St George.

20. Cit. Christopher Walter in *The warrior saints in Byzantine art and tradition* (Aldershot, 2003), p. 112.

21. For a general survey of St George plays see Muir, 'The saint play in medieval France', pp. 146–52.

22. For plays on Edward III and the Order of the Garter, see Part Three, p. 117.

23. A *Jeu de monseigneur St Georges*, performed on the Grand Place at Mons in 1491 by the *confrairie S. Georges*, may have included both the dragon and the martyrdom (Cohen, *Mons*, p. xv). For the background to the episode of the dragon see Walter, *Warrior saints*, pp. 140ff. He makes it quite clear that there is no connection with the story of Perseus and Andromeda and that the event took place during George's lifetime. It is not a post-mortem miracle.

24. Not all the titles are identical so there may also be some variations in the texts. Only four stanzas survive of Feo Belcari's fifteenth-century *St Giorgio ferisce el drago*.

25. For details of these performances during the 1420s, the period of English domination in France, see Muir, 'The saint play in medieval France', pp. 149–50. Stegmann lists performances of a Jesuit play of St George in 1562, 1586, 1589 and 1609. These seem all to be martyrdom plays.

26. For the Spanish *auto* see Rouanet, XXVI; the German play is in Ukena, I, pp. 384–439.

27. The school play is listed by Stegmann among the non-Jesuit plays (p. 667). The Jesuit text has a French title: *St George combattant le dragon*. As Gratz is in German-speaking Austria I conclude that the text is untitled and has been given a suitable descriptive title in French by Stegmann.

28. In the French play, St Margaret defeats her own dragon in fine style – see Muir, 'The saint play in medieval France'. St George was also venerated in the Burgundian Netherlands.

29. Neumann, *Geistliches Schauspiel*, p. 296.

30. The most useful survey of the hagiographical sources is H. Delehaye's *Légende de St Eustache* (Mélanges d'hagiographie Grecque et latine), *Subsidia Hagiographie*, 42 (1966). pp. 212–39) in which he lists all the different MSS in Greek and Latin as well as the vernacular versions in prose and verse and concludes that the source is definitely not historical but will be found in the *contes populaires* from which so many legends have descended. Following this conclusion, Delehaye goes on to indicate the many oriental stories with similar elements.

31. A *spel van Senta Joos Staess* is included in the list of plays belonging to the Dutch guild of St Kathelinen in the fifteenth century. (*Spel en spektakel*, p. 123); a play of *Placy Dacy als St Ewe Stacy* was performed in Braintree, Essex, to raise funds for church building in 1534 (Lancashire, 1523) and the representation of *Santo Stagio* was performed by the boys of the Purification company in Florence during carnival-tide in 1477 (Newbigin, p. 144). A lost French play of S. Eustace is listed as item 193 in a fifteenth-century Tours bookseller's catalogue (*Mainte belle œuvre faite*, p. 405). Stegmann records a school performance at Louvain in 1631 and Jesuit school performances at Evora (1635) and Malines (1636). Jesuit plays of St Eustace were performed in Germany over a period of 180 years from 1584 to 1766 (Szarota, II, 2, p. 2269).

32. 'They are put in the bull and a cloud comes down from the sky and carries away their souls, singing.'

33. Extensive extracts from the diary (with English translation) are included in Mara Nerbano's 'Play and record: Ser Tomasso di Silvestro and the theatre of Medieval and early modern Orvieto', *EMD*, 8, (2004) pp. 127–72. Several other saints' plays are mentioned, mostly of local saints.

34. For details of the *Moralitas* and the cult of Eustace in Provence see Henrard, pp. 264–76, and J. Chocheyras, *Le théâtre religieux en Dauphiné du Moyen Age au XVIIIe siècle* (Geneva, 1975), pp. 88–90. There were several French plays of St Eustache in the seventeenth century, including one by the Belgian, Pierre Bello, in Liège in 1632 (Lancaster, I, ii, p. 679). A play by the Jesuit-educated Nicholas Desfontaines was performed in 1642 and another play on the subject, by Baro, was published in 1649. Baro omits the Job parallels, the second emperor and the lions and draws a comparison between the execution of Eustace and that of Charles I of England (Lancaster, II, i, p. 174).

35. Chocheyras, *Dauphiné*, pp. 172–6.

36. St Hubert (3 November, not included in the *Legenda*) was an eighth-century courtier who entered religion and became bishop of Maestrecht. According to a late legend he was converted by seeing the stag with the crucifix and was punished for spending too much time hunting. He shares the emblem of the stag and crucifix with Eustace.

37. I have used the forms of the names found in the English *Legenda*. They vary slightly but not substantially from the spellings in Latin, Greek and French.

38. The theme of the testing of the hero and the need for patience links Eustace with Job – indeed for the Jesuits he became the New Job – and particularly with the *Testament of Job*, a late Greek variation on the story where Job wants to destroy a temple dedicated to the Devil but is warned by God that if he does so he will have to endure the Devil's wrath and revenge. However, God assures him that he will be rewarded eventually if he endures the suffering without rejecting God. For details of this and other Job stories see my article: 'The sufferings of impatient Job', in *Mainte belle œuvre faite*, pp. 419–20. Many of the Testament details are found also in the *La vie de Saint Eustace*, ed. Jessie Murray, CFMA (Paris, 1929), a thirteenth-century French prose translation of the Latin *Vita*.

39. These events can be paralleled in the opening chapter of the Book of Job.
40. The adventures of Eustace and his family have many parallels in romance and especially in the English tale of *Sir Isumbras* and the French *Guillaume d'Angleterre* which are secular versions of the Eustace legend. There are many studies on the subject. Laura Braswell, '"Sir Isumbras" and the legend of Saint Eustace', *Medieval Studies*, 27 (1965), pp. 128–51, is one of the more recent and includes a good bibliography.
41. This part of the story between the conversion and the martyrdom of Eustace and his family is a classic tale of a family separated and eventually reunited. In many ways it is the reversal of the accused queen story (see Part Three) for here it is the husband who is forcibly separated from first his wife and then his children who, like Valentine and Orson, are carried off by wild animals and brought up as strangers to each other and their parents. The animals in this story do not bring up the children, who are rescued and reared by shepherds, but it is noticeable that the animals mentioned, especially the wolf, are the classic rearers of lost children from Romulus and Remus to Kipling's Mowgli. As Antigonus reminds himself when orderd to abandon Perdita, 'Wolves and bears they say . . . have done like offices of pity' (*Winter's tale*, Act II, scene 3).
42. Genesius (I have used the Latin form throughout except in direct quotations) is not in the *Legenda*, but the undated Latin *Passio* is included in the *Acta Sanctorum* for 25 August. I have used the translation of the *Passio* in Oscar M. Villarejo, 'Lope de Vega and the Elizabethan and Jacobean drama' (Doctoral dissertation, 1953, UMI dissertation services, Ann Arbor), pp. 440–1.
43. The first martyrs to be saved by the 'baptism of blood' were the Holy Innocents – the children killed by Herod's soldiers. In a royal entry of 1484 in Paris there was a scene of Herod and the Innocents where the archangel Gabriel 'baptise les aisnels en leur sang don't Dieu est loué' (baptises the lambs in their blood to the glory of God). Cit. Josephe Chartrou, *Les entrées solennelles et triomphales à la renaissance 1484–1551* (Paris, 1883), p. 21.
44. The references to the instruments and the use of the term 'ludant' suggests a musical performance rather than a play.
45. The only surviving MS is full of annotations and repetitions which suggest it was a producer's copy used on several different occasions, but no performances of the play are recorded and no printed edition was published. It was edited by Mostert and Stengel in 1895.
46. A Jesuit play on a similar subject was Bidermann's *Philemon* (1608) based on the story of an Egyptian comic actor who was martyred in the early days of Christianity. The play, like *St Genis*, develops scenes of a clash between the Roman gods led by a statue of Jupiter and the Christians who destroy the statues. Philemon is an actor but not converted by acting as is Genesius (Best, *Bidermann*, pp. 114–39). In *Künstler Grübler und Rebellen. Studien zum Europäischen Martyrdrama des 17 Jahrhunderts* (Bern and Munich), a study of martyrdom plays in the baroque period, Szarota compares *Philemon* with the Genesius plays of Lope de Vega, Rotrou and Desfontaines.

47. Weaver, p. 70 n. 64. He also wrote a play on St Agata sometime between 1614 and 1623 and probably *S. Ginesio* was written during the same period. See Antonio Grimaldi, *Il chiostro e la scena. Michelangelo Buonarroti il giovane e il Convento Di Sant'Agata*, Studi Italiani, XI (1998), pp. 149–98.

48. All citations are from the translation by Michael McGaha, entitled *Acting is believing* (San Antonio, Tex., 1986). I am most grateful to Professor McGaha for sending me a photocopy of his out-of-print text which includes an extensive introduction on Lope's life and works.

49. The story of Diocletian and the prophetess, probably taken from Vopiscus, is also the basis of Fletcher and Massinger's play *The prophetess* (1622).

50. Performed in Paris c. 1645. For Rotrou's debt to Lope, see Ladborough's introduction (*Le véritable St Genest* (Paris, 1988), pp. xiv–xv).

51. The martyrdom of *St Hadrian and his companions* (*Legenda* 8 September, cult limited to local church in 1969) took place in the reign of Maximin. He was a Roman soldier in charge of imprisoned Christians who was converted by their faith and martyred with them, together with his wife, Natalie, who has a major role in the *Legenda* and in the French play *St Adrien* written in 1485 (*Mystères*, II, p. 466).

52. Bidermann's *Adrianus* is known only from *perioche*. Act IV shows the on-stage martyrdom of Adrian: his feet are crushed and his hand cut off; his wife Natalia follows the corpse, catching the dripping blood and seeking relics: Natalia is the most dominant woman in any of Bidermann's plays (Best, *Bidermann*, pp. 120–1).

53. He is generally accepted as the same person as the actor who played with Molière in 1635 (Lancaster, II, i, p. 78) and headed a troupe of actors – the *Troupe Desfontaines* which performed in Nantes in 1651 (Lancaster, I, ii, p. 704).

54. While deciding what to act for the emperor, Genesius cites the stories of Dardaleon and Porphyrie 'who followed our profession'. Dardaleon and Porphyrie are mentioned in the *Passio*. The former is not listed in BSS but the latter was an actor who was converted, while acting a mockery of Christian baptism before Julian the Apostate (BSS 15 September).

55. For a detailed account of the festivities see Bertha von der Lage, *Studien zur Genesiuslegende* (Berlin, 1898–9), pp. 12–14.

56. James A. Parente, *Religious drama and the Humanist tradition. Christian theater in Germany and in the Netherlands 1500–1680* (Leyden, 1987) pp. 140–1. Vondel was an Anabaptist converted to Catholicism.

57. Szarota, III, p. 329. Stegmann lists a performance of *Genesius* by Laski at Poznan in 1619, and others at Fribourg (Switzerland) in 1634 and at Malines in 1638 without any details.

58. St Genesius is mentioned in the title of the second version but he does not feature in the play except for references by the Spaniards to the Chapel of St Genesius in a church in Madrid dedicated to the Virgin Mary, the Aurora of the play, who appears in visions to the Incas. I am grateful to Penny Robinson for help in analysing this unusual text.

59. Villarejo, 'Lope de Vega', p. 339. Ed. cit. vol. III, p. 3, sources. In addition to Suetonius and other Latin historians, Massinger has made use of a range of stories including the theme of the woman scorned which is echoed by Domitia's anger when Paris rejects her advances.

60. Villarejo, 'Lope de Vega', p. 342.

2 WHITE MARTYRDOM – THE HERMITS

1. Although I have given references to the *Legenda* for these stories, Hrotsvitha would have used one of the early Latin works on the lives of the Desert Fathers.

2. For a play on a hermit who despaired and turned to sin see Tirso de Molina, *El condenado por desconfiado*.

3. The scene is common in art including the celebrated triptych by Jeronimus Bosch.

4. Cioni, *Bibliografia*, lists the printed editions, some of which have detailed summaries of the play. The Italian text is published in D'Ancona, II, and an English translation by J. W. Cook is published in *Florentine drama*. The *Legenda* includes a series of miracles and marvels connected with the saint and drawn from the *Lives of the Fathers*.

5. In the *Le cento novelle antiche*, LXXXIII (Milan, 1825), the story is told of Christ with his disciples. When they want to take the gold he tells them this is the material 'che toglie al regno nostro la maggiore parte de l'anime' (which takes the greater part of the souls from our kingdom). The following day they pass by again and see two men who have killed each other for the money.

6. The same story is the subject of *Der Tod im Stock*, a Shrovetide play by Hans Sachs which is printed in W. F. Bryan and Germaine Dempster's *Sources and analogues of Chaucer's Canterbury tales* (Chicago, 1941; repr. New York and London, 1958), pp. 429–36. D'Ancona also refers to a legend of the Buddha who, seeing a precious treasure lying on the ground, referred to it as a 'venomous snake'.

7. Henrard, pp. 234–63. Henrard mentions a reference to a performance of a play of St Anthony at Compiègne in 1457, the *Vie et invention de sainte Antoine*, but rejects any link with the Provençal play which does not include the 'Invention' or discovery and veneration of the relics of the saint (p. 263).

8. 'Quant a la mise en scene de l'intervention de l'oiseau elle est laissée à l'inspiration du meneur de jeu' (the staging of the bird's appearance is left to the director's inspiration) (Henrard, p. 256).

9. D'Ancona, II. The story of Onofrio alternates with a series of scenes of everyday life with innkeepers and robbers. Onuphrius (BSS 12 June) was the patron saint of weavers because he wore only a mat of hair and loin cloth of leaves. Panuzio is probably Paphnutius, a hermit (BSS 12 September), said to be the father of the woman hermit, St Euphrosyne, whose life is

dramatised in the Lille plays (*Lille*, v). Cioni mentions a fifteenth-century play by an unknown author and twelve printed editions up to 1610.

10. The Cangé spelling of the name is a corruption of 'poilu', hairy, but the original form in the French thirteenth-century texts (see n. 12) is Jehan Paulus. There is no Latin source. The play calls him simply Jehan which led to some interesting later developments of the story.

11. Losing contact with a hunting party is a common opening of a story, in both saints' plays and romances.

12. An account of the German legends of these strange penitents is given in Charles Allyn Williams, *The German legends of the Hairy Anchorite* (Urbana, Ill., 1935), which also includes two narrative versions of the French story of St Jean Paulus. Williams includes many illustrations of the story by Dürer and other major artists of the fifteenth to sixteenth centuries showing Jehan as the animal and the princess with her child, often sitting on a rock.

13. The play is described by Hummelen in the *Repertorium*, item 7 18. *Jan van Beverley* (published in Brussels by Boekenoogen, 1903).

14. For other examples of these motifs see the woman scorned (p. 106) and the severed hand (p. 93). There is an element of truth behind these stories in that Chrysostom, as bishop of Constantinople, was in a constant conflict with the empress Eudoxia and many churchmen over the Aryan controversy (*Legenda* 27 January).

15. St John Damascene, *Barlaam and Joasaph*. See also Hippolyte Delehaye, *The Legends of the saints*, trans. Donald Attwater, with new introduction by Thomas O'Loughlin (Dublin, 1998), p. 51. In the AASS, among the *rejecti* for 2 April there is listed Barlaam, hermit and confessor, with the note 'Nobis ignotus nisi sit Barlaaam qui cum Josaphat in India vixit' (unknown to us unless this is the Barlaam who lived in India with Josaphat).

16. Several printed editions of each play are listed by Cioni up to 1655. A performance of the Barlaam play in San Marco (Venice) in September 1474 is listed by Newbigin (p. 142). It was also a popular subject with the Jesuits. School performances of *Barlaam and Josaphat* are listed by Stegmann in 1571, 1591, 1602 (2), 1613, 1616 and 1620. Andrzej Dabrowka 'Polish saint plays of the sixteenth and seventeenth centuries', *EDAM Review*, 23:1 (2000), pp. 23–4, lists a Jesuit *Barlaam* in Latin at Poznan 1616, with c. fifty performances. Bidermann's *Josaphatus rex* follows the standard story by John Damascene but omits the temptation by women. Performances are recorded in Innsbruck and Eichstatt (Szarota, II, 2, pp. 1645, 1721).

17. In the history of the Buddha there is a description of one of his incarnations in which he is the son of a king who is told that the child 'will become an ascetic as the result of seeing old age, sickness, death and a hermit'. The king does not want the child to become an ascetic so he has him kept in a guarded palace full of delights and where the words 'sorrow' and 'death' may not be mentioned. (*Myths of the Hindus and Buddhists*, by the Sister Nivedita and Ananda K. Coomaraswamy (London, 1913), p. 261).

18. I am grateful to Nerida Newbigin for sending me a copy of an unpublished Italian play about a king's son, named Tiberio, which includes many details probably borrowed from Barlaam and Josaphat.

19. In the story of the martyrs Daria and Grisante (*Legenda* 25 October) the latter's father also tries women to turn his son away from Christianity but in vain.

20. The name, of Indian origin, is spelt either Advenir or Avenir.

21. These *sarrasins* had been encouraged by Hugues, count of Provence, to settle there and block the pass against Berenger, his rival for the crown of Italy, a deed that called down on Hugues the curses of the chronicler Liutprand who deems him worse than Herod (*Le mystère de St Bernard de Menthon*, ed. A. Lecoy de la Marche, SATF (Paris, 1888), introduction, p. 12). The story of Bernard is set in the mid-tenth century.

22. The clash between a religious vocation and family pressure to marry most commonly affects daughters. However, Bernard's rejected fiancée declines her father's offer of a more important bridegroom and chooses to enter religion herself. There is a parallel here with the popular tenth-century legend of St Alexis, who left his wife on the wedding night, became a beggar and lived as a hermit under the staircase of his family home in Rome for many years. *La rappresentazione di Santo Alesso* (De Bartholomaeis, II) dates from the late fifteenth century. Cioni also lists many printed versions up to 1620. The legend has no foundation and the cult was suppressed in 1969.

23. In the last poem of the cycle, *Le moniage Guillaume*, William first enters a monastery at nearby Aniane but his hot temper make him so unpopular that he moves to a hermitage at Gellone a few miles away and now called St Guillem-le-desert, where there is a fine romanesque church containing his tomb. For details of the last years of this William see my introduction to William, count of Orange, *Four Old French epics*, ed. Glanville Price, trans. Glanville Price, Lynette Muir and David Hoggan (London, 1975).

24. Jeanroy (*HLF*, XXXIX, pp. 72–3) describes the confusion also between the different dukes of Aquitaine, Guillaume VII and Guillaume VIII, who were both approximate contemporaries of Bernard and notes that the *Vita* first published by Surius is 'suspecta' (AASS 11 February). Guillaume is not listed in BSS.

25. In the *Legenda* (20 August) St Bernard, having been rejected by William, says Mass and then brings the consecrated Host to William saying: 'Here is thy Judge at whose name every knee shall bow.' William is imediately overcome and falls to the ground.

26. An Italian *Rappresentazione di san Bernardo d'uno signore facea rubare le strade* is based on a miracle of the Virgin listed in the *Legenda* (Annunciation, p. 207). Bernard (an unnamed monk in *Legenda*) defeats a devil who is haunting a highwayman but cannot seize him because he says 'Ave Maria' constantly. Bernard reveals the devil to the highwayman who repents his wicked life

and is saved. (Nerida Newbigin, *Sacre rappresentazioni fiorentine del Quattrocento* (Bologna, 1983)).

27. There are obvious parallels here with the story of Robert le Diable, see p. 56.
28. In the *Moniage Guillaume*, the hero has chosen the religious life and is not doing penance. He agrees to come to the help of the French against the Saracens and then returns to the monastery. Later he retires to a small secluded hermitage where he builds a bridge over a gorge for the benefit of pilgrims. When the devil keeps destroying his work William throws him into the water. The Bollandistes' entry for Guillaume d'Aquitaine makes it clear that from the beginning there was confusion of these stories: 'prima et antiquissima facta est confusio' (AASS 10 February, p. 435).
29. John Tailby, 'Ein vernachlässigter Luzerner Bühnenplan', in *Ritual und Inszenierung*, ed, Hans Joachim Ziegler (Tübingen, 2004), pp. 255–60.
30. This *perioche* is a rare example of one in German and French but not in Latin. It was performed at the consecration of a bishop.

3 SOLDIERS OF CHRIST: THE CHURCH MILITANT

1. The manuscript of Pulci's plays, one of the earliest Florentine collections, dating from 1490–5, is described by Weaver, pp. 97–104. Cioni lists four printings up to 1559. There is an English translation in Cook's *Florentine drama*. The Spanish *Aucto di San Francisco* (Rouanet, II, 670 lines) presents brief scenes from the beginning of Francis' life, some episodes with the brothers and his death.
2. *Come apparve Christo a Santo Francesco* (De Bartholomaeis, I). Lope de Vega wrote a play about St Francis called *El serafin humano* (see Rennert, *Life of Lope de Vega*, p. 530). In Milan in 1475 a resurrection play was performed by some Florentines in *La Piaza del seraphico e divo Frances* (Newbigin, p. 142).
3. Shergold, *History of the Spanish stage*, pp. 64–5.
4. Preaching was also important to the Franciscans, of course, and a Spanish play on *El divino Portugues San Antonio de Padua. Comedia Famosa del Doctor Juan Perez de Montalvan* is listed in Edward M. Wilson and Don W. Cruickshank, *Samuel Pepys's Spanish plays* (London, 1980), No. 19 p. 155. The Pepys edition was published not later than 1638. Anthony was born in Lisbon and became a monk but then transferred to the Franciscans, and travelled to Italy where under Francis' guidance he became a noted preacher especially against heresy. He died in 1231 and was canonised the following year (BSS 13 June).
5. In the introduction to the *Mistere*, the editors draw interesting conclusions from the relationship of the Dominicans in the play and in the sixteenth century, when the play was written and the heresies of the thirteenth century had become the more wide-spread and lasting 'heresies' of the Reformation.
6. The play is for performance on the feast of St Dominic. *Come converti I Patarini con la sperienza del libro che pose nel fuocu* (De Bartholomaeis, I). There is also a one-act convent play of the *Exemplo del gloriose padre San Domenico come converti dua giovanie ricevette alla sancta religione* (Weaver, p. 263).

7. The MS (Vit. Em. 483) is in the Biblioteca Nazionale in Rome. For the play's links with Bologna see M. Calore, 'Rappresentazioni sacre a Bologna nel XV secolo', *Strenna Storica Bolognese*, 28 (1978), pp. 101–10.

8. The rosary is divided into fifteen decades of Ave Marias grouped in three 'chaplets' of five decades. The young man had told his uncle that at one time he had made a chaplet of roses each day to put on the Virgin's statue.

9. See Hüsken, *Everaert*.

10. For details of the performance see TIE *Medieval*, E.104. Cioni also records an unpublished Italian play on Catherine which was printed eleven times between 1515 and 1623.

11. *La devozione e festa de santo Petro martire* (De Bartholomaeis, II, and *Abruzzese*, XIV). The texts are identical apart from some dialectal spelling variants. A *Dialogus D. Petri Martyris* treating of the Arian heresy was performed at the Jesuit college of Mallorca (Calore, 'Rappresentazioni sacre a Bologna nel XV secolo').

12. This lengthy account of a comparatively minor saint is explained by the fact that the author of the *Legenda* was himself a Dominican. St Thomas Aquinas is not in the *Legenda* because Jacobus died in 1298 and Aquinas was not canonised until 1323 (BSS 28 January). However, Dante found him a place in Paradise (canto 12) and in the fifteenth century a tragi-comedy of the saint was performed by the students at the Dominican college 'Lirino' as Ugo Giordana describes in the introduction to *Le jeu de Saint Thomas d'Aquin* (Paris, 1939).

13. At almost 2,000 lines this is one of the longest Italian saints' plays. Like several others it exists in two versions: De Bartholomaeis, II, pp. 44–114, and *Abruzzese*, XIV.

14. For the miracle of Bolsena and the founding of the feast see p. 53.

15. Justo García Soriano, 'El teatro de colegio en España. Noticia y examen de algunas de sus obras', *Boletín de la real academia española*, 14 (1927), p. 261. Details of the play are given in E. Roux, *Le théâtre dans les colleges des Jésuites en Espagne. Dramaturgie et société*, II (Paris, 1968), pp. 503–5.

16. T. H. Vail Motter, *The school drama in England* (New York, 1929), p. 225. Motter also quotes the account of the school plays there, written in 1557 by bishop John Bale, himself a noted dramatist. In Bohemia, Huss became a national hero.

17. The Vaudois or Waldenses, a small Christian community which still survives in Piedmont, had its origins in the 'Poor men of Lyons' in the twelfth century (*Oxford dictionary of the Christian church*).

18. Anon., *La tragédie du sac de Cabrière, ein Kalvinistiche drama des Reformationszeit*, ed. Karl Christ (Halle, 1928), pp. 8–9.

19. The anonymous play, edited by Renée Gimenez, was published in 1989.

20. 19 January. Limited to local cult since 1969.

21. The surviving text includes the only known speech in Shakespeare's own hand. In the introduction to the text prepared for the Stratford production of the play in 2005, Martin White discusses the severe censorship of the period

and the many revisions this involved with evidence in the surviving text of five anonymous different authors. He concludes 'there is no conclusive evidence that the play was ever staged in an Elizabethan or Jacobean playhouse'.

22. Louis A. Schuster in the introduction to his edition and English translation of *Henry VIII* (p. 370). Schuster treats the play in great detail and has much of interest to say about Vernulaeus and his school plays. There are also Jesuit plays on St Thomas who was seen as a martyr of the clash between church and state.

23. Lancaster, I, ii, p. 671. La Serre was the first French dramatist to write his plays in prose.

24. Vernulaeus, *Henry VIII*, trans. Schuster, pp. 37–9. Stegmann records performances of another Jesuit play on Thomas à Becket in 1610 in Lille and 1622 in Ghent.

25. The cult was suppressed in 1538 and briefly revived during the reign of Mary Tudor (Davidson, 'Middle English saint play' pp. 52–8).

PART TWO: INTRODUCTORY SECTION

1. The Meriasek and Genevieve plays are both divided into a series of incidents describing episodes of the saint's life and miracles. The sixth-century Celtic saint, Meriasek, was born in Cornwall but ended his days in Brittany. In addition to those (mainly healing) miracles performed by Meriasek, the episodes interpolated in the play of *Beunans Meriasek* (composed c. 1500), include the conversion of Constantine by St Sylvester, the latter's subduing of a dragon (see p. 158); and the legend of the woman who stole the statue of Jesus (see p. 43). The fifteen playlets that make up the St Genevieve collection were written in Paris in the early fifteenth century. See p. 218.

2. The story of St Andrew helping a bishop who is tempted by the Devil disguised as a woman is included in the saint's life in the *Legenda* and dramatised in the *Auto de un milagro de Sancto Andres* (Rouanet, XXIX) and the *Miracolo di Sant'Andrea* (De Bartholomaeis, III, Bologna). An English play of St Andrew performed in a church at Braintree, Essex, in 1525 (Lancashire 395) may also be based on this miracle. There are three Italian plays of miracles of St James, involving respectively one, two or three pilgrims (D'Ancona, III, pp. 445–85). All three are taken from the *Legenda*. For Spanish, French and Provencal plays of the miracle of the pilgrim saved from hanging by Santiago, see 'The woman scorned' p. 106.

3. A recently discovered MS of plays of St Nicholas, now in the library at Yale University, has eight St Nicholas plays, three unique ones, set in the saint's life-time, and five post-mortem miracles which are also found elsewhere (see Lynette R. Muir, 'St Nicholas: a newly discovered French play cycle', *EDAM newsletter*, 11 (Fall 1998), pp. 1–4). A total of eight Latin plays have survived. All the dramatised stories are recorded in the *Legenda*. Best known are probably the stories of the resuscitation of the 'pickled boys' – given new life in the twentieth century by Benjamin Britten – and of Nicholas throwing balls of

gold through the window of a house, to provide dowries for three girls who are preparing to prostitute themselves to win money for their aged father. For texts see Young, *The drama of the medieval church*, 2 vols. (Oxford and London, 1933), II, ch. XXVI. There are also a few vernacular plays (see below) as well as performance references such as *Le miracle de St Nicolas* (prologues), ed. C. Samaran, *Romania*, 51 (1925), pp. 191–7. A *jeu et feste* of St Nicholas was performed in Nancy in 1496 but we do not know which play was given.

4. See Rutebeuf's *Le miracle de Théophile*, ed. Grace Frank CFMA (Paris, repr. 1975). The most important French texts are the forty plays of the fourteenth-century Cangé MS, discussed in the Introduction.

5. García Soriano, 'El teatro de colegio en España', p. 245 n. 3.

6. Typical of this group of Marian miracles is the tale of the pregnant abbess (Cangé, XX) also included in the *Mystères de Lille* (no. 71). A Dutch version of this story is mentioned in De Bruyn, p. 29.

4 MIRACULOUS CONVERSIONS OF JEWS (AND A FEW PAGANS)

1. By the thirteenth century, Jews were an integral part of French urban life (although expelled in 1306 they were soon allowed back) and were much involved in borrowing and lending money, with sometimes disastrous effects on the Christian population.

2. In many stories, Jews and pagans are seen as interchangeable. In addition to the *Iconia* plays, see *infra* the miracles of *Agnolo ebreo* (p. 17), of the Devil's children (p. 58) and the rash bargain (p. 65).

3. The 'Amiraus d'Orkenie' is forced into baptism but warns the saint that 'Par parole devieng vostre hom / Mais li creanche est en Mahom' (I will be your man in word / But my belief is in Mahomet). Jean Bodel, *Jeu de St Nicholas*, ed. F. J. Warne (Oxford, 1951), ll.1515–16.

4. D'Ancona, III, pp. 485–98.

5. There is an interesting variant on this theme in the memoirs of Sir Osbert Sitwell. As a child he was given a shilling a week pocket money and told he should give half of it to the poor. According to the nanny, he understood this 'to mean that each gesture of charity brought in a substantial and immediate cash return from Heaven'. 'The impression was confirmed a few days later when his grandmother gave him a five shilling tip. But although he parted with future sixpences, none of them brought in celestial dividends.' (Quoted in Adeline Hartcup, *Children of the great country houses* (London, 1982), p. 97.)

6. John. E. Tailby, 'Hans Sachs and the Nuremberg Fastnachtspiel tradition of the fifteenth century', in *Hans Sachs and folk theater*, ed. Aylett and Skrine, p. 193.

7. There is a classical parallel with Junius Brutus who carried a gold rod to offer to the gods inside a hollow wooden staff as a sign that he was not the fool he appeared to be (Livy I, 56).

8. In Beroul's version of the Tristan legend, Iseult escapes condemnation by a similar trick when swearing an oath that she is chaste. Iseult gets away with it: the romances were much less moral than the saints' lives and legends.

9. This same story occurs in *Don Quixote* related by Sancho Panza in the chapter when he talks of being king of his island (Part II, ch. 45).

10. A performance of 'L'usurier *alias* le trésorier' in Draguignan may be a version of this story (Chocheyras, *Dauphiné*, p. 162).

11. This of course is a Muslim rather than a Jewish belief.

12. The parallel with Shakespeare is discussed below p. 49. For the bargain see also the story of Theophilus.

13. The earliest version of the casket scene is recorded in John Damascene's *Barlaam and Joasaph* (p. 75). The story of the pound of flesh was already widely known by the twelfth century. See Bullough, I, pp. 446–7.

14. See De Bruyn, pp. 62–7. Some of her parallels seem exaggerated, especially the equating of Portia's submission to Bassanio with the Virgin Mary's 'behold the handmaid of the lord'.

5 SACRAMENT PLAYS

1. For the text in English and Latin and details of the promulgation of the Bull, see P. Meredith and L. Muir, 'The Corpus Christi Bull', *MeTh*, 26 (2004), pp. 62–78.

2. The *auto sacramental* is peculiar to Counter-Reformation Spain; the plays were written for and performed at Corpus Christi but unlike such plays from other countries and from earlier Spain, they were not based on biblical stories and saints' lives but explicitly treated of miracles and allegories and moralities about the sacrament itself, with special reference to the doctrines challenged by the Protestants of Transubstantiation and the Real Presence of Christ in the sacrament, the need for auricular Confession before receiving it and the sacrament of Penance. See Andrachuk, 'The *auto sacramental* and the Reformation', *Journal of Hispanic Philology*, 10 (1985), pp. 8–38. Among the major writers who composed this kind of *auto* are Lope de Vega and Calderon. An interesting variant on these texts is to be found in the Chantilly play of the *Moralité du pèlerinage de vie humaine*, based on the *Pèlerinage de vie humaine* by Guillaume de Deguilleville. Nature complains to Grace de Dieu because, instead of accepting that no substance can be changed except by the power of Nature, yet Grace de Dieu has given to some of her followers the power to change bread into flesh and wine into blood. Grace de Dieu explains that she has the right to grant such power to whom she will since, as Nature has said, she is the Mistress and all others are her servants (see *Nativités et moralités liégeoises du moyen âge*, ed. G. Cohen (Brussels, 1953), p. 268).

3. When, in the early seventeenth century, the church of St Etienne du Mont (which contained the relics of St Genevieve, patron saint of Paris) was rebuilt, one of the windows in the gallery behind the high altar commemorated the

miracle of the profaned Host. In 1664, a small pamphlet was published: *Le miracle de la Sainte Hostie de 1290 a Paris* (with engravings by F. Ragot) and this was reprinted for the sexcentenary commemoration of the original event in 1890. For a rare modern analogue from Poland see Judith A. Krane-Calvert, 'A twentieth-century analogue of the *Play of the sacrament*', *EDAM Review*, 20:1 (Fall 1997), pp. 24–7.

4. Edited with a preface and notes by André Mary (Paris, 1929), trans. Janet Shirley: A *Parisian journal 1405–1449* (Oxford, 1968), p. 353. See also Lynette R. Muir, 'Further thoughts on the tale of the profaned host', *EDAM Review*, 21:2 (1999), pp. 88–97. The Host had originally been stolen from the church of St Jean (in the *mystère* from St Merri) and the sacred relic was subsequently preserved there. According to Michel Félibien, 'The Knife, the Blood and other relics were still to be seen in the *Chapelle des miracles*, built on the site of the Jew's house by a bourgeois of Paris, then in the fourteenth century given into the care of a charitable order known as Les Billettes. In 1632 they were disbanded and the chapel was taken over by the Carmelites' (*Histoire de la ville de Paris*, 5 vols. (Paris, 1725), I, pp. 458–9).

5. In the fourteenth and fifteenth centuries many Jews especially in Germany were accused of abusing the sacrament. See Miri Rubin, *Gentile tales* (Yale, 1999).

6. Graham Runnalls, *Les mystères français imprimés*, Bibliothèque du XVe siècle (Paris, 1999). A modern edition of *La Sainte Hostie* is currently being prepared by Robert Clark to whom I am indebted for an advance copy of the text of the play. A detailed summary is given in *Mystères*, II, pp. 574–6.

7. I am grateful to Nerida Newbigin for sending me an advance copy of her edition of the play. She also records a performance in Rome in 1473 'di quello judeo che rosti il corpo di Christi' and suggests the text was similar to that printed at the end of the century (p. 141).

8. Norman Davis, ed., *Non-cycle plays and fragments*, Early English Text Society, Extra Series, Supplementary Text 1 (London, 1970), p. lxxiv.

9. In the French accounts, the Host when thrown into the fire 'ne se veult tenir' (will not stay there). The English oven parallels the French story of the cauldron, vividly described in another of the Metz stage directions: when flung into a cauldron of boiling water: 'l'hostie se elevoit en 1'air et montoit en une nuée et devint ung petit enfant en montant a mont' (the Host then rose in the air and went up in a cloud and became a little child as it rose). An interesting cross-reference between the French and English texts is in the description of the seventeenth-century Eucharistic tapestry at the Chateau de Langeais (near Tours). The description in the modern leaflet available at the Chateau lists a series of images including the meeting of Abraham and Melchisedek, the Jewish Passover and the *Miracle des Billettes*, showing the profanation of the Host by 'l'usurier Juif Jonathas en 1290'. The Jew in the French miracle is never named but Jonathas is the name used in the Croxton play.

10. Davis, ed., *Non-cycle plays and fragments*, p. lxxiv.

11. See Georg Liebe, *Das Judentum in der deutschen Vergangenheit*, Monographien zur deutschen Kulturgeschichte (Leipzig, 1903) (unpaginated). Six of the most significant episodes are shown in illustration No. 5.

12. Cioni refers to *La rappresentatione d'un miracolo del sagramento*, by Bernardo Cungi. This is a different play in which a Christian sells a Host to a Jew, gambles away the money and becomes a bandit – he is killed by a lion. The Jew is converted by the Capucins.

13. There are paintings and carvings in the chapel of the miracle in Orvieto cathedral (constructed 1323 44) which include citations from the Office composed by Thomas Aquinas (who died in 1265). His authorship of at least some of the Propers of the feast is generally accepted.

14. Steven Berkoff's play *Ritual in Blood* (Steven Berkoff, *Plays 3* (London, 2000), performed in 2001) is based on the supposed ritual murder of nine-year-old Hugh of Lincoln by the Jews in 1255, for which Henry III had eighteen Jews hanged. (The cult of 'Little Saint Hugh' is now not kept as being an example of anti-Semitism.) It has a scene which echoes Macharius' actions. The different parishes are fighting over who should have the body of the 'martyr', but the father of the boy who was killed now knows that really his son died as the result of a fall while playing with his brother. He has kept quiet because he thinks he will get a lot of money from it all, but begins to feel doubts about all the things the priest has said about the Real Presence of Christ in the Bread and Wine. He obtains a Host (Berkoff does not say how) then he says: 'Sorry Jesus, I have to know' and stabs the Host to see if it will bleed. Nothing happens and then he begins to fear he has countenanced a terrible crime. 'Go on then, bleed, bleed, I want to see it! Bleed you bastard!' He takes a knife up and continues stabbing, groaning with frustration and doubt. End of the scene (p. 74).

6 YOUR ADVERSARY THE DEVIL: THE SAVED AND THE DAMNED

1. In addition to the plays on the Last Judgement and the Trial in Heaven, neither of which have a major role for the Virgin Mary, there are the plays of the Judgement of Jesus Christ, in which she tries, and fails, to prevent the condemnation of her Son. (See Muir, *Biblical drama*, pp. 123–5).

2. Graham Runnalls, 'The mystère de l'advocacie Nostre Dame: a recently discovered fragment', *Zeitschrift für romanische Philologie*, 100:2 (Tübingen, 1984), pp. 41–77.

3. A useful outline of the different doctrines of Augustine and Anselm on this subject is given by Kevin J. Ruth in 'Juridical language and the Devil's rights in the Maastrichter (ripuarisches) Passionsspiel', *EMD*, 8 (2004), pp. 19–34.

4. Runnalls, 'The mystère de l'advocacie', p. 46.

5. The three accounts are compared and analysed in J. P. Wickersham Crawford's 'The Catalan "Mascaron" and an episode in Jacob van Maerlant's "*Merlijn*", *PMLA* 26, (1911). Crawford argues convincingly for the Catalan

version to be older than the Dutch. He does not mention the parallels with the *Advocacie Notre Dame.*

6. 'Jatsia que jo sia mare no son mare axi con los altres cor jo son mare sens corrumpcio e fuy preys sens to greuje e infante sens dolor.' I am grateful to Lenke Kovaks for help in translating this text.

7. See Alexandre Micha, 'The vulgate Merlin', in *Arthurian literature in the Middle Ages*, ed. R. S. Loomis (Oxford, 1959), p. 319.

8. *Robert le Diable, roman d'aventures*, ed. E. Löseth, SATF (Paris, 1903).

9. Cf. Cangé, XVII, where an excommunicate man is saved by a holy fool. Like St Alexis he lives in extreme poverty under the staircase and eats only food left by the dogs.

10. For details of the legend see *Robert le diable*, ed. Löseth, pp. xvii–xix.

11. *The tragedy of Ecerinus* has been edited with a facing English translation and a useful introduction by R. W. Carrubba *et al.* and published by the Department of Classics, Pennsylvania State University (Philadelphia, 1972). I have quoted from the English text throughout. The play was a huge success and 'Mussato was crowned with laurel by the grateful Paduans' (ed. cit. p. iv).

12. For studies of *Ecerinis* and its links with Seneca, see *Studi sul teatro medioevale* (Viterbo, 1979).

13. There is an echo here of Plutarch's account of the marriage of Alexander's parents: 'The night before the consummation of their marriage she [Olympias] dreamt that a thunderbolt fell upon her body, which kindled a great fire.'

14. The story is found in many early collections of Marian miracles including those of Gautier de Coinci.

15. At one point in the play, the young man declares that he is called a 'Jew or a pagan' because he has not been baptised – another example of the confusion between the two in early stories. See the *Iconia* plays above p. 45.

16. This is an echo of the lament of the foolish Virgins in the *Sponsus*: 'helas chetives trop i avons dormies' (woe to us wretched ones, we have slept too long).

17. Ed. cit. pp. 231–46: the stage direction specifies the use of a child of about three years old.

18. This was a well-known theological view, see, for example, the *Sentences* of Robert de Melun, XVII, cit. C. William Marx, *The devil's rights and the redemption in the literature of medieval England* (Cambridge, 1995), p. 153.

19. I have used the parallel Latin/English text by Peter Dronke in *Nine medieval Latin plays* (Cambridge, 1994), accepting his claim that this musical play was intended for performance.

20. A number of French 'Everyman' texts are included in *Répertoire*, which despite its title includes many serious morality plays (e.g. nos. 13, 14, 22, 26). See also Fortune's wheel, p. 179.

21. *Ancien théâtre françois*, III. Ed. Viollet le Duc Bibliothèque Elzevirienne III (Paris, 1854), pp. 5–86. This parable with its basic theme of sin, repentance and forgiveness has been dramatised numerous times from *Courtois d'Arras* in the thirteenth century (see Muir, *Biblical drama*, p. 122) to Gnaephius' *Acolastus*

in the sixteenth. For the plot and staging see Alan Hindley, 'Staging the old French *moralité*. The case of *Les enfants de maintenant*', *METh*, 16 (1994), pp. 77–90.

22. Hindley, 'Staging the old French *moralité*', p. 78. The unique feature of the *Enfants* which links it with this section is the damnation of one of the brothers. There is also an interesting role for their mother (Mignotte) who does not often feature in plays of the prodigal son.

23. Dietrich Schernberg, *Ein schön spiel von Frau Jutten*, ed. Manfred Lammer (Berlin, 1971). This most recent edition of *Frau Jutta* is based, not on Schernberg's lost original text, but on the 1565 printed version by a Lutheran preacher, Hieronymus Silesius, which emphasises the anti-Catholic elements of the legend (Ukena, II, p. 161). The form Jutta for Joan is peculiar to this text.

24. A recent and detailed study of the legend is Peter Stanford's *The she-pope; a quest for the truth behind the mystery of pope Joan* (London, 1998). He provides convincing evidence that the story was not, as often claimed, entirely a creation of Protestant writers inserted into the late copies of early Catholic chronicles (pp. 29–31).

25. This was a serious sin in the Middle Ages as is recorded in the trial of Joan of Arc, for example. Nor were men allowed to wear women's clothes. Actors had to have special dispensation for this, as is shown in the charter of the *Confrérie de la Passion* who may pass freely 'dressed as the play requires' (*Mystères*, I, p. 417). In Henslowe's *Diary* (ed. W. W. Greg, 2 vols. (London, 1904–8), II, p. 152) there is a reference to 'poope Jone' being performed by Strange's men, as an old play (1 Mar. 1591/2). This play is lost but Elkanah Settle's *The female prelate* (London, 1680), which has survived, begins where she is about to be elected pope and presents a complex plot of the struggle between Joan and the duke of Saxony, whose father she had murdered. The theme of this play is the corruption of the papacy and the conflict between Protestant and Catholic. Only in the final act where there is a detailed narration of her giving birth during the procession are we brought close to the main legend. Some of the remarks both in the text and the dedication to the earl of Shaftesbury (leader of the anti-Catholic Whig party) are clearly warnings to Charles II and his very pro-Catholic brother James.

26. Leo IV 847–55 was succeeded by Benedict III. There have not been any popes called Basil. According to J. N. D. Kelly, *Oxford dictionary of popes* (Oxford, 1986; updated edition with new material by Michael Walsh, Oxford, 2006), the legend of pope Joan first appeared in the fourteenth century in a Dominican chronicle which sets her reign in the eleventh century. This would fit in quite well with Schernberg's reference to the university of Paris.

27. The stage direction reads: 'the devil reveals that Pope Jutta . . . is pregnant' (p. 54).

28. According to the legend, it was during a procession that Joan went into labour and died giving birth in the street. Thereafter, that part of the route was always by-passed by papal processions (Stanford, *The she-pope*, p. 6).

29. De Bruyn claims that according to the stage directions 'the pageant must have been highly spectacular' (p. 154) but I do not think such very simple directions as 'Now they put the crown on Pope Joan' (p. 53) support her case. It is interesting to compare this with a scene in Barnaby Barnes, *The Devil's charter* (1608) which opens with Rodrigo Borgia tempted by the Devil with a papal tiara and signing a pact with his blood in order to get it. See below p. 72.

30. For the background to the two versions and latest edition of the English text, see Margaret M. Raftery, *Mary of Nemmegen* (Brill, 1991). For the play-text I have used the edition by Saalborn in *Toneelglorie der Middeleeuwen* (Naarden, n.d.).

31. There are several parallels here with the *Advocacie Nostre Dame* including the objection by Masscheroen, on the grounds that Mary is the judge's mother.

32. Mariken begins to weep – a sign of her repentance for the inability to cry was one of the signs of witchcraft and devil worship according to the *Malleus Maleficarum* (see Raftery, *Mary of Nemmegen*, p. 12 n. 43).

33. A detailed study of the play by Stephen Wright was published in *Comparative Drama*, 27 (1993), pp. 4–16. It is to be published in an anthology of translations of Danish plays currently being prepared by Thomas Pettitt and Leif Søndergaard, with the provisional title: *Interludes and miracle plays*.

34. The habit of swearing by the Body or Wounds of Christ (including such exclamations as 'swounds' and 'zounds') was already widespread in the fourteenth century as can be seen, for example, in several *Ballades* by Eustache Deschamps (c. 1346–1406): 'May he be damned and lost who shall break the body of God in pieces, it is forbidden to dismember it for the sake of God who was transfigured' (Eugene Deschamps, *Œuvres complètes*, ed. Gaston Raynaud, SATF, 11 vols. (Paris, 1878–1903), I, p. 276, my translation).

35. Wright links the play with a number of pictorial versions of Marian miracles in an attempt to identify the character of Sir Procopius, and other unusual features of the play.

36. De Bartholomaeis, II, pp. 403–22.

37. The play was written c. 1620. I have used the English text printed in *Three plays by Tirso de Molina*, trans. by F. Minelli and J. D. Browning, Carleton Plays (Ottawa, 1991). The introduction includes a detailed analysis of the theological background to the play with special reference to the contemporary argument on free will versus predestination.

38. An interesting contrast to the Virgin's freely given pardons is found in one of the St Genevieve plays. A nun comes to visit Genevieve who questions her about her life. She claims she lives celibate, but Genevieve tells her the name of her seducer. The nun claims it was her destiny to sin, and Genevieve is horrified. God has given man free will! The nun claims God 'm'a faite . . . pour moy dampner'. There follows a long and interesting argument with Genevieve insisting that the nun should not despair. Finally convinced, the nun makes her confession and is pardoned by the bishop.

39. In Pedresco's final speech he tells the audience that if they want to read the original story they will find it in the *Vitae patrum*. The story referred to may

well be that of the previous play of the faithful *monaco* or, more likely, the story of San Panunzio (D'Ancona, II, pp. 55–60).

40. The loose-living womaniser first appeared in Tirso de Molina's *Il burlador de Sevilla* (c. 1623) and soon ousted both Theophilus and Faust as the archetypal unrepentant sinner.

7 WHO SUPS WITH THE DEVIL: THE RASH BARGAIN

1. The earliest version of the Christian story of the rash bargain is found in the life of St Basil of Caesarea and tells of a young slave who makes a pact with the Devil in order to win the love of his master's daughter. St Basil subsequently redeems him from his pact. The version of the story featuring Theophilus first appears in Greek in the sixth century and as St Theophilus the penitent (4 Feb.) he was included in the tenth-century collection of saints' lives by Metaphrastes. For details of these and the later narrative versions in Latin, French and Spanish, see Annette Garnier's edition of Gautier de Coinci's *Le miracle de Théophile, ou comment Théophile vint à la pénitence*, ed. and trans. Annette Garnier, CFMA (Paris, 1998), pp. 7–8. The best-known medieval version must be that included with other miracles of the Virgin Mary in the *Legenda* under 8 September, Feast of the Nativity of the Virgin Mary. The post-medieval survival of the Greek story is interestingly revealed by William Dalrymple in his book *From the Holy Mountain* (London, 1997). He reports that the Byzantine version of the Faust tale involved a Jewish necromancer leading a presbyter who has been sacked from his position as *oikonomos* (treasurer) by the new bishop, to the Hippodrome in the middle of the night (p. 55). The Jew there summons up the Devil who promises to help the presbyter who has to kiss his cloven foot in submission and thus sells his soul to the Devil. It is intriguing to see how many motifs are included and, especially, what is excluded: the name of the presbyter, the written bond and any suggestion of salvation – it is indeed more Faust than Theophilus.

2. The 'theatre of the devils' is described in Roger of Wendover's *Flowers of History* of 1206 (trans. J. A. Giles, 2 vols. Bohn's Antiquarian Library (London, 1849), II, p. 227). His vision of the torments of Hell and Purgatory is 'far superior to any of the preceding ones. Here the cruelty of the torments is not so preponderant as in many other visions of the same period, especially Tundalus'. A. B. Van Os, *Religious visions: the development of the eschatological elements in medieval English religious literature* (Amsterdam, 1932), p. 74. For a Jesuit play of Tundalus see Szarota, I, 2, p. 1815.

3. Rutebeuf, *Le miracle de Théophile*.

4. Ibid., ll. 22–6. This is an interesting echo of the reactions in the *Iconia* plays and the beating of the statue in *Le jeu de S. Nicolas*.

5. For the confusion of Jews and pagans see also the *Enfant donné au diable* and the story of Agnolo Ebreo.

6. For details of the sources and play texts, see Petsch, *Theophilus* (Heidelberg, 1908). Discussed in chronological order, the MSS are labelled for their

current location: Helmstadt (H. 745 lines), Stockholm (S. 998 lines) and Trier (T. 824 lines but not complete). There are also records of performances of a Latin *Theofilus Spull* in a Deventer school in 1436 and 1453 (Worp, I, p. 194).

7. These two are also among the biblical sinners invoked by Frau Jutta when she is begging for forgiveness.

8. This motif goes back to Gautier's poem.

9. The seven devils feature in the English Magdalene play. For this and other medieval Mary Magdalene plays see Muir, *Biblical drama*, pp. 238–41. They also appear in the play of St Anthony, see p. 23, and in a very unusual carnival *lauda* from Orvieto in which each in turn they all confess their sin and ask for help to do better so that they shall not lose eternal joy. *Avarizia*, for example, asks for the virtue of *largitade*: generosity. De Bartholomaeis, I, pp. 366–7.

10. For other examples of this motif see *L'Advocacie Notre Dame* and the Swedish *Peccatore*.

11. *Teofilo* is printed in D'Ancona, II, pp. 445–67. He used the first of the three printed editions (1498, 1500 and 1517) listed in Cioni, *Bibliografia*, pp. 291–2.

12. The popularity of Theophilus in the sixteenth century was helped by Celsis' publication, in 1501, of Hrotsvitha's poem *Lapsus et conversio Theophilii vicedomi* along with her plays. Two versions of Theophilus are recorded among the German *perioche* edited in Szarotza, I, 2, pp. 1449–62. For details of the Theophilus legend and the Jesuits, see Valentin, II, pp. 544–51. He also cites K. Plenzat, *Die Theophilus legende in den dichtungen des Mittelalters* (Berlin, 1926).

13. Valentin suggests that the earlier texts may also be by Rader though the matter is not susceptible of proof.

14. The play is described as a *Comoedien*. See Szarota, I, 2 pp. 1449ff.

15. The Jesuits also dramatised another miracle of the Virgin, the story of Udo of Magdeburg. Udo was granted intelligence by the Virgin Mary so that he could rise to the rank of bishop; unfortunately he then gave way to pride in his achievements, fell from grace and was eventually damned.

16. This Scotus is Hieronymus Scotus, a celebrated sixteenth-century Italian magician (Fidel Rädle, *Faustsplitter aus lateinischen Dramen im Clm 26017*, Festschrift B. Bischoff (Stuttgart, 1971), p. 48). The sudden appearance of these two characters in what Rädle (p. 490) calls the 'epilogue in Hell' is to serve as a warning to sinners of their fate. The characters lament in alternate couplets finally addressing mankind: Scotus: 'Take heed, oh, take heed. There is but a moment of delight and enjoyment but an eternity of anguish, suffering and death!' Both: 'Ah, take heed, you mortals, take heed.' Rädle compares this in general, though not in detail, to Faust's *wehe von der Hellen* (lament from Hell), in the 66th chapter of the German *Faustbuch*.

17. *Mystères*, II, pp. 335–6. There are several partial editions in modern French but the most recent complete edition is that by Viollet le Duc in the *Ancien théâtre françois*, III, pp. 425–78. A performance of the play at Die in 1541 is listed by Chocheyras in *Dauphiné*, p. 162. He suggests that *Le chevalier désesperé* performed at Brignoles in 1598 may be the same play.

18. There is a marked resemblance here to the story mentioned in the English play fragment known as the Durham prologue (Davis, ed., *Non-cycle plays and fragments*, p. 118). The story is also extant in Dutch, see C. G. N. De Vooys, *Middelnederlandsche Maria legenden*, 2 vols. (Leiden, 1903), I, p. 22. For other versions see De Bruyn, p. 29, notes: *de milite qui pactum fecit cum diabolo*, English version in *The life of St Katharine*, ed. J. Orchard Halliwell (Brixton Hill, 1848).

19. The seven-year delay is also mentioned in the miracle of the child vowed to the Devil, see above p. 58.

20. I have used the translation by Michael McGaha which has a detailed and useful introduction by José M. Ruano (Carleton Renaissance Plays in translation 16, Dovehouse editions (Ottowa, 1989)).

21. The importance of filial obedience especially of daughters is a constantly recurring theme in early seventeenth-century Spanish drama. See Melveena McKendrick, *Woman and society in the Spanish drama of the Golden Age. A study of the mujer varonil* (Cambridge, 1974), pp. 28–30.

22. An alternative safeguard is made by the wife in *The late Lancashire Witches*, a comedy by Heywood and Broome. Having admitted to her husband that she has made a pact with the Devil she explains:' What interest in this soul myself could claim, / I freely gave him; but his part that made it / I still reserve, not being mine to give.' The Devil is also tricked in the French comedy *La merveille* (Rouen, 1612, Lancaster, I, i, p. 139).

23. For other examples of Mary Magdalene as the model for the female penitent, see *Frau Jutta* and p. 61.

24. The Dominican order was at this time at loggerheads with the Jesuits over questions of grace and free will, so this appearance would have been meaningful to the audience.

25. This tableau and the scene of Don Gil with the skeleton are reminiscent of the tableau that ends the Dutch play of *Man's desire and fleeting beauty*. 'HERE the bower is opened and Man's Desire and Fleeting Beauty sit together embracing. And Death stands by them with skull . . . but the lovers both turn away from Death in horror', trans. from the Dutch by Robert Potter and Elsa Strietman, Leeds Medieval Studies, University of Leeds (Leeds, 1994), p. 89.

26. A useful outline of the origin and development of the Faust legend is given in the introduction to the Everyman translation of Goethe's *Faust* by A. G. Latham (London, repr. 1912). He mentions the links with the biblical story of Simon magus (Acts 9:8) and the legend of St Justina who converted a sorcerer, Cyprian (*Legenda* 29 September). The cult was suppressed in 1969.

27. *Studies in Philology*, 63 (1966), pp. 565–77. Gabriel Bailey, in her study of 'Medieval saint-play metamorphoses in English drama 1490–1642', (Ph.D. thesis, University of Bristol, 1984), has a substantial chapter on this and other changes in saints' plays during the sixteenth century. This thesis provides an interesting explanation of the dramatic (and narrative) weakness of the central part of the play which has led some editors to suggest it was not by

Marlowe at all. 'I suggest that when Marlowe died he left his play on Dr Faustus unfinished' (ed. R. Gill (Oxford, 1990), p. xviii).

28. Faustus uses more medieval terms – he talks of mercy but soon succumbs again to despair. Prospero says he will abjure this 'rough magic', break his staff and drown his book and he does it, intending thereafter to retire to Milan where 'every third thought shall be my grave'.

29. For more on these players see *supra* the martyrdom of St Dorothea, p. 10. It is generally accepted that all early German Faust plays were based on Marlowe's play and the first original versions date only from the early eighteenth century and belong to the popular *puppentheater* tradition as in the text from Ulm, which was predated by a Dutch version of c. 1700 by Reindorp; it is likely that the popular tradition continued even after the appearance of Goethe's Faust (Robert Petsch, *Faustsage und Faustdichtung* (Dortmund, 1966) pp. 67–71). Goethe changed the situation completely by having Faust saved, not damned. As Dorothy Sayers puts it in the preface to her Faust play 'for Goethe it was impossible to accept the idea that desire for knowledge could be in itself an evil thing' (*The devil to pay* (London, 1939), p. 11).

30. *Le pape malade*, attributed to Théodore de Bèze is listed by Petit de Julleville among the *moralités* though he admits this violently anti-papal pamphlet may not have been staged (*Répertoire*, 54, p. 92).

31. There is an interesting echo of this scene in the libretto of Gounod's Faust. Margareta, who has been seduced by Faust, kills her child, but dies repentant. Mephistopheles declares she is damned (*Jugée!*) but the chorus of angels reply 'she is saved' (*Sauvée*)! As in Goethe's play, Faust is also apparently saved.

32. An interesting French moralité of the late fifteenth to sixteenth centuries has recently been edited by Alan Hindley and Graeme Small. 'Le ju du grand dominé et du petit, *Revue belge de philologie et d'histoire*, 80 (2002), pp. 413–56, is a free adaptation of the parable of the talents (Matthew 25) in which the servant (*le petit dominé*), who buried the talent instead of using it, is 'cast out into outer darkness' – the standard biblical term for damnation – by the *grand dominé*. I am grateful to Alan for sending me a copy of this play.

33. *Cenodoxus* has been published with a facing English translation by D. G. Dyer, with a useful introduction on the Jesuit drama. Jacob Bidermann was one of the greatest of the early Jesuit playwrights, a pupil of Matthaus Rader, author of the Theophilus play discussed above, he entered the order in 1594 and taught in several colleges before ending his life in Rome as official theologian and censor of the Order (Jakob Bidermann, *Cenodoxus*, ed. and trans. D. G. Dyer, Edinburgh Bi-Lingual Library 9 (Edinburgh, 1974), p. 9). Unusually for Jesuit drama, his collected plays were published in 1666. There is a useful analysis and discussion of all the plays in Best, *Bidermann*.

34. The stress on spectators to take warning from the plays is emphasised in the Sterzing play of the parable of Dives and Lazarus (see Muir, *Biblical drama*, p. 122). There is a final speech by the Herald (Einschreiher) in which we are told that the five brothers are now squandering their inheritance, gambling, drinking, cursing, swearing and womanising. His final words make clear the

local relevance: 'This scene is unfortunately seen daily, that is why it is shown here in public. In all wisdom it is acknowledged that such a lifestyle leads to a bad end.' . . . It is a message for a society in which there were enough prosperous citizens to whom this message applied (John Tailby in 'Drama and community in South Tirol', in *Drama and community: people and plays in medieval Europe*, ed. Alan Hindley (Turnhout, 1999), pp. 148–60). A similar attack on worldliness is found in Wager's *Enough is as good as a feast*. See Robert Potter *The English morality play: origins, history and influence of a dramatic tradition* (London, 1975), p. 118.

35. The *perioche* for these plays are in Szarota, II, 2, pp. 879–86. The Ametano play was performed at Augsburg in 1615 and Humphredus at Dusseldorf in 1664. A play of the damnation of a player (*Spiler*) was performed in Trepano, Sicily, in 1623 (Szarota, II, 2, pp. 887–93) and there are a number of semi-allegorical plays on the Dance of Death and related themes.

36. Szarota (II, 1, p. 1815), cites the *Visio Tungdali* translated from Irish into Latin by the Irish monk Marcus c. 1150–60, but prefers Vincent de Beauvais as the likely source. The *perioche* of *Tundalus redivivus* (Szarota, II, 1, pp. 1441–8) mentions many descriptions of the horrors of Hell as Tundalus' guardian angel tries to win him back from his evil doing and eventually succeeds.

PART THREE: INTRODUCTORY SECTION

1. Ed. R. M. Lumiansky, David Mills, *The Chester mystery cycle*, Early English Text Society, Supplementary Series (London, 1974), p. 424 'They were no myracles but mervelles thinges / that thou shewes unto these kinges / through the fyendes crafte.'

8 HAPPILY EVER AFTER: FRIENDS AND LOVERS

1. Marriage between Christians and pagans was justified by St Paul: 'for the unbelieving husband is sanctified by the wife; the unbelieving wife is sanctified by the husband' (I Corinthians 7:14). Several early saints' lives, including the story of St Ursula (*Legenda* 21 October) indicate the potential dangers of these marriages.

2. The *seraglio* setting is also found, sometimes with a tragic ending, in many plays in the sixteenth and seventeenth centuries, as well as eventually finding its way into Mozart's opera, which has many similarities to the medieval *Floire et Blanchflor* story in which Floire tells the guard he is an 'ingenieur' with an interest in the tower where Blanchflor is imprisoned, just as Mozart's Belmonte claims to be an architect. For the background romances see Patricia E. Grieve, *Floire and Blancheflor and the European romance* (Cambridge, 1997).

3. The story is also the basis of Boccaccio's novel of *Filicolo*.

4. There are no French plays on this theme but a Dutch play, *'tSpel van Florijsse ende van Blanchefloere* is recorded from 1483 (Worp, I, p. 145). Lancashire, p. 81, has a reference to a play of a 'knight cleped Florence' in 1444 which may

be a *Floire et Blanchfleur* story. A convent drama on the subject, *Amor di vertu* by Beatrice di Sera (1548), is analysed in Weaver (pp. 152–3); she points out that the quest of the lovers, Florido and Aurabeatrice, 'has at least three concurrent allegorical meanings' (p. 152).

5. An English translation of the Italian play is included in *Florentine drama*.

6. This scene is possibly based on the legend of Mary Magdalen and the king of Marseilles, found in the *Legenda* and in the *Digby Mary Magdalen* play.

7. Apart from its length and the introduction of the conflict between Christian and pagan, this is very like a number of romance play openings, such as those based on the *Manekine* (see below), which show the heroine's birth and her mother's death.

8. However, a friend of Ulimentus sees what happens and sends a messenger to him in Paris.

9. In the Abruzzese version of Rosana there is also a scene where a champion appears to save Rosana's life.

10. There is here a probable influence of the story of Joseph.

11. Three anonymous German Arthurian plays are based on a chastity test involving a drinking horn, a mantle or a crown. There is also a *spruch* on the same theme by Hans Sachs entitled *König Artus mit der Ehbrecherbrugk* (King Arthur and the adulterer's bridge). See John E. Tailby, 'Arthurian elements in drama and Meisterlieder', in *The Arthur of the Germans*, ed. W. H. Jackson and S. A. Ranawake (Cardiff, 2000), pp. 243–7.

12. In the *chanson de geste* of the *Prise d'Orange*, Guibourg, a Saracen princess gives a potion to her husband on the wedding night so that he thinks he has possessed her, and thus remains a virgin till she marries Guillaume d'Orange, the man she loves.

13. Esmeré and Gloriant are the names of two brothers in one of the stories from the cycle of the crusades, *Baudoin de Sebourc*, written down about 1350 in Hainault. The name of Esmoreit's beloved, Damiate, also appears in Baudoin. See W. Gerritsen, *A dictionary of medieval heroes*, trans. from the Dutch by Tanis Guest (Woodbridge, 1998), pp. 53–4.

14. Abelant is also the name of the pagan emperor of Constantinople in the romance of *Théseus de Cologne* (cf. Robert Bossuat, '*Théseus de Cologne*', *Le moyen age*, 65 (1959), p. 103).

15. This situation is reminiscent of *Baudoin* which also includes a battle between the Christians and the Red Lion of Abelant, in which the former are victorious, though in *Baudoin* the daughter of the Red Lion, after many adventures, marries Esmeré not his brother Gloriant.

16. This is a reversal of the *Floire et Blanchfleur* story and other tales of the heroine in the harem.

17. Another variant on the theme is found in Louvet's Marian miracle IX (1547): three Christians are imprisoned by the Soldan who tries to convert them with the aid of his daughter. Instead she becomes Christian and all four of them reach home safely, courtesy of the Virgin Mary.

18. For details of the sources and history of this Burgundian Romance see Alphonse Bayot, *Le roman de Gillion de trazegnies* (Louvain, 1903).

19. The fifteenth-century prose version of the romance includes also the adventures of the boys, Gerard and Jean, which closely resemble those of their father.

20. See *Spel en spektakel*, pp. 112–13.

21. A useful modern edition, with information on the background of the play by Gordon McMullan, was prepared for the Royal Shakespeare Company's performance of the play in 2002.

22. Yver's tales were translated into English by Sir Henry Wotton under the title *Cupid's Cautels*.

23. Many different reasons have been given for this change, see Henry Piard 'Adaptations de la "Tragédie Espagnole" dans les Pay Bas et Allemagne', in *Dramaturgie et société*, 2 vols. (Paris, 1968), II, pp. 635ff.

24. This is Sultan Soliman II, the magnificent (1520–66), who supported François 1er of France against the Holy Roman Emperor, Charles V.

25. The play includes many minor characters, especially a boastful knight in the group of Christians in Rhodes which also includes the Champions from England (St George), France (St Denys) and Spain (St James). For Richard Johnson's tale of the *Seven champions of Christendom* (1596–7) see p. 201. A play of the *Seven champions of Christendom* by John Kirke was printed (and probably performed) in England in 1638.

26. For details of all these texts see C. D. Rouillard, *The Turk in French history, thought and literature* (Paris, 1938).

27. Also the episode called 'The captive's story' in *Don Quixote*, Part I, xxxix–xli, published in 1605, and translated into English in 1612; the story 'The liberal-Lover' was published in 1613 as one of the *Novelas exemplares*, and translated into French in 1615 and into English in 1640. *Los Baños d'Argel* was published in *Ocho comedias y ocho entremeses nuevos* (1615), and never translated in full. A partial French version appeared in 1862 and a facsimile reprint of the 1615 text was published in Madrid in 1986.

28. Constanza is, of course, the name of the heroine in Mozart's *Seraglio*. See *supra* n. 2.

29. Massinger's principal alterations to the Spanish narrative consist of the substitution of comic and satirical scenes for a number of episodes displaying Spanish heroism and faithfulness.

30. *Les folies de Cardenio*, ed. J.-P. Leroy, TLF (Geneva, 1989). Guillén de Castro, *Obras de Don Guillén de Castro y Bellvis*, 3 vols. (Madrid, 1925–7), II, pp. 331–72. Despite the similarity of names, the tragedy *Cardenio und Celinde* by Gryphius has no connection with *Don Quixote*.

31. I am grateful to Alan Hindley for providing me with a copy of this fascinating play which was published by Emile Picot in Paris in 1901. Picot mentions a wide range of other versions of the story from different parts of Euriope up to the eighteenth century (ed. cit. pp. 1–14).

32. I am grateful to Elsa Strietmann for letting me have copies of the translations she and Peter Happé are making of these and other Dutch plays.

33. Théophile de Viau, *Pyrame et Thisbe* (*Théâtre du XVIIe siècle, t.2*). The sudden bathos would certainly raise a laugh today and probably did then. The *Pyrame* of Pujet de la Serre (1633) is virtually a prose version of Théophile's work (Lancaster, I, i, pp. 169–79).

34. Groto's *Adriana* is published in *Il teatro Italiano*, ed. Marco Ariani (Turin, 1977), II: *La tragedia del cinquecento* pp. 287–424. Ten editions were printed between 1578 and 1619 (ed. cit. p. 284).

35. For Chateauvieux see Lanson, p. 199. The French pastoral genre includes many other love stories with tragic endings including the *Amours de Dalcméon et de Flore* by Estienne Bellone (1610).

36. Translated into English by Cynthia Rodriguez-Badendyk, Lope's play is very different from Webster's grim tragedy. In the early acts especially there is a good deal of humour. Whereas in Webster the duchess is the focal character, in Lope it is the steward.

37. There is also a Latin *Vita de Amicus et Amelius* first mentioned in 1190 in which they are killed while crusading with Charlemagne (*The life of the dear friends Amicus and Amelius* trans. Mathew Kuefler, in *Medieval hagiography an anthology*, ed. Thomas Head (New York and London, 2000). p. 441). They were canonised as martyrs of the crusades in 1486, but rejected by the Bollandistes in 1794. I am grateful to Alexandra Johnson for a record of a performance of 'Amys and Amylon' at Bicester Priory in 1423–4 (*REED Newsletter*, 18:2 (1993), pp. 15–18).

38. The use of innocent blood as a cleansing for leprosy appears also in one of the Santiago miracle plays, *Le due pellegrini* (D'Ancona, III), and in medieval tales including the *Conte del Graal* where it is Perceval's maiden sister who pays the price.

39. *Spel en spektakel*, p. 115 and p. 333 n. 16.

40. Sachs, VIII, pp. 219–60. The French chronicle was translated into German in 1521 so would have been available to Sachs. See *The historye of Oliver of Castylle*, ed. Gail Orgelfinger (New York, 1988).

41. The only other instance of a play which includes this well-known folk motif of the 'Grateful Dead' is George Peele's *Old wives tale*. See Elizabeth Williams, 'The White Knight, the ungrateful dead and two Jacks', in *Essays in honour of Peter Meredith*, Leeds Studies in English, XXIX (Leeds, 1998), pp. 411–26.

42. Emile Roy, *Etudes sur Le Théâtre français*, III: *Les miracles de Notre Dame. Le recueil de Jean Louvet* (Paris, 1902), no. 2 (1537).

43. Harbage also lists English plays of the well-known friendship of Damon and Pythias in 1565, 1600 and (a puppet play) 1614. Sachs' play of *Agatocli und Clinia*, is based on a *Historia* from Lucian's *Dialogue of friendship*. Agatocli renders himself penniless and is imprisoned for debt bcause he has given all his money to a friend, to woo a courtesan who shows him favours while he has money and then rejects him.

44. Louis Sorieri, *Boccaccio's story of Tito e Gisippo in European literature* (New York, 1937). Friends as rival lovers also feature in Boisrobert's complex play of *Les rivaux amis* (1637) (Lancaster, I, i, p. 526).
45. The story is partly based on Montemayor's pastoral *Diana*.

9 PREMARITAL PROBLEMS

1. The 'substitute bride' motif was well known from the prose *Tristan* in which Brangane takes the place of Yseult when she marries Mark. Shakespeare uses a variation on the motif in both *Measure for measure* and *Alls well that ends well*, the latter being based on a Boccaccio story (Decameron Day 3, novella 9) which was also dramatised by Sachs and others.
2. The story line in *La comtesse d'Artois* (Louvet I), is virtually identical, the Devil as well as the Virgin Mary appears in person on the stage.
3. For other examples of this kind of violent revenge see David Blamires, 'Victim heroines in Hans Sachs' plays' in *Hans Sachs and folk theatre*, ed. Aylett and Skrine, p. 126. For the 'monstrous ransom' see p. 115.
4. The story of Dux Moraud and his daughter whom he seduces and who later kills both her father and her mother is known from a number of Latin and English versions, which make it possible to suggest an ending for the incomplete play text. See Davis, ed. *Non-cycle plays and fragments*, p. ciii. Brousse claimed he had used the version of the story in *Gesta Romanorum CLIII* (Lancaster, I, ii, pp. 122–3). See also George Wilkins, *The painful adventures of Pericles, prince of Tyre*, ed. Kenneth Muir (Liverpool, 1967).
5. In *Chaucer's Constance and accused queens*, (New York repr., 1973), Margaret Schlauch provides a useful guide to themes and motifs in the romances. She lists many narrative versions of the story, including folk tales. Dekker's lost play of *Fair Constance of Rome* (1600) is based on Chaucer's story. See also Black (pp. 272–3) for the Burgundian variant of the story of *La belle Helene de Constantinople* who escapes her father's desires, marries an English king called Henry and in due course succumbs to the wicked mother-in-law who orders her to be burnt. The executioner cuts off Helen's arm to 'prove' he has killed her but then changes his mind, burns his own niece instead and sends Helen off in the usual boat with her children, one of whom, known henceforth as *Bras*, has her arm fastened round his neck. Helen's other son becomes St Martin of Tours.
6. This rare example of a Latin romance play was composed in the end of the fourteenth or early fifteenth century. A miniature at the beginning of the MS shows a Dominican friar presenting it to a cardinal identifiable by the armorial blazon as belonging to the Colonna family (Roy, *Etudes*, p. v).
7. In the Cangé play the king goes so far as to appeal to the pope for permission to marry his daughter so as to appease his barons who insist on the need for a male heir to the throne. The pope agrees that it is necessary!
8. Uliva not only cuts off *both* her hands but does it alone on stage: a nice problem for the producer.

9. It is at this point that Stella's hands are restored by the doctors. In the French play the hand is fished out of the Tiber and miraculously restored at the very end of the story.

10. For the theme of infanticide see Schlauch, *Chaucer's Constance and accused queens*, p. 60.

11. The play is based on a sequel to the romance of *Huon de Bordeaux* where the 'magic' element is provided by the fairy Auberon. Yde (as she is called in the romance) actually has a sex change and marries the emperor's daughter. This was evidently considered inappropriate for a play described as a miracle of the Virgin (though she hardly appears in it). The same subject, we may assume, was dramatised in the *Jeu et exemple d'Yde et Olive* recorded as having been performed in Metz on the feast of St Waudrue in 1488–9. See Cohen, *Mons*, p. xxv.

10 THE FALSELY ACCUSED QUEEN AND OTHER SUFFERING WIVES

1. The epithet is used more in its original sense of suffering than its modern meaning of enduring without complaint. It is thus in many ways a feminine analogue of the book of Job who is also 'suffering' rather than 'patient', indeed he is explicitly referred to as 'impatient' (Job 4:5). For plays on Job see Muir, 'The sufferings of impatient Job'.

2. There is a play by Hans Sachs and a Dutch play *'t Spel van Gryselle*, recorded from 1489 with other plays or performances in 1498, 1541 and 1546 (Worp, I, p. 142). Latin school plays on Griselda were also popular (ibid., p. 202) as well as numerous later versions.

3. See Peggy McCracken, *The romance of adultery: queenship and sexual transgression in Old French literature* (Philadelphia, 1998), pp. 52ff.

4. Schlauch, *Chaucer's Constance and accused queens*, lists more than twenty romance versions from different countries of this story as well as many folk tales and other source material. In the Dutch dialogue *De Deucht en Constantia* (*Virtue and Constantia*), the other characters are Adulation and Calumny (*Repertorium*, 1S14). As Constance is a common name for the accused queen, it seems probable that this is also a version of that story.

5. In Sachs' *Die vertrieben keyserin*, the mother-in-law slanders the wife by telling her son that twins are always born of two different fathers – a well-known folk motif. When he refuses to reject his wife, the queen arranges for a scullion to be found naked in her bed; he is killed and the king then banishes her and her children. In the forest the children are stolen by an ape and lion. The motive of the scullion (or other servant) reappears in several versions including Genevieve of Brabant and Sachs' plays of *Ritter Galmi* and of the *Königin von Frankreich*. The children carried off by animals is also a common motif, see *St Eustace* and *Valentine and Orson*.

6. For *Théseus de Cologne* see Bossuat, 'Théseus de Cologne'. The best-known medieval source for the animal story is the *Dolopathos* account of the birth of

the swan-children which became part of the Godefroy de Bouillon/Swan Knight cycle; see Johannes de Alta Silva, *The seven sages of Rome and the Dolopathos* (Binghampton, N. Y., 1981). For obvious reasons the Swan children tales were not dramatised.

7. See Simon Eckehard, *Die Anfänge des weltlichen deutschen Schauspiels 1370–1530* (Tübingen, 2003), pp. 21–2. Jacob Ayrer dramatised the story in three parts and Lope de Vega in two parts, known only by a reference in Lope's own list of plays. See Arthur Dickson, *Valentine and Orson. A study in late medieval romance* (New York, 1929). The main versions are French, printed in Lyon by Jacques Maillet in 1489, and a Middle Low German text by Wilhelm Zieley. This, in conjunction with *Olivier und Artus* is the version used by Ayrer.

8. In the seventeenth-century play by N. Desfontaines, *Bellissante ou la fidélité reconnue*, a version of Valentine and Orson, no animal actually appears on stage.

9. See *Florentine drama*. An undated Croatian drama on this little-known local saint, almost certainly based on Antonia Pulci's play, is mentioned in *New approaches to European theater of the Middle Ages* (New York, 2004), (p. 133).

10. Kathleen Krause, 'The falsely accused heroine in the *Miracles de Notre Dame par personnages*', EMD (Camerino, 1999), treats of the theme in the Cangé plays. In some versions of the story the empress pretends to offer the brother-in-law a rendezvous in a tower room and then locks him in. Unfortunately for her, she releases him when the king's return is announced and he immediately denounces her to her husband.

11. As David Blamires points out, 'the husband is always ready to believe the worst of his wife' ('Victim heroines in Hans Sachs' plays', p. 122).

12. In Sachs' play the herb is brought by an angel – there is no place for the Virgin Mary in reformed Nuremberg.

13. This change is probably due to the fact that Pulci wrote plays for a convent. At the beginning of the play, Guglielma reluctantly agrees to the marriage proposed for her, although she would prefer to enter a nunnery. For a detailed study of this theme see also Weaver, pp. 99–104.

14. See Schlauch, *Chaucer's Constance and accused queens*, p. 109 n. 37.

15. Other examples of the unexpected champion are to be found in the Abruzzese version of *Rosana*, and the *Marquise de Gaudine*. A late version of the false accusation which also involves a champion is *La Polixene* (1597) by Jean Behourt who wrote it for his pupils to act. The story is based on the sixth *Histoire tragique* by Boaistuau telling of the duchess of Savoy and a Spanish lord, Mandozza.

16. An element of comedy is introduced by Frischlin who gives Talandus a servant based on the typical Italian parasite, whose only concern is where his meals are coming from. Even when the blind Talandus asks him to accompany him to Rome, the parasite only agrees if he can go by cart since he is too fat to travel on horseback.

17. Graham Runnalls, Jean Louvet: compositeur de mystères et homme de théâtre Parisien, 1536–50, *Bibliothèque d'Humanisme et Renaissance*, 62 (2000).

18. For details of the romance see Schlauch, *Chaucer's Constance and accused queens*, pp 110–11.
19. The theme is used by Sachs in *Der ritter Galmi* (VIII).
20. The story of 'St Genevieve' is recorded under 2 April in *Natales sanctorum Belgii* by Johannes Molanus (Louvain, 1595) (Black, p. 192). In later editions of Molanus she is referred to only briefly (1616) or not at all (1626). In the *Acta sanctorum* Genevieve is listed under the 'rejecti' for 2 April with the comment: 'totam historiam habet suspectam'. It is not surprising therefore that in her index, Szarota confuses her with St Genevieve, the patron saint of Paris (II, 2).
21. There are many medieval plays on the biblical story of Susannah and the Elders, the earliest being by John Damascene in the late seventh century, see TIE *Medieval*, C.67. In the sixteenth and seventeenth centuries the story was especially popular in Protestant countries.
22. A *zwerglein* (dwarf) also features in Hans Sachs' accused queen play of *Die königin von Frankreich* (VIII, p. 54). Later plays in German were the sources used by Schumann for the libretto of his opera *Genoveva*. In Painter's English story of *The lady falsely accused* (XLI, based on a Bandello story), the would-be lover, a hitherto faithful retainer, sends an innocent youth to the lady's chamber and then kills him. See also Schlauch, *Chaucer's Constance and accused queens*, pp. 104–6.
23. *Pandosto: the triumph of time* by Robert Greene (in *The descent of Euphues. Three Elizabethan romance stories*, ed. James Winny (Cambridge, 1957)).
24. The two-day French play of *Pandostes* by Hardy is lost, but one by Pujet de la Serre (1631) closely follows Greene's story, including having Pandosto fall in love with and seek to marry his daughter. However, La Serre, like Shakespeare, prefers a happy ending and when the truth is revealed, Pandostes joins all the other characters in rejoicing at the wedding of Doraste and Favvye (Lancaster, I, ii, pp. 671–5).
25. Lancaster, II, i, pp. 243–5. This is the only text I have found which explicitly claims that the supposed relationship with the brother-in-law would be incestuous.
26. See also M. Valency, *The tragedies of Herod and Mariamne* (New York, 1940).
27. *La mort des enfants d'Hérodes ou la suite de Mariane* (Lancaster, II, i, p. 188). The Paris Jesuits staged *Alexander et Aristobulus* in 1663 (Boysse p. 142).

11 DOMESTIC DRAMAS

1. For a more detailed account of this early detective story see TIE *Medieval*, p. 162.
2. See the article: '"La buena guarda" de Lope de Vega y 'Felix Culpa', in *La comedia de Magia y de Santos*, ed. F. J. Blasco, E. Caldera, J. Alvarez Barrientos and R. de la Fuente (Madrid, 1992), pp. 97–106. I am grateful to Ann Rees for this reference.

12 THE WAGER

1. Gaston Paris, 'Le cycle de la gageure', *Romania*, 32 (1903), pp. 481–551, is based on a series of lectures given by Gaston Paris at the Sorbonne on the *romans d'aventure*. The wager material was later edited for *Romania* by Bédier. Paris gives detailed analyses of many texts from different parts of Europe which he groups according to common motifs. More recently, the wager story is examined from a feminist and legalistic point of view in R. L. Krueger, 'Double jeopardy: the appropriation of women in four Old French romances of the *Cycle de la gageure*', in *Seeking the woman in late medieval and renaissance writings. Essays in feminist contextual criticism*, ed. S. Fisher and J. E. Halley (Knoxville, 1989), pp. 21–50.

2. Paris does not know of any original source for this theme but cites a number of other similar stories (ibid., pp. 486–90). A comic variant of the ring story may be found in *The merchant of Venice*.

3. In his sources of Cymbeline, Bullough (VIII, pp. 79–85) includes several scenes from *Eufemia* in his own English translation.

4. In the thirteenth-century French romance of *Guillaum de Dole* a servant tells the villain of a rose on the heroine's leg and in the derivative *Roman de la violette*, the villain peeps through a hole while the heroine is bathing and sees a violet on her right breast (Paris, 'Le cycle de la gageure', pp. 539–42).

5. Gaston Paris describes the plot of Cymbeline as being 'la plus compliquée et la plus invraisemblable qu'on puisse voir' but praises the characterisation of Imogen and Iachimo and the poetry (ibid., p. 511). *Ostes d'Espagne* he puts in a different group of texts and denounces it as being 'd'une extrême faiblesse et d'une inseigne gaucherie' with no redeeming features at all (ibid., pp. 530–1).

6. Probably Lothaire I (840–55), grandson of Charlemagne. This would fit in with the partial Christianisation of Spain while Granada is still ruled by the Muslims.

7. The girl who disguises herself as a boy is a very common figure in medieval and Renaissance literature, though she gradually disappears during the classical period. In Corneille's second play, *Clitandre* (1630), 'une tragédie romanesque assez extravagante', one of the heroines disguises herself as a man and starts to fight with one of the villains. Unfortunately he notices a hairpin with which she has fixed her hair and realises who she really is. When he tries to assault her, however, she pulls the pin out of her hair and thrusts it into his eye, thus giving herself an opportunity to kill him with her dagger.

8. For other examples of 'beating God' see the miracles of St Nicholas (p. 48).

9. Although the Virgin has her customary angelic train and musical tribute as in all the Cangé plays, it is God who actually speaks to Ostes.

10. In a fourteenth-century Franco-Provençal poem on the same subject, *Elena*, the wife, herself fights and cuts off the traitor's arm. He confesses the truth (Paris, 'Le cycle de la gageure', p. 527).

11. Paris (ibid., p. 506) cites an anonymous fourteenth-century Italian *novelle* in which the characters finally meet up in Alexandria and the lady strips off her masculine clothes before her husband, the 'Can' (or ruler) and the traitor.

12. Paris mentions this parallel in a detailed study of Ohle's creation of a hypothetical *Posthumus* play as the source of *Cymbeline* (Ohle, p. 70 cit. Paris, 'Le cycle de la gageure', p. 514 n. 4). Nosworthy, in the Arden edition of *Cymbeline*, refers simply to a *Miracle de Notre Dame* by Gautier de Coinci (p. xx). I can find no trace of such a miracle.

13. In the fifteenth-century fable of *The wright's chaste wife* (ed. F. J. Furnivall, Early English Text Society, Original Series 12 (London, 1865), the shirt is replaced by a wreath of roses which only guarantees the wife's chastity. Furnivall quotes a number of analogues from different countries. In *L'empereur Henry et Kunégonde* performed by the Jesuits at Malines in 1616 (Lanson, p. 227) the queen, accused of adultery by her husband, took the test of walking on red-hot iron and was proved innocent (AASS 1 March).

14. For other examples of the wrath of the woman scorned see below p. 106.

15. This is obviously a variant on the empress of Rome and the tower.

13 HELL HATH NO FURY: THE WOMAN SCORNED

1. The twelfth-century *Sept sages de Rome* is the earliest western version of the story which became widespread in Europe with constantly changing series of tales.

2. For the medieval plays of Joseph see Muir, *Biblical drama*, pp. 76–7 and notes.

3. For plays by Crocus, Macropedius, Diether and Balticus, see Creizenach, II, pp. 105–8. For Ruf and Rute's versions see ibid., III, p. 243.

4. Best, *Bidermann*, p. 94. The play was first performed in Munich in 1615.

5. *Le mythe de Phèdre* (ed. A. G. Wood (Paris, 1996)) includes three seventeenth-century plays on this theme between Garnier's *Hippolyte* (1585) and Racine's *Phèdre* (1677).

6. Dabrowka, 'Polish saint plays of the sixteenth and seventeenth centuries', p. 182.

7. *Le théâtre complet de Tristan l'Hermite*, ed. Claude Kurt Abraham, Jerome William Schweitzer and Jacqueline van Baelen (Tuscaloosa, 1975).

8. Sachs (VIII, pp. 107–30). The story is set in the reign of Otto II, c. AD 990.

9. The theme also features in Massinger's *The Roman actor* (see p. 21), and in the classical tale of *Cephalus and Procris*: Cephalus rejects the goddess Aurora because he loves his wife Procris. In revenge Aurora arranges for him to kill Procris in a shooting accident. Plays survive in Dutch (*Repertorium*, 2.24) and French: Hardy, *Procris* (Lancaster, I, i, pp. 53–6) and Chrestien des Croix, *Le ravissement de Céphale* (Lancaster, I, i, p. 128).

10. See Lebègue, p. 272. Marie de France's *Lanfal* has a similar plot but with a happy ending as the knight rides away to fairyland with his lady.

11. For other plays on St John Chrysostom see p. 25.

12. *Legenda*, pp. 539–43.

13. D'Ancona, III, pp. 465–85.
14. This is obviously borrowed from the story of Benjamin and Joseph (Genesis 44: 1–12). In the *Legenda* and other early versions, the pilgrims are a father and son, the innkeeper puts the goblet in the father's sack so he can claim all their goods when they are arrested. The 'scorned' daughter was soon added and so is the story of the cock that crows. There are records of French and Provençal plays on the same miracle, see Henrard, pp. 332–6; an Italian play on St James is recorded from Florence in 1473, and the miracle was performed in Ferrara in 1476 'by a Florentine together with some people of this city' (Newbigin, p. 143). Two other plays of miracles of St James, *I due pellegrini* and *Di uno pellegrino*, are both based on stories in the *Legenda*.
15. The episode is traditionally linked with the town of Santo Domingo de la Calzada and to this day a white cock and hen live in a glass-fronted nest in the cathedral – in the Middle Ages pilgrims could purchase a feather as a relic. The cooked bird which gets up and crows is also found in the English carol of 'King Herod and the cock'.

14 FAMILY FEUDS

1. For the plays of Jacob and Esau which deal with inheritance, see Muir, *Biblical drama*, p. 213 n. 10. See also Herod and his sons p. 99.
2. For the historical details of the marriage of Clovis and Ste Bathildis see Jeanroy (*HLF*, XXXIX, p. 83).
3. This may be the inspiration behind Hans Sachs' treatment of the Oedipus legend in his play of *Die ungluckhafften königin Jocasta*. In the last act the two sons of Oedipus attack and kill each other on stage, leaving Jocasta to make the final speech emphasising the tragedy's moral lessons (Peter Skrine, 'The Greek tragedies of Hans Sachs', in *Hans Sachs and folk theatre*, p. 93).
4. This suggests a link with the origin of the Roman fastes, a bundle of rods surrounding an axe used as the symbol of the king's authority.
5. I am grateful to Alan Knight for supplying me with a copy of this interesting dialogue, which is almost certainly based on the story of King Lear in Geoffrey of Monmouth's *History of England* (Bullough, VII, p. 311) which itself is a reworking of the folk tale of the daughter who declared she loved her father as meat loves salt.
6. Simon, *Die Anfänge*, p. 158.

15 THE THEATRE OF CRUELTY

1. The first French translations of Seneca were by Garnier whose plays were themselves translated into English by Lady Pembroke and members of her circle which included Thomas Kyd. See A. M. Witherspoon, *The influence of Robert Garnier on the Elizabethan drama*, Yale Studies in English 65 (New Haven, repr. 1968).

2. The article is one of a group which Lebègue identifies with the term baroque – the period between the humanist drama of the sixteenth century and the establishment of the classical French theatre c. 1640.

3. Creizenach (III) lists one in Spanish, and several in German. Bullinger was head of the *kloster schule* in Zurich from 1523 to 1528; his Lucretia was a work of the Zurich Reform and includes a scene of peasants demanding justice against kings, while Sextus is in Lucretia's house (Creizenach, III, p. 255). French texts in the sixteenth century are mentioned by G. Lebègue in *La tragédie religieuse en France. Les débuts 1514–73* (Paris, 1929), and plays in Dutch are recorded in *Repertorium* (1U1)and Worp, I, p. 307.

4. 'Comment centurion romain tenoit en captivité une dame nommee Orgia et la viola par force, dont laditte orgia print vengeance terrible dudit centurion' (fo. 290r). The play will be published in vol. V of Knight's edition of the Lille plays. The story is given here from Valerius Maximus, *Memorable doings and sayings*, Bk vi: 1 ext. 2, Loeb Classical Library, 2 vols. (Harvard, 2000).

5. *Le viol de Tamar* (Lille II:25). *Amnon et Thamar* by Chrestien des Croix was published in Rouen in 1608 (Lancaster, I, i, p. 128). There are two Dutch plays, one, *Ammon en Thamar*, in the collection of the Rhetoricians group of the *Roode Roos* from Hasselt (*Repertorium*, 1S9) is dated 1610, the other, *Amon*, in the collection of the *Fiolieren* of 's-Gravenpolder is undated but probably also early seventeenth century (*Repertorium*, 1U13). Peele's play of *David and Bethsabe* includes the story of Thamar. In *Thamara* (1611), the German writer, Honerdus, emphasised the sorrows of David rather than the violence stressed by the Senecan imitator Lummennaeus in *Amnon*, 1611. See also Parente, *Religious drama*, p. 53.

6. Tirso's play, translated by James Fenton as *Tamar's revenge*, was performed at Stratford in 2004. Information about Tirso and his work can be found in the introduction to the translation of *The doubter damned* cited above.

7. *Lanseloet van Danmark* is in many ways different from the other *abele spelen* for it does not have the traditional happy ending – at least not for the hero, who is, it turns out, not really a proper hero at all. The play is such an unusual mixture of motifs that it cannot truly be called a tragi-comedy or even a tragedy. Everything in it is topsy-turvy, a reversal of the usual themes and characters. The only parallel to such inversions may perhaps be found in the quasi-dramatic thirteenth-century *chantefable* of *Aucassin et Nicolete*, but there the changes are pleasant and humorous: Nicolete is the active partner who, when they are separated, makes all the efforts to find her way back to Aucassin but he remains entirely faithful in his intention to marry Nicolete.

8. All quotations are from the translation by Johanna Prins (1999) though I have retained the Dutch spelling of Lanseloet to avoid confusion with the better known Arthurian hero. The reference to wealth, before mentioning birth, may be significant here. Walter Cohen, in *Drama of a nation: public theater in Renaissance England and Spain* (Ithaca, 1985), is one of the few scholars to include this play in a general discussion of medieval and Renaissance theatre. He concludes that it provides 'a class-based moralized conclusion: bourgeois

virtue is rewarded and aristocratic vice punished' (p. 76). This, however, suggests that the queen's objection to Sanderijn's rank is justified, though the author makes it clear she was, if not aristocratic, at least not of bourgeois parentage.

9. *L'empereur qui tua son neveu* (Lyon, 1543). (*Ancien théâtre françois*, ed. Le Duc, III.) No source is given for the story, which is set in a Christian German empire and is part morality and part miracle play.

10. The term 'Monstrous ransom' was coined by Mary Lascelles in her study: *Shakespeare's Measure for measure* (London, 1953).

11. Daniel's interrogation of the two elders, in which he leads them to give different accounts of the scene of the 'adultery', is one of the oldest pieces of courtroom detection on record.

12. An ancient version of the story is cited by St Augustine to show the difficulty of making moral judgements about fornication. For the text of this and other analogues see Bullough, II, *Measure for measure* (p. 400).

13. Eusebius, *The history of the Church*, trans. G. A. Williamson and ed. with a new introduction by Andrew Louth (Harmondsworth, 1989), ch. 8, Diocletian to Maximian, p. 350.

14. Ukena, p. 722. The MS of Cysat's play ends here at line 4465, though the extant summary shows another three and a half Acts. This and other plays of the Invention of the Holy Cross are discussed elsewhere, but Cysat is the only author to have intercalated such an incident in the story.

15. The play was performed at Trinity College, Cambridge, in 1564/5 in either French or Latin (Bullough, II, p. 400).

16. Mariana in *Measure for measure* pleads, successfully, for Angelo's life. Her loss of virginity is less serious, since they were already betrothed and he marries her.

17. In Livy, the judge is called Appius Claudius and his false witness is unnamed. Though mid-sixteenth century in date, the form of the play is still that of the old moralities with a Vice and other allegorical and comic characters.

18. Cueva's Spanish play *La muerte de Virginia y Appio Claudio* has 'tragic force' (McKendrick, p. 56). Bullinger's *Apius und Virginia* was performed in Berne in 1565–70 (Creizenach, III, p. 255).

19. *Répertoire*, no. 56, p. 95.

20. For details of the relationship between the play and the story see P. R. Horne, *The tragedies of Giambattista Cinthio Giraldi* (Oxford, 1962), ch. 7.

21. An English translation and details of Whetstone's dramatisation of the story in *Promos and Cassandra* are given in Bullough, II, *Measure for measure*.

22. Lycurgus was a (probably legendary) ruler of Sparta famous as a lawgiver. For another version of this story see *Gesta Romanorum*, Tale IV.

23. John Fletcher, *The dramatic works in the Beaumont and Fletcher Canon*, ed. F. Bower, 8 vols. (Cambridge 1966–79), VIII, p. 87. Hardy's plays of *Scédase* and *Timoclée* (both based on stories in Plutarch) also include themes of rape and revenge (Lancaster, I, i, pp. 46–7).

24. See 'The alleged rape by Edward III of the countess of Salisbury', in Antonia Gransden, *Legends, traditions and history in medieval England* (London, 1992),

pp. 267–78. For full details see Hugh E. L. Collins, *The Order of the Garter 1348–1461: chivalry and politics in late medieval England* (Oxford, 2000).

25. Coppée's play of the *Sanglante bataille entre les impériaux et Bohèmes* refers to an episode in the Thirty Years War, in which the Protestant Winter King of Bohemia lost his kingdom to the Catholic Holy Roman Emperor (Lancaster, I, i, p. 227).

26. 'An order set up by a king, as while dancing he went to pick up the Countess's garter saying: "shame be to him who thinks ill of this" thus showing to his subjects her innocence.' The 'romantic account of the origins of the garter' (ibid., p. 271) was first mentioned in *Tirant lo blanc* (c. 1460) and then popularised by Polydore Vergil: 'About the origin, however, of the instituting of the Order there is considerable uncertainty. Vulgar rumour now has it that Edward once picked up from the floor the garter of the queen or a (female) friend, which having by chance come undone as happens from use had fallen. Several courtiers observed this and made joking remarks and he [Edward] said a short time in the future the highest honour should attach to them by this same garter, and not long after he instituted this same order and added the motto to it by which he showed these courtiers that this matter was contrary to the way they had judged.' *Anglica historia*, 1534, p. 379. I am most grateful to Peter Meredith for the translation.

16 LE *CŒUR MANGÉ* AND OTHER CULINARY SURPRISES

1. For the history of this popular medieval story see the introduction to *Le roman du châtelain de Couci et de la dame de Fayel*, ed. Gaston Paris, SATF VIII (Paris, 1879), pp. xlvi–lviii. In a number of late medieval texts including verses by Christine de Pisan, the name of the Chatelain de Couci is linked with that of the Chastelaine de Vergi (ibid., pp. lxxviii–lxxix). There is also a detailed study of the text by Gaston Paris in *Romania*, 8 (1879) (pp. 343–71).

2. The lady's refusal ever to eat again and her speedy death continues to feature in the many variants on the story. (ed. cit., p. xlviii). Retellings of the story appeared in French and English (where the love was always chaste, see Helen Cooper, *The English romance in time: transforming motifs from Geoffrey of Monmouth to the death of Shakespeare* (Oxford, 2004), p. 397) in the seventeenth and eighteenth centuries. The most ludicrous is a version of the story published in London in 1707 featuring monsieur and madame Butler in which the lover sends his heart home in powder form and it is served to the lady in her tea (ed. cit., p. xcv)!

3. *Spel en spektakel*, p. 123. The introduction to the poem includes references to versions of the story in the Low Countries (p. lxxix).

4. There is no surviving Greek play but the story was dramatised in three Latin plays, by Ennius, Accius and Varius before the best-known version by Seneca.

5. The play was translated into Dutch by Jan Vos with the title *Aran en Titus*.

6. The spelling of Philomela's name varies considerably. Lavinia, in *Titus Andronicus*, manages to explain what has happened to her by picking out a copy of this story from a pile of books. With deliberate irony, Imogen in *Cymbeline* is shown reading the story in bed when Jachimo is hidden in the chest in her bedroom.

7. *Progne* by Jacques de la Taille, composed in 1562, is lost (Lebègue, *Tragédie*, p. 28). Harbage mentions an English version from Corraro performed at Christchurch, Oxford, in 1566.

8. Simon, *Die Anfänge*, p. 93. The form 𝕮𝖔𝖓𝖈𝖗𝖊𝖙𝖎 is probably a misreading by Sachs of the Gothic printed text: 𝕮𝖔𝖓𝖈𝖗𝖊𝖇𝖎 for 𝕿𝖆𝖓𝖈𝖗𝖊𝖇𝖎. See Tailby, 'Arthurian elements in drama', p. 246, for another example: 𝕽𝖆𝖒𝖊𝖘𝖎𝖘 for 𝕿𝖆𝖒𝖊𝖘𝖎𝖘 – London's river.

9. For the influence of Seneca on these English plays see Willard Farnham, *The medieval heritage of the Elizabethan tragedy* (Oxford, 1956), p. 356. He points out that in the second chorus in *Gismond* the young widow is criticised for succumbing to lust and her failure 'to show the chaste steadfastness of such famous women as Lucrece and Penelope' (pp. 360–1).

10. Joseph Spencer Kennard, *The Italian theatre*, 2 vols. (New York, 1931; repr. 1952), I, p. 144. The popularity of the subject in France is attested by the publication in quick succession of Chrestien des Croix's *Rosemonde* of 1603, repr. as *Albouin* in 1608 (Lancaster, I, i, p. 128). Claude Billard's *Alboin* followed in 1610 (Lancaster, I, i, p. 147) and Baro's *Rosemonde* in 1651 (Lancaster, I, ii, p. 356).

11. Kennard, *Italian theatre*, I, p. 141. See P. R. Horne *The tragedies of Giambattista Cinthio Giraldi* (Oxford, 1962), p. 49. Giraldi used a very similar theme in *Altile* where the heroine marries against the will of her brother but escapes his revenge by the arrival, just in time, of her husband's father who turns out to be a man of rank and wealth, so all ends happily. The daughter's/sister's secret and unsuitable marriage and children are reminiscent of the *Duchess of Malfi* and Giraldi's novella may have influenced Bandello in his development of what is said to be a true story.

12. *Orbecche*, ed. Ariani, *Il teatro italiano*, I: *La tragedia del cinquecento* pp. 85–184 (Turin, 1977). A French translation by Du Mounin was printed in 1585 (Stegmann, p. 682).

13. Horne, *The tragedies of Giambattista Cinthio Giraldi*, p. 56. Horne also explains the quite substantial differences between the play and the novella.

14. Julius von Braunschweig, *Die Schauspiele des Herzogs Heinrich Julius von Braunschweig*, ed. Julius Tillman (Leipzig, 1880).

17 THE SIEGE OF TROY

1. Useful information about the many narratives of Troy in Latin and French is given in the introduction by Jean-Yves Tilliette to *L'Iliade*, an edition by Francine Mora of the Latin poem by Joseph of Exeter, with facing French translation (Brepols, 2003). This thirteenth-century text combines material

from Homer with substantial extracts from the works of Dares and Dictys and details from Benoit de Ste Maure.

2. G. Cohen, *Etudes d'histoire du théâtre* (Paris, 1956), pp. 164–5. This was obviously a substantial play but unfortunately we have no information about it, though Benoit's *Roman de Troie* was probably the source. In 1400 the duke of Anjou would have been Louis II, father of René d'Anjou, who was a great patron of the arts including drama.

3. In 1389 during a banquet held as part of the celebrations for the arrival of queen Isabel of Bavaria in Paris, a fleet of Grecian ships attacked the 'chastel d'Ilion' which bore the banners of Priam, Hector and other Trojan kings. The room was so hot and the crowds so great that the queen felt faint and broke a window near her to get some air. Roy, *Etudes*, p. cxxxii. See also n. 6.

4. For details of the MSS and editions see Runnalls, *Les mystères français imprimés*, p. 84. Although the title page spells Milet with only one 'l' it is customarily spelt with two.

5. This was a very suitable choice of play for a Prince of the Blood, becaue of the tradition that the French kings descended from Hector. See below p. 145.

6. Lanson, pp. 224–5.

7. Benoit de St Maure, *Le Roman de Troie*, ed. Leopold Constans, SATF, 6 vols. (Paris, 1904–12). For details of the MSS and printed versions of the *Roman* and the sources, derivatives and translations, see Marc Jung, *La légende de Troie en France au moyen âge*, Romanica Helvetica 114 (Basel, 1996). Jung also gives a very detailed analysis of Benoit's poem including the post-siege fate of both Greeks and Trojans (pp. 40–77), a number of illustrations and details of the Latin and French related texts.

8. For Dares and Dictys I have used the translations by R. M. Frazer Jr: *The Trojan war. The chronicles of Dictys of Crete and Dares the Phrygian* (Bloomington, Ind., 1966). Frazer's introduction gives full details of the differences between their accounts and the *Iliad*, as well as their influence on the later narratives, including that of Guido delle Colonne, one of the major sources of Shakespeare's *Troilus and Cressida*.

9. The narration by Paris of the 'judgement' scene, Benoit took from Dares who does not introduce the gods and goddesses as Homer did. Dictys, writing from the Greek point of view, omits the judgement episode completely and describes Paris's actions as greed and treachery. Dares and Millet's account say that the apple is for the 'worthiest'. The *Iliade* like many older versions says it is for the most beautiful (ed. cit., pp. 237–50).

10. The story is dramatised in Euripides, *Iphigenia in Aulis*, and there are a number of Latin and Vernacular versions in the sixteenth century. For a chronological list of the many post-classical plays see J.-M. Gliksohn, *Iphigénie, de la Grèce antique à l'Europe des lumières* Littératures Modernes 37 (Paris, 1985), pp. 228–32.

11. 'Lors d'un costé et d'autre sonneront les trompettes et ce commencera la bataille tellement que d'un chascun cote en doit cheoir plusieurs morts et

puis cessera le bruit' (Then the trumpets will sound on both sides and the battle will begin so that several will fall dead on each side, then the noise will stop) (p. 90). There is no modern edition of Millet's play and many of the early printed texts are not paginated, so I have taken all quotations from Stengel's nineteenth-century copperplate, transcript edition (Jacques Millet, *La destruction de Troye la grant* (Paris, 1484), transcript by E. Stengel (Marburg, 1883)).

12. Millet's story of Troilus and Briseida was taken direct from Benoit who probably invented it. There is no classical version of the story though the names Briseida and Criseida both occur in Homer. In the fourteenth century the romance of Troilus and his unfaithful beloved, now called Criseida, was treated as a separate story especially by Boccaccio in his *Filostrato*, whence it passed via Chaucer to Shakespeare.

13. Dares makes the planner of the ambush Hecuba rather than Paris (*The Trojan war*, pp. 160–2). See below Heywood's *Iron Age* where Paris and Hecuba plan the ambush together. The only Greek source is the scene at the end of Euripides' *Hecuba*, when after the destruction of Troy, Pyrrhus, the son of Achilles, claims that the Ghost of Achilles cannot rest unless Polyxena, youngest daughter of Priam, be sacrificed on his grave, which is done. In Ovid's *Metamorphoses* Book XIII, the death of Polyxena closely follows the Greek play version.

14. In Dares and Dictys he is called Neoptolemus. In Dictys, Penthesilea appears earlier and is killed by Achilles, in Dares she is killed by Pyrrhus.

15. A rare later French play on the Trojan war is Montchrestien's *Hector* (1604) set entirely inside Troy, involving Priam and his family, with messengers and a chorus. There is no stage action and the chorus is mainly involved in discussions of abstract themes of courage, disaster and honour. The play begins with Cassandra's prophecies of disaster and ends with the death of Hector and the lamentations of his wife and family.

16. Franz Schnorr von Carolsfeld, 'Vier ungedruckte Fastnachtspiele des 15. Jahrhunderts', *Archiv fur Litteraturgeschichte*, 3 (1874), pp. 1–25, nos. 2 and 4. I am most grateful to Cora Dietl for sending me details of these and the other German plays.

17. *Die zerstörung der statt Troya*, in six Acts with thirteen characters (Sachs, XII, pp. 279–316). The prologue specifies the sources.

18. See Skrine 'The Greek tragedies of Hans Sachs', p. 97. Skrine also describes Sachs' other plays on Greek themes including the stories of Clitemnestra and Jocasta.

19. Sachs' version of the name 𝕯eop𝕳ebus as 𝕻𝕳leow𝕻𝕳ebus is probably the result of misreading the Gothic print. See also p. 135.

20. In Dares' account of the fall of Troy, the gate the traitors open has a horse's head on the outside. In Dictys a very large horse is built as an offering to Minerva; the Trojans have to pull down the walls to allow the horse to be brought in. Neither Dares nor Dictys uses the story of the men hidden inside the horse which is described by Odysseus in *Odyssey*, Book VIII, but an

illustration in Millet's play makes the presence of the Greeks in the horse quite clear.

21. The story of Achilles and Polyxena was very popular in early seventeenth-century France: in *Achille* by Nicholas Filleul of Rouen, performed in 1563, Achilles sees the ghost of Patroclus, promises revenge, and kills Hector. Then follows the betrothal of Achilles with Polyxena and his death as a result. There is no stage action – everything is narrated (Creizenach, II, p. 422). Hardy's *Mort d'Achille* (1605–15) also includes the luring of Achilles to his death by the promise he shall marry Polyxena (Lancaster, I, i, p. 47). The lost play of *Ajax and Ulysses* listed by Harbage (in 1572) and Benserade's *Mort d'Achille et la dispute de ses armes* (Lancaster, II, i, p. 308, 1637) are based on the episode described in the *Odyssey*: when the arms of the dead Achilles were awarded to Ulysses, Ajax went mad and killed himself, as Ulysses explains to Achilles when Ajax refuses to speak to Ulysses when he visits the Elysian fields (*Odyssey*, Book XI).

22. There is no modern edition of the play which is described in Petra Fochler, *Fiktion als Historie. Der Trojanische Krieg in der deutschen Literatur des 16. Jahrhunderts* (Wiesbaden, 1990), pp. 130–56.

23. The story of the quarrel and Ajax's madness and death is described in Ovid, *Metamorphoses*, Book XIII.

24. Harbage, Supplementary List II k, mentions a performance of the destruction of Troy in Germany by Spencer's touring company in 1613, and suggests it might be Heywood's *Iron Age* but the dates do not fit.

25. This must be a deliberate echo of Richard III. Duke Julius frequently entertained the English travelling companies of *Commödianten*.

26. This scene is in *Aeneid*, Book II, but not mentioned in other plays.

27. This is a unique version of the death of Agamemnon, and Orestes' revenge; Hans Sachs'*Clitemnestra* is a straight version of the original legend.

28. In the prologue, Banks appeals to the audience and hopes: 'you will be kind to hear / the Lives of those whose Successours you are: / For when Troy fell, its remnant here did plant / and built this place, and call'd it Troynovant.' A few years later Heywood's account of a pageant presented in London in 1603 for the new king, James I, and his queen, includes a song with the refrain: 'Troynovant is now no more a Citie' because, as Heywood explains, it has become a royal bower during the king's visit (John Heywood, *The dramatic works of John Heywood*, modernised edn by J. S. Farmer, 2 vols. (London, 1905), I, p. 302)

29. The theft of the Palladion (I have used Benoit's spelling throughout) comes from Dictys pp. 100ff. where the episode is much further on in the story, after the deaths of both Hector and Achilles.

30. The term seems to be used here in the sense of Inigo Jones' 'scena versatilis', a front piece which swivelled to reveal a different scene on the reverse side, or the 'scena ductilis', a scene painted on shutters, which could be pulled apart to reveal another scene behind. See Inigo Jones in *Cambridge Guide to World Theatre*, ed. Martin Banham (Cambridge, 1988), p. 528.

31. This is in many ways one of the most original and freely developed of the Troy plays. Despite the prologue the play actually emphasises the role of Achilles and the other Greeks, and Banks has no qualms about altering many details of the story.

32. All quotations are from Cora Dietl's edition. I am grateful to her for letting me have advance copies of the Latin play text and the very useful German commentary.

33. The reference to Peleus is interesting as there is an element of confusion in some versions of the story between Peleus, father of Achilles, and Pelias, uncle of Jason. Dictys ignores this early history of Troy and mentions neither. Dares on the other hand begins his story with an account of Jason and the Argonauts setting off at the orders of Pelias, and this arrangement is followed by Benoit de St Maure, whose poem begins with a prologue on his sources, Dares and Dictys. Benoit follows this with a brief résumé of the whole story from Jason Troy (ed. cit. ll. 145–714). 'I'll begin by speaking of Peleus and his wife Thetis.' These two were the parents of Achilles (ll. 145–50). However, when at the end of the résumé Benoit actually starts his full story-telling he makes no mention of Achilles and goes straight into the episode of the Golden Fleece.

34. Locher intercalates a number of these comments to emphasise the decadence of the contemporary world.

35. Jan Kochanowski, *The dismissal of the Greek envoys*, trans. and commentary by Barry Keane (Szczecin, 1999). I am grateful to Rob Zulewski for drawing my attention to this interesting play.

36. Following the example of Dictys, Paris is called Alexander throughout the play. Homer sometimes called him Alexandros.

37. The Dutch playwright Vondel also used a Trojan theme to present a political subject in his seventeenth-century play of *Palamedes* (1625). The popular Greek captain, falsely accused of taking bribes and treacherously killed by jealous rivals Diomedes and Ulysses in Dictys, is seen as a forerunner of the tragedy of the Dutch hero, Oldenbarnefeld (Worp, I, p. 266). The slaughter of Palamedes is described by Aeneas in the *Aeneid* 'Him the Greeks framed on a monstrous charge of being a traitor / and put him down to death, an innocent man, because he was against the war, (Virgil, *The Aeneid. The Eclogues, Georgics and Aeneid of Virgil*, trans. C. Day Lewis (Oxford, 1966), ll. 83–5).

38. D. Stone, *French humanist tragedy: a reassessment* (Manchester, 1974), p. 98. The theme rarely appears, however, in the seventeenth century, possibly because gods and goddesses ceased to be acceptable in serious classical drama. For Sophonisba see below p. 186.

39. Elsa Strietman, 'Van Eneas en Dido. *Two* amorous plays performed in Antwerp, 1552', *EMD*, 3, ed. Sydney-Higgins, pub. Tempo di Spettacolo (1999), pp. 261–83.

40. D. Stone, 'Didon se sacrifiant', in D. Stone *Four Renaissance tragedies* (Cambridge, Mass., 1966), p. 241. For Fortune and her wheel see below, p. 182.

41. Towards the end of the play, when the Greeks have been urging Priam to pull down the city walls so they can bring inside the great wooden horse created as a gift to Pallas Athene, Agamemnon actually addresses king Priam as 'francoys'. Stengel, either as a correction or because he is transcribing one of the other editions, writes 'franc roys' (p. 414, v. 26654). The legend, 'which is quite without historical substance', describes how Hector's son, Francus, was saved from death by a trick and smuggled away from the city and eventually founded the Frankish nation from whom the Merovingian kings of France descended (*The fourth book of the chronicle of Fredegar with its continuations*, trans. from the Latin with introduction and notes by J. M. Wallace-Hadrill (London and New York, 1960), p. xii). The *Liber historiae francorum* has an even more surprising version, claiming that 'the city of the Trojans in the region called Illium . . . was where Aeneas reigned . . . When the city was conquered, the tyrant Aeneas fled to Italy to obtain men to carry on the fighting . . . Priam and Antenor, two of the other Trojan princes also fled and settled near the river Don' (ed. and trans. Bernard S. Bachrach (Kansas, 1973), p. 23). There is no mention here of Francus, instead we are told that 'because of the hardness and the daring of their hearts the Emperor Valentinian called the Trojans Franks' (ibid., p. 24). A detailed analysis of these traditions and their sources is given by Claude Nicolet in chapter II of his *La fabrique d'une nation. La France entre Rome et les Germains* (Paris, 2003).

42. Jean le Maire de Belges in his *Singularités de Troie* (1510–13) cites numerous authorities from classical to Boccaccio (Georges Doutrepont, *Jean Lemaire de Belge et la Renaissance* (Brussels, 1934). Beginning with Ronsard, a number of poets treated the story in epic poems, many of them with the same title: *La Franciade* (R. E. Asher, *National myths in Renaissance France: Francus, Samothes and the Druids* (Edinburgh, 1993), pp. 122–40). One writer, Jean Godard, produced instead a unique play based on the story of Francus also called *La Franciade œuvres de Jean Godard* (Lyon 1594). Godard omits the early part of the story of Francus' escape from Troy and begins at the point when Francus and his followers prepare to fight the Gauls (Asher, *National myths*, pp. 142–4).

43. For an account of this and other plays by Chastelain see Estelle Doudet's 'Un dramaturge et son publique au XVe siècle', *EMD*, 9 (2005), pp. 61–86. For references to Achilles' treachery see Millet, *La destruction de Troye*, Day Two.

44. According to Walter Fitzstephen in the twelfth century, London is a much older city than Rome, 'for by the same Trojan forefathers this was founded by Brutus before that by Romulus and Remus', cit. John Stow, *Survey of London*, introduction by H. B. Wheatley (London, 1956), I, p. 80. An amusing, indirect rejection of London's primacy is created by the German playwright Jacob Ayrer, writing in the late sixteenth century. In a cycle of seven Roman plays 'based on Livy', Ayrer has a scene of Romulus preparing to build up Rome as a seat of power. Enter Aeneas and Achilles who have fled together from Troy and landed in Italy with a small band of followers. Aeneas offers their services to Romulus who welcomes their help but asks if they have any

women among them as there is a great shortage of wives. Aeneas says their wives were carried off by the Greeks, so the two leaders together plan and carry out the celebrated rape of the Sabine women! Jacob Ayrer, *Dramen*, ed. Adalbert von Keller, 3 vols., Bibliothek des literarischen Vereins, lxxvi–lxviii (Stuttgart, 1865), I, pp. 84–92. Lope's *Romulo y Remo* seems to be the only Spanish play that comes anywhere near to the Trojan tradition.

45. 'How the Trojans were descended from Japhet and shows by signs how four groups of people left Troy the great after it was destroyed who settled in and peopled countries and lands . . . and founded several cities, towns and castles, notably Rome, Paris and London', cit. Oliver Pickering, 'The crusades in Leeds University Library's genealogical History roll', in *From Clermont to Jerusalem: the crusades and crusader societies, 1095–1500*, ed. Alan V. Murray, International Medieval Research 3 (Turnhout, 1998), p. 258. I am grateful to Oliver Pickering for showing me this manuscript and his article on it.

46. There are a number of references to performances in Venice of Troy plays including one on the occasion of the visit of Anne of Britanny, wife of Louis XII, in 1502, when Italian reports mention the tradition of Trojan links wih Venice. I am indebted to Cora Dietl for this information from her forthcoming book.

47. J. Day's *The conquest of Brute*, I (Harbage, 1598), is unfortunately lost. A detailed genealogy from Aeneas to Brute and the creation of the Troynovant is described in the opening paragraph of Richard Johnson's *The seven champions of Christendom: 1596–7*, ed. Jennifer Fellows (Aldershot, 2004), first printed in the 1590s. See below p. 201.

48. There is some argument as to whether it is Aeneas or Antenor who is described here. In Millet, after the destruction of Troy, Aeneas declares 'Et men yray en ytalie' (I shall go to Italy), but Antenor, who traditionally founded Padua and had the Circle of Traitors called after him in Dante's *Inferno* Canto XXXII, is setting off for Britain: 'Et je menray ma compaignie / Es ylles devers les angloys / si feray la dedans troys moys / Une cite forte et garnie' (and I shall lead my company towards the English islands where within three months I shall build a strong and well-found city), *La destruction de Troye*, p. 433, ll.27904–7.

49. *Edward I*, Act I, scene 2. *The works of George Peele*, ed. A. H. Bullen (1888, repr. Port Washington, N.Y., 1966), p. 97).

50. Hummelen provides a detailed summary of this play in the *Repertorium*, IC3. A Dutch play of *De brand van Trojen* (The burning of Troy) by Govert Bidloo was first published in 1719. Worp, I, p. 346.

51. The same collection also includes a play commemorating the birth of Margaret of Burgundy, Charles' sister, in which the giving of gifts is linked with the three Magi, who represent the three estates. E. de Bock, 'Een presentspel van Collin Cailleu', *Spiegel der Letteren*, 4 (1963), pp. 241–69. Margaret married the duke of Savoy, another dynasty which claimed Trojan ancestry. See Bossuat, 'Théseus de Cologne', p. 105.

18 THE SIEGE AND DESTRUCTION OF JERUSALEM IN AD 70

1. In *The Vengeance of Our Lord*, Stephen Wright discusses plays on the subject in six languages from the fourteenth to the seventeenth century. For detailed studies of the English narrative versions see B. Millar, *The siege of Jerusalem in its physical, literary and historical contexts* (Dublin, 2000). For the many Vengeance texts, including plays from the Iberian peninsula, see D. Hook, *The destruction of Jerusalem: Catalan and Castilian texts*, Kings College London Medieval Series (London, 2000).

2. Voragine includes several incidents from the events that followed the crucifixion, some of which he explicitly describes as fictional, but which are also found in other narrative versions. Wright, pp. 28ff, and Alvin Ford, *La vengeance de nostre-seigneur. The Old and Middle French prose versions and the version of Japheth*, Pontifical Institute of Medieval Studies 63 (Toronto, 1984).

3. See Runnalls, *Les mystères français imprimés*, pp. 167–9. There is no modern edition of the play so I have followed Runnalls and Petit de Julleville in using the spelling 'Vengeance' rather than 'Vengance'. Both spellings are found in the original texts.

4. A new study of the Vengeance plays has just been published by J.-P. Bordier: 'La composition de la vengeance de notre seigneur. Un aspect de l'art dramatique d' Eutrache Marcadé', in *Mainte belle œuvre faite*.

5. For an English version and variants of Pilate's letter to the emperor Claudius see E. Hennecke, *New Testament Apocrypha*, ed. Wilhelm Schneemelcher, English trans. R. McL. Wilson, 2 vols. (London, 1963), I, pp. 477–8.

6. In the *Vindicta salvatoris*, it is Titus, king of Acquitaine, who is ill with an incurable face cancer. The emperor Tiberius also has cancer. The siege and conquest of Jerusalem takes place before the healings by Veronica's cloth.

7. In the Towneley *Play of the dice*, Pilate plays at dice for the 'gowne' with the soldiers; when he loses he forces the winner to give it to him by threats (*The Towneley plays*, ed. Martin Stevens and A. C. Cawley (Oxford, 1994), Play 24).

8. The third day of the *Cornish ordinalia* includes, after the 'Death and resurrection of Christ', a play of 'The death of Pilate' which shows the same episodes, though the leprous emperor is Tiberius whom Veronica heals with the 'Veronica'. Then follows the summons to Rome of Pilate and the influence of the robe which Tiberius forces him to remove. Pilate is imprisoned and commits suicide. The earth will not accept his corpse so it is wrapped in iron and flung into the Tiber. The devils take his soul to Hell and the play ends with Christ's entry into Heaven at the Ascension (*The Cornish ordinalia*, trans. Markham Harris (Washington DC, 1969), III: *The resurrection of our Lord*).

9. Petit de Julleville points out the need to show or mention all events because there is no interval in the play for them to happen off stage and it is necessary to show the passing of time. Tiberius died in AD 37 and Vespasian succeeded in AD 69 – the 'year of the four emperors'.

10. Graham Runnalls, 'Civic drama in the Burgundian territories in the later Middle Ages', *Revue Belge de Philologie et Histoire*, 78 (2000), pp. 41–422.

11. In his edition of the play, Graham Runnalls describes its interesting history – it was printed in Paris, and in 1536 the only surviving copy was bought in Lyons by Fernard, son of Christopher Colombus, a well-known collector of books which are now preserved in the Biblioteca Colombina in Seville.

12. Ed. Rouanet, I, play 30. It follows the French version very closely but avoids the difficulty of linking the stories of Veronica healing emperor Tiberias, with the same woman healing *emperor* Vespasian more than twenty years later, by not naming the emperor or specifying where he is living. There is also recorded a Mexican translation of the play dating from the late seventeenth century: *Destruición de Jerusalén. Auto en lengua mexicana*, ed. Francisco del Paso y Troncoso, Biblioteca Nahuatl I: IV (Florence, 1907). I am grateful to Penny Robinson for this information from her edition of the Portuguese narrative *Estoria do muy nobre Vespesiano* (Exeter, 1983).

13. Ford, *La vengeance de nostre-seigneur*, p. 149.

14. *Estoria do muy nobre Vespesiano*, ed. Robinson, p. 43. Josephus, *The Jewish war*, trans. G. A. Williamson (Harmondsworth, 1959), p. 319. Hook, *Destruction of Jerusalem*, pp. 2–5, gives interesting details of tapestries on the themes of the Vengeance, owned by kings of Spain and England. They include the episode of the cannibal mothers which is almost certainly derived from the Old Testament account of the siege of Samaria (4 Kings 6: 26–9) which was dramatised at Lille (*Lille*, III, 46) and in *Die belegerung Samarie* by Hans Sachs 1552 (X, p. 454).

15. Josephus, *The Jewish war*, pp. 300–11.

16. *Códice de autos viejos*, ed. Miguel Ángel Pérez Priego (Madrid, 1988).

17. For a detailed account of the probable link with the order of *The Teutonic knights of the order of the Virgin*, see Wright, pp. 62–7.

18. The scene must refer to the war against the Jews, but not necessarily the destruction of the city which terminated it (ibid., p. 74). Subsequent speeches in the Rolle refer to the challenge of Peter and Paul by Simon Magus and their subsequent martyrdom under Nero. For other plays on this theme see Muir, *Biblical drama*, p. 145.

19. I have followed the spelling of Ruf's name used in the *Schauspiele schweizerische* edition of 1893. The form Rueff is also sometimes found.

20. The introduction of these avengers is probably based on the parable of the guests who do not come to the wedding and kill the messengers: 'But when the king had heard of it, he was angry, and sending his armies, he destroyed these murderers and burnt their city' (Matthew 22:7).

21. The account comes from the *Mémoires de Pierrefleur* p. 348. Wright, p. 111.

22. R. W. Ingram, ed. REED: Coventry (Toronto and Manchester, 1981), p. 303.

23. Ibid., p. 308.

24. Thomas Sharp, *Dramatic mysteries of Coventry* (1825), repr. with new fore-word by A. Cawley (Totowa, N.J., 1973), p. 41. I have only included the main characters, most of whom appear in Josephus. For other information

about the actors, costumes and waggons see Ingram, ed., *REED: Coventry*, pp. 307–9.

25. Both Corneille (*Tite et Berenice*) and Racine (*Berenice*) wrote plays on this theme and the latter had just been translated into English as Crowne says in his preface, where he rejects suggestions he had made use of it. The English play still contains much more action and violence than was acceptable on the French stage. A Jesuit play of Titus, performed in Munich in 1713, emphasised only his goodness and almost saintly behaviour as emperor (Szarota, III, 2, p. 2163).

26. For Judith plays see p. 173.

27. McKendrick, *Woman and society*, pp. 88–90.

19 EARLY CHRISTIAN EUROPE: CONSTANTINE TO THE CRUSADES

1. A Dutch play of *Het Heilig Kruis* was performed by the Chamber of Saint Barbara in Kortrijk in 1451 (Worp, I, p. 159). A *Spel van den Helighen Cruce* was performed in 1505 and 1541–2, in Thielt, and in 1558 in Rousbrugge-Haringhe (ibid., pp. 34–5). In Antwerp in the first half of the fifteenth century, the Corpus Christi procession included the history of Constantine the Great in three tableaux (ibid., p. 45). The Corpus Christi procession in Barcelona in 1424 included in the representations by the Monastery of St Anne 'St Helen with the Emperor Constantine, with his wise men [*doctors*] and knights'. TIE *Medieval*, I.17.

2. The Arian heresy was widespread at this date and despite the teaching of St Athanasius and the council of Nicea on the true nature of the Trinity, many of the invading tribes in Eastern Europe remained wedded to the heretical views of Arius.

3. For another interpolation in this text, the miracle of the Virgin, see p. 43.

4. A similar episode in the life of St Martha (*Legenda* 29 July) tells how she tamed the Tarasca (a dragon-like monster) that was terrorising the land in southern France. René d'Anjou established an annual procession and representation of the scene in the town of Tarascon which is still performed today (Muir, 'René d'Anjou and the theatre in Provence').

5. The author obviously does not know that Constantine was in fact in Britain at this time. The site of the formal declaration in the Roman barracks at York can be seen today under the crypt of York minster. In 2006, York celebrated the 1,700th anniversary of the event. A Jesuit play in Paris in 1681 presented the battle between Constantine and Maxentius and the triumph in the Sign of the Cross (Boysse, p. 179).

6. A play on the holiness of Constantinus was performed in Vienna in 1659 to the glory of the Holy Roman Emperor Leopold (Szarota, III, 2, p. 1049).

7. The famous 'in hoc signum vinces' vision is told in *Legenda* under *Invention of the Holy Cross* 3 May. In this version Constantine is not given a cross but told there will be a sign and before the battle he sees a cross in the sky.

8. Constantine's building of churches is mentioned by Eusebius (*History of the Church*, trans. Williamson, pp. 393–4).

9. Stegmann lists a number of Latin plays on Constantine the Great, one by Reuchlin (1513) and another by Schilting in Cologne (1602). A Jesuit play *Constantinus magnus* by Agricola was staged in Munich in 1574–5.

10. D'Ancona, III, pp. 1–120. The acts were interspersed with interludes, printed by D'Ancona at the end of the play (pp. 121–38).

11. All three plays, together with commentaries, cast lists and staging details, are printed in Ukena, II.

12. The *Legenda* gives details of this action and it seems probable this was copied in performance: 'Chosroes, seating himself upon the throne as the Father, set the wood of the Cross at his right side in the Son's stead and a cock at his left side as the Holy Ghost (*Legenda*, p. 544).

13. This story is briefly told in the *Legenda* and in great detail in narrative versions in many languages. The only other dramatisation of this part of the story is in the first day of the *Cornish Ordinalia*.

14. Tapfer makes Constantinus the emperor who has the vision and is baptised. Then there is a direction: the *alt keyser* disappears and the *jung* one is crowned.

15. There is no pope Silvester at this date. Silvester I was pope from 324 to 335 and Silvester II from 999 to 1003.

16. In her commentary (pp. 725–6), Ukena lists eight different sources used by Cysat including Josephus and Eusebius but not the *Legenda*.

17. See p. 115.

18. The cast list also includes Constantine's son Crispus, which suggests that the play may have included the story of the false accusation against Crispus by Constantine's scorned wife (see p. 107).

19. Jesuit plays in Germany on the Exaltation of the Cross include a *Tragedy of the Roman Emperor Heraclius*, in Munich in 1617 (Szarota, II, 1, p. 25), and the *Triumphus sanctis crucis*, a century later in Regensburg (Szarota, III, 3, p. 14). Stegmann also lists a play of *Heraclius* at Tournai in 1596 and *Chosroes* (probably the same subject) at Anvers (1629) and Munich (1638).

20 CHRISTIANITY GOES WEST

1. *Le mystère de Saint Remi*, ed. Jelle Koopmans (Droz, 1997), p. 29.

2. Ibid., pp. 410–509.

3. The ampulla was preserved in Rheims cathedral and used for the consecration of all subsequent French kings.

4. Several of the group of St Genevieve plays are healing and similar miracles and are cited in Part One. St Didier was the bishop of Langres in the fourth century. *La vie et passion de Monseigneur St Didier*, a play on his life and martyrdom at the hands of the invading pagan hordes from Germany was specially composed by Guillaume Flamang for the inhabitants of Langres to perform in 1482.

5. In 510 Clovis founded a rich basilica where he and his wife were buried, together with the saint who had died in 501. Later a great abbey grew up there from whose library this play manuscript comes.

6. The church of St Fiacre in Paris, nowadays better known for its cab rank than as a place to eat, is certainly the only location that rhymes with *archediacre*.

7. A miniature in the *Chroniques de St Denis* shows all the details described (Roy, *Etudes*, p. cxxxii).

8. The three day *Mystère de St Louis* was edited in 1871 by Francisque Michel and published in England for the Roxburghe Club. Petit de Julleville suggests that the decision to publish it in England is linked with the passages in mock English with odd pronunciation which appealed to 'des rancunes mal assoupies de la guerre de Cent Ans' (unhealed rancour from the Hundred Years War).

9. The battle scenes are played out in formal style: the opponents only two or three on each side (including *Outrage*) insult each other and then fight 'Icy bataillent'. 'Apres la bataille' they return to their verbal quarrel.

10. One of the miracles involved raising from the dead a mason and a carpenter which explains the choice of St Louis as their guild patron.

11. John Wasson, 'The secular saint plays of the Elizabethan era', in *The saint play in medieval Europe*, ed. Davidson, p. 248. Wasson also lists Heywood's 'If you know not me you know nobody', a play of the miraculous survival of Elizabeth during the reign of Mary (p. 250).

21 THE WORTHY, THE PROUD AND THE POPULAR

1. For pageants of the Worthies in England see Lancashire, 31, and many later references. They also appear in other countries, for example in 'A civic reception for Fernando the Catholic', Valladolid, 1509. *Fama* was placed at its highest point and 'Under her were placed in good order all those famous forbears deserving of her company with their crowns and signs.' Among those listed are Julius Caesar, Octavius, Alexander the Great, Trajan, King David, Constantine, King Solomon, Hannibal, Judas Maccabeus, Scipio, Hector and the Cid. Gómez Moreno (TIE *Medieval*, I. 41 pp. 153–8).

2. Hardy's trilogy consists of the *Mort de Daire*, *Mort d'Alexandre* and *Timoclée*, in the last of which there is a battle with 'fusées' (guns) (Lancaster, I, i, p. 46). Lope de Vega, *La grandezas de Alejandro*, c. 1582.

3. David Price, *The political dramaturgy of Nicodemus Frischlin. Essays on Humanist drama in Germany* (Chapel Hill and London, 1990), p. 63.

4. See vols. II and III of Alan Knight's edition.

5. When Charles V visited Douai in 1516 he was greeted with a series of tableaux. On one side of the road were representations of the victories of Joshua and on the other the victories of the emperor himself (Gustave Lhotte *Le théâtre à Douai avant la révolution* (Douai, 1881), pp. 18–28).

6. McCabe, p. 205. Godefroy appeared in lost plays based on Tasso's *Jerusalemme liberata* in 1614 and 1657 (Edelman, p. 145). He was also included

among the 'Cavaliers' in a *Cour sainte* by the French Jesuit Nicholas Caussin, and with other French heroes, including Charlemagne and Joan of Arc, in the *intermèdes* of Chrestien des Croix's *Grandes amantes* pastoral in 1613 (ibid., p. 182).

7. Lope de Vega *Arcadia, prosas y versos de Lope de Vega Carpio* (Madrid, 1653), p. 125. Surprisingly, certain of the versions of the prose *Tristan* describe how Charlemagne conquers England and sees statues of Arthur's knights and considers Arthur a 'child' not to have conquered all of Europe with such warriors. See Lynette Muir, 'Le personnage de Charlemagne dans les romans en prose arthuriens', *Boletin de la real Academia de Buenas Letras de Barcelons*, 31 (1965–6), pp. 233–41.

8. Such parallels were not uncommon. In 1686, the ballet which provided the interludes for the performance of the play of *Clovis* at the Collège Louis-le-Grand in Paris presented the labours of Hercules as parallels with the victories of Louis XIV: the first labour, the slaying of the Nemean lion, was a favourable augury for Hercules' successes, as the conquest of Flanders was for the victories of Louis (Boysse, p. 189). Two centuries earlier, in 1468, for the marriage of Margaret of York to duke Charles the Rash of Burgundy, a series of plays based on the Labours were presented during the evening banquets. Each play had an epilogue linking the deeds of Hercules with the duties of a good ruler. Olivier de la Marche, *Mémoires*, Collection des mémoires relatifs à l'Histoire de France (Paris, 1825), III, pp. 114–201.

9. Sachs' play of Tristan was composed in 1553 and includes all the main events found in the romances. The potion only lasts four years, but their love continues afterwards showing that it was not only the result of the drink. Sachs, XII, pp. 142–86.

10. A lost play of *Arthur, king of England* by Hathway is recorded by Harbage, in 1599. For Arthur's role in tournaments and other shows see R. S. Loomis, 'Chivalric and dramatic imitations of Arthurian romance', in *Medieval studies in memory of A. Kingsley Porter*, ed. Wilhelm R. W. Koehler (Cambridge, 1939), pp. 79–97.

11. Millet, *La destruction de Troy*, Day 4. For the establishment of the *Neuf preuses* and their changing membership see M. Warner, *Joan of Arc. The image of female heroism* (London, 1981), pp. 205–8. A number of Amazons featured in Spanish plays described by McKendrick in her study of the *Mujer Varonil* or masculine woman: *Woman and society*, ch. 6: 'The Amazon, the leader, the warrior'. Among the women listed here is Ariosto's Bradamante who became popular also in French drama (Lancaster, I, i, pp. 191–8).

12. Lope de Vega, *Arcadia*, p. 124.

13. Judith and Jael both featured in a Dutch *Ommegang* in Ypres in 1483 as part of a group of 'figueren' denoting deliverance (TIE *Medieval*, H.45, p. 537). Hans Sachs wrote the only play I have found on Jael, who killed Sisera, the general attacking the Jews, by hammering a nail through his head while he is hiding in her tent (Sachs, X, pp. 130–46).

14. Marina Warner's book includes a picture of Judith and Joan from the *Champion des Dames* showing them as comparable female warriors *Joan of Arc*, ch. 8, Illustration 22).

15. It is tempting to see here the influence of the stories of the siege of Jerusalem where lack of water was also a deciding factor. See the Jerusalem plays, p. 147.

16. No MSS of these plays survive. Further editions were printed between 1515 and 1519 and in 1542. The whole *Viel Testament* was published in the nineteenth century by James de Rothschild. Runnalls edited the Judith and Holofernes play in 1995, and published a translation into English in 2002, with a useful introduction. The theme was very popular in Spain and McKendrick lists several Spanish plays and many other narrative accounts (p. 310 n).

17. Runnalls' translation has a detailed analysis of the text which he says follows the Book of Judith 'reasonably closely' (p. 13).

18. The relevant quotation from Luther is printed by Sommerfeld in *Judith-Dramen des 16/17. Jahrhunderts* (Berlin, 1933): 'Und mag sein das sie solch gedicht gespielet haben wie man bei uns die Passio spielet' (and it may be that they acted such a poem as we in our time have acted the Passion). The Lutheran text precedes a group of six German 'Judith' plays from 1539 to 1710 including at least one Jesuit text. For details of Luther's attitude to plays and the Bible see Parente, *Religious drama*, pp. 26–7.

19. Cioni lists thirteen editions of plays on *Giuditta/Judith Ebrea* between 1486 and 1612.

20. See Valentin, I, p. 17, and Michela Messineo, 'Primordi del teatro di collegio in Sicilia', in *I Gesuiti e il primordi del teatro barocco in Europa*, ed. F. Doglio and M. Chiabo (Rome, 1994), p. 109. See also Jean-Michel Gardair, 'Giuditta e i suoi doppi', in ibid., p. 458. Much information on the school plays is given in these and other papers from the Viterbo conference.

21. Boyer, a prolific rather than inspired author, first achieved success with plays written for the school at St Cyr and suffered therefore from critics comparing his plays unfavourably with those of Racine (Loukovitch, p. 436).

22. *Le mistère du siège d'Orléans*, ed. V. L. Hamblin, TLF (Geneva, 2002).

23. This is surely a useful hint to the property-maker.

24. I have used the summary given by Schuster in his study (Nicolaus Vernulaeus, *Henry VIII*, a neo-Latin drama by Nicolaus Vernulaeus, trans. and ed. Louis A. Schuster (Austin, Tex., 1964), p. 42) with some details from Latour's translation.

25. The performance should have taken place in the spring before Henri III but he did not attend (Lanson, p. 206).

26. For details of these, mostly lost, texts see Lancaster, II, i, p. 357. For other plays and poems on Joan in France in the seventeenth century see Edelman, pp. 245–74.

22 PRIDE AND THE WHEEL OF FORTUNE

1. Adam de la Halle, *Le jeu de la feuillée* ed. E. Langlois (rev. edn, Paris, 1970), p. 135. The role of Fortune is discussed in H. R. Patch, *The Goddess Fortuna in medieval literature* (Cambridge, Mass., 1927). There is an indirect reference to Fortune's wheel in Cangé, III: 'Miracle de l'evesque que l'arcediacre murtrit', a play about a bishop who is murdered, but is avenged by the Virgin Mary. The murderer is carried off by the devils and the dead bishop is taken to Heaven by angels. In the opening speech of the play the bishop addresses his clergy – and the audience – on the danger of power and reminds them that: 'when a man has climbed higher than he should / he falls from higher than he would'.

2. *Moralités françaises*, I, p. 79. (Facsimile reprint Slatkine, Geneva, 1980.) Fortune appears in several Jesuit plays, including one on Job in which, however, she is explicitly under the control of *Divina Providentia*. See Muir, 'The sufferings of impatient Job'.

3. Lady Macbeth sums up the situation:'Thou wouldst be great / art not without ambition but without / the illness should attend it' (Act I, scene 5).

4. In Munday's *Sir Thomas More*, the hero, newly raised to high office, talks of the dangers of Fortune: 'And that which we profanely term our fortunes / Is the provision of the power above . . . But More, the more thou hast / either of honour, office, wealth, and calling, / which might excite thee to embrace and hug them, / The more do thou in serpents' natures think them (Act III:1).

5. *Premier discours sur le poème dramatique* (Pierre Corneille, *Théâtre*, ed. G. Couton, 3 vols. (Paris, 1942), I, pp. lx–lxi. Corneille, like other dramatists, allowed the appearance of classical deities in the *pièces à machines*, such as his *Andromède*, just as they appeared in Jacobean masques or Italian interludes.

6. A variant of this story, told by Peter Damian, is cited in *Legenda* at the end of the story of St Maurice (22 September). A proud clerk who had taken over the church of St Maurice heard one day at the end of Mass the words 'Everyone that exalteth himself shall be humbled.' The clerk declared: 'It is false, for if I had humbled myself before mine enemies I should not now have so many riches.' Immediately a flash of lightning entered the mouth that had uttered such blasphemy and the clerk was no more.

7. I have used the edition of the *Gesta* translated by Charles Swan which also includes Robert of Sicily and other English texts. The story of Jovinian is told in Tale LIX 'Of too much pride', pp. 100–6.

8. Picot presented a copy to the British Library. His introduction adds several more texts and manuscripts to D'Ancona's list including an *auto sacramentale* by Pedroso – see below.

9. In 1675, *Jovinianus* (a tragedy with pastoral interludes) was performed by the pupils of the second class at the Jesuit College in Paris (Boysse, p. 167). It is possible that the author knew the earlier printed French version.

10. D'Ancona, III, pp. 175–98. Ciono lists eighteen editions of the *Re superbo* between 1530 and 1619. A Latin play of the *Rex superbus* by the Jesuit father Louis Cellot was performed at St Omers in 1623; it included the traditional Magnificat and bathing scenes (McCabe, p. 84).

11. 'He has put down the mighty from their seats and hath exalted the humble and meek' (Luke 2:15, English translation from the Book of Common Prayer).

12. There is also a German play by Giovanni Rümoldt (1564) which I have not been able to see and Szarota lists *perioche* for four different Jesuit plays of *Jovinian* from Germany. They vary in detail but all include the Magnificat and the bath (Szarota I, 2, pp. 1790–6).

13. Details of the Robert of Sicily legend and many comparisons and sources are given by L. Hornstein in her article: 'King Robert of Sicily: analogues and origins', *PMLA*, 79 (1964), pp. 13–21. In the fourteenth-century French poem, *Le dit du magnificat*, by Jean de Condé, the hero is also *de Sicile* and like Robert has two noble brothers though their titles are different. In contrast to the English texts, however, the poem does include the bath scene.

14. Rodrigo de Herrera, *Del cielo viene el buen rey*, Biblioteca de Autores Espanoles 45 (1858), p. 250. Luzbel or Lucibello is used elsewhere for the pre-fallen Lucifer, see Muir, *Biblical drama*, p. 204 n. 13.

15. In Munday's *Sir Thomas More*, the hero, newly raised to high office, talks of the dangers of Fortune: 'And that which we profanely term our fortunes / Is the provision of the power above . . . But More, the more thou hast / either of honour, office, wealth, and calling, / which might excite thee to embrace and hug them, / The more do thou in serpents' natures think them' (Act III:1).

16. An English play on Belisarius entitled *Fortunae ludibrium* (Fortune's plaything) is listed by Harbage in 1651. The history of the general's life was told by his secretary, Procopius, in two separate books: *The war against the Vandals* and *The secret history*.

17. Fortuna enters the plaza, drawn in a chariot by four attributes of her two-sided nature – Favour, Contempt, Felicity and Calamity (Best, *Bidermann*, p. 75).

18. She appears in several Jesuit plays including one on Job, in which, however, she is explicitly under the control of Divina Providentia. See Muir, 'The sufferings of impatient Job'.

19. Theodora also supported the monotheistic heresy which the pope and, of course, the Jesuits, opposed. The emphasis on religious disputes is not found in the other plays on Belisarius, where the stress is on personal relations and a power struggle.

20. According to John Julius Norwich: 'the authority for this story dates from more than five centuries later and can be rejected' (*Byzantium: the early centuries* (London, 1988) p. 261).

21. See Best, *Bidermann*, p. 89. Szarota (II, 2, p. 2334) also lists a *perioche* for a different play of *Belisarius* in Munich, 1740.

22. For these themes in drama see Part Two, p. 106. Jean Rotrou's *Théâtre complet*, ed. V. Lochert and L. Picciola, 6 vols., Société des Textes Francais Modernes (Paris, 2000), I, has a scene by scene parallel analysis of the two plays, showing the similarities and differences (pp. 179–99).
23. Rotrou, *Théâtre complet*, p. 141.
24. Ibid., p. 161.
25. Though Hardy's play is inevitably similar to Shakespeare's in subject matter there is no evidence of direct borrowing.
26. I have used the text prepared by Martin Butler for the performance at Stratford in 2005.

23 AFFAIRS OF STATE

1. Boccaccio's account of her in his *De claris mulieribus* was a major source of these plays which were especially popular in Spain; see McKendrick, *Woman and Society*, pp. 203–4.
2. The rich materials used for the costumes and décor cost the queen 1,349 *livres* ('Sophonisbe au chateau de Blois', Lebègue, pp. 160–5). In view of Mary's later marital/political problems this is an ironic choice of subject. (For the story of Sophonisba see *infra*.)
3. Michael G. Paulson, *The fallen crown: three French Mary Stuart plays of the seventeenth century* (Washington DC, 1980), includes full texts of plays by Montchrestien, Regnault and Boursalt, as well as extensive commentary on Mary's life and death.
4. Joost van den Vondel, *Mary Stuart or tortured majesty*, trans. Kristiaan P. Aercke, Carleton Plays (Ottawa, 1996).
5. Gryphius, in his *Carolus Stuardus*, also sympathised with Charles but was more concerned with the politics than the religious elements that Vondel stressed (Parente, *Religious drama*, pp. 202–4).
6. For this subject see van der Lust's *Ongheblanckette Maria Stuart* (Worp, I, p. 299) and Karl Kipka, *Maria Stuart im drama der Weltliteratur*, Breslauer Beiträge zur Literaturgeschichte (Leipzig, 1907).
7. I have not found any in Spanish or Dutch.
8. See Paola Guerrini, 'Iconografia di Sofonisba: storia e teatro'. In *Nascita della tragedia di poesia nei paesi Europei*, ed. F. Doglio and M. Chiabò (Viterbo, 1991).
9. The later Italian plays on Sophonisba are mostly inferior, the decadence terminating in tragi-comic operas (Ricci, *Sophonisbe*, pp. 210–22).
10. A. José Axelrad, *Le thème de Sophonisbe dans les principales tragédies de la littérature occidentale: France, Allemagne, Angleterre* (Lille, 1956), p. 19. Axelrad discusses a score of plays on Sophonisba in Italian, French, English and German from the sixteenth to the twentieth century.
11. Ibid., p. 45.
12. Ibid., p. 55 n. 23.
13. Ibid., p. 62.

14. Ibid., p. 129.
15. Ricci, *Sophonisbe*, p. 209.
16. Published in *Porci ante Margaritam, Essays in Honour of Meg Twycross*, ed. Sarah Carpenter, Pamela King and Meredith, Leeds Studies in English, New Series XXII (Leeds, 2001), pp. 151–70. Hüsken explains that unexpected choice of subject by the Chamber *De Fiolieren* in 's-Gravenpolder in Zeeland, as a tribute to the role that Essex played in defending the United Provinces against the Spaniards in the 1580s. Hüsken's paper includes historical references and many details of the story and its sources.
17. Ibid., p. 157.
18. It is tempting to see in this very early Dutch reference to Elizabeth's ring the original of the episode cited in most of the plays: see below nn. 21 and 22. Interestingly, in Shakespeare's *Henry VIII* (1613, Act V, scene 3), Henry gives Archbishop Cranmer a ring to use if threatened by Wolsey. When Cranmer shows the king's ring Wolsey immediately abandons his attempt to imprison Cranmer for heresy!
19. Hüsken, 'Queen Elizabeth and Essex', p. 157.
20. The play was first performed in 1637 and was still in the repertory of the Hotel de Bourgogne in 1647. La Calprenède wrote two other plays based on English history, *Jeanne d'Angleterre* on Lady Jane Grey and *Edouard* about Edward III (see p. 117). These and other French plays on the Tudors are examined in detail in L. Alfreda Hill's *The Tudors in French drama*, Johns Hopkins Studies in Romance Literatures and Languages 20 (Baltimore, 1932).
21. The reason for this revival of an episode out of English history is linked by the editor, Wendy Gibson, with the alliance between Charles II and Louis XIV at this date, encouraged by the latter's hope that Charles would openly declare himself a convert to Catholicism.
22. I am most grateful to Wendy Gibson for sending me a copy of Charles Boyer's *Le comte d'Essex* which was staged shortly after Thomas Corneille's play at a rival theatre in Paris. Boyer explains that he started composing his play a few weeks before the first performance of Corneille's play and borrowed names and even actual lines of verse from La Calprenède in his haste to complete the play. He included the episode of the ring, because, he explains in the *au lecteur*, 'je le tiens historique'. He also suggests that the audiences at Thomas Corneille's play had difficulty in recognising the story for lack of this famous episode.
23. John Banks, *The unhappy favourite or, the eart of Essex*, ed. Thomas Marshall Howe Blair (New York, 1939). A French two-part translation, *Le comte d'Essex, histoire anglaise*, had been published in Paris in 1678. See Thomas Corneille, *Le comte d'Essex*, ed. Wendy Gibson, Textes Littéraires CX (Exeter, 2000), p. xvii. A copy in the British Library is entitled: *The history of the most renowned queen Elizabeth and her great favourite the earl of Essex. A romance*. For details of the 'romance' see Hill, *The Tudors in French drama*, p. 133. Hill points out that the story is already cited in 1623 in Webster's *The Devil's lawcase*, Act III, scene 3).

24. Charles, earl of Nottingham (1536–1624), was the son of Lord Howard of Effingham, and a cousin of the duke of Norfolk.

25. Walther Baerwolff, *Der Graf von Essex in deutschen Drama* (Stuttgart, 1919).

26. A. Coello Y Ochoa, 'El conde de sex: the earl of Essex', trans. and edited J. B. Graham (MA dissertation, Birmingham University, 1968).

24 PATRIOTS AND POPULAR HEROES

1. I am grateful to Alan Knight for sending me advance copies of the texts which will be published in vol. v of his edition of the Lille plays.

2. Porsenna has ordered the secretary to sit by him and give the men their pay. With a nice touch of dramatic irony the secretary insists he is not worthy to be dressed like the king and set down by his side (ll. 189–96).

3. In Livy, the main source of the play, Porsenna only threatens to have Mucius burnt and not on the altar. The author also mentions Valerius Maximus, who has a brief reference to Mucius, and St Augustine, who in the *City of God* (v:18) questions how many Christians would behave so boldly if threatened for their faith.

4. *Mucius Scaevola* has only been dramatised a few times. A Spanish play by Cueva, *La libertad de Roma por Mucio Cevola* was published in 1582 (see McKendrick, p. 56); a Dutch *Treuerspel* by Mucius Scaevola (presumably a pen-name) in Amsterdam in 1727; and one in French by Roentgen, Paris, 1821.

5. The author quotes Valerius Maximus (I:14) among other Roman historians and St Augustine *City of God* (I:14) as sources. Regulus is more concerned with his country's welfare than with his own glory which makes him an interesting subject for a play at any period.

6. Schweizerische Schauspiele des sechzehnten Jahrhunderts, III (Zürich 1803).

7. The play is described in Creizenach, III, p. 154. There is also a later play on the *Eidgenossenschaft*, Ruf's *Etter Heini* (1538) which includes debate on the religious divisions in Switzerland between the Protestants and Catholics (ibid., p. 258).

8. *Playing Robin Hood. The legend as performance in five centuries*, ed. Lois Potter (Newark, N.J., and London, 1998), includes a range of articles on aspects of the dramatic treatment of the legend including Alexsandra Johnston's 'The Robin Hood of the records'. See also John Wasson, 'The St George and Robin Hood plays in Devon', *Medieval English Theatre*, 2:2 (1980), pp. 66–8.

9. Other extant plays of the period are: *George a greene*, printed in 1599, *Look about you*, printed 1600, and the unfinished and never performed *The sad shepherd or a tale of Robin Hood* by Ben Johnson, printed 1641. I am most grateful to John Marshall for information about these plays. See also Marshall, '"Goon in to Bernysdale". The trail of the Paston Robin Hood Play', in *Essays in honour of Peter Meredith*, Leeds Studies in English, XXIX (Leeds, 1998).

10. George Peele, *The works of George Peele*, ed. A. H. Bullen (1888, repr., Port Washington, N.Y., 1966).

11. This is the first appearance of 'Maid Marian' (Johnston, 'The Robin Hood of the records', p. 23) and of the idea of Robin as an outlawed nobleman.

12. The events following Robin's death are also told in a separate play, *King John and Matilda* by Robert Davenport (1655).

13. For details of the plays and the 'St George Ridings', see Davidson, 'The Middle English saint play and its iconography', pp. 60–9.

14. Jennifer Fellows, 'St George as romance hero', *Reading Medieval Studies*, 19 (1993), pp. 27–54, at p. 35.

15. I am most grateful to Jennifer Fellows for giving me a copy of her new edition of Johnson's book and for general help with St George and the *Seven champions*. It is probable that Johnson also drew on Spencer's *Fairy Queen* and the Red Cross Knight.

16. Johnson, *Seven champions*, ed. Fellows, p. 145.

17. *Gothic art for England 1400–1547*, ed. Richard Marks and Paul Williamson (London, 2003), p. 397.

18. In his study of *The English mummers' play* (Woodbridge, 1981), the late Alex Helm claims that 'one of the saddest features . . . of the Ceremonial' is the impossibility of finding any reference to it before the 1700s (p. 7). Helm's book includes a range of texts and references to the subject matter of these plays, as well as the history of the genre.

CONCLUSION: FROM QUEEN OF HEAVEN TO FAIRY QUEEN

1. The revival of religious drama in England with the formation of the Religious Drama Society by E. Martin Browne in 1930, under the auspices of Bishop Bell of Chichester, encouraged the staging of new plays, including Sayers' *The devil to pay* – a version of the Faust legend (see p. 71), and *idem, The emperor Constantine: a chronicle* (London, 1951) (see p. 156), and Christopher Fry's *The boy with the cart*, a legend of St Cuthbert. The most important work of the Society was to obtain permission to revive the medieval cycles, and in 1951 the York plays were staged for the first time for more than 400 years – the rest is history.

2. The term *contes de fées* was first used for the volume published in 1698 by Madame D'Aulnoy (see *The classic fairy tales* by Iona and Peter Opie (London, 1974) p. 14). The problem of the relationship between folk and fairy tale is beyond the scope of this book.

3. Probably the earliest love story to be dramatised is the twelfth-century Latin play by William of Blois, described by his brother Peter in a letter unanimously dated to 1170, as 'tragoedia vestra de Flaura et Marco' (Letter 93, ed. Migne Pat. Lat. 207 col. 292). The tragedy has not survived but Gustave Cohen in his study of *La 'Comédie' latine en France au xiie siècle*, 2 vols. (Paris, 1931), mentions it in conjunction with William's Latin comedy, *Alda*, also referred to in Peter's letter. Cohen suggests that 'Flaure' may be a celebrated 'courtisane du xii siècle' (i, p. 112). The 'prostitute Flora' is included

in Boccaccio's *Famous women*, ch. LXII. Boccaccio describes her story, which is set in imperial Rome, as confused and variable and concludes: 'This disagreement does not matter to me as long as it is clear that Flora was a rich prostitute' (p. 139). Marcus is never identified.

4. A number of fairy tales have very ancient roots, including Sleeping Beauty which is included in the fifteenth-century romance of *Perceforest*. The parallel of the Italian story of *Stella* and her jealous step-mother has associations with Snow White (see p. 93) and other tales also stress the importance of goodness and patience. To turn the story of Patient Griselda into a fairy tale it would only be necessary to reveal at the end that she was originally of noble birth, as occurs in Marie de France's *Lai de Fresne*.

Bibliography

PLAYS CITED UP TO 1700

Collections of plays are listed under the name of the editor: e.g. D'Ancona.

Adam de la Halle. *Le jeu de la feuillée*. Ed. E. Langlois. Rev. edn, Paris, 1970.

Anon. *La tragédie du sac de Cabrières, ein Kalvinistiche drama des Reformationszeit*. Ed. Karl Christ. Halle, 1928.

Anon. *Das Urner Spiel von Wilhelm Tell*. Ed. Hans Bodmer (1520–4). Schweizerische Schauspiele des sechszehnten Jahrhunderts, III. Zurich, 1893.

Arboreda, Alejandro. *El mas divino remedio y Aurora de san Ginés*. Ed. Pasqual Mas y Uso. Teatro de Siglo de Ora, 83. Kassel, 1997.

Auto de Sant Jorge quando mato la serpiente. See Ukena.

Ayrer, Jacob. *Dramen*. Ed. Adalbert von Keller. 3 vols. Bibliothek des literarischen Vereins lxxvi–lxxviii. Stuttgart, 1865.

Banks, John. *The unhappy favourite or, the earl of Essex*. Ed. Thomas Marshall Howe Blair. New York, 1939.

Beaubreuil, Jehan. *Regulus*. Limoges, 1582.

Belcari, Feo. *Saccre rappresentazione e laude*. Turin, 1920.

Bergmann, R. *Katalog der deutschsprachigen geistlichen spiele und Marienklagen des Mittelalters*, Munich, 1986.

Bidermann, Jakob. *Cenodoxus*, Ed. and trans. D. G. Dyer. Edinburgh Bi-Lingual Library 9. Edinburgh, 1974.

Bodel, Jean. *Jeu de St Nicholas*. Ed. F. J. Warne. Oxford, 1951.

Boyer, Charles. *Le comte d'Essex*. Paris, 1678.

Braunschweig, Julius von. *Die Schauspiele des Herzogs Heinrich Julius von Braunschweig*. Ed. Julius Tillman. Leipzig, 1880.

Brooke, Henry. *The earl of Essex*. Dublin, 1761.

Castellani, Castellano. *La rappresentazione di San Venanzio*. Ed. N. Newbigin. Camerino, 2000.

Castro, Don Guillén de. *Obras de Don Guillén de Castro y Bellvis*. 3 vols. Madrid, 1925–7.

Castro, Don Guillén de. *Comedia de Don Quijote de la Mancha*. Obras II. Real Academia España. Madrid, 1926.

Cervantes, Miguel de. *Ocho comedias y ocho entremesos nuevos*. Facsimile edition. Madrid, 1984.

Coello Y. Ochoa, A. *El conde de sex: the earl of Essex.* Trans. and ed. J. B. Graham. MA dissertation, Birmingham University, 1968.

Cohen, Gustave. *Le livre de conduite du régisseur . . . pour le mystère de la passion à Mons en 1501*. Paris, 1925.

Collin, Heinrich Joseph von. *Regulus.* Berlin, 1802.

The comedy of George a Greene, 1599. London, 1911.

Comment ceulx de Cartaige mirent a tourment inhumain Actilius Regulus. See Mystères de Lille.

Comte d'Essex, histoire angloise. Paris, 1678. Trans as *The secret history of the most renowned queen Elizabeth and her great favourite the earl of Essex.* London, 1695.

Consueta de Sant Jordi. See Ukena.

Corneille, Pierre. *Théâtre.* Ed. G. Couton. 3 vols. Paris, 1960.

Corneille, Thomas. *Le comte d'Essex.* Ed. Wendy Gibson. Textes Littéraires CX. Exeter, 2000.

The Cornish ordinalia. Trans. Markham Harris. Washington DC, 1969.

Courtois d'Arras. Ed. E. Faral. CFMA 3. Paris, 1922.

Crown, John. *Regulus.* London, 1694.

Crowne, John. *The destruction of Jerusalem.* London, 1677.

Cysat, Renward, *Spil des heiligen Crützes erfindung. See* Ukena.

D'Ancona, A. *Sacre rappresentazioni dei secoli XIV, XV, XVI.* 3 vols. Florence, 1872.

II

Rappresentazione di S. Panunzio
di Teofilo
di SS. Giovanni e Paulo di Lorenzo de Medici
di SS Grisante e Daria
di Costantino imperatore, San Silvestro papae Sant' Elena

III

L'Esaltazione della Croce di Govianmaria Cecchi
Rappresentazione del Re Superbo
di Santa Guglielma, di Madonna Antonia Pulci
di Santa Uliva (also in De Bartholomaeis, III)
di Stella (also in De Bartholomaeis, III)
di Rosana (also in De Bartholomaeis, III)
di un Pellegrino
di un miracolo di due Pellegrino
di un miracolo di tre Pellegrino
di Agnolo ebreo

Davenport, Robert. *King John and Matilda.* In *Elizabethan history plays.* Ed. William A. Armstrong. London, 1965.

Davis, Norman, ed., *Non-cycle plays and fragments.* Early English Text Society, Extra Series, Supplementary Text 1. London, 1970.

De Bartholomaeis, V. *Il teatro abruzzese del medio evo.* Bologna, 1924.

De Bartholomaeis, V. *Laude drammatiche e rapprezentazioni sacre*. 3 vols. Florence, 1943.

I

    Orvieto: *Come le sette peccata mortali si conducono a contrizione*
             Come apparve Christo a Santo Francesco
             Come converti I Patarini con la sperienza del libro che pose nel fuocu

II

    La devozione e festa de S. Petro martire
    La legenna di Santo Tomascio (also in *Il teatro abruzzese*)
    La leggenda di un Monaco qui ando al servizio di dio.

III

    Un miracolo di Sant'Andrea

De Bock, E. Een presentspel van Collin Cailleu. *Spiegel der Letteren*, 4 (1963), pp. 241–69.
Delehaye, H. *Légende de St Eustache*. Mélanges d'Hagiographie Grecque et Latine. *Subsidia Hagiographie*, 42 (1966).
Desfontaines, Nicolas Mary, sieur. *Tragédies hagiographiques*. Ed. Claude Bourqui and Simone de Reyff. Société des Textes Français Modernes. Paris, 2004.
Destruiciòn de Jerusalén. Auto en lengua mexicana. Ed. Francisco del Paso y Troncoso. Biblioteca Nahuatl I: IV. Florence, 1907.
Dronke, Peter, ed. and trans. *Nine medieval Latin plays*. Cambridge Medieval Classics I. Cambridge, 1994.
Les enfants de maintenant. Ancien théâtre françois. Ed. Viollet le Duc. Bibliothèque Elzevirienne III. Paris, 1854.
Esmoreit. See Medieval Dutch drama.
Euripides, *Iphigeneia in Aulis*. In *The war plays: Iphigenia at Aulis, the Women of Troy, Helen*. Trans. and introd. Don Taylor. London, 1990.
Fletcher, John. *The dramatic works in the Beaumont and Fletcher canon*, Ed. F. Bowers. 8 vols. Cambridge, 1966–79 (VIII: *The queen of Corinth*; IX: *The prophetess*).
Fletcher, John. *The island princess*. Ed. Gordon McMullen for the Royal Shakespeare Company. Stratford, 2002.
Florentine drama for convent and festival. Ed. and trans. J. W. and B. C. Cook. Chicago, 1996.
Les folies de Cardenio. Ed. J.-P. Leroy. TLF. Geneva, 1989.
Les fragments du mystère Auvergnat de St Agathe. Etude et Texte par G. Runnalls. Montreal, 1994.
Giordana, Ugo, *Le jeu de Saint Thomas d'Aquin*. Paris, 1939.
Gloriant. See Medieval Dutch drama.
Herrera, Rodrigo de. *Del cielo viene el buen rey*. Biblioteca de Autores Espandes 45 (1858).
Heywood, John. *The dramatic works of John Heywood*. Modernised edn by J. S. Farmer. 2 vols. London, 1905.

Heywood, Thomas. *The Iron Age*. Ed. Arlene W. Weiner. New York, 1979.

Hindley, Alan and Small, Graeme. Le ju du grand dominé et du petit. *Revue belge de philologie et d'histoire*, 80 (2002), pp. 413–56.

Hrotsvitha, *Opera*. Ed. Conrad Celtis. Nűrnberg, 1501. Trans. Christopher St John, *The Plays of Roswitha*. New York, 1966.

Hüsken, W. M. N. *De spelen van Cornelis Everaert*. 2 vols. Hilversum, 2005.

Jones, Henry. *The earls of Essex. A tragedy*. London, 1753.

Jonson, Ben. *Sejanus his fall* (adapted by Martin Butler for for the Royal Shakespeare Company, 2005).

Kirke, John. *The seven champions of Christendom*. London, 1638.

Kochanowski, Jan. *The dismissal of the Greek envoys*. Trans. and commentary Barry Keane. Szczecin, 1999.

La Calprenède. *Le comte d'Essex*. Paris, 1639.

Lanseloet van Danmark. See *Medieval Dutch drama*.

Lascelles, Mary. *Shakespeare's Measure for measure*. London, 1953.

The life of Meriasek: a medieval Cornish miracle play. Trans. Markham Harris. Washington DC, 1977.

Longtin, Mario. Edition critique de la cinquième journée du mystère de sainte Barbe. Doctoral thesis, Edinburgh 2001.

Lope de Vega, *El mayordomo de la duquesa de Amalfi* (1618). Trans. Cynthia Rodriguez-Badenyk: *The duchess of Amalfi's steward*. Carleton Plays. Ottawa, 1985.

Lope de Vega. *Lo fingido verdadero*. Trans. Michael McGaha: *Acting is believing*. San Antonio, Tex, 1986.

Ludus de Sancta. *Dorothea*. See Ukena.

Lumiansky, R. M. and David Mills, eds. *The Chester mystery cycle*. Early English Text Society, Supplementary Series. London, 1974.

Man's desire and fleeting beauty. Trans. from the Dutch by Robert Potter and Elsa Strietman. Leeds Medieval Studies, University of Leeds, Leeds, 1994.

Mariken van Nieumeghen. Ed. Saalborn in *Toneelglorie der Middeleeuwen*. Naarden, n.d.

Marlowe, Christopher. *Doctor Faustus*. Ed. R. Gill. Oxford, 1990.

Mary Magdalen: the late medieval religious plays of Bodleian MSS Digby 133 and E Museo 160. Ed. Donald C. Baker, John L. Murphy and Louis B. Hall Jr. Early English Text Society 283. London, 1982.

Massinger, Philip. *Plays and Poems*. Ed. Philip Edwards and Colin Gibson. 5 vols. Oxford, 1976.

Medieval Dutch drama. Four secular plays and four farces from the Van Hulthem Manuscript. Trans. Johanna Prins. Asheville, N.C., 1999.

Millet, Jacques. *La destruction de Troye la grant*. Paris, 1484. Transcript ed. E. Stengel. Marburg, 1883.

Mira de Amescua, Antonio. *El esclavo del demonio (The Devil's slave)*. Trans. Michael McGaha with introduction by José M. Ruano. Carleton Renaissance Plays in translation 16. Dovehouse editions. Ottawa, 1989.

Le miracle de la Sainte Hostie de 1290 à Paris. 1664, with engravings by F. Ragot; reprinted for the sexcentenary commemoration of the original event in 1890.

Miracles de Notre Dame par personnages. Cangé MS. Ed. G. Paris and U. Robert. 8 vols. SATF. Paris, 1876–93.

Le mistère du siège d'Orléans. Ed. V. L. Hamblin. TLF, Geneva, 2002.

Molina, Tirso de. *Obras, dramaticos completas.* 3 vols. Madrid, 1946–58.

Molina, Tirso de. *The doubter damned (El condenado por desconfiado).* C. 1620. In *Three plays by Tirso de Molina.* Trans. F. Minelli and J. D. Browning. Carleton Plays. Ottawa, 1991.

Molina, Tirso de. *Tamar's revenge.* English version for Royal Shakespeare Company, by James Fenton. Stratford, 2004.

Montchrestien, Antoine de. *Hector* (1604). In *Two tragedies: Hector and la reine d'Ecosse.* Ed. C. N. Smith. London, 1972.

Moralité de l'orgueil et presomption de l'empereur jovinien, Ed. Emile Picot. Paris, 1912.

Moralité des enfants de maintenant. Ed. Viollet le Duc. Ancien théâtre français III. Paris, 1854.

Moralité du pèlerinage de vie humaine. Ed. G. Cohen. In *Nativités et moralités liègeoises du moyen âge.* Brussels, 1953.

Moralités françaises, I. Facsimile reprint Slatkine, Geneva, 1980.

Munday, A., and Chettle, H. *Sir Thomas More.* Ed. Martin White for Royal Shakespeare Company, 2005.

Munday, Anthony. *The downfall of Robert, Earl of Huntingdon.* 1601. Malone Society Reprint. Oxford, 1965.

Munday, Anthony. *The death of Robert, earl of Huntingdon.* 1601. Malone Society Reprint. Oxford, 1967.

Le mystère de Judith et Holofernés. Ed. Graham Runnalls. TLF 461. Geneva, 1995. Trans: *Judith and Holofernes, a late 15th-century French mystery play.* Trans. into English with introduction and commentary by Graham Runnalls. Early European Drama in Translation. Asheville, N.C., 2002.

Le mystère de Sainte Barbe: tragédie bretonne: texte de 1557 / publié avec traduction française, introduction et dictionnaire par Emile Ernault. Nantes, 1885–7.

Le mystère de St Bernard de Menthon. Ed. A. Lecoy de la Marche, SATF. Paris, 1888.

Mystère de St Louis. Ed. francisque Michel. Roxburghe Club. London, 1871.

Le mystère de Sainte Venise. Ed. Graham Runnalls. Exeter University Textes Litteraires XXXVIII. Exeter, 1980.

Le mystère du Viel Testament, ed. J. de Rothschild. 6 vols. SATF. Paris, 1878.

Les mystères de la procession Lille. Ed. Alan Knight. 5 vols. (I–III pub.) Geneva, 2001– (in progress).

Le mythe de Phèdre. Ed. A. G. Wood. Paris, 1996.

Newbigin, Nerida. *Sacre rappresentazioni fiorentine del Quattrocento.* Bologna, 1983.

Passion S Genis: l'ystoyre et la vie de saint Genis. Ed. W. Mostert and E. Stengel. Marburg, 1895.

Paulson, Michael G. *The fallen crown: three French Mary Stuart plays of the seventeenth century.* Washington DC, 1980.

Peele, George. *The works of George Peele.* Ed. A. H. Bullen. 1888, repr., Port Washington, N.Y., 1966.

Pettitt, Tom and Sondergaard, Leif, trans. *De uno peccatore qui promeruit gratiam* (in preparation).

Pra, Canon Siboud. *Le mystère des trois doms.* Ed. P. E. Giraud and Ulysse Chevalier. Lyon, 1885.

Pradon, Jacques. *Regulus.* Paris, 1688.

Raftery, Margaret M. *Mary of Nemmegen.* Brill, 1991.

La rappresentazione di Santo Alesso (late fifteenth century) *See* De Bartholomaeis II.

Rosete, Niño, Pedro, *et al. El mejor representante San Ginés,* by three *Ingenios.* 1688. Place of Publication not given.

Roswitha. *See* Hrotsvitha.

Rotrou, Jean. *Le véritable St Genest.* Texte établi et commenté par José Sanchez; preface de Jacques Morel. Paris, 1988.

Rotrou, Jean. *Théâtre complet.* Ed. V. Lochert and L. Picciola. 6 vols. Société des Textes Français Modernes. Paris, 2000.

Rouanet, L. *Autos, Farsas y Coloquios del siglo XVI.* 4 vols. Barcelona and Madrid, 1901.

    Aucto de la destruicion de Jerusalem (Rouanet, XXX).

    Aucto di San Francisco (Rouanet, XXXIX).

    Auto de Sant Jorge quando mate le serpiente (Rouanet, XXVI).

    Auto de un milagro de Sancto Andres (Rouanet, XXIX).

    Auto della visitacion de Sant Antonio a Sant Pablo (Rouanet, LXXVI).

Ruf, Jacob. *Das neuer Tellenspiel,* and *Von des Herren Weingarten.* Schweizerische Schauspiele des sechszehnten Jahrhunderts, III. Zurich, 1893.

Runnalls, Graham. The mystère de l'advocacie Nostre Dame: a recently discovered fragment. *Zeitschrift für romanische Philologie,* 100:2 (Tübingen, 1984), pp. 41–77.

Rutebeuf, *Le miracle de Théophile.* Ed. Grace Frank. CFMA. Paris, repr., 1975.

Sachs, Hans. *Werken.* Ed. A. V. Keller and E. Goetzer. Bibliothek des literarischen Vereins. Stuttgart, Stuttgart, 1866–92.

Sachs, Hans. *Der Dot im Stock.* In Bryan and Dempster, eds., *Sources and analogues.*

Scaevola, Mucius. *Treuerspel.* Amsterdam, 1727.

Schernberg, Dietrich. *Ein schön spiel von Frau Jutten.* Ed. Manfred Lammer. Berlin, 1971.

Schnorr von Carolsfeld, Franz, 'Vier ungedruckte Fastnachtspiele des 15. Jahrhunderts'. *Archiv fur Litteraturgeschichte,* 3 (1874), pp. 1–25.

Settle, Elkanah. *The female prelate.* London, 1680.

Shakespeare, William. *The complete works.* The Oxford Shakespeare, general eds. Stanley Wells and Gary Taylor. Oxford, 1999.

Sharp, Thomas. *Dramatic mysteries of Coventry* (1825). Repr. with new foreword by A. Cawley. Totowa, N.J., 1973.

Sommerfeld, M. *Judith-dramen des 16/17 Jahrhunderts*. Berlin, 1933.
Spel van den Helighen Sacramente van der Nieuwverwaart. Ed. Saalborn in *Toneelglorie der Middeleeuwen*. Naarden, n.d.
Spil von St Jörigen und des künigs von Libiba tochte und wie sie erlöst war. See Ukena.
Le '*Sponsus*'. *Mystère des vierges sages et des vierges folles*. Ed. L.-P. Thomas. Paris, 1951.
Sterzing play of the parable of Dives and Lazarus. In *Die geistlichen Spiele der Sterzingearchivs*. Bern, 1981 (in progress).
Stone, D. 'Didon se sacrifiant'. In *Four Renaissance tragedies*. Cambridge, Mass., 1966.
Strietman, Elsa. *Van Eneas en Dido. Two amorous plays performed in Antwerp, 1552*. EM Drama, 3, ed. Sydney Higgins, pub. Tempo di Spettacolo (1999), pp. 261–83.
Le théâtre complet de Tristan l'Hermite. Ed. Claude Kurt Abraham, Jerome William Schweitzer and Jacqueline Van Baelen. Tuscaloosa, 1975.
The Towneley plays. Ed. J. England. Early English Text Society, Extra Series 71. Oxford, 1897. Repr. Millwood, N.Y., 1978.
Tragédie du Bon Kanut roy de Dannemarch, 1575. Ed. Renée Gimenez. Saint-Etienne, 1989.
La tragédie du sac de Cabrières. In *Kalvinistiche drama des Reformationszeit*. Ed. Karl Christ. Halle, 1928.
The tragedy of Ecerinus, with a facing English translation and introduction by R. W. Carrubba *et al*. Published by the Department of Classics, Pennsylvania State University. Philadelphia, 1972.
Ukena, E. *Die deutschen Mirakelspiele des Spätmittelalters. Studien und texte*. 2 vols. Bern, 1975.
Urueña. *Ingenio y representante S. Ginés y S. Claudio*. 1771.
Vernulaeus, Nicolaus. *Henry VIII*, a neo-Latin drama by Nicolaus Vernulaeus. Trans. and ed. Louis A. Schuster. Austin, Tex., 1964.
Vondel, Joost van den. *Mary Stuart or tortured majesty*. Trans. Kristiaan P. Aercke, Carleton Plays. Ottawa, 1996.
Webster, John. *The Devil's law case*. In *The complete works of John Webster*. Ed. F. L. Lucas. 4 vols. Rev. edn, London, 1958.

PLAY RECORDS AND REFERENCE WORKS

Adam of Cobsam. *The wright's chaste wife*. Ed. F. J. Furnivall, Early English Text Society, Original Series 12. London, 1865.
Axelrad, A. José. *Le thème de Sophonisbe dans les principales tragédies de la littérature occidentale: France, Allemagne, Angleterre*. Lille, 1956.
Aylett, R. and Skrine, P. *Hans Sachs and folk theatre in the late Middle Ages. Studies in the history of popular culture*. Lampeter, 1995.
Baerwolff, Walther. *Der Graf von Essex in deutschen Drama*. Stuttgart, 1919.
Bailey, Gabriel. *Medieval saint-play metamorphoses in English drama 1490–1642*. Ph.D. thesis, University of Bristol, 1984.

Best, Thomas W. *Jacob Bidermann*. Twayne's World Authors Series 314. New York, 1975.

Blamires, David. Victim heroines in Hans Sachs' plays. In *Hans Sachs and folk theatre*. Ed. R. Aylett and P. Skrine.

Bordier, Jean-Pierre. La composition de la vengeance de notre seigneur. Un aspect de l'art dramatique d'Eutrache Marcadé. In *Mainte belle oeuvre faite*.

Boysse, E. *Le théâtre des Jésuites*. Slatkine repr. Geneva, 1970.

Bryan, W. F., and Dempster, Germaine, eds. *Sources and analogues of Chaucer's Canterbury tales*. Chicago, 1941. Repr. New York and London, 1958.

Bullough, Geoffrey. *Narrative and dramatic sources of Shakespeare*. 8 vols. London, 1957–75.

Calore, M. Rappresentazioni sacre a Bologna nel XV secolo. *Strenna Storica Bolognese*, 28 (1978), pp. 101–10.

Chocheyras, J. *Le théâtre religieux en Dauphiné du Moyen Age au XVIIIe siècle*. Geneva, 1975.

Chocheyras, J. *Le théâtre religieux en Savoie au XVIe siècle*. Geneva, 1971.

Cioni, A. *Bibliografia delle sacre rappresentazioni*. Biblioteca Bibliografia Italica 22. Florence, 1961.

Clark, R. The 'Miracles de Nostre Dame par parsonnages' of the Cangé manuscript and the sociocultural function of confraternity drama. UMI dissertation services, 1994.

Cohen, G. *Etudes d'histoire du théâtre*. Paris, 1956.

Cooper, Helen. *The English romance in time: transforming motifs from Geoffrey of Monmouth to the death of Shakespeare*. Oxford, 2004.

Correale, R. M., ed. *Sources and analogues of the Canterbury tales*. 2 vols. Cambridge, 2002–5.

Corneille, Pierre. *Théâtre choisi précédé des discours sur le poème dramatique (avec notes et préfaces de Voltaire)*. Paris, 1924.

Creizenach, W. *Geschichte des neueren Dramas*. 3 vols. Halle, 1911–23.

Dabrowka, Andrzej. Polish saint plays of the sixteenth and seventeenth centuries. *EDAM Review*, 23:1 (2000), pp. 33–48.

Davidson, ed. *The saint play in medieval Europe*. EDAM Monograph Series, 8. Kalanazoo, 1986.

Davidson, Clifford, The Middle English saint play and its iconography. In *The saint play in medieval Europe*. Ed. Davidson.

Falvey, Kathleen. The Italian saint play. In *The saint play in medieval Europe*. Ed. Davidson.

García Soriano, Justo. El teatro de colegio en España. Noticia y examen de algunas de sus obras. *Boletín de la real academia española*, 14 (1927), pp. 235–77.

Gautier de Coinci. *Le miracle de Théophile, ou comment Théophile vint à la pénitence*. Ed. and trans. Annette Garnier. CFMA. Paris, 1998.

Gliksohn, J.-M. *Iphigénie de la Grèce antique à l'Europe des lumières*. Litteratures Modernes 37. Paris, 1985.

Guerrini, Paola. Iconografia di Sofonisba: storia e teatro. In *Nascita della tragedia di poesia nei paesi Europei*. Ed. F. Doglio and M. Chiabò. Viterbo, 1991.

Harbage, Alfred. *Annals of English drama, 975–1700*. London, 1964.

Henrard, Nadine. *Le théâtre religieux médiévale en langue d'oc*. Geneva, 1998.

Henslowe Philip. *Diary*. Ed. W. W. Greg. 2 vols. London, 1904–8.

Hill, L. Alfreda. *The Tudors in French drama*. Johns Hopkins Studies in Romance Literatures and Languages, 20. Baltimore, 1932.

Hindley, Alan. Staging the old French *moralité*. The case of '*Les enfants de maintenant*'. *METh*, 16 (1994), pp. 77–90.

The Historye of Oliver of Castylle. Ed. Gail Orgelfinger. New York, 1988.

Horne, P. R. *The tragedies of Giambattista Cinthio Giraldi*. Oxford, 1962.

Hummelen M. M. *Repertorium van het Rederijkersdrama, 1500–c. 1620*. Assen, 1968.

Hüsken, W. M. N. Queen Elizabeth and Essex: a Dutch rhetoricians' play. In *Porci ante Margaritam. Essays in honour of Meg Twycross*. Ed. Sarah Carpenter, Pamela King and Peter Meredith. Leeds Studies in English, New Series XXII. Leeds, 2001.

Ingram, R. W., ed. *REED: Coventry*. Toronto and Manchester, 1981.

Journal d'un bourgeois de Paris. Ed. with a preface and notes by André Mary. Paris, 1929. Trans. Janet Shirley. *A Parisian journal 1405–1449*. Oxford, 1968.

Jung, Marc. *La légende de Troie en France au moyen âge*. Romanica Helvetica 114. Basel, 1996.

Kennard, Joseph Spencer. *The Italian theatre*. 2 vols. New York, 1931; repr. 1952.

Kipka, Karl. *Maria Stuart im drama der Weltliteratur*. Breslauer Beiträge zur Literaturgeschichte. Leipzig, 1907.

Knight, Alan. *Aspects of genre*. Manchester, 1938.

Krane-Calvert, Judith A. A twentieth-century analogue of the *Play of the sacrament*. *EDAM Review*, 20:1 (Fall 1997), pp. 24–7.

Krause, Kathleen. The falsely accused heroine in the *Miracles de Notre Dame par personnages*. EMD. Camerino, 1999.

Krueger, R. L. Double jeopardy: the appropriation of women in four Old French romances of the *Cycle de la gageure*. In *Seeking the woman in late medieval and renaissance writings. Essays in feminist contextual criticism*. Ed. S. Fisher and J. E. Halley. Knoxville, 1989.

Lancashire, Ian. *Dramatic texts and records of Britain. a chronological topography to 1558*. Cambridge, 1984.

Lancaster, H. Carrington. *Théâtre français du 17e siècle*. Part I, 1610–35, 2 vols. Part II, 1635–42, 2 vols. Baltimore, 1992.

Lanson G. Etudes sur les origines de la tragédie classique en France. *Revue d'histoire littéraire de la France*, 10 (1903), pp. 177–231 and 413–36.

Lebègue, G. *La tragédie religieuse en France. Les débuts 1514–73*. Paris, 1929.

Lebègue, G. *Etudes sur le théâtre français*. Paris, 1977.

Linke, Hansjürgen. A survey of medieval drama and theater in Germany. In *Medieval drama on the continent of Europe*. Ed. Clifford Davidson and John Stroupe. Medieval Institute Publications. Kalamazoo, 1993.

Lohmann, W. Untersuchungen über Jean Louvets 12 Mysterien zu Ehren von Notre Dame de Liesse. Dissertation. Greifswald, 1900.

Look about you: a pleasant commedie called Looke about you. A critical edition by Richard S. M. Hirsch. New York, 1980. (Orig. printed 1600; unfinished and never performed.)

Loomis, R. S. Chivalric and dramatic imitations of Arthurian romance. In *Medieval studies in memory of A. Kingsley Porter*. Ed. Wilhelm R. W. Koehler. Cambridge, 1939.

Lope de Vega. *Arcadia, prosas y versos de Lope de Vega Carpio*. Madrid, 1653.

Lope de Vega. *El serafín humano. Life of Lope de Vega*, p. 530. *See* Rennert.

Loukovitch, K. *L'évolution de la tragédie religieuse classique en France*. Paris, 1933.

McCabe, W. H., SJ. *An introduction to the Jesuit theater*. The Institute of Jesuit Sources, Missouri, 1983.

McKendrick, Melveena. *Woman and society in the Spanish drama of the Golden Age. A study of the mujer varonil*. Cambridge, 1974.

McKendrick, Melveena. *Theatre in Spain, 1490–1700*. Cambridge, 1989.

Mainte belle œuvre faite. Etudes offertes à Graham Runnalls. Orleans, 2005.

Marshall, John. 'Goon in to bernysdale'. The trail of the Paston Robin Hood play. In *Essays in honour of Peter Meredith*. Leeds Studies in English XXIX. Leeds, 1998.

Meredith, P. and Tailby, J., eds. *The staging of religious drama in Europe*. EDAM. Kalamazoo, 1983.

Messineo, Michela. 'Primordi del teatro di collegio in Sicilia'. In *I Gesuiti e il primordi del teatro barocco in Europa*. ed. F. Doglio and M. Chiabo. Rome 1994.

Metz, G. H. *Sources of four plays ascribed to Shakespeare*. Columbia, 1989.

Le miracle de St Nicolas (prologues). Ed. C. Samaran. *Romania*, 51(1925), pp. 191–7.

Motter, T. H. Vail. *The school drama in England*. New York, 1929.

Muir, Lynette R. The saint play in medieval France. In *The saint play in medieval Europe*. Ed. Davidson.

Muir, Lynette R. *The biblical drama of medieval Europe*. Cambridge, 1995.

Muir, Lynette R. Further thoughts on the tale of the profaned host. *EDAM Review*, 21:2 (1999), pp. 88–97.

Muir, Lynette R. René d'Anjou and the theatre in Provence. *EMD*, 3 (1999), pp. 57–72.

Muir, Lynette R. St Nicholas: a newly discovered French play cycle. *EDAM Newsletter*, 11 (Fall 1998) pp. 1–4.

Muir, Lynette R., The sufferings of impatient Job. In *Mainte belle oeuvre faite*. Etudes offertes à Graham Runnalls. Orleans, 2005.

Nerbano, Mara. *Play and record: Ser Tomasso di Silvestro and the theatre of medieval and early modern Orvieto*. *EMD*, 8 (2004), pp. 127–72.

Neumann, von Bernd. *Geistliches Schauspiel im Zeugnis der Zeit. Zur Aufführung Mitteralterlicher religiöser Dramen im deutschen Sprachgebiet*. 2 vols. Munich, 1987.

New approaches to European theater of the Middle Ages. Ed. Barbara I. Gusick and Edelgard DuBruck. New York, 2004.

Newbigin, N. *Feste d'Oltrarno. Plays in churches in fifteenth-century Florence*. 2 vols. Florence, 1996.

Newbigin, N. Agata, Appollonia and other martyred virgins. *EMD*, 1 (1997), pp. 175–97.

Nicolet, Claude, *La fabrique d'une nation. La France entre Rome et les Germains*. Paris, 2003.

Parente, James A. *Religious drama and the Humanist tradition. Christian theater in Germany and in the Netherlands 1500–1680*. Leyden, 1987.

Paris, Gaston. Le cycle de la gageure. *Romania*, 32 (1903), pp. 481–551.

Petit de Julleville, L. *Répertoire du théâtre comique en France au moyen âge*. Repr., Geneva, 1967.

Petit de Julleville, L. *Les mystères*. 2 vols. Repr., Geneva, 1969.

Petsch, *Theophilus*. Germanische bibliothek 2. Heidelberg, 1908.

Playing Robin Hood. The legend as performance in five centuries. Ed. Lois Potter. Newark, N. J., and London, 1998.

Potter, Robert. *The English morality play: origins, history and influence of a dramatic tradition*. London, 1975.

Rädle, Fidel. *Faustsplitter aus lateinischen Dramen im Clm 26017*. Festschrift B. Bischoff. Stuttgart, 1971.

Rennalls, Graham. Le dernier mystère originale. In *Mémoire en temps advenir. Hommage à Theo Venckeleer*. Leuven, 2003.

Rennert, H. A. *The life of Lope de Vega*. Glasgow, 1904 (repr. 1937). Includes a catalogue of the surviving plays.

Ricci, C. *Sophonisbe dans la tragédie classique Italienne et française*. Grenoble, 1904.

Rouillard, C. D. *The Turk in French history, thought and literature*. Paris, 1938.

Roux, Lucette Elyane. Cent ans d'expérience théâtrale dans les collèges de la compagnie de Jésus en Espagne. In *Dramaturgie et Société XVI et XVII siècles*, II. Editions CNRS. Paris, 1968.

Roy, Emile. *Etudes sur le théâtre français*, III: *Les miracles de Notre Dane. Le recueit de Jean Louvet*. Paris, 1902.

Runnalls, Graham. *Les mystères français imprimés*. Bibliothèque du XVe siècle. Paris, 1999.

Runnalls, Graham. Civic drama in the Burgundian territories in the later Middle Ages. *Revue Belge de Philologie et d'Histoire*, 78 (2000), pp. 41–422.

Runnalls, Graham. Jean Louvet: compositeur de mystères et homme de théâtre Parisien, 1536–50. *Bibliothèque d'Humanisme et Renaissance*, 62 (2000), pp. 561–89.

Ruth, Kevin J. Juridical language and the Devil's rights in the Maastrichter (ripuarisches) Passionsspiel. *EMD*, 8 (2004), pp. 19–34.

The sad shepherd; or a tale of Robin Hood by Ben Jonson. A fragment. With continuation, notes, and an appendix by G. F. Waldron. London, 1783. (Unfinished and never performed.)

Settle, Elkanah, *The female prelate*. London, 1680.

Simon, Eckehard. *Die Anfänge des weltlichen deutschen Schauspiels 1370–1530*. Tübingen, 2003.

Skrine, Peter. The Greek tragedies of Hans Sachs. In *Hans Sachs and folk theatre*. Ed. Aylett and Skrine.

Snyder, Susan. Marlowe's Doctor Faustus as an inverted saint's life. *Studies in Philology*, 63 (1966), pp. 565–77.

Spel en spektakel: middleeuws toneel in de Lage Landen. Ed. H. van Dijk and Bart Ramakers. Amsterdam, 2001.

Stegmann, A. *L'héroisme Cornélie*, II: *L'Europe intellectuel et le théâtre, 1580–1650*. Paris, 1968.

Stone, D. *Four Renaissance tragedies*. Cambridge, Mass., 1966.

Szarota, E. M. *Das Jesuitendrama im deutschen Sprachgebiet*. 3 vols. (in two parts each). Munich, 1979–83.

Tailby, John E. Arthurian elements in drama and *Meisterlieder*. In *The Arthur of the Germans*. Ed. W. H. Jackson and S. A. Ranawake. Cardiff, 2000.

Tailby, John E. Drama and community in South Tirol, In *Drama and community: people and plays in medieval Europe*. Ed. Alan Hindley. Turnhout, 1999.

Tailby, John. Ein vernachlässigter Luzerner Bühnenplan. In *Ritual und Inszenierung*. Ed. Hans Joachim Ziegeler. Tübingen, 2004.

Tailby, John. E. Hans Sachs and the Nuremberg Fastnachtspiel tradition of the fifteenth century. In *Hans Sachs and folk theatre*. Ed. Aylett and Skrine.

Il teatro Italiano. Ed. Marco Ariani. Turin, 1977.

The German and Dutch theatre, 1600–1848. Ed. G. Brandt. Cambridge, 1993.

The medieval European stage, 500–1550. Ed. W. Tydeman. Cambridge, 2001.

Umstead, Douglas R. *Carnival comedy and sacred play. The Renaissance dramas of Giovan Maria Cecchi*. Columbia 1986.

Valency, M. *The tragedies of Herod and Mariamne*. New York, 1940.

Valentin, Jean-Marie. *Le théâtre des Jésuites dans les pays de langue allemande (1554–1680)*. 3 vols. Bern, 1978.

La vie de Saint Eustace, ed. Jessie Murray. CFMA. Paris, 1929.

Villarejo, Oscar M. 'Lope de Vega and the Elizabethan and Jacobean drama. Doctoral dissertation, 1953. UMI dissertation services. Ann Arbor, USA.

Wasson, John. The St George and Robin Hood plays in Devon. *Medieval English Theatre*, 2:2 (1980), pp. 66–8.

Wasson, John. The secular saint plays of the Elizabethan era. In *The saint play in medieval Europe*. Ed. Davidson.

Weaver, E. B. *Convent theatre in early modern Italy. Spiritual fun and learning for women*. Cambridge, 2001.

Wickersham Crawford, J. P. The Catalan 'Mascaron' and an episode in Jacob van Maerlant's '*Merljin*'. *PMLA*, 26 (1911).

Williams, Elizabeth. The White Knight, the ungrateful dead and two Jacks. In *Essays in honour of Peter Meredith*. Leeds Studies in English, XXIX. Leeds, 1998.

Wilson, Edward M. and Cruickshank, Don W. *Samuel Pepys's Spanish plays*. No. 19, p. 155. *El divino Portugues San Antonio de Padua. Comedia Famosa del Doctor Juan Perez de Montalvan*. London, 1980.

Witherspoon, A. M. *The influence of Robert Garnier on the Elizabethan drama*. Yale Studies in English 65. New Haven, repr. 1968.

Worp, J. A. *Geschiedenis van het Drama en van het Toneel in Nederland*. 2 vols. Rotterdam, 1903.

Wright, Stephen. *The Vengeance of Our Lord. Medieval dramatizations of the destruction of Jerusalem*. Pontifical Institute of Medieval Studies. Toronto, 1949.

Wright, Stephen. De uno peccatore qui promeruit gratiam. *Comparative Drama*, 27 (1993), pp. 4–16.

Young, K. *The drama of the medieval church*. 2 vols. Oxford and London, 1933.

OTHER WORKS CITED

Aarne, A. *The types of the folktale: a classification and bibliography*. FF Communications No. 184. Trans. and enlarged by Stith Thompson. Helsinki, 1961.

Acta sanctorum. Collegit Johannes Bollandus *et al.* 61 vols. Brussels, 1965–70.

Alta Silva, Johannes de. *The seven sages of Rome and the Dolopathos*. Binghampton, N.Y., 1981.

Andrachuk, G. P. The *auto sacramental* and the Reformation. *Journal of Hispanic Philology*, 10 (1985), pp. 8–38.

Bayot, Alphonse. *Le roman de Gillion de Trazegnies*. Louvain, 1903.

Bede, the Venerable. *Bede's ecclesiastical history of the English people*. Ed. Bertram Colgrave and R. A. B. Mynors. Oxford, 1969.

Benoit de St Maure. *Le Roman de Troie*. Ed. Leopold Constans, SATF, 6 vols. Paris, 1904–12.

Berkoff, Steven. *Ritual in Blood*. In *Plays Three*. London, 2000.

Black, Nancy B. *Medieval narratives of accused queens*. Gainesville, Fla., 2003.

Boaistuau, Pierre. *Histoires tragiques*. Ed. Richard A. Carr. Société des Textes Français Modernes. Paris, 1977.

Boccaccio, Giovanni. *De claris mulieribus*. Trans. and ed. as *Famous Women* by Virginia Brown. Cambridge, Mass., and London, 2001.

The book of saints. A dictionary of servants of God canonised by the Catholic Church. Compiled by the Benedictine monks of St Augustine's Abbey Ramsgate. Sixth edition, London, 1989.

Bossuat, Robert. Theséus de Cologne. *Le moyen âge*, 65 (1959).

Braswell, Laura. 'Sir Isumbras' and the legend of Saint Eustace. *Medieval Studies*, 27 (1965) pp. 128–51.

Cambridge guide to world theatre. Ed. Martin Banham. Cambridge, 1988.

Le cento novelle antiche, LXXXIII. Milan, 1825.

Cervantes Saavedra, Miguel de. *Don Quixote de La Mancha*. Trans. Charles Jarvis, ed. with an introduction by E. C. Riley. Oxford, 1992.

Chartrou, Josephe. *Les entrées solennelles et triomphales à la renaissance 1484–1551*. Paris, 1928.

Chastellain, Georges. *Chroniques du duc de Bourgogne*. Ed. J. A. Buchon. Paris, 1883.

Códice de autos viejos, ed. Miguel Ángel Pérez Priego (Madrid, 1988).

Cohen, Walter. *Drama of a nation: public theater in Renaissance England and Spain*. Ithaca, 1985.

Collins, Hugh E. L. *The Order of the Garter 1348–1461: Chivalry and politics in late medieval England*. Oxford, 2000.

Dalrymple, William. *From the Holy Mountain*. London, 1997.

Dante. *Divine comedy*. Trans. Dorothy L. Sayers. 3 vols. Penguin Classics, 1962.

Dares and Dictys. *The Trojan war. The chronicles of Dictys of Crete and Dares the Phrygian*. Trans. with introduction and notes by R. M. Frazer Jr. Bloomington, Ind., 1966.

De Bruyn, Lucy. *Woman and the Devil in sixteenth-century literature*. Tisbury,, 1979.

De la Marche, Olivier. *Mémoires*. Collection des mémoires relatifs à l'Histoire de France, Paris, 1825. III, pp. 114–201.

De Vooys, C. G. N. *Middelnederlandsche Maria legenden*. 2 vols. Leiden, 1903.

Delehaye, Hippolyte. *The legends of the saints*. Trans. Donald Attwater, with new introduction by Thomas O'Loughlin. Dublin, 1998.

Deschamps, Eustache (c. 1346–1406). *Œuvres complètes*. Ed. Gaston Raynaud. SATF. 11 vols. Paris. 1878–1903.

Dickson, Arthur. *Valentine and Orson. A study in late medieval romance*. New York, 1929.

Doudet, Estelle. Un dramaturge et son publique au XVe siècle'. *EMD*, 9 (2005), pp. 61–86.

Doutrepont, Georges. *Jean Lemaire de Belges et la Renaissance*. Brusells, 1934.

Edelman, Nathan. *Attitudes of seventeenth-century France towards the Middle Ages*. New York, 1936.

Estoria do muy nobre Vespesiano. Ed. Penny Robinson. Exeter, 1983.

Eusebius. *The history of the Church*. Trans. G. A. Williamson. Rev. and ed. with a new introduction by Andrew Louth. Harmondsworth, 1989.

Farnham, Willard. *The medieval heritage of Elizabethan tragedy*. Oxford, 1956.

Félibien, Michel, *Histoire de la ville de Paris*. 5 vols. Paris, 1725.

Fellows, Jennifer. St George as romance hero. *Reading Medieval Studies*, 19 (1993).

Fochler, Petra. *Fiktion als Historie. Der Trojanische Krieg in der deutschen Literatur des 16. Jahrhunderts*. Wiesbaden, 1990.

Ford, Alvin. *La vengeance de nostre-seigneur. The Old and Middle French prose versions and the version of Japheth*. Pontifical Institute of Medieval Studies 63. Toronto, 1984.

The fourth book of the chronicle of Fredegar, with its continuations. Trans. from the Latin with introduction and notes by J. M. Wallace-Hadrill. London and New York, 1960.

Fox, David Scott. *Saint George. The saint with three faces*. Windsor Forest, Berkshire, 1983.

Frazer, R. M. *The Trojan War: the chronicles of Dictys of Crete and Dares the Phrygian*. Bloomington, Ind., 1966.

Gardair, Jean-Michel. Giuditta e i suopi doppi. In *I Gesuiti e il primordi del teatro barocco in Europa*. Ed. F. Doglio and M. Chiabo. Rome, 1994.

Gerritsen, W. *A dictionary of medieval heroes*. Trans. from the Dutch by Tanis Guest. Woodbridge, 1998.

Gesta Romanorum. Ed. and trans. Charles Swan. London, 1912.

Giordana, Ugo, ed. *Le jeu de Saint Thomas d'Aquin*. Paris, 1939.

Goethe. *Faust*. Trans. A. G. Latham. London, (repr.) 1912.

The Golden Legend of Jacobus de Voragine. Translated by Granger Ryan and Helmut Ripperger. New York, 1969.

Gransden, Antonia. *Legends, traditions and history in medieval England*. London, 1992.

Greene, Robert. *Pandosto: the triumph of time*. In *The descent of Euphues. Three Elizabethan romance stories*. Ed. James Winny. Cambridge, 1917.

Grieve, Patricia E. *Floire and Blancheflor and the European romance*. Cambridge, 1997.

Grimaldi, Antonio. *Il chiostro e la scena. Michelangelo Buonarroti il giovane e il Convento Di Sant'Agata*. Studi Italiani XI. Florence, 1998, pp. 149–98.

Guillaume, P. 'Le mystère de St Eustache'. *Revue des langues romanes*, 3rd series, 7 (1882).

Hartcup, Adeline. *Children of the great country houses*. London, 1982.

Helm, Alex. *The English mummers' play*. Woodbridge, 1981.

Hennecke, E. *New Testament Apocrypha*. Ed. Wilhelm Schneemelcher. English trans. R. McL. Wilson. 2 vols. London, 1963.

Hook, D., *The destruction of Jerusalem: Catalan and Castilian texts*. King's College London Medieval Studies. Londan, 2000.

Hornstein, L. King Robert of Sicily: analogues and origins. *PMLA*, 79 (1964), pp. 13–21.

St John Damascene. *Barlaam and Joasaph*. Edited with an English translation by G. R. Woodward and H. Mattingly. London and Cambridge, Mass., 1914.

Johnson, Richard. *The seven champions of Christendom: 1596–7*. Ed. Jennifer Fellows. Aldershot, 2004.

Josephus. *The Jewish war*. Trans. G. A. Williamson. Harmondsworth, 1959.

Kelly, J. N. D., *Oxford dictionary of popes*. Oxford, 1986. Updated edition with new material by Michael Walsh. Oxford, 2006.

Le moniage Guillaume. Ed. W. Cloetta. 2 vols. Paris, 1906–11.

Le roman du châtelain de Couci et de la dame de Fayel. Ed. Gaston Paris. SATF VIII. Paris, 1879.

Lefèbvre, Léon. *Histoire du théâtre de Lille des origines à nos jours*. 5 vols. Lille, 1907.

Liber historiae francorum. Ed. and trans. Bernard S. Bachrach. Lawrence, Kans., 1973.

Liebe, Georg. *Das Judentum in der deutschen Vergangenheit. Mit 106 Abbildingen und Beilagen*. Leipzig, 1903.

The Life of St Katharine. Ed. J. Orchard Halliwell. Brixton Hill, 1848.

Marx, C. William. *The devil's rights and the redemption in the literature of Medieval England*. Cambridge, 1995.

McCracken, Peggy. The romance of adultery. *Queenship and sexual transgression in Old French literature*. Philadelphia, 1998.

Meredith, P. and Muir, L. The Corpus Christi Bull. *METh*, 26 (2004), pp. 62–78.

Micha, Alexandre. The vulgate Merlin. In *Arthurian literature in the Middle Ages*. Ed. R. S. Loomis. Oxford, 1959.

Millar, Bonnie. *The siege of Jerusalem in its physical, literary and historical contexts.* Dublin, 2000.

Muir, Lynette R. Le personnage de Charlemagne dans les romans en prose arthuriens. *Boletin de la real Academia de Buenas Letras de Barcelona,* 31 (1965–6), pp. 233–41.

Muir, Lynette R. Rhetoricians and the francophone tradition. In *Urban theatre in the Low Countries 1400–1625.* Ed. Elsa Strietman and Peter Happe. Brepols, 2006.

Mystère de St Barthélemy. See Nadine Henrard.

Myths of the Hindus and Buddhists. By the Sister Nivedita and Ananda K. Coomaraswamy. London, 1913.

Ovid. *Metamorphoses.* Trans. A. D. Melville, with introduction and notes by E. J. Kelly. Oxford, 1986.

Painter, William. *The palace of pleasure.* 3 vols. Dover Publications. New York, 1966.

Patch, H. R., *The Goddess Fortuna in medieval literature.* Cambridge, Mass., 1927.

Petsch, Robert. *Faustsage und Faustdichtung.* Dortmund, 1966.

Piard, Henry. Adaptations de la 'Tragédie Espagnole' dans les Pays Bas et en Allemagne. In *Dramaturgie et société.* 2 vols. Paris, 1968.

Pickering, Oliver. The crusades in Leeds University Library's genealogical history roll. In *From Clermont to Jerusalem to Jerusalem: the crusades and crusader societies, 1095–1500.* Ed. Alan V. Murray. International Medieval Research 3 (Turnhout, 1998).

Plenzat, K. *Die Theophilus legende in den dichtungen des Mittelalters.* Berlin, 1926.

Price, David. *The political dramaturgy of Nicodemus Frischlin. Essays on Humanist drama in Germany.* Chapel Hill and London, 1990.

Prise d'Orange. See William, count of Orange.

Rädle, Fidel. *Faustsplitter aus lateinischen Dramen im Clm 26017.* Festschrift B. Bischoff. Stuttgart, 1971.

Robert le Diable, roman d'aventures. Ed. E. Löseth. SATF. Paris, 1903.

Roger of Wendover. *Flowers of History,* 1206. Trans. J. A. Giles. 2 vols. Bohn's Antiquarian Library, London, 1849, II, p. 227.

Roux. E. *Le théâtre dans les colleges de la Jésuites en Espagne. Dramaturgie et société,* II. Paris, 1968.

Rubin, Miri. Gentile tales. Yale, 1999.

Sayers, Dorothy L. *The Devil to pay.* London, 1939.

Sayers Dorothy L. *The emperor Constantine: a chronicle.* London, 1951.

Schlauch, Margaret. *Chaucer's Constance and accused queens.* New York, Repr., 1973.

Shergold, N. D. *A history of the Spanish stage from medieval times until the end of the seventeenth century.* Oxford and London, 1967.

Sorieri, Louis. *Boccaccio's story of Tito e Gisippo in European literature.* New York, 1937.

Stanford, Peter. *The she-pope: a quest for the truth behind the mystery of pope Joan.* London, 1998.

Stegmann, A. *L'héroisme Cornélien,* II: *L'Europe intellectuel et le théâtre, 1580–1650.* Paris, 1968.

Stow, John. *Survey of London*. Introduction by H. B. Wheatley. London, 1956.

Studi sul teatro medioevale. Viterbo, 1979.

Szarota, E. M. *Künstler Grübler und Rebellen. Studien zum Europäischen Martyrerdrama des 17 Jahrhunderts*. Bern and Munich, 1967.

Tasso, Torquato. *Gerusalemme liberata*, con introduzione e commento di Giovanni Ziccardi. Turin, 1936.

Valerius Maximus, *Memorable doings and sayings*. Ed. and trans. D. R. Shackleton Bailey. Loeb Classical Library. 2 vols. Harvard, 2000.

Van Os, A. B. *Religious visions: the development of the eschatological elements in medieval English religious literature*. Amsterdam, 1932.

Virgil. *The Aeneid. The Eclogues, Georgics and Aeneid of Virgil*. Trans. C. Day Lewis. Oxford, 1966.

Von der Lage, Bertha. *Studien zur Genesiuslegende*. Berlin, 1898–9.

Walter, Christopher. *The warrior saints in Byzantine art and tradition*. Aldershot, 2003.

Warner, Marina. *Joan of Arc. The image of female heroism*. London, 1981.

Wilkins, George. *The painful adventures of Pericles, prince of Tyre*. Ed. Kenneth Muir. Liverpool, 1967.

William, count of Orange, four Old French epics. Ed. Glanville Price. Introduction by L. R. Muir. London, 1975.

Williams, Charles Allyn, *The German legends of the Hairy Anchorite*. With two Old French texts of *La vie de St Jehan Paulus*. Ed. Louis Allen. Urbana, Ill., 1935.

Index